Chanel

An Intimate Life

LISA CHANEY

FIG TREE
an imprint of
PENGUIN BOOKS

For Anna
and in memory of my mother, Elizabeth (1923–2009)

FIG TREE

Published by the Penguin Group
Penguin Books Ltd, 80 Strand, London wc2r orl, England
Penguin Group (USA) Inc., 375 Hudson Street, New York, New York 10014, USA
Penguin Group (Canada), 90 Eglinton Avenue East, Suite 700, Toronto, Ontario, Canada m4p 2y3
(a division of Pearson Penguin Canada Inc.)
Penguin Ireland, 25 St Stephen's Green, Dublin 2, Ireland (a division of Penguin Books Ltd)
Penguin Group (Australia), 250 Camberwell Road,
Camberwell, Victoria 3124, Australia (a division of Pearson Australia Group Pty Ltd)
Penguin Books India Pvt Ltd, 11 Community Centre,
Panchsheel Park, New Delhi – 110 017, India
Penguin Group (NZ), 67 Apollo Drive, Rosedale, Auckland 0632, New Zealand
(a division of Pearson New Zealand Ltd)
Penguin Books (South Africa) (Pty) Ltd, 24 Sturdee Avenue,
Rosebank, Johannesburg 2196, South Africa

Penguin Books Ltd, Registered Offices: 80 Strand, London wc2r orl, England

www.penguin.com

First published 2011

1

Copyright © Lisa Chaney, 2011

The moral right of the author has been asserted

This book is not affiliated with, authorized or endorsed by the Chanel group of companies or any of them.
'Chanel' is a trademark of Chanel Limited and other Chanel group companies.

Every effort has been made to trace copyright holders and to obtain their permission for the use of
copyright material. The publisher apologizes for any errors or omissions and would be grateful to be
notified of any corrections that should be incorporated in future editions of this book.

Set in 12/14.75pt Monotype Dante by
Palimpsest Book Production Limited, Falkirk, Stirlingshire
Printed in Great Britain by Clays Ltd, St Ives plc

A CIP catalogue record for this book is available from the British Library

ISBN: 978–1–905–49036–3

www.greenpenguin.co.uk

MIX
Paper from
responsible sources
FSC
www.fsc.org   FSC™ C018179

Penguin Books is committed to a sustainable
future for our business, our readers and our
planet. This book is made from paper certified
by the Forest Stewardship Council.

Chanel

By the same author

Elizabeth David

Hide and Seek with Angels:
A Life of J. M. Barrie

'Capel said, "Remember that you're a woman."
All too often I forgot that.'[1]

Contents

Contents

Illustrations

1. View from Ponteils; author's photo.
2. The Chanel inn, Ponteils; author's photo.
3. Aubazine; author's photo.
4. Gabrielle and Adrienne Chanel *c.* 1904. Courtesy *LIFE* ©. All rights reserved.
5. Etienne Balsan *c.* 1903. Courtesy of Antoine Balsan and Philippe Gontier.
6. Gabrielle Chanel *c.* 1910. Hulton Archive © Getty Images.
7. Emilienne d'Alençon, 1875. © Getty Images.
8. Royallieu. ©. All rights reserved.
9. Arthur Capel *c.* 1910. Courtesy of Christopher Osborn.
10. Arthur Capel and Gabrielle Chanel on horseback *c.* 1910. Courtesy *LIFE* ©. All rights reserved.
11. Arthur Capel on horseback, *c.* 1910. Courtesy of Christopher Osborn.
12. Gabrielle in her own hat designs; *Comoedia Illustré,* 1910. ©. All rights reserved.
13. Gabrielle Dorziat in 'Marie-Louise' hats; *Comoedia Illustré,* 1910. ©. All rights reserved.
14. Gabrielle Dorziat in a Chanel hat, 1912. ©. All rights reserved.
15. Gabrielle Dorziat in a Chanel hat; *Journal des Modes,* 1912. ©. All rights reserved.
16. Adrienne and Gabrielle Chanel in front of her Deauville shop. Courtesy *LIFE* ©. All rights reserved.
17. *Tangoville sur mer,* caricature of Coco Chanel and Arthur Capel by Sem; © Archives Charmet, Bridgeman Art Library.

18. Gabrielle and friends outside Deauville shop, *c.* 1914. Courtesy Ville de Deauville ©. All rights reserved.

19. Coco Chanel playing golf *c.* 1913; © Hulton Archive, Getty Images.

20. Coco Chanel and Arthur Capel on the beach at St-Jean-de-Luz, 1915; © Hulton Archive, Getty Images.

21. Pablo and Olga Picasso, 1917; © Poperfoto, Getty Images.

22. Diana Capel by John Sargent; © Private Collection.

23. The Capel Polo Trophy. Courtesy Polo de Paris; photo Adelia Sabatini.

24. Sergei Diaghilev and Igor Stravinsky; © Victoria and Albert Museum, London.

25. Igor Stravinsky, José Maria Sert, Gabrielle Chanel and Misia Sert, 1920; Igor Stravinsky Collection; © Paul Sacher Foundation, Zurich.

26. Grand Duke Dmitri Pavlovich. From *Chanel: A Woman of Her Own*, Axel Madsen ©. All rights reserved.

27. Gabrielle and her dog at the Faubourg St-Honoré; Henri de Beaumont; ©. All rights reserved.

28. Gabrielle Chanel and Dmitri Pavlovich *c.* 1921; ©. All rights reserved.

29. Chanel N°5 by SEM; © Getty Images.

30. Dancers from *Le Train bleu*, 1924; © Hulton Deutsch Collection, CORBIS.

31. Dancers from *Le Train bleu*, 1924; © Hulton Deutsch Collection, CORBIS.

32. Lubov Tchernicheva in *Apollon musagète*. Courtesy *Dancing Times* Archive.

33. Pierre Reverdy; © Roger Viollet, Topfoto.

34. Paul Morand *c.* 1910; © Roger Viollet, Getty Images.

35. Duke of Westminster; *Sunday Telegraph*, all rights reserved.

Introduction

Gabrielle (Coco) Chanel was a woman of singular character, intelligence and imagination. These attributes enabled her to survive a childhood of deprivation and neglect and to re-invent herself to become one of the most influential women of her century. Unlike any previous female couturier, her own life quickly became synonymous with the revolutionary style which made her name. This style was pared down, seductive and elegant. Many of its elements, which have become indispensable to every modern woman's wardrobe, were already developed by the early years of the First World War.

But dress was only the most visible aspect of more profound changes Gabrielle Chanel would help to bring about. During the course of an extraordinary and unconventional journey – from abject poverty to the invention of a new kind of glamour – she helped to forge the idea of modern woman.

Leaving behind her youth of incarceration in religious institutions, Gabrielle became a shop assistant in a town thronging with well-to-do young military men from the regiments stationed on its perimeter. She then threw away any chance of respectability by becoming mistress to one of them and, over the years, her numerous subsequent liaisons were much talked about. Her relationship with the Grand Duke Dmitri Pavlovich was a remarkable reflection of changing times, while that with the fabulously wealthy Duke of Westminster was the stuff of legend. Her love affair with one of Europe's most eligible men, the enigmatic playboy Arthur Capel, enabled her to flourish, but would end in tragedy.

Aside from her dark beauty, Gabrielle was described as 'witty, strange, and mesmerizing'. She would become the muse, patron, collaborator or mistress to a number of remarkable men, including some of the most celebrated artists of modern times. These included Picasso, Cocteau, Stravinsky, Visconti, Dalí and Diaghilev.

In addition, Gabrielle rose to the highest echelons of society; created an empire; acquired the conviction that 'money adds to the decorative pleasures of life, but it is *not* life'; became a quintessential twentieth-century celebrity; and was transformed into a myth in her own lifetime.

To those already interested in her, the general outline of her life is well known, and I was reluctant to add to the large number of publications already out there. But Gabrielle's story is one of drama and pathos, and I had become intrigued. It was doubtful, however, that there was much left to discover.

Her first biographer, Edmonde Charles Roux, appeared to have found all that the passage of time and Gabrielle's concealment of her past would permit. Subsequent biographers had accepted this state of affairs and, thus, various periods in her life remained unknown. My interest had been caught, though, amongst other reasons, by the variety and calibre of artists whom she had known, artists instrumental in the creation of Modernism in early-twentieth-century bohemian Paris. Using Gabrielle's well-known story, my aim has been to draw out the remarkable connections between her and these artists and to give a broader interpretation of Gabrielle the woman and her legacy. Simply retelling the rags to riches narrative and listing the sartorial changes she is credited with inventing don't do justice to a woman who played a part in the formation of the modern world, not only in clothes but in its culture.

As I became more familiar with her story, however, the gaps were more tantalizing. In addition, while that first biographical interpretation had stamped itself upon the general perception of Gabrielle, intuition told me things were subtly different. Gabrielle left behind few letters and no diaries. Believing, nevertheless, that I might be able to turn up some new details, little did I know the trails I was to follow and the raft of discoveries I would be fortunate enough to make over the next three years. As these new elements of her story gradually fell into place, more light was in turn thrown on Gabrielle's character.

Her dreadful childhood was obviously critical, but while her own versions of it shifted like the sands, I found treasures once I had learned how to filter her own storytelling. Gabrielle often tells us as much about herself in what she left out or 'altered' as in what she told. Approaching her from a peripheral viewpoint was also fruitful. Had so and so known her? If so, what had been written up in their diaries or letters? One line here, another there, in a letter, or an interview, became crucial to the expanding story.

Once, I travelled to Ireland to meet Michel Déon, who had spent much time with Gabrielle sixty years before. As a successful young novelist, he had been commissioned to write her biography. I returned with no new 'facts', but something more important. Michel Déon had regaled me with anecdotes, interspersed with the sharpest of observations. At the same time, his compassion for Gabrielle was instrumental in the development of my own and my ability to look beyond her fantasies to comprehend her life-long emotional plight. Her vulnerability was largely concealed, but it contributed to her isolation.

The reminiscences of those who had known Gabrielle were invaluable, but other sources were also critical. My introduction to the American Russianist William Lee, for example, brought about his translations of a number of Duke Dmitri Pavlovich's diary entries, sent to me via instalments over several weeks. These have revised our understanding of Dmitri and Gabrielle's affair. They reveal quite a different relationship from the one traditionally described, which has Gabrielle the man-eater being mooned over by the young aristocrat.

My confirmation of Gabrielle's rumoured bisexuality and drug use is important, but as much as anything because their denial related to Gabrielle's refusal to face certain realities; publicly, anyway. Meanwhile, other discoveries were more significant, because they opened up deeper, sometimes disturbing, questions about her.

After months of searching, one day I sat with the son-in-law and grandson of Arthur Capel, unquestionably the great love of Gabrielle's life. His family had no more than snippets of information about their elusive forebear. This included the complex triangular relationship between him, Gabrielle and the woman he would marry instead, Diana Wyndham. But what I heard that day set me on the trail of this extraordinary man – whom Gabrielle said had made her – and the discovery of the poignant details of their affair.

During part of the Second World War, Gabrielle lived in occupied Paris at the Ritz with Hans von Dincklage, a German. The other 'guests' were German officers. It was already established that von Dincklage carried out some pre-war spying for his government. On meeting Gabrielle, apparently this had ceased and he was 'anti-war'. Gabrielle and von Dincklage's affair, and whatever his activities really were, have only been partially known. However, a cache of documents on von Dincklage in the Swiss Federal Archives, some in the French Deuxième Bureau, and yet more information in other, unlikely, places, have made it possible to give a fuller account of this reprehensible man than ever before. A master of seduction and deception, he was without question a spy. Yet while Gabrielle was undoubtedly a survivor, I don't believe she ever knew this. Nevertheless, post-war, she thought fit to remove herself to neutral Switzerland, to avoid any possible proceedings against her.

Having closed her couture house during the war, in 1954 she returned to it. At first a failure, Gabrielle once again became a world-class couturier. Her myth, which she nurtured, grew until it was sometimes impossible to distinguish it from the real woman. As one of the pioneers of modern womanhood, Gabrielle personified one of its greatest dilemmas: fame and fortune versus emotional fulfilment. Her myth was sometimes a substitute; she now had little else. Besides, her carapace of inviolability, her wall of self-protection, raised up over the years, meant that few were able to 'reach' her. In her last years, increasingly autocratic, Gabrielle remained formidable. Her loneliness was also sometimes tragic.

After her death, Chanel continued with increasing success, constantly reinventing Gabrielle's themes. As a result, the myth 'Coco Chanel' is now a global icon far outstripping her status in her own lifetime. I make no claim to have covered everything, or solved all the mysteries Gabrielle left behind. But in illuminating some of them, while she is presented without sentimentality, I hope the reader can feel compassion for this deeply complex woman; one of the most remarkable of the last century.

Gabrielle Chanel moved to Switzerland after the Second World War. It was here that she asked a friend, the writer and diplomat Paul Morand, to take down her memoirs. She left behind no diaries and only a handful of letters but, after her death, Morand was persuaded to publish the notes from those evenings in Switzerland. No other primary source gives as much insight into Gabrielle's extraordinary life as Morand's book, her memoir, The Allure of Chanel. *Gabrielle's own words ring out in the description which follows of an event that would alter the course of her life.*

Prologue: You're proud, you'll suffer

One night, just over a century ago, a couple made their way past the Tuileries, the oldest of Paris's gardens. They were to dine in St-Germain, the neighbourhood where the loftiest nobility still kept a mansion in town.

The young woman was straight and slender. Her heavy black hair was caught up at the nape of a long neck, dark eyes revealed little, and an unusually simple hat set off her angular beauty. She looked younger than her twenty-six years. Her English lover's gaze was sceptical, amused, revealing the confidence of privilege. His manner was, intentionally, less polished and urbane than that of his French peers.

As they went on, Gabrielle (who was to become known to some as Coco) talked. Enjoying her new-found independence, acquired with the progress of her little business, she remarked on how easy it seemed to be to make money, and was unprepared for her Englishman's response.

He told her she was wrong. Not only was she not making any money, she was actually in debt to the bank.

She refused to believe him. If she wasn't making any money, why did the bank keep giving it to her?

Her lover, Arthur Capel, laughed. Hadn't she realized? The bank only gave her money because he'd put some there as a guarantee. But she challenged him again.

'D'you mean I haven't earned the money I spend? That money's *mine.*'

'No, it isn't, it belongs to the bank!'

Gabrielle was shocked into silence. Keeping stride with her

quickened pace, Arthur told her that, only yesterday, the bank had telephoned to say she was withdrawing too much.

While her talk of business had provoked Arthur to reveal the truth of her situation, he didn't much care and told her it really wasn't important. This attempt to mollify her only renewed her defiance.

'The bank rang you? Why not *me*? So I'm dependent upon you?'[1]

In despair, she now insisted they go back across the river, but this brought her no respite. Looking around their well-appointed apartment, she saw the objects she had purchased with what she had thought to be her profits and was faced with the illusion of her independence. Everything had really been bought by Arthur. Her despair turning to hatred, she hurled her bag at him, ran down the stairs and out into the street. Heedless of the rain, she fled, intent on seeking refuge several streets away in her shop on the rue Cambon.

'Coco, you're crazy!' Arthur called out.

By the time he reached her, though they were both soaked, his instruction to her to be reasonable was useless and she sobbed, inconsolable.

In his arms, she was at last calmed. 'He was the only man I have loved,' she would say in later years. 'He was the great stroke of luck in my life . . . He had a very strong and unusual character . . . For me he was my father, my brother, my entire family.'[2] Yet only after much persuasion would she return to their apartment. In the early hours, when Arthur believed he had soothed the wound to her pride, at last, they both slept.

This experience transformed her purpose. A few hours later, arriving early at rue Cambon, she made a pronouncement to her head-seamstress, Angèle: 'From now on, I am not here to have fun; I am here to make a fortune. From now on, no one will spend one centime without asking my permission.'[3]

When Arthur shocked Gabrielle out of her fantasy and laughed at her self-delusion, even he, who understood her well, could not have predicted the ferocity of her response. He had done her a harsh favour, had compelled her to face reality. This was the catalyst that would release her most intense creative energies.

Coco Chanel would never forget Arthur's part in initiating her transformation. And if he had at first underestimated the degree to which her pride was the force that drove her, he was nonetheless the one who said to her, 'You're proud, you'll suffer.'[4]

In these words, he had singled out Gabrielle's most significant driving force, and foreseen that it would be the source of her vulnerability. Yet, while her pride was indeed to make her suffer, she believed it was the key to her success. 'Pride is present in whatever I do,' she would later say. 'It is the secret of my strength . . . It is both my flaw and my virtue.'[5]

Some time after the night that drove her to her new purpose, her business began to make a profit, and she would emerge from her understudy role as a kept young woman with a hat shop. As her rebellious and progressive style gradually became synonymous with her controversial life, Coco Chanel would embody an influential and glamorous new form of female independence. Later, she would say, 'But I liked work. I have sacrificed everything to it, even love. Work has consumed my life.'[6]

In the meantime, as her profits became substantial, she proudly told Arthur she no longer needed a guarantor and that he could withdraw all his securities. His reply was melancholy: 'I thought I'd given you a plaything, I gave you freedom.'[7]

I

Forebears

While state roads have carved up landscapes with a rigorous effi-ciency, leaving few places distant or mysterious, the region of Gabrielle Chanel's paternal ancestors, the Cévennes, retains a strong sense of its earlier remoteness. One of France's oldest-inhabited regions, it is that complex network of peaks, valleys and ravines forming the south-eastern part of the Massif Central. To the east it is cut off from the Alps by the cleft of the river Rhône, to the west lies the high, open-skied emptiness of the Causses. Here, vast lime-stone plateaux, dissected by deep river gorges, were traditionally the preserve of shepherds and their sheep.

By the eighteenth century, the valleys of the Cévennes were dependent upon silk farming and weaving and the cultivation of the mulberry. Below the highest Cévennes peaks, only fit for pasture, the chestnut still dominates this landscape. For a few centuries, it was this tree that provided any riches the high-Cévennes dwellers might possess.

Patches of misty cloud hang above dripping trees as the road makes a final twist and reaches Ponteils, a hamlet of stone houses. An immense rainbow arcs out over a mountainous distance, here vis-ible for the first time. Everywhere there are chestnut trees: thousands upon thousands – millions of them; impenetrable greenery reach-ing to the horizon and tempering the contours of these great heights.

Dwarfed by a church of incongruous proportions, the cluster of houses huddles against the mountain. In the high Cévennes, build-ings follow the incline of the slopes and are usually built on several levels. Their massive walls and roof-tiles are made from local stone, whose iridescent undertones sparkle in the sunlight after rain. When times were good, houses were rendered then painted with lime coloured with sheep's raddle in pale pink, ochre or indigo blue. Patches of this exquisite palette can sometimes still be found, in an old barn or some other forgotten corner. In the past, close by the houses a spring fed a stone water-reservoir; close to that was a vegetable garden; and, on a nearby terrace, the orchard.

Remote from the highways and their easier carriage of goods, the Cévenols long ago learnt to take full advantage of their local resources. The most precious of these was the sweet chestnut, the region's food staple, whose harvest was the barometer of prosperity and governed the daily round. Around the chestnuts' terraced orchards, one can still see the little stone buildings where the harvested fruits were carefully laid out to dry. Almost the only source of wood, the trees provided sturdy timbers for floors, doors, shutters, and supporting beams for the stone roof-tiles. In order to survive the formidable terrain, the peasants kept bees, a few sheep, goats or cattle.

Isolation creates independence and, for a long time, the Cévennes was one of those French regions stubbornly resistant to the national drive to unify this diverse country. In spite of the great road-building project of the first half of the nineteenth century, hamlets as remote as Ponteils would have to wait many years before their turn came around. For centuries, the inhabitants of such regions had moved around their native land – their *pays* – via myriad paths and tracks. Out of sight of the more populous carriageways, these 'routes' criss-crossed France, often invisible to all but local people, and the traders and shepherds making their seasonal journeys.

In 1792, only three years after the Revolution, Joseph Chanel, Gabrielle Chanel's great-grandfather, was born in Ponteils. As a journeyman carpenter, his betrothal enabled him to use his fiancée's modest dowry to rise above the perennial status of employee and become, at least partially, his own man. Joseph set himself up as the Ponteils tavern-keeper, in part of a large farmhouse standing on a little knoll above the hamlet. In time, the farmhouse became known as 'The Chanel', the name it retains to this day. The tough and forthright Cévenol mentality that had enabled the local early Protestants, the Huguenots, to withstand their terrible persecution would seem to have passed down the Chanel line to their descendant Gabrielle. One of her immediately noticeable traits was the directness of her manner, and the simplest definition of 'Protestant' – 'I protest' – would become one of the most significant aspects of her life. In years to come, her friend Jean Cocteau would say: 'If I didn't know she was brought up a Catholic, I would imagine she was a Protestant. She protests inveterately, against everything.'[1]

Today, the only memorial to any of the Chanels is the church records and Joseph's tavern. The Chanels of Ponteils were unexceptional; theirs were the lives of countless country people. But between 1875 and 1900, their region was hit by a series of exceptional natural disasters. Phylloxera ravaged the vines in the lowlands, the silkworm farmers reeled from the effects of a silkworm disease epidemic, and the vast chestnut forests of the uplands were eaten up by *la maladie de l'encre,* a disease specific to the species. With the core of the rural economy devastated, the villagers of Ponteils could only struggle on for so long. Thousands in the region forsook their birthplace in search of work and, between 1850 and 1914, the population of the Cévennes dropped by more than half.

Of Joseph Chanel's sons, only the eldest remained. The second, Henri-Adrien – Gabrielle's grandfather – and two younger brothers were among those whom *la maladie de l'encre* forced to leave Ponteils. As mountain dwellers, their skills weren't much use down in the valleys but, eventually, Henri-Adrien found work with a silk-farming family, the Fourniers, in Saint-Jean-de-Valériscle. The self-reliance of the mountain dweller sustained Henri-Adrien, and he survived his new life. Youth, ignorance and a taste for adventure permitted him the luxury of confidence. This same confidence soon led his employer's sixteen-year-old daughter to fall pregnant.

Virginie-Angélina's parents' fury became insistence that Henri-Adrien should marry their compromised offspring. The prospect of

9

Virginie-Angélina's dowry may have been the deciding factor in the young man's compliance. Soon after the ceremony, however, the newlyweds left the silk farm for Nîmes.

While only fifty miles distant from Ponteils, Nîmes was a world away from Henri-Adrien's life in the mountains. Even so, he knew that here there were already other refugees from Ponteils. The town might be frightening, but it was also a powerful lure, with the prospect of higher wages and an escape from tough country life. Although at first the town was lonelier, the work was easier, the hours shorter and medical care and charity were more available. In addition, not only were there 'coarse and dissolute delights',[2] but the country dweller experienced a new feeling, anonymity: 'In the crowd no one knows you.'[3] What befell Gabrielle Chanel's forebears was part of that great drift towards France's towns. And, as the countryside became sparsely populated, a slow but irrevocable change was taking place in the national mindset, the corollary of France's transformation into an industrial and metropolitan nation.

As for Henri-Adrien, aside from beggary there were few options and, almost inevitably, he turned to market trading. Markets and fairs were still essential elements in the economy, serving the majority of everyday needs. Some people bought enough for just one day at a time; others travelled miles to market to store up their provisions. Many made the journey to the markets and fairs simply for the contact with the outside world. Everything was there, from clothes – or the wherewithal to make them – to livestock, food and tools, to the strolling players: 'charlatans, magicians, musicians, singers . . . and gamblers'.[4] Some fairs even functioned as marriage marts, where, effectively, one could buy a wife.

For almost a year, Henri-Adrien and his Angélina stayed put at Nîmes. Then, one day, collecting up their meagre belongings, and their little boy, Henri-Albert (always known as Albert), they were gone. For years, the Chanels were to continue as itinerant market traders, eventually producing nineteen children in a series of cheap lodgings across the south of France.

Meanwhile, helped by the extension of roads and the spread of the railways, a revolution was sweeping across the land. Life in the provinces had continued in much the same way for centuries but, in the fifty years before 1914, it was set to change out of all recognition. What had customarily been the gradual and sporadic nature of change would be swept away by an avalanche of modernization. France was almost catapulted into the machine age; it was entirely different from anything the country had previously experienced.

In the spaces left by the country's transformation, Henri-Adrien and Angélina Chanel cobbled together an existence, but their class would be left behind, rendered virtually obsolete by the changes. Like many others', their minds remained in the old world they were unable to relinquish. As for the children, their lives were to straddle two entirely different worlds, one ancient, predominantly rural and agrarian; the other, modern, industrial and urban. Real success depended upon firmly grasping the new. And, a generation later, one member of the family would show that only through absolute acceptance of the new world could a person transcend mere survival and prosper. Henri-Adrien and Angélina's granddaughter Gabrielle would not only grasp this world, she was to become one of its architects.

Henri-Adrien combined the traditional wiliness of the peasant with the quicker-witted worldliness of the town dweller. He added the trader's patter and showmanship necessary in the markets. Although Henri-Adrien now often travelled by the new-fangled train, his life remained wedded to the traditional markets and the fairs; tied, like them, to the season-bound rhythms of rural life. Leaving behind his mountain hamlet and joining the exodus from the country to the towns, Henri-Adrien exhausted his ability to change by that one momentous move. And, as the century progressed, and with it the industrial centres, peasant life was increasingly perceived as inferior. In turn, by the early years of the twentieth century, many country dwellers were beginning to see themselves as somewhat inadequate.

As the Chanels' children grew up in their succession of back-street lodgings, they were soon put to work. The eldest, Albert, and his younger sister Louise worked with their parents from earliest childhood. Life was hard for the children, encouraging neither root-edness nor the ability to stick at much. The Chanels' nomadic lifestyle stoked in Albert a desire for the romance of the road and a constant urge for movement. He, too, became a market trader like his father, and sold haberdashery and domestic tools.

Taking the new railway out of the south, he was able to follow the progress of the ancient fairs. One November, he stopped at Courpière, a village in the region of Livradois. With winter's approach, itinerant traders and pedlars did their best to settle down. Albert found a room for himself with a young man called Marin Devolle, left fatherless at seventeen. That November of 1879, Marin was twenty-three and, while his carpentry went well enough, he could do with the extra money from hiring out a room. Albert was full of bonhomie, and he and Marin were soon firm friends. Marin's younger sister, Eugénie Jeanne (called Jeanne), lived close by with their maternal uncle, Augustin Chardon, a winegrower. Jeanne also kept house for her brother.

Family tradition has it that the twenty-six-year-old Albert was, like his father, a typical Chanel man. Essentially, he was a charmer, a showman who had a way with words and also with unwary women. Whether on the market 'stage' or playing the exhilarating game of seduction, Albert was unwilling to shoulder any responsi-bility besides the maintenance of his stock. Setting down the shallowest of roots, he was charismatic; inhabiting the world of per-formance, he juggled fantasies about who he wanted to be. And, each time his pool of buyers, and admirers, was exhausted, Albert collected his belongings and took off. In January 1880, as he had done before, and would do again, he left behind him a love-sick girl. This time it was Marin's sixteen-year-old sister, Jeanne, who was paying the price for succumbing to the young lothario's advances.

As the spring wore on, Jeanne was unable to hide her pregnancy, and her family was incensed. Uncle Augustin threw her out, and she went to live with Marin. By no means all working people saw the need to formalize their relationships – particularly if neither land nor worthwhile possessions were involved. However, as respectable property-owning artisans, Jeanne's family felt a cut above the country peasants, that class from which Albert Chanel sprang, and which was increasingly condescended to in newly metropolitan France. While the Devolles didn't live in Courpière's poorest quarter, their proximity to the bottom of the social ladder meant that anything pushing them down a rung was taken very seriously.

The mayor was enlisted to find the father of Jeanne's child. He tracked down Albert's parents, Henri-Adrien and Angélina, twenty-two miles away in Clermont-Ferrand but, with no response to his letter, Marin and two male relatives set off in pursuit. Either Albert Chanel was to marry their kinswoman, or he must recognize paternity of the child. If Chanel refused, they would have him up in court. These threats sufficiently frightened Albert's parents and they divulged Albert's whereabouts.

No sooner had Marin and his kinsmen returned to Courpière with Albert Chanel's current address than Jeanne set off after her errant lover, to Aubenas, 125 miles to the south. Now in the final month of her pregnancy, she believed Albert was more likely to make a respectable woman of her if she presented herself without family. The intrepid girl (who had never before left Courpière) travelled across country and found Albert established at a tavern. Here, a short time later, now turned seventeen, she gave birth to a baby girl, whom she named Julia-Berthe.

Albert was not pleased at being reunited with his conquest. His aim was to conquer, not to commit, and he absolutely refused to marry Jeanne. He did, however, acknowledge paternity of the child, and conceded to Jeanne's promotion as his companion: she was young, and he could do with help in the markets. At a time when the majority of marriages were based above all upon practicality, the loss of Jeanne's heart to her lover was seen by her community as soft-headed. But, even without her thraldom to Albert Chanel, the thought of her reception, on returning home with an illegitimate child, made going back impossible. Despite Albert's lack of welcome, Jeanne accepted his refusal to commit to her and stayed at his side. This episode would set the tone for their relationship, and the girl from Courpière was now constantly on the move.

In August of 1883, Jeanne was about to give birth once again. This time, she was in Saumur, the western provincial town that played host to the nation's elite cavalry regiment and the famed school of horsemanship, the Cadre Noir. Saumur was devoted to its permanent 'visitors', and the tailors, blacksmiths and farriers; the smart cafés, the elegant restaurants, the pretty 'working girls', all catered to the whims of the 'gentlemen officers'. The contrast between the officers' privileged lives and that of Jeanne and Albert in their garret lodgings, nearby the central market, could not have been greater.

On 18 August, during the greatest heat of the summer, Jeanne began her labour. Albert wasn't around but, somehow, his mistress got herself to the one place the poor were assured of assistance, the charity hospital run by the Sisters of Providence. One suspects that Jeanne arrived without a friend, and with her little girl, Julia-Berthe, in tow. The following day, the birth of a baby girl was registered at the town hall. Not only was Jeanne too unwell to attend but the father's signature is absent from both the child's registration and birth certificates. Albert was recorded as 'travelling'. With neither parent present, the child's name was misspelt and became 'Chasnel' instead of 'Chanel'. When, on the following day, the hospital chaplain christened the baby, in the mistaken belief that her parents were married, the little girl was named Gabrielle Jeanne Chasnel. This, then, was the inauspicious start to the life of a woman who was to become one of the celebrated figures of her century.

2

The Bad One

For the first year of her life, Gabrielle's parents remained in Saumur. One can't call it home, as there never was one. With a baby at Jeanne's breast and a toddler at her feet, she helped Albert in the town's markets. Albert frequently left behind his woman and children and set up his stall in another town. Jeanne knew Albert had other women and, while her desire to possess more of her man than he was ever prepared to give took its toll upon her health, her objections had little effect upon his conduct.

With her babies in tow, Jeanne was often obliged to supplement the family's meagre income by working as a domestic. For the rest, with few markets covered over, traders of this sort had no more than an awning to keep off the sun and rain, and mother and children were outside in all weathers. Yet, although Jeanne's life was one of unceasing labour, for the moment, youth and determination were on her side.

Jeanne's uncle Augustin Chardon now agreed to have her, Albert and the children to stay for a while, but only on one condition: that Albert marry his niece. After much discussion, and depressing evidence of Albert's reluctance in the matter, the banns were published at Courpière.

When the day arrived, Jeanne waited in vain with her family at the town hall: Albert did not appear. To their embarrassment and fury, he refused to attend, overcome at the thought of being shackled. Nothing like it could be recalled in Courpière, and Jeanne's relations' subsequent threats drove Albert Chanel to flee. A feckless man, who preferred a good yarn and a fast woman to anything more lasting, nevertheless, he showed extraordinary tenacity of purpose in his refusal to enter wedlock.

Following a series of pretty sordid negotiations, a deal was finally struck. Jeanne's family united, effectively, to pay Albert to marry her. As a precautionary measure, Albert would only receive his windfall of 5,000 francs, plus Jeanne's personal possessions and her furniture, once he had actually signed the contract. Whatever Jeanne's behaviour to the contrary, she nonetheless craved respectability, and her goal was achieved when Albert finally wed her, in November 1884.

Incapable of thrift, Albert quickly squandered his 5,000 francs on drink and swagger, thus curtailing his dream of advancement from market stall to his own haberdasher's shop.[1] Remaining in proximity to his in-laws now caused Albert still greater discomfort, and he set off for the south-west with his wife and little daughters to Issoire, a market town on the Couze river. Here, in 1885, Jeanne gave birth to their first son, Alphonse, who would become Gabrielle's favourite brother.

The Chanels usually found lodgings in the districts largely occupied by artisans' workshops, and the children thus grew up amidst the noise and smell of these last vestiges of pre-industrial France. They were familiar with the leather workers, the candle makers, the joiners, cobblers, tailors and seamstresses: traders whose hand skills – like those of the weavers, button makers, ribbon makers and cutlers from whom Albert bought his wares – were to become largely redundant as the factory machines far outstripped their rate of production.

In 1887, a third daughter was born to Jeanne and Albert at Issoire; they named her Antoinette. By now, the strain of caring for four young children, working outside and living in rundown accommodation was affecting Jeanne's health. The asthma from which she had long suffered had grown worse, and she persuaded Albert to return to Courpière, where Uncle Augustin again took them in. (Gabrielle would remember the misery of enforced silence, because of her mother's illness.)

Albert's unpopularity with his wife's family wasn't the only reason he soon left Courpière. It wasn't simply that his job involved constant travel; the young hustler was constitutionally incapable of remaining still. In stillness, he would have been obliged to face himself. This was something Albert strenuously avoided; a trait that would have an echo in his daughter Gabrielle's future life. Meanwhile, Jeanne's sense of self-preservation paled beside her obsession with her husband and, after a brief recuperation, she left the children behind and went in search of her no-good man. She returned periodically to Courpière, but the three older children – Julia-Berthe, Gabrielle and Alphonse – remained with their relations for some time. Jeanne's constant anxiety about her errant husband must have made her distracted; quite probably, she was depressed.

Aside from the children's extended interlude at Courpière, physical hardship, constant upheaval and a dysfunctional parental relationship were their lot. Little Gabrielle's response to this seems clear: she was angry. As a way of incorporating and managing her predicament, she resorted to the healthy habit of childhood: make-believe. Years later, she told of acting out her fantasies in an overgrown Courpière churchyard, over which she ruled, and where the dead were her subjects. Sometimes, she took along her rag dolls to join in her conversations with the dead. In a way, the dead and her dolls were Gabrielle's only fixed points; her only sense of certainty in a world where the living were so miserably failing her.

While the instability of Gabrielle's world gave her little sense of control, her consequent feelings of impotence were made worse by what she would later describe as her relatives' 'insensitivity'. Discovering that she had stolen kitchen objects and flowers as 'offerings' for her lonely games, her elders thwarted Gabrielle's make-believe world by locking things away out of reach. She reacted with disobedience and, in due course, was stigmatized as the 'bad one'. Her older sister, Julia-Berthe, was never very bright and, although Alphonse was Gabrielle's favourite, it takes little to see that she was angry and frustrated at her powerlessness. She felt lonely, abandoned and, most of all, unloved.

In 1889, Jeanne gave birth to her second son, Lucien. Eighteen months later, again pregnant, and in poor health, she made her way back to Courpière. Here, she gave birth to a third boy, named Augustin, in honour of her uncle. The baby, however, was sickly and soon died. Jeanne's family now dissuaded her from returning to Albert and, for a year or so, she saw little of her reprobate husband. At the same time, Jeanne was jealous of the liaisons she knew he would be conducting, and pined for him. In due course, with an awful inevitability, the old pattern reasserted itself and, in 1893, against her family's wishes, Jeanne set off in search of her Albert.

He had sent word that he was running a tavern with his brother at Brive-la-Gaillarde, in the Limousin, many miles from Courpière. Jeanne now made the journey of over a hundred miles, hoping, against all odds, that Albert's new trade signified a change in their fortunes for the better. This time, either Jeanne's family refused to look after Julia-Berthe and Gabrielle, or Jeanne wanted them with her, because she took her eldest girls along.

Typically, Albert's story was a fabrication and Jeanne's optimism proved unfounded. Rather than managing the tavern, Albert was nothing more than its waiter. However dispirited Jeanne must have felt, she didn't have the strength of mind to go back to her relations in Courpière. Neither would she have had the money for the fare. With thirteen-year-old Julia and ten-year-old Gabrielle as assistants, Jeanne applied herself to the old routine.

A life of unrelenting work, bad living conditions, consistent neglect and almost certain physical abuse from a man was the lot of so many of Jeanne's female compatriots. As a result, their lives followed an almost inevitable path. By the winter of 1894, Jeanne was in a very poor state of health, and frequently confined to bed with asthma. Eventually, she developed bronchitis, and lay ravaged by a fever and without medical help. Finally, she could take no more and was released from her struggle, dying in a Brive-la-Gaillarde garret in February 1895. Albert's wanderlust and need for money had sent him out on the road again, and he was absent when his wife died. Jeanne had long since lost her youth to a punishing physical and emotional schedule. Now, at a mere thirty-one years of age, she had also lost her life.

Her daughters Julia-Berthe and Gabrielle would have seen the awful decline in their mother's health and been powerless to halt it. Quite probably, they shared the room in which she slept. Almost certainly, it was they who discovered her death. In the absence of their father, it was his brother, Hippolyte, who signed the death certificate and made the arrangements for Jeanne's funeral.[2] Those in the family who could have told more never would.

3
The Lost Years

Jeanne Chanel's death was to usher in perhaps the most mysterious period in her children's lives. Gabrielle's early childhood is obscure enough but, for the next six or so years, there is virtual silence – an ominous silence, because instituted by Gabrielle herself. Throughout her life, she would remain self-conscious about her background. Indeed, it was rumoured that she paid some of her family and her associates not to speak about her past and negotiated the destruction of certain documents. Whatever the truth, while Gabrielle failed to hide it completely, she did succeed in disguising her early life. In doing this, she not only censored the most formative period of her life but, by extension, tried to destroy her early self.

Despite this self-imposed silence, the life Gabrielle told her friend the writer Paul Morand, while often a remoulding of events, is nonetheless a remarkable 'memoir'. Although Gabrielle was a supreme realist, following her fantasist father's example, she was always driven to hide from the childhood that had damaged her. Thus she would say, 'Reality doesn't make me dream . . . and I like to dream.'[1] Her miserable beginnings, combined with her artistic nature, meant that Gabrielle didn't have too much time for the past. As a creator, it was the present and the future that held the most meaning for her. In retelling her past, Gabrielle did more than simply survive its horrors; she used her intelligence and imagination to create a new one. Yet, while unwary Chanel biographers have read her extraordinary memoir, given to Paul Morand, too literally, when one has the key, one discovers much treasure there.

In searching for reality in Gabrielle's stories, what one repeatedly finds is that the truth of an event for her lay not in the *fact* but in the *feeling*. She retained the emotional and psychological *residue* of the past. As a result, at the heart of her tales one often discovers the tenor of what happened; what Gabrielle chose to tell often revealed far more than it appeared at first sight. Bearing this in mind, one is left with the impression of an overwhelmingly sad childhood: 'My earliest childhood. Those words . . . make me shudder. No childhood was less gentle. All too soon I realized that life was a serious matter.'[2]

In her recollections, Gabrielle recalled her mother in no more than a handful of anecdotes. Among them we notice the little girl's capacity for destructiveness, and her mother's telling response, as in this incident when the children were staying with their mother at Uncle Augustin's. The adults had shut the children out of the way. Bored with their seclusion, they noticed how easily the damp wallpaper could be removed. At first it was just a little strip they took off, but then, to their great amusement, they found they could pull off whole sections at once. They peeled off more, then clambered on chairs they'd piled up, gradually revealing the pink plaster. Then they stripped the ceiling! Their mother eventually came in to discover this 'disaster'. She didn't reprimand the children, just stood silently weeping. Little Gabrielle was so taken aback by her poor mother's response that she 'ran away howling with sorrow'. And Gabrielle soon recognized that life was indeed 'a solemn affair, since it caused mothers to cry'.[3]

On another occasion, the children were put to bed in a workroom. Bunches of grapes were hanging from the rafters in paper bags, preserving them for the winter. Throwing a pillow, Gabrielle brought down a paper bag. This was hilarious. Felling another one, she then set to work with a bolster. Finally, she had 'brought the entire harvest of grapes down, so that they were strewn over the wooden floor . . . For the first time in my life I was whipped. The humiliation was something I would never forget.'[4]

Jeanne's family scorned her ramshackle life with Albert, and her aunts made superior remarks, such as 'These people live like travelling circus folk.' As for the children, Gabrielle sensed particular disapproval of herself, borne out when one aunt prophesied that she would 'turn out badly'. Another talked of 'selling her to the gypsies' and 'discussed beating her with nettles'. Gabrielle's defence was 'stubborn defiance'. Thus upping the stakes, she provoked still greater chastisement, which in turn 'only made me more uncivilized, more fractious'.[5] One of the saddest legacies of this pattern of behaviour was the self-loathing Gabrielle described. In childhood and youth, she believed she was ugly, almost cursed. Only much later was she proud of whom she had become.[6]

At Jeanne Chanel's death, while neither aunts nor uncles nor grand-parents were willing to take responsibility for Albert's children, neither was he going to himself. Perhaps no one could afford to feed and house these extra mouths; perhaps their impoverished and semi-nomadic lifestyle had left them unacceptably feral in the eyes of their relatives. Clearly, the bond between the children and their extended family wasn't strong, or a way would have been found to take in at least one or two of them. Gabrielle was left with an undying grudge against her family. It was her father's behaviour, however, that was to scar her with a morbid fear of abandonment. She struggled to camouflage this handicap, but it was to haunt Gabrielle, revealing its corrosive power over and over again.

As for Gabrielle's father, for whom, most of the time, she felt such longing, the pain of blaming him was more than she could bear. So she did the only thing that gave her any control: she *retold* their story. In the retelling, Albert was absolved of almost all blame, because Gabrielle projected her anger and disappointment at the rest of her family.

Another aspect of Gabrielle's early life that caused her much suffering was her lack of social status. Over time, she would convert her sense of inadequacy over her missing father, and her lack of social status, into a most creative set of fantasies. These would become crucial to her psychic health by permitting her to believe that she was loved.

Gabrielle would tell how, after her mother's death and still in deep mourning, she arrived with her father at the miserable house of some unwelcoming old aunts. Albert ignored his six-year-old daughter's pleas and left without more ado. He then sailed for America, where he went to seek his fortune. Having succeeded, he returned and visited his pining daughter, or wrote to her when he could. But he never took her to the new home he had promised, and Gabrielle remained with her aunts; effectively, an orphan.

The more accurate details of the story are these: Albert never travelled to America; neither did he make anything resembling a fortune. He was a drunken braggart; his life one of fantasy and evasion. When Gabrielle's mother died, Gabrielle was in fact eleven, not six. Neither was she alone in the place where her father so callously left her. She was accompanied by two sisters, Julia and Antoinette. But who were these aunts? According to family memory, they were the nuns of the convent orphanage at Aubazine, a small village in the Corrèze, not far from Brive-la-Gaillarde, where the children's mother had died. While the records from this period are lost, it was in this convent of Aubazine that Gabrielle would be cloistered, with her sisters and other orphan girls, for the following six or so years.

The young Gabrielle was desperate at her father's imminent departure and cried out, 'Take me away from here! Take me away!' Albert told her not to worry, everything would be all right; he would return and take her with him as soon as he was able. But he had no intention of returning. Over the years, Gabrielle usually kept to the story about Albert's journey to America; it enabled her to maintain her pride. But, on other occasions, she communicated her sense of abandonment, saying, 'Those were his last words. He did not come back.'

Sometimes, she would say that he wrote telling her to trust him and that his business was doing well, but the other, more level-headed Gabrielle would say, 'We didn't hear another word from him.' Almost certainly, Albert Chanel never wrote to Gabrielle, nor to any of his other children, and Gabrielle waited in vain for the father whom she never saw again. This final rejection somehow

sealed her fate. Although she was to become a woman of great fortitude, Gabrielle would never prove emotionally resilient when
'left'; particularly when the leaving was by a man. In summing up
her childhood, she would say she knew 'no home, no love, no father
and mother. It was terrible.'[7] And, as she had in that childhood, in
adulthood, she would weave herself new stories in order to survive.

When the eleven-year-old Gabrielle was deposited in the convent,
she sought refuge in thoughts about dying, or destruction, or injur-
ing those who had cruelly betrayed her. In her impotent rage, she
dreamed of setting fire to the convent's great barn. Yet, for all her
misery and longing to destroy this 'awful place', in many ways,
Gabrielle and her sisters were to fare better than their brothers,
Alphonse and Lucien.[8]

Unable to enter the convent, at the tender ages of ten and six they
were placed with peasant farmers, becoming two more of the thousands of children abandoned by their parents each year into this
then-still-acceptable form of semi-slavery. Authorities frequently
placed orphaned or deserted boys with foster families, whose modest payments for their charges' board and lodging traditionally
supplemented the family's income, while the boys' hard labour supplemented the workforce. These young children were seldom
nurtured, and remained, literally, outsiders, more often than not
sleeping in the barns. In winter, they slept close to the animals in
their attempts to keep warm. Remonstration with foster parents by
the parish priest had little effect, and it wasn't uncommon for these
shunned, abused and neglected children to die while in the care of
these families.

Jeanne and Albert Chanel's five children may have suffered emotional and physical deprivation when tramping the roads with their
parents. But their mother's death, their father's abandonment and
the harshness of their new lives initiated a period of even greater
hardship. Added to this, the girls were separated from their brothers, and they may not have seen one another for several years.

A small compensation for the Chanel children's life of nomadic poverty had been the companionship of other families like themselves. But life in the convent for Gabrielle and her sisters could not have been more different. Aubazine was the largest girls' orphanage in the region, and behind its high walls they must truly have felt imprisoned. From the moment of waking to the moment of falling asleep, from early mass to prayers before bed, life was rigidly prescribed.

Unlike the young women whose moneyed parents could afford to pay for their convent schooling, these were charity children at an orphanage. A good fraction of the Aubazine girls were also illegitimate, a state bringing with it yet further stigma. Neither would the nuns have held back from reminding their charges that their condition was indeed shameful.

Before the Chanel sisters' incarceration at Aubazine, coming and going from Courpière, as they had, their school attendance can only have been sporadic. One of the most significant reasons for this, however, was not simply that the Chanels moved around so much. For the poor, schooling was seen as next to useless for any practical purposes. A child not earning was a burdensome mouth to feed. In addition, what use to them was the metric system they were taught in school? When Gabrielle was young, market traders and the ordinary people still weighed their goods in *toises*, *cordes* and *pouces*, and counted out in *Louis* and *écus*. They didn't use the *franc*, the currency imposed since the Revolution as a tool to unite France.

While the recent drive to educate more French children had radically shaken up the system, nowhere near all school-age children regularly attended school in the 1890s. Many of the poor simply couldn't afford books, paper, ink and pens, and none were provided by the state. It was all just further strain on the already depleted family purse, and the response was often truancy. In 1884, a year after Gabrielle's birth, the future president of France, Georges Clemenceau, asked a peasant why his son didn't go to school. The retort came quickly: 'Will *you* give him a private income?'[9]

If reading and books were of little use for many country people, because they had little practical application,[10] the French language itself, the most basic tool of the educational system, presented one of the greatest difficulties for people such as the Chanels. French, the language intended to unite the regions of this large and disparate country, and therefore the one used in schoolbooks and school lessons, was *not* the language of most people in the provinces. Like the Chanels, they spoke in their own dialect. As one teacher put it in 1894, the year before Gabrielle arrived at Aubazine, 'In the great majority of our rural schools, children come ... knowing little French and hearing only *patois* spoken.'[11]

To make matters worse, Gabrielle's lessons were taught by dictation and rote learning, the core teaching method since the Middle Ages. Learning things by heart, *patois*-speaking children often failed to *understand* what it was they were learning. 'Parrot fashion' was an apt description. Eventually, the people from the provinces would learn the language of their nation but, at the end of the nineteenth century, one teacher despaired of these *patois* speakers. 'Our children ... have no way to find enough French words to express their thoughts.'[12] Thus, when Gabrielle was young, few in the regions could either read or write French well. And, while Gabrielle would always remain grateful to the sisters at Aubazine for helping her to lose her *patois* and teaching her to speak the 'language of well-bred people', it is most unlikely she was ever comfortable *writing* in her national language.

One might reasonably assume that, one day, a cache of Gabrielle's letters or diaries will turn up. In years to come, she would know the painter Salvador Dalí, and in one of his letters to her he said he'd been told that 'you never, never, never write, which I'm already starting to notice.' This is not an anomaly. In the small number of letters we know of in Gabrielle's hand, her unfamiliarity with written French is confirmed. In comparison with the finesse of her personal manner, her written French is neither very well expressed nor particularly grammatical. My own belief is that almost no letters from Gabrielle will ever be found, because she actually wrote very few. By committing as little as possible to paper, she was hiding another source of her sense of inadequacy.

★ ★ ★

The twelfth-century hermit Etienne de Viezaux (St Stephen) founded the convent of Aubazine at a remote spot, in his words, 'to be far from the concourse of men'. Even today, Aubazine feels distant from any great 'concourse' and, soon after its founding, the monastery became a welcome resting place on the great pilgrim route to Santiago de Compostela.

During the terrors of the Revolution, a new religious order, the Congregation of the Sacred Heart of Mary, was founded to care for the poor and rejected, including running homes for abandoned and orphaned girls. At Aubazine, whose towering chapel reflects its prominence as church to the Romanesque abbey, the sisters restored the austere buildings. The long, white-washed corridors and convent rooms are high, wide and airy, and the doors are a contrast in black; the colour worn by nuns and pupils alike. When Gabrielle arrived at Aubazine, seven centuries, and many feet, had worn a beautiful dip in the great central stone staircase.

Aubazine's isolation meant that, aside from the odd festival, guided walk or occasional visit to relations, there was little respite from the girls' regimented and cloistered existence. State education wasn't always up to much, but religious institutions such as this were often woefully behind even that. The educational drive of such orphanages was the moulding of their charges into devout Christians and devoted future employees. Long hours were spent at catechism and the prayer book. Given the convent's rural location, the majority of its girls were, like Gabrielle, the offspring of peasants. Social hierarchy inside religious institutions rigidly followed life outside them, and social mobility was not, therefore, something the nuns expected of their charges. They became servants, shop assistants or, if they were lucky, the wives of peasant farmers. Aubazine pupils were an underclass and such it was presumed they would remain.

Beyond a limited proficiency in reading, arithmetic, and possibly French history and geography, lessons were of a very basic nature. What orphanage sisters did, however, regard as essential were housekeeping skills for the girls' hardworking future lives. They also tried to ensure that their pupils left with the modest trousseau including household linen they had sewn for themselves during their years under the nuns' care.

Life at Aubazine was busy but deeply uneventful. By contrast, Gabrielle's first eleven years had been spent in a round of ceaseless activity, either travelling or in the noisy, gaudy bustle and repartee of the markets. She was accustomed to people whose rough and precarious lives were lived on a public stage. Those who succeeded best had the keenest sense of showmanship, the quickest sense of humour and the greatest flair for holding their audience with a tale or a joke. Capturing the imagination, these people knew that the business of selling was, in large part, performance. And aspects of this upbringing would not go amiss in Gabrielle's future life.

Transplanted as cruelly as she had been to the seclusion of a convent, Gabrielle was intelligent and curious enough about the world to chafe at her incarceration. One rare form of escape did, however, provide a feast for her imagination.

In the last quarter of the nineteenth century, as village communities were much reduced and the urban mentality became dominant in France, the hugely expanded popular newspapers developed a vast circulation. Counter to tradition and the rural way of life, these organs of mass communication celebrated speed, spontaneity and all that was unpredictable. They exemplified the city, and Paris in particular. Celebrating modernity, the popular press enabled people to make some sense of their newly urbanized world. It also introduced a new concept, the serial novel, the *feuilleton*, and it soon became something of a national obsession. While many families collected their instalments, until they had grown into a book, critics lamented the *feuilletons'* formidable influence.

Along with thousands of others, Albert's younger sister, Gabrielle's Aunt Louise, decamped from the daily round by immersing herself in the latest *feuilleton*, and Gabrielle remembered: 'We never bought books . . . we cut out the serial from the newspaper and sewed them all together.'[13] She also smuggled these back to the attics at Aubazine, where she hid from reality in their glamour and romance. Her adolescent dreams were fuelled by these torrid fictions, crammed with scenes of passion and love that always triumphed. When Gabrielle's shameful worldliness was discovered, she was severely chastised by the nuns but, years later, while saying that the writers were 'ninnies', she also claimed to have learnt more from these popular fictions than from anything in her impoverished education. She added meaningfully that the romances 'taught me about life; they nourished my sensibility and my pride'.[14]

For the most part, however, Gabrielle's time at Aubazine was to remain a poorly healed wound. To contemporaries, an illegitimate birth, impoverished childhood and abandonment to an orphanage were slurs upon one's reputation and, once out in the world, Gabrielle set about concealment. If, once or twice, the burden of this anxious secret left her feeling so alone she was driven to confide it in full, her confidants were decent enough to tell no one.

Yet, while we catch only glimpses of the crucial years that formed Gabrielle, over time she found covert ways to express herself and tell her story. She described repeatedly, for example, a profound antipathy for a group of women she called her 'aunts'. Unpicking the web of misinformation Gabrielle wove around herself, one sees that these 'aunts' were not one but two sets of women. They were a conflation of her real aunts and the sisters of Aubazine. Together, they took the brunt of Gabrielle's youthful resentment, the memory of which still rankled over half a century later. Above all, she believed that, for her 'aunts' – in other words, her family, and the nuns – 'Love was a luxury and childhood a sin.'[15] Surrounded as she was by unloving authority figures, Gabrielle's early experience was one of consistent disharmony, repression and neglect.

4

Things that I should be and which I am not

In their eighteenth year, when the girls left the confines of Aubazine, the nuns saw themselves as responsible for their continuing welfare. First Julia-Berthe, then Gabrielle and, finally, Antoinette, left behind this remote place that had held them for so long. What we don't know is why, on leaving Aubazine, they didn't set off, along with the thousands of other girls from humble backgrounds, in search of work. Instead, the nuns arranged for the Chanel girls' transfer to *another* convent. This was at Moulins, a small town over a hundred miles to the north.

The Moulins convent of Notre Dame was a local finishing school of sorts, with a contingent of charity pupils, whom Gabrielle joined in 1901. Seated in a lower position at table and in church, and wearing clothes of poorer quality, the charity pupil was seldom permitted to forget her inferior status. At Moulins, young Gabrielle's position was even more irksome to her than at Aubazine, where at least the girls had all sprung from similarly modest backgrounds. As a final humiliation, the Moulins charity girls were obliged to fulfil domestic duties to supplement their keep.

Despite the fact that Gabrielle's sisters were at Aubazine, when later speaking covertly of her time there, she always gave the impression that her childhood and youth were spent without siblings or friends. At Moulins, however, she found a friend.

Adrienne Chanel was the youngest of Henri-Adrien and Angélina Chanel's nineteen children. Their eldest, Albert, was Gabrielle's father, twenty-eight years older than Adrienne. With only two years between the two girls, Gabrielle and Adrienne looked like sisters. Adrienne, a boarder at Notre Dame since the age of ten, made Moulins more acceptable for Gabrielle. The older girl's self-possession and tranquil nature were strongly contrasted with the defensiveness and pent-up energy of her niece Gabrielle. A photograph of the girls together, taken shortly after this period, is a striking illustration of their different personalities. Adrienne places one hand fetchingly on her hip; the other is behind Gabrielle's head, as if showing her to the camera. Adrienne looks a little concerned, and pleased, smiling lovingly at her friend, who keeps her own hands firmly behind her back. With the barest hints of a smile, Gabrielle looks fiercely into the camera.

What had made these young women so unalike, when they had so much in common? Both were the children of impoverished, nomadic market traders. Adrienne boarded at a convent at ten; Gabrielle joined Aubazine at eleven. Adrienne's parents couldn't scrape together the money to spare their daughter the stigma of charity status, also borne by Gabrielle during her years at Aubazine and Moulins. There was, though, one significant difference between them: Adrienne had always felt cared for. Her parents made regular visits to Moulins to see their favourite daughter. In addition, Adrienne often visited her older sister Louise (second-born, after Gabrielle's father, Albert), who lived not far away with her husband, the stationmaster at Varennes. Adrienne made the best of her lot, and a lovable and vibrant personality had endeared her to the nuns at Notre Dame. Rather than regretting her time there, Adrienne benefited and became a charming and competent young woman.

Her sister Louise, having long since rejected the ramshackle, nomadic life that was her birthright, didn't mind that Varennes was a one-street, nowhere place consisting of her husband's railway station, an inn, a church and a short straggle of houses. She happily occupied herself with her children, the housekeeping and maintaining the niceties of her improved social position. And it was she who drew the Chanels together, at Varennes, where they had the semblance of a home. Even Gabrielle's recalcitrant father called in on occasion (albeit secretly, so as to avoid seeing his children). Gabrielle's disillusionment intensified when, one day, Louise let slip this information.

While Gabrielle was at Aubazine, she and Adrienne may possibly have met each other when visiting Louise on the odd occasion but, after Gabrielle's arrival at Moulins, she and Adrienne became firm friends. Nearby were Adrienne's parents (Gabrielle's grandparents), Henri-Adrien and Angélina, who had finally come to a halt in Moulins. That summer of 1901, a young woman's reputation still required her being chaperoned in public and, accordingly, Louise would have obliged on their visits to her home.

Louise, both an adept with her needle and a woman of some artistic flair, had a great passion for hats. Following her periodic orgies of window-shopping in the fashionable spa town of Vichy, nearby, she then visited the haberdasher's and bought the wherewithal to conjure the latest stylish hat. Adrienne and Gabrielle were willing pupils, their imaginations fired by these flights of fancy. In contrast, Gabrielle recalled with venom the needlework her 'aunts' imposed upon her at 'their gloomy house' (presumably, the convent). Such sewing had angered her beyond measure, and she was elated when she was able to abandon working on her trousseau, 'embroidering initials on towels . . . and sewing crosses in Russian stitching on my nightdresses, for a hypothetical wedding night', which made her 'spit'.[1]

Meanwhile, despite the new proximity to her grandparents and the home-loving Aunt Louise, the only extended-family member for whom Gabrielle developed any real affection was the lovely Adrienne. For the rest, Gabrielle's doleful history made her pretty well impervious to any advances from her family. Although we can't be certain, it appears that Gabrielle's mother's relations in Courpière had virtually no contact with Gabrielle and her siblings after Jeanne's death. Gabrielle may, however, have simply erased them from the story because she resented them for not having taken them in.

Moulins, an ancient cathedral town situated in central France, was previously seat to the dukes of Bourbon. In 1901, it was, above all, a garrison, whose livelihood largely depended upon the military regiments stationed on its perimeter. Following Gabrielle's years of seclusion, this bustling provincial centre, made urbane by its attachments of officers, must have seemed a bright prospect indeed. But, before Gabrielle could savour it, she had to watch from the sidelines, in the convent, for one last, frustrating year. Finally leaving religious institutions behind, on the mother superior's recommendation Gabrielle joined Adrienne as an assistant in a smart draper's shop in town. Lodging with their earnestly respectable employers, M. and Mme Desboutin, the girls were obliged to ape them in being disdained by local society women while serving in the shop.

After a year and a half under the Desboutins' watchful eyes, at the age of twenty-one, Gabrielle could bear it no longer. Escaping her lifetime of being under surveillance, she set off to live somewhere of her own choosing. Although her room was in the most downmarket Moulins neighbourhood, her liberty must at first have felt quite heady, and she persuaded Adrienne to strike out from the Desboutins and join her. As seamstresses, the Chanel girls had joined the thousands upon thousands of others working at what was then, along with domestic service, the most common of all female employment. Regardless of frequently considerable skills, a seamstress's wages were pitiful. Like many another seamstress, the girls took on a Sunday job to bolster their paltry earnings, working at one of the town's several tailor shops.

With hundreds of officers stationed around Moulins, there was a lot of work available, tailoring, altering uniforms and kitting out local worthies for the racing each season. The most exalted of the cavalry regiments was the 10th Light Horse, whose intake was drawn from the highest echelons of Parisian society, plus the landed gentry. Although forward-thinking politicians now regarded cavalry regiments as outdated, the old guard saw them as the most distinguished in all France.

The story is told that, one Sunday, Gabrielle and Adrienne were at work in the tailor's shop when a party of six young lieutenants turned up for some last-minute alterations. Standing around, some in their shirt-tails, they noticed the two pretty girls busy in the next room. Despite determined overtures from the young men, they

remained studiously absorbed in their sewing. Intrigued, the officers quizzed the tailor, discovered the girls' other place of work and
waylaid them with an invitation to watch the horse-jumping. The
girls agreed, but with an *hauteur* only serving to fascinate the distinguished young men still further. All went well, and soon Gabrielle
and Adrienne were being escorted to La Tentation to eat sherbets,
or passing the time flirting with their admirers at the smart set's
favourite rendezvous, the art nouveau Grand Café.

The Chanel girls were enthralled by these encounters, savouring
this unfamiliar admiration from their socially superior escorts, some
of the most eligible young men in France. Men supremely confident in their youth, their wealth and their pedigree, with ineffable
style the officers exuded the casual charm of those accustomed to
having their own way. Towards girls lower down the social scale,
however, that charm often held an undercurrent of condescension.

The Chanels were invited to evenings at La Rotonde, a large café
functioning as a kind of small-scale music hall, a type of *café-concert*
(*caf'conc*) for entertaining the army in garrison towns. Deriving
from the far more worldly seductiveness of Parisian *café-concerts*
such as the Alcazar and the Eldorado, which played host to celebrated performers such as Yvette Guilbert and the great Mistinguett,
the entertainment in the *beuglants* (the name given to provincial
caf'concs) was an altogether less sophisticated and heartier affair.

Café-concerts had developed around mid-century as simple shows
for the populace at ordinary cafés on Paris's boulevards. The aim
was sociable drinking, light music and performance concentrating
on the travails of everyday urban low life, including erotic innu-
endo, love and catchy, nonsensical choruses. Before the cinema took
off in a big way, the *caf'conc* was the pivot of social life for the newly
urban working classes. The cafés, music hall and literary cabaret
variations they spawned, such as the Folies Bergère, the Moulin
Rouge and the Mirliton, became popular with other sections of
society. Not only did the bohemian painters, poets and writers rou-
tinely patronize these café-clubs, the bourgeoisie got a frisson from
their raffish and anarchic atmosphere.

Unaccustomed as the Chanel girls were to the more high-brow opera and theatre, they relished their visits to the *beuglants*. Indeed, the noise, the strangers and the bawdy, quick-talking showmanship were reminiscent of the atmosphere in the fairs and markets of their childhood.

With the pianist, the singer belted out her numbers over the cheery din of the crowd. Behind her sat a ring of *poseuses* – young hopefuls who stepped forward, one by one, to fill in with popular refrains while the lead took her much-earned break. The *poseuses* were there above all to strike poses, the more suggestive the better. Yet, despite the frequent indignity of these occasions – the audience booed and threw cherry pips if the girl didn't pass muster – life on stage beckoned to these young women as one of the few available escape routes from lives of certain servility.

The celebrities at the great *caf'concs* in Paris were invariably from impoverished backgrounds. Armed with singular personalities, they cloaked themselves in a shimmer of glamour and sang with black humour and pathos of the exacting lives of the poor. Fantasies of becoming such a celebrity were what Gabrielle was harbouring when she persuaded the manager of the Moulins *beuglant* to take her on as a *poseuse*. Not a girl with come-hither eyes nor the traditionally prized voluptuous female form, Gabrielle nonetheless possessed her own particular allure. So too did Adrienne, whom Gabrielle next persuaded to join her.

While Gabrielle can't have had much of a voice, the story is told that, at this juncture, she acquired the sobriquet by which the world came to know her. One of the songs she is supposed to have sung to greatest effect was a verse from a popular *caf'conc* revue called 'Ko Ko Ri Ko'. Another was '*Qui qu'a vu Coco dans l'Trocadéro?*' (Who's Seen Coco at the Trocadéro?). Gabrielle was game and determined, with a quick sense of humour, and character and individuality were what the cabarets wanted above all. Her admirers were noisy in their approval. For an encore, they simply chanted the word found in both her songs: 'Coco! Coco! Coco!' And at La Rotonde she was soon La petite Coco. Gabrielle herself always insisted that her nickname had originated with her father. While this may have been wishful think-ing, Coco *was* a known diminutive for a child.

In a short time, the spirited and entertaining Chanel girls became favourites of the officers and their crowd; an indispensable comple-ment to an evening. Amongst Gabrielle and Adrienne's aristocratic companions at Moulins was a young *haut bourgeois*, Etienne Balsan, whose family's considerable fortune derived from astute invest-ments in wool. At Châteauroux, in the Indre, in the centre of France, where fine wool had been made for centuries, the Balsan family's vast textile factory produced cloth for military uniforms (and the British police) with great success. While virtually owning the town, the Balsans also kept a number of fine houses in the environs. The three sons were expected to enter the family business, but their social lives as well-to-do *fin de siècle* bachelors were also permitted. In time, both Etienne Balsan and his older brother, Jacques, were to make names for themselves far beyond the family trade in wool.

Following their father's premature death, Etienne was sent to private school in England by his uncle, Charles, in an attempt to instil some discipline into the boy. From England, he sent home a telegram from his dog, Rex, saying, 'My master has arrived safely, Rex.' He then bought two horses, which he used in regular and popular attendance at the local fox-hunting meets. Etienne was obsessed with horses and, during his time away, paid little attention to his lessons. Neither, after the initial telegram from his dog, did he make any more contact with his family. Summoned home by Uncle Charles, Etienne was unconcerned. His despairing relation, mean-while, failed to appreciate that beneath Etienne's apparent lack of purpose was the seed of a serious and disciplined calling. He was simply not interested in the same things as his uncle and informed him that under no circumstances would he enter the family firm. Indeed, it was only with great reluctance that the young man was cajoled into military service.

To Etienne's horror, his service saw him stationed with a foot regiment rather than the cavalry. This was insupportable, and he soon had himself transferred to a place where he could spend his time with horses. A series of events led to a posting to Algeria, in the African Light Cavalry, and here Etienne found himself one day very hot and very bored. Caught sleeping on sentry duty by the regimental governor, whom he failed to recognize in civilian dress, he was reprimanded for dereliction of duty. Etienne foolishly answered back, was thrown in the lock-up and was then to put on fatigues to clean out the latrines. This dented neither the young cavalryman's confidence nor his unwavering purpose.

It so happened that the regiment's horses were suffering from an unpleasant skin ailment, and the wily Etienne made a deal with one of his superiors. If he cured the animals, he was to be transferred to a regiment back in France. To the vet's amazement, Etienne succeeded, with a prescription he had learnt in England. And thus we find him in the 10th Light Horse at Moulins. It was probably around 1904 that he met the pretty shop assistant Gabrielle Chanel and became one of the group of officers around her and Adrienne. Gabrielle would always remain secretive about this period, including whom she took as her first lover. All we know is that, at some point in the near future, she and Etienne Balsan would begin their affair.

Meanwhile, the Chanel girls' troupe of followers no doubt encouraged Gabrielle in her belief that the stage was her calling. Accordingly, she left the relative safety of her job as a seamstress to try her luck on a grander scale. After much persuasion, the more cautious Adrienne followed Gabrielle's example and, together, they set off to Vichy for the season.

Only thirty miles distant from Moulins, Vichy was then one of the most fashionable spa towns in the world. While the restorative properties of its spring waters had long been recognized, by the 1880s, acres of landscaped gardens were well established, having replaced the old marshes near the river, boulevards and streets had been laid out, elaborate chalets and pavilions had risen up, and a rail link connected the flourishing spa town with Paris. By the end of the century, Vichy had become a resort renowned for its worldliness, its sophistication, and its visitors. Amongst these were many of Europe's most eminent society figures and most notable celebrities.

To while away the hours between one's 'cure', there were recreational activities as suave as any that could be found in the capital. Monotony was forbidden at Vichy, and performers of the highest rank came, ready to oblige for the season. The greatest of the courtesans, plus their less exalted sisters, saw millions won, and lost, at the lavishly appointed casino, while theatres catered to every taste, and the recently opened opera house drew some of the most distinguished singers of the day. The racecourse was one of the finest in France, and old and new money flocked to take the waters and entertain itself with lovers, mistresses, and sometimes wives, too.

The visitors wanted mansions for their annual stay, and Vichy's architects ransacked the history of architecture in a series of gestures, each more outlandish than the last. The anarchic mix of styles, from Byzantine to Classical to the most grandiose Art Nouveau, reflected the baroque atmosphere of this glamorous and unreal town. Yet Vichy was not only for the rich; here, all stations of society were accommodated and entertained.

The Chanel girls' ignorance partially shielded them from their limitations, and they felt themselves prepared. In outfits made by their own hand, Gabrielle strode about airily with her 'nose up in the air'. By contrast with the modest pleasures of Moulins, the girls saw that Vichy was a world unto itself. Its lavish indulgence made a deep impression upon Gabrielle and, although, years later, she described it as a 'ghastly fairyland', for now, it was utterly 'wonderful to fresh eyes'. Comparing Moulins to this 'heart of the citadel of extravagance', with astonishment Gabrielle realized that 'cosmopolitan society is like taking a journey without moving: Vichy was my first journey.'[2]

Adrienne, meanwhile, quickly realized that the stage was not for her and made her way back to Moulins. Gabrielle was now alone for the first time in her life, and struggled on. Even the support acts, the *poseuses*, in Vichy, were superior to the proper singers of Moulins. Gabrielle paid for lessons, was obliged to hire expensive gowns for auditions and tried to find her forte. Doggedly persevering, she longed for a Vichy manager to hire her.

How Gabrielle supported herself in this venture we don't know, but any savings from her paltry wages can't have gone very far. There has been speculation that she indulged in some discreet prostitution, as did some of her colleagues living in the backstreet rooms nearby.[3] Another, more likely, possibility is that it was Etienne Balsan who partially supported her venture. We know that he visited her in Vichy and, by this point, they must have become lovers.

While Gabrielle complained that the resort was full of the elderly, she remained enchanted by its fantasy, admiring everything, even the engraved glasses used for the foul-smelling water gushing from the curative springs. Marvelling at the cosmopolitanism of the town, she was entranced by the unintelligible foreign tongues she heard all around: 'It was as if they were the passwords of a great society.' And in the midst of this 'great society', Gabrielle was led to a crucial personal insight: 'I watched the eccentric people parade past and I said to myself, "There exist in the world things that I should be and which I am not."'[4] But for an epiphany to really change a life, it must be acted upon, and that may take time.

At the end of that season, gravely disappointed, Gabrielle had to admit that no one was going to hire her, and she followed Adrienne back to Moulins. In spite of her retreat, she would always say it was Vichy that had taught her about life, opening her eyes and giving her a new goal. Meanwhile, Adrienne had fared well.

Maud Mazuel was a woman whom she and Gabrielle had known before they left for Vichy. Of undistinguished origin and looks, she had, nonetheless, created a discreet position as chaperone and matchmaker at the centre of local society. Acting as cover for the establishment, in her pleasant villa near Souvigny, outside Moulins, she also brought women together with their lovers, without rousing the suspicion of their families. The local gentry and officers from the Moulins garrison knew that, at her gatherings, they would find an entertaining mix of people appropriate to their own caste.

They could also find attractive young women whose backgrounds had none of the lustre of the other guests. Though without social distinction, Adrienne was nonetheless beautiful, well dressed and sparkled in company, and Maud had made her the offer of respectability by inviting her to be her live-in companion.

No less strong-minded or characterful than Gabrielle, Adrienne combined her quiet ambition with an uncomplicated femininity. Yet, without a name or a dowry behind her, unless Maud Mazuel could find her a well-to-do suitor, Adrienne knew her prospects were few. She loved her family but, like Gabrielle, wished to move beyond her roots and find acceptance with a social stratum significantly higher than the one into which she was born. Not only was she aiming at an almost impossible target, unlike many socially ambitious women Adrienne was also in search of love. For girls from Adrienne and Gabrielle's background, their looks and personality really were their only fortune.

Adrienne was soon courted with entertainments and outings by no fewer than three aristocratic admirers. She became one of the daring, finely dressed beauties seen with their lovers at the Vichy races. Adrienne's three most ardent admirers invited her to Egypt, where, away from prying eyes, she would be free to choose her man. Gabrielle, too, was invited on this adventure, but said it would gain her nothing.[5] By the time the Egyptian party returned, Adrienne had indeed made her choice. She had become mistress to the Baron Maurice de Nexon, and would faithfully devote herself to him for the remainder of her life.

A courtesan might bankrupt a family's son and also break his heart, but she rarely lived with her lover for any length of time. An *irrégulière* (a permanent mistress), on the other hand, was a threat involving a family's honour in a different way: a son might be mad enough to ask for his lover's hand, leaving his family's name stained for a generation and more. Adrienne's lover, the Baron de Nexon, would do just this. Despite the de Nexon parents' outrage and the lovers' subsequent humiliation when the de Nexon family and society figures refused to 'receive' Adrienne, the young baron stood firm by his choice. He wanted Adrienne. But he also wanted his inheritance, which he would forfeit should they wed. Thus, the couple lived discreetly in Paris and Vichy for many years, until the baron's parents' deaths meant he finally felt able to marry.

When Gabrielle returned to Moulins, she was, as Adrienne had been, alone and without prospects. She had set her heart on the stage, where success would have given her that self-determination she longed for so heartily. Her failure left the normally vibrant and energetic Gabrielle rather insecure, unsure of what to do next. This must have been exacerbated by Adrienne's effectiveness in bringing her own aims to fruition; her happiness was self-evident. Adrienne's success almost certainly spurred Gabrielle on to make her next move. Etienne Balsan, in the background for several months, had set up house and now invited Gabrielle to live with him as his mistress. One suspects she accepted without too much hesitation, relieved, and grateful for a means of escape from the servitude to which she would otherwise have been forced to return. (Etienne may already have asked Gabrielle before she went to Vichy and been refused.)

Some time before, first Etienne's father then his mother had died, each leaving him a large inheritance, making him a very wealthy young man. Immediately after completing his military service, he had launched himself into his life's work – breeding and training horses. To this end, he had bought and restored a small château, Royallieu, in the department of Oise, and it was here that Gabrielle now travelled with Etienne to begin a new life.

While Adrienne's co-habitation with her lover must have shocked her sister Louise, and the rest of their family, Louise would also have appreciated Adrienne's great discretion and, one hopes, been unprudish enough to rejoice at her sister's good fortune. Gabrielle's situation, however, was rather different. We don't know whether she hid her new life from her family for a time and was subsequently found out, or if she told them immediately she was going to live openly with a man out of wedlock. (As so often, it wasn't quite so much what one did but the way one did it that mattered; discretion counted above all.) Years later, when Gabrielle came to tell of her installation at the château of Royallieu, despite garbling the truth to throw her audience off the scent, one catches a hint of her misrepresentation, which clearly provoked considerable family disapproval.

Gabrielle told how she had run away; that her grandfather in Moulins believed she had returned to Courpière; that her aunts thought she was at her grandfather's house; and that, finally, someone 'would realize that I was neither with one nor the other'.[6] Although nomadic, and at the lower end of the social scale, the Chanel family would have been quite aware that (unlike Adrienne), Gabrielle was jettisoning any chance of a good name by going to live at Royallieu.[7] In being disapproved of, however, Gabrielle was not to be alone: her new lover's family regarded him, too, as its black sheep.

From an early age, Etienne Balsan, a most sympathetic character, was both easy-going and provocative, habitually unsettling his *haut bourgeois* family. They, meanwhile, put his intermittent irritability down to the fact that he often starved himself so as to keep his weight down as a jockey (Etienne frequently rode as the only gentleman rider with the professional jockeys). When he wasn't working hard, one of Etienne's favourite pastimes was women. Then, he was relaxed and amusing, with a famously caustic wit. Women responded to his cheerful force, and were seduced by his lack of romance and an unflinching confidence in victory. One of his stable lads, describing him as a champion jockey, said his only criticism of Etienne was with regard to women. 'He focused on them too much. And it tired him out, sometimes.' When this stable lad mistakenly gave Etienne the benefit of this opinion, he was called an 'idiot', and Etienne informed him: 'It's no more tiring than riding horses!'

As a man of eminently respectable pedigree and great means, Etienne could afford not to care about status. His own gave him the freedom to do pretty much as he pleased, something very few women, particularly those from Gabrielle's background, were permitted to any degree. While Adrienne had subtly maintained her reputation, Gabrielle's arrival at Royallieu to live with Etienne Balsan had made her entirely disreputable in the eyes of contemporary society.

During the second half of the nineteenth century, under Louis Napoléon's Second Empire, Paris became associated with an ostentatious theatricality and a luxuriant, new kind of spectacle. Louis's mission was to promote his country's magnificence and superiority to the world, and in this he was assisted by his urban planner, Georges-Eugène Haussmann. This promotion of magnificence in turn contributed towards a period of feverishly self-absorbed luxury. Gratification was the imperative, and entertainments of all kinds proliferated. Many of the now famous great restaurants and grand cafés appeared, as did sumptuous new theatres and concert halls, playing nightly to packed houses.

Another form of entertainment – prostitution – also grew dramatically. At the end of the century, about a hundred thousand women plied their trade to a Parisian population of just under three million.[8] At that time, Paris had one of the most highly organized and regulated systems of prostitution in the world. The penal code discriminated against women, and female adultery was considered far worse than when committed by a man. The state's double standard assumed that male extramarital sex was inevitable – in fact, necessary. At the same time, the *demi-monde*, the half-world beyond the bounds of respectability inhabited by women selling their sexual favours, was rigorously controlled. In doing so, the state believed it was contributing towards the stability of the institution of marriage and simultaneously reducing the incidence of grim syphilis.

The myriad names for these women subtly delineated their variety, hierarchy and position in male fantasy. Many, such as the 'kept' women, the *irregulières* or *femmes galantes*, did their utmost to avoid being registered as prostitutes. Each category of the trade had its own epithet, including the street prostitute, the brothel prostitute, the *fille libre*, *fille en carte*, *fille de maison* or *fille de numéro*.

Then there was the *grisette*, the young milliner, glover or seamstress, who often took lovers to boost her pitiful earnings.

Higher up the scale was the *lorette*, found in the fashionable cafés and restaurants of Paris's *grands boulevards*, who often dreamed of becoming an actress, or might even dare to aim for the status of courtesan. The courtesan, the most highly prized prostitute, had many names: *cocotte*, *biche*, *chameau*, *camélia* (as in *La Dame aux camélias*), etc. In an era of conspicuous and ostentatious consumption, these women flourished as never before. At the pinnacle of the courtesan class itself were the *grandes horizontales*, *lionesses*, *mangeuses d'homme*, *Amazones* and the *grandes cocottes*. In lives of previously unimagined refinement and extravagance, they were a living myth, the image of desire. The loving recorder of the *demimonde*, the Comte de Mournay (pseudonym, Zed), aptly described the courtesan as 'a luxury that surpasses all one's wildest dreams'.

While many men kept a mistress from a lower class than themselves, they rarely lived with her, or not openly anyway. De Nexon and Etienne Balsan were two of the exceptions. While Etienne had already brought the celebrated courtesan Emilienne d'Alençon to the Château de Royallieu, he had now asked Gabrielle to join her. With so few men willing to risk their reputation by marrying their mistress, if a woman flaunted the loss of her reputation, as Gabrielle was now doing, there was little she could ever do to regain it.

Etienne was the least conventional of the three Balsan brothers and cared little that his behaviour was seen as scandalous. He was stubborn and determined, with a fiery temper. He was also generous spirited, with a rare gift for friendship. Demonstrating his disdain for propriety, at Royallieu sociability was arranged with as much freedom from convention as possible.

Although the *demi-mondaine* was generally shunned at private gatherings of respectable society, society women, just as much as men, were fascinated by the secrets of their success. As Balzac would observe, 'Nothing equals the curiosity of virtuous women on this subject.' Unlike the common prostitute, available to any takers, or the ordinary mistress, the *irregulière*, normally confined to one man, the courtesan had such power that she chose for herself those privileged enough to share the delights of her company. Indeed, men could offer a fortune for the pleasure of one night.

Emilienne d'Alençon was one of these, and had earned for herself huge sums. She was a concierge's daughter who had worked her way up from circus performer to *caf'conc* dancer to her final position of renown. Like many courtesans, her 'payment' was often in the form of pearls or precious stones, giving rise to the grand courtesan's sobriquet, *croqueuse de diamants*, or 'diamond cruncher'. Caroline Otero, a beautiful and eccentric Spaniard, owned a stupendous jewel collection and famously said, 'No man who has an account at Cartier could ever be regarded as ugly.' She had made for herself a notoriously revealing bodice made entirely of precious stones, and kept it stored in the vaults of her bank. At the sighting of one of these costly *Amazones* on a son's horizon, his family was in dread lest he should squander his inheritance.

Nonetheless, 'at once exclusive, alternative and forbidden',[9] the courtesan was worshipped as a status symbol and a trophy. At the same time, courtesans' sexual tastes were wide ranging; they were often bisexual. The exquisite Liane de Pougy, for example, one of Emilienne's numerous female lovers, wrote of her: 'With an impudence as great as her beauty, she . . . installed herself in my bed, at my table, in my carriages . . . vicious and ravishing . . . Nothing about her was banal or vulgar, not her face nor her gestures, nor the things she dared to do.'[10]

And while courtesans pursued a life of independence and sexual liberation unthinkable for all but the smallest fraction of other women, the tension between success and the tenuousness of their position often left them struggling. While majestically overcoming typically impoverished and unstable backgrounds, they were, more often than not, ill equipped to deal with their fevered lives. Frequently mismanaging their celebrity and huge earnings, they regularly squandered them on a life even more lavish than the one they could actually afford. In addition, a secret yearning for acceptance usually deluded the courtesans into believing that marriage would gain them an entrée to society as equals. Seeking anaesthesia against their ultimate ostracism, these memorable women all too often became mired in addiction to alcohol or drugs. Indeed, it was not uncommon for the courtesan, and her 'lesser' sisters, to die destitute and forgotten. Liane de Pougy and Emilienne d'Alençon were two who kept their wits about them, not only hanging on to their fortunes but also making impressive marriages.

In living with Etienne Balsan, Gabrielle eschewed the path of the courtesan and became an *irrégulière*, a mistress, entirely dependent upon her lover. Yet, while she secretly longed for independence, her rejection of the courtesan's jewel-encrusted path was significant. Over time, she came to understand the courtesans' lives, would admire and be influenced by them, but she would also strive to distance herself from their glamorous dependence. Instead, Gabrielle was groping her way towards an idea of self-determination that might bring her a more genuine autonomy. In one sense, the courtesan's life was a heightened, more dramatic version of the usual power-broking taking place in relations between men and women. This drama involved the power of the courtesan's lover over the courtesan, the mutual power she and her lover acquired by association and, finally, the power wielded by the courtesan in her potential to damn a man's life if he should fall in love with her.

Gabrielle was unusual in that she wasn't interested in that kind of power – power for its own sake. For this reason, although she was aware of her ignorance of château life – and set to learning about it – her interest in status was limited. Ultimately, this gave Gabrielle great confidence. However unconsciously, people sensed this and treated her more 'equally' than they might otherwise have done. What really interested Gabrielle was influence. Over the span of her life, her interest in influence would be misconstrued over and over again as a desire to wield power. But Gabrielle would come to wield power above all as a means to an end, the creation of her art, her work, and, through work, she would gain her independence.

* * *

If Gabrielle remained stubbornly coy about the identity of any earlier lovers, Etienne Balsan was probably not the first of her Moulins officers. And, while payment may have been involved, one suspects that, for Gabrielle, it would also have been about sex and luxuriating in her youthful body. Hinting darkly at a brief entanglement when still an adolescent, she said that girls of this age 'are terrible. Anyone can have them who uses a little subtlety.'[11] Meanwhile, though the young officers at Moulins may have entertained liberally, the expectation of a reward was implicit. Gabrielle's move to Royallieu, however, originated in far more long-sighted ambitions.

In part, it was realism. Not cynicism, but simply the realization that the world Etienne inhabited represented a heaven-sent means of escape. For this reason, Gabrielle referred to it as 'a dream'. She liked Etienne, and he found her exotic in her difference. His mixture of drive, devil-may-care attitude and antipathy towards bourgeois proprieties made him a dynamic and attractive lover for someone in Gabrielle's position. While Etienne was never outrageously unconventional, he was nonetheless regarded by his fellow officers as a sympathetic outsider, a quality that also endeared him to Gabrielle, the outsider from a different class. And, if it so happened that Emilienne d'Alençon was staying at Royallieu when Gabrielle arrived, there was no question of Gabrielle making any objection.

By 1906, we find Gabrielle's name on the census returns for Royallieu. The household was large, with the jockeys, grooms and servants, but Gabrielle's name is placed immediately after Etienne's. She is described as *sans profession*: she is a kept woman, a luxury. Yet, in the early years of the new century, change was in the air. A crucial aspect of this concerned the position of French women. In 1906, still denied rights of citizenship, they were neither permitted to vote nor to stand for political election. Married women in particular were second-class citizens, minors in the eyes of the law. In 1900, only 624 women gained entry into higher education. Despite rumblings of discontent, across the political spectrum, the shrill moralist response was that a woman's place was 'by the hearth'. Most men were extremely reluctant to contemplate an alternative order, believing the present traditional one was natural and unalterable. Meanwhile, on terms of massive inferiority, women made up a third of the French workforce. Over half those working in textile factories, for example, were women; their wages were half the men's.

If Etienne Balsan could afford to maintain a life similar to his forebears, he wasn't, however, to be left behind with the old order. And probably the most significant example of Etienne's apprehension of a new order was his fascination with Gabrielle. With hindsight, one sees that the image of woman as siren, as *femme fatale*, was competing with a new one. This would become more recognizable as the new century wore on, and it was an image that Gabrielle herself was to embody.

A few years before Gabrielle's jettisoning of her good name by her co-habitation with Etienne Balsan, however, another young woman whose work would influence her times was making her first steps in this direction.

5

A Rich Man's Game

In 1900, a notorious Parisian hack, Henry Gauthier-Villars (known as Willy), published a novel claiming to be the work of a sixteen-year-old schoolgirl, Claudine. *Claudine à l'école* and the follow-up novels were hugely successful. Heralded for their style, their frankly sexual subject matter also tainted their author's reputation with scandal. Willy's cynical claim that *Claudine at School* had been written anonymously would eventually be exposed by its real author, his wife, Sidonie-Gabrielle Colette, writing to order for her husband. (By then, she had left him.)

That some find the sexual promise of an adolescent arousing is nothing new. But the traditional French view, in which a woman becomes more seductive as she grows beyond her teens and twenties and gains experience, had an unorthodox competitor in the raw young Claudine. On the surface, the *Claudine* novels served as soft porn for the bourgeoisie but, below the titillation and sexual heresy, Colette was articulating an unsettling version of a gnawing contemporary problem: the battle between the sexes.

Many men were ambivalent about women. On the one hand, woman was Venus, whose corseted and exaggerated hourglass figure was worshipped; on the other, the male *fin de siècle* mindset had become increasingly preoccupied with the image of the *femme fatale*, the man-consuming sphinx. One of the best examples of this was the proscribed, ritual drama played out between the *fin de siècle* courtesan (the *femme fatale*) and her lover. And many found this a more insidious relationship than the traditional balancing act of man–woman relations described in earlier literature.

In the provocatively unorthodox Claudine, Colette had captured something in the contemporary mind, and versions of the character became common in literature. Nothing like the seductive and majestic *grandes courtisanes*, this younger woman, with her unripe allure, had an edgy, anarchic femaleness, her ignorance and unself-consciousness liberating her from constraint. In the future, a man of experience would write, 'Today, I miss . . . the time one spent waiting. The penitence and the continence that society imposed on us imparted an unbelievable flavour to the opposite sex, and they conferred something sacred that has been lost.'[1] In contrast, devoid of cultivation, Claudine was confrontational, revealed her confidence in a caustic sense of humour, cared little for tradition, and was utterly impervious to the notion of maturity. While encapsulating an important aspect of the sexual flavour of the period, the anarchic Claudine would also emerge as its most unsettling female image.

There is no doubt that Gabrielle's particular allure lay somewhere in this mould.

Nevertheless, for all the apparent unorthodoxy of Royallieu, she had no more real scope than any traditional mistress. She was 'kept' by Etienne and, with her solemn, elfin beauty, in photographs Gabrielle often looks fiercely at the camera with an air of studied defiance. Whatever Claudine's influence, like other women with any ambition, Gabrielle was faced with 'a choice as dramatic as it was contrived: between retaining the prestige of their femininity, which left them at the mercy of their men; and renouncing it for the sake of man's autonomy . . . which set them adrift in an environment hostile both psychologically and economically to emancipated women'.[2]

The constant stream of visitors to Royallieu brought a cheerful mix of aristocratic sportsmen, stars of the turf, actresses, singers and *demi-mondaines* – young people whose lives revolved around entertainment of one kind or another. Etienne's friends were strongly discouraged from showing up at Royallieu with their wives. Mistresses were preferred. But, if Etienne's life appeared a carefree round of riding to hounds and house parties, this omits an important detail: in many ways, he wasn't a carefree soul at all. While his love of playing the fool went in tandem with an aversion to emotional responsibility, in fact, a vein of absolute commitment ran seamlessly through his life: Etienne was dedicated to horses. He knew them, loved them, understood their foibles, their worth, and was capable of fierce competitiveness about them too. When purchasing one or taking part in a race, he was a formidable adversary. As a result, his rise to prominence as both trainer and gentleman rider was rapid, and would eventually make him one of the most famous horse breeders in France. His obsession also left Etienne prepared to live in the country, something most young men of his status were loath to do.

The country house to which he brought Gabrielle was a handsome one. First a hunting lodge for kings, it became La Maison du Roy and, eventually, simply, Royallieu. A priory, then an abbey, it was extended and altered over time. Finally, the château became a stud farm, which perfectly suited Etienne's needs. Royallieu was close to the Chantilly racetrack, in the province of Oise, regarded as the best thoroughbred training ground in France.

At Moulins, while the rich young officers had been flattering and fun, the reality of Gabrielle's life had been servitude as a lowly shop assistant, with lodgings in a poor part of town. At Royallieu, she experienced for the first time the elements of grandeur, and also a certain public notice. While never the mistress of the house, she was to remain there as Etienne's *irrégulière* for several years to come. Absorbing the standards and conventions of Royallieu, however, was a considerable struggle and, for some time, Gabrielle felt out of her depth. She later admitted lying to camouflage her inadequacy.

The contrast between Gabrielle's old life and Royallieu was almost unimaginable. Sloughing off virtually overnight a life ruled by figures she found unsympathetic, it is no wonder that Gabrielle saw Royallieu's privilege, its servants and its sophisticated company as a kind of dream. No longer did she need to rise early and cross town to her *petit bourgeois* employers, bowing and scraping subservience to their condescending clients. Slowly comprehending her new position, Gabrielle learnt, for example, to negotiate the thorny problem of the Royallieu domestics, of whom she would say, 'I was afraid.' Social hierarchies may have been under attack in 1906, but Etienne's servants would have disdained to treat their master's lower-class mistress with much deference. Meanwhile, if she chose, this ex-shop-girl need do nothing all day except lie in bed, reading her trashy novels.

At first, Gabrielle worked hard at this leisure, something alien to both her nature and her upbringing. Etienne was too active to cultivate the art of languor, and marvelled at her ability to read in bed until noon. But Gabrielle was doing more than simply reading popular fiction, she was learning. Since childhood, this highly intelligent young woman had found no one to guide her. Admitting later that her early reading matter was 'rubbish', she added, 'The very worst book has something to say to you, something truthful. The silliest books are masterpieces of experience.'[3] Indeed, Gabrielle said that she 'learnt about life through novels . . . There you find all the great unwritten laws that govern mankind . . . From the serial novels to the greatest classics, all novels are reality in the guise of dreams.'[4] Permitting herself the time, previously in such short supply, to luxuriate in her dreams, Gabrielle devoured her cheap romances, the only imaginative fodder that had so far come her way. One wonders if this orgy of immersion in fantasy may also have signalled something about the inadequacy of her relationship with Etienne.

Meanwhile, Gabrielle was that rare thing: a person who changes little over time. One could say that, as a child, she was an old soul: she was already grown. In this way, her character would not really change much; it was precociously well formed. As a result, growing up for Gabrielle did not come, as it does for most people, through *events*, which bring about personal change. Her particular voyage of self-discovery came through her *environment*, the situation in which she found herself. And of this, as of people, she was always an unusually good observer.

What was outside her – the world outside her – *that* was what Gabrielle had to learn. Her unusual mentality in turn provided her with a ruthless attention to the texture of the present. This would become an invaluable asset in her life's work, for fashion is, as much as anything, about illuminating and articulating the present *moment*. In years to come, Gabrielle would articulate this precisely when she said, 'Fashion should express the place, the moment . . . fashion, like opportunity, is something that has to be grabbed by the hair.'⁵

Life at Royallieu was to prove an important catalyst for this singular young woman. Immersing herself in her new environment, she began a process of separation from the impoverished world of her origins, projecting herself on to a far more expansive stage. Indeed, without Etienne Balsan and Royallieu, we might never have heard of Gabrielle Chanel. Later, she said of those early days at Royallieu: 'I was constantly weeping. I had told him a whole litany of lies about my miserable childhood. I had to disabuse him. I wept for an entire year. The only happy times were those I spent on horseback, in the forest.'⁶ This is undoubtedly an exaggeration, but clearly what Gabrielle went through hinted at some kind of emotional crisis during that first year and, in his own way, Etienne must have been supportive. Certainly, whatever she might say of her friends in the future, Gabrielle would never criticize him.

And, on whatever basis the intimate life of Royallieu was organized, for a brief period, the courtesan Emilienne d'Alençon and Gabrielle amicably shared Etienne and his home.

Emilienne knew she would eventually be deposed as one of the most fêted *grandes courtisanes*, but what did she have to fear from this young Gabrielle Chanel? Yes, the girl had sumptuous hair, a long neck and a striking profile, but she was far too thin and flat chested; she just didn't look the part. Yet, while Gabrielle didn't look or dress like any *cocotte* Emilienne had ever known, with her wit and talent for mimicry, her intelligence and sheer animal force, she could be a most entertaining and seductive companion. She was also happy to remain silent. This, combined with her mix of defiance and cool reserve, gave Gabrielle an enigmatic quality that Emilienne may well have found attractive.

Unlike Britain, France didn't punish homosexuality, which was a major feature of Belle Epoque society. Indeed, by 1900, French tolerance had not only made Paris an international refuge for homosexuals, it was also dubbed 'Paris-Lesbos' for its reputation as the lesbian world capital. There were a number of married society women who enjoyed lesbian affairs, leading one society hostess to say, 'All the noteworthy women are doing it.'[7] While it wasn't against the law, there were very strict social conventions against the sexual experimentation in which both men and women indulged freely. If upper-class women were protected by their social status and greater freedom, sexual deviance had to be acted out with the utmost discretion away from the public sphere. Financially dependent women were obliged to preserve themselves from public scandal. Above all, they had to give the appearance of normality.

In his novel *Nana*, Emile Zola's description of the widespread Parisian subculture of lesbian courtesans reflected a contemporary fascination with these transgressive relationships. Watching a lesbian couple perform was a popular 'turn' at brothels and burlesque shows, and in *À la recherche du temps perdu*, Proust's Marcel finds his courtesan mistress, Albertine, more desirable when he discovers that she is bisexual. For many men, lesbianism was 'seen as a charming caprice, a sensual vice from which he too may profit'.[8] Colette's notorious experimentation with sexual identities introduced her to that Parisian lesbian subculture which included Emilienne d'Alençon. Indeed, Colette would remember a Mardi Gras ball in Nice in 1906 where Renée Vivien and the courtesans Emilienne d'Alençon, Liane de Pougy and Caroline Otero were with 'a crowd of courtesans, actresses, corps de ballet members . . . down from Paris, most of them part-time members of le Tout Lesbos'.[9] No prosecution was brought against Liane de Pougy, for example, when her sensational novel *Idylle saphique* trumpeted her affair with that suave seducer of women, the beautiful and highly intelligent American heiress Natalie Barney. One of Barney's many lovers was the same Renée Vivien at that lesbian Mardi Gras ball in Nice, who died at the age of thirty-two from anorexia, drink and drugs. Renée Vivien and Barney were two of Emilienne d'Alençon's most famous female lovers.

Though lesbianism wasn't illegal, the rigid social conventions against its public display included a very intolerant attitude towards cross-dressing – indeed, female transvestism was held in great public contempt. A woman on a Parisian boulevard in trousers ran the risk of immediate arrest. Two of those who notoriously flaunted this rule were George Sand and, later, Sarah Bernhardt. (As a writer and an actress, they were considered outsiders and thus managed to avoid public censure.)[10]

But, in private, women in men's clothes had for long been a common theme in erotic art and was seen as highly suggestive when practised by the *demi-mondaine*. When playing at being a man, rather than threatening the superiority of her client, she provoked an erotic frisson. When Emilienne d'Alençon took to cross-dressing in the early years of the century, however, she may well have been trading on a double message. Her regulation ties and stiff collars, set off by pert female hats, were possibly as much a covert sign of sisterhood to fellow lesbians as they were an appeal to voyeuristic male fantasies.

Etienne Balsan was a man with worldly and sophisticated friends who brought their lovers to have fun at Royallieu. Virtually all the female visitors whom Gabrielle would befriend there were, like her, skirting the edges of society. Society still looked askance at actresses and singers, regarding them as little different from kept women; they often were. The courtesans' sexual attitudes, in combination with the cheerfully liberated sexual atmosphere at Royallieu, may have a bearing on what we will discover about Gabrielle's own sexuality in the future. It is quite possible that, at Royallieu, she succumbed to the advances either of Emilienne or another of the bisexual female visitors who found Gabrielle's delicate androgyny seductive. And Gabrielle and Emilienne were to remain friends long after Etienne and Emilienne had separated.

In comparison with the drama expected of female dress at that time, Gabrielle's lack of flamboyance was understated to the point of sobriety. This austerity was, in part, a determination to distance herself from the ostentation of the courtesan, or the more subtle flaunting indulged in by a mistress. But it should also be remembered that Gabrielle's attitude was an identification with certain social movements of the period. There was a small number of other young women reacting against the tendency to overstatement in contemporary dress who were presenting themselves with greater simplicity.

Living openly as Etienne's mistress, Gabrielle had signalled that she was unconventional, something accentuated by her unusual style of dress. By contrast, Adrienne, who was also averse to being taken for a *cocotte*, dressed as she would like to be perceived – as a woman of good taste and breeding. She was not interested in making a new world; what Adrienne wanted was to find a better place for herself in the old one. Thus, she looked elegant and uncontroversial, presenting an understated version of the contemporary female drama of lace, draperies, trimmings and triumphal hats. This held no interest for Gabrielle.

While, in living at Royallieu, she may have sacrificed any respectability, she had also been given a unique opportunity to leave behind her miserable beginnings. However, it didn't take Gabrielle long to recognize that country-house life could be an indolent one for the masters. Living as Etienne's mistress failed to consume enough of her prodigious energy, so she launched herself into an activity that both did this and also contributed towards the refashioning of Gabrielle Chanel. The most successful courtesans were those who mimicked best the attributes of higher class women. Only better off women rode and, with Etienne's tutelage, Gabrielle now set about becoming a horsewoman.

Etienne taught her about the handling of the horse at all stages of its training. Gabrielle proved a most willing and able pupil, luxuriating in an experience that took her outside her normal self. A personality of extremes, once she had decided to apply herself to something, it was done with a fierce intensity. And, in her determination to ride, on the days when she and Etienne weren't training together, Gabrielle was up at dawn and off with his apprentice jockeys and the trainers. With these men she felt at ease, understanding their working-man's language. She rapidly became not only a fearless and skilful rider, but also a fine polo player, at that time unusual for a woman.

Gabrielle would say that her fine horsemanship didn't spring from an obsession with horses; that she wasn't like Etienne, or those English women who 'loved hanging around the stables'. Nonetheless, it was for her horsemanship that she was remembered by Valéry Ollivier, one of Etienne's friends, himself a distinguished horseman. He and the other visitors to Royallieu hadn't regarded Etienne's young mistress as particularly significant: 'She was a tiny little thing, with a pretty, very expressive, roguish face and a strong personality. She amazed us because of her nerve on horseback, but aside from that there was nothing remarkable about her.'[11]

Valéry Ollivier was correct: Gabrielle did have a strong personality. And, as a character of outstanding force and intelligence, she could also have excelled at a number of things. In the future, she would say of her couture business, 'I could easily have done something else. It was an accident.'[12]

After the mid-nineteenth century, it had become increasingly fashionable for women of means to go horse riding. Both female riders and lesbians were called Amazons, referring to those sexually suspect women in Greek mythology. This was because their riding habits had for many years been quasi-masculine ensembles and were regarded as an especially forward-thinking, modern aspect of female dress.[13] The riding habits were made of woollen cloth and dark, sober colours (then uncommon for women of means in their daily attire). The women wore severely tailored jackets, and skirts over chamois trousers, attached to a corset, frequently made by men's tailors. It was accepted that these outfits were *intentionally* masculine, made even more so with the addition of a man's bowler or top hat. But, while the adoption of semi-male attire for riding had remained much the same for years, some of the women who hunted were more radical in their appropriation of men's clothing. For several years, they had worn shorter skirts or even breeches – and rode astride their horses.

Not long after Gabrielle began learning to ride with Etienne, she was to make another gesture revealing her capacity for non-conformity: she went to the tailor at La Croix St-Ouen, in the forest of Compiègne, whose usual clients were stable boys and huntsmen, and had him make her a riding outfit. She didn't request a female ensemble of fitted tailored jacket and a long skirt; she wanted a pair of trousers – in other words, jodhpurs. Years later, she remembered the tailor's confusion at her request.

A photograph shows her sitting astride her horse in her new riding gear: a short-sleeved, mannish shirt, a knitted tie and those rather shocking men's jodhpurs. Nudging again at tradition, Gabrielle has also substituted the woman's riding hat – either a top hat or a bowler, – for one both less formal and more feminine looking, wide brimmed and made of soft felt. With her slight figure and broad young face, in this outfit, she could almost have been mistaken for a boy.

If Gabrielle's part in the evolution of women's dress was not always as outrageous as others have suggested, while riding astride her horse was in the vanguard, most shocking was her wearing *men's* riding trousers, and not *only* when she was hunting. And Gabrielle was famously to take this idea further. Rather than confining her blurring of male–female sartorial boundaries to horseriding, it was to become one of her great trademarks: with a hint of that frisson given by cross-dressing, femininity and seductiveness were heightened by borrowings from a man's wardrobe.

Etienne Balsan was neither a man of politics, nor a man of letters. He was a most gifted and dedicated sportsman whose favourite reading was the racing and the gossip columns in the daily papers.

Most important of all the equine pursuits at Royallieu was the racing timetable. From Royallieu, it was possible to visit a racetrack most days of the week, and Gabrielle did so with Etienne and his friends. Mondays at St-Cloud, Tuesdays at Enghien, Wednesdays at Tremblay, on through the end of the week to Sunday at Longchamp, the most elegant of racecourses, in the Parisian park of the Bois de Boulogne.

Spectating at the races had become an immensely popular pastime across the social spectrum. One writer went so far as to say that, in France, sport *was* the turf. As an activity with great social prestige, racing had quickly become a stage on which to vaunt one's social position. This, of course, included the competitive spectacle of fashion. Indeed, many of those who regularly attended the races were far more interested in the promenade of fashion and society than the racing itself. A microcosm of Parisian society, racetrack meetings attracted enormous crowds and, by the early 1900s, the Longchamp racecourse was one of the most fashionable public venues in France. A huge draw for other forms of entertainment, race days were rich pickings for prostitutes of all kinds.

While a respectable woman was obliged to be escorted in public, the *demi-mondaine* usually arrived unaccompanied and was consequently forbidden access to the enclosure. Yet, as the most seductive celebrities of the day, these women were also major attractions. The Second Empire had flourished and, with it, the *demi-monde* had flowered, and the grandest of its denizens met with society women, with whom they now frequently shared the same couturier. 'At first glance they were the same women dressed by the same dressmakers, the only distinction being that the *demi-monde* seemed a little more *chic*.'[14]

By contrast with the worldly image of these exotic *fin de siècle* creatures, Gabrielle always appeared unadorned, modest and neat; without exception, her dress was very simple. At the racecourse, intent on watching one of Etienne's horses in training, she might wear a loose, mannish coat over a tailored jacket, collar and tie, with an undecorated straw boater. She made a practical, sporty look appear most desirable.

A good many American women appear to have adopted tailored outfits for practical activities as far back as the 1880s. This was well ahead of France. As late as 1901, the influential French magazine *Les Modes* was still describing the female suit as 'a revolutionary development', adding the caution that 'gentlemen have not fully appreciated the tailored costume. They have found it too closely resembling their own.'[15]

Gabrielle would say in the future that she had been unaware of being watched and gossiped about as Etienne Balsan's mistress at the races. She also said, 'I looked like nothing. Nothing was right on me . . . Dresses didn't fit me and I didn't give a damn.'[16] Gabrielle didn't wear the traditionally exaggerated female get-ups for the races, and instead stuck to her simple tailored outfits. Again, it wasn't that wearing a tailored outfit was unheard of, but it was seen as unconventional for a woman to wear it to the races.

Despite her belief that, if she didn't dress like a kept woman, she wouldn't be seen as one, Gabrielle was, nonetheless, a mistress. As for her looks, opinion was divided. While some didn't find her particularly attractive, others were in thrall to her unconventional beauty. She was told she 'looked noble' and that she possessed an 'authentic exoticism'.[17] Gabrielle was never very adept at the simpering demeanour of many contemporary women; with hindsight, her manner was an intimation of the future.

She had chosen to leave behind her previous servitude by becoming a kept woman, but her intelligence was too keen and her energies too restless for her to find the passiveness of this existence rewarding for very long. And, after a time, the entertainments at Royallieu would come to bore her too. If, by any chance, Gabrielle articulated her dilemma to herself, for the moment, she could find no answer. Living with the trappings of luxury and the apparent freedom that many women from her background would have fought for, she recognized that, really, she had simply swapped one kind of bondage for another. Yet, while her ambivalence about her position is sometimes revealed in photographs of her at this time, in others, her expression displays by turns her confidence, her wit and an unusual ability to appraise herself and her audience. What the photographs show, too, is the odd glimpse of her diffidence and vulnerability, and also of her most elusive and feminine allure.

In one such photograph Gabrielle walks along the promenade at Nice. Dressed almost head to toe in black, she sports a muff, a huge-brimmed hat, white shirt and tie. A beautiful young woman, she is attended by three highly eligible young men – Comte Léon de Laborde, Miguel de Yturbe and Etienne Balsan. All wealthy horse-men, they are charming cynics who speak the language of a sophisticated, knowing elite. Gabrielle was learning and, at Nice, she was also luxuriating in the only power then available to her, a sexual one emanating from the possession of great character and unusual beauty. And her eyes tell us that she knows it.

At the races, we see Léon de Laborde holding Gabrielle's chin in a gesture both intimate and proprietary. Another photograph shows Gabrielle, Léon and Etienne at the Royallieu stables. Léon has his arm around Gabrielle's waist and stands between her and her lover. Here, and in other photos, one could be forgiven for assuming that Léon, not Etienne, was her lover. (Almost certainly, at some point, he was.)

If a rich man played the game, when he grew tired of his mistress from a lower class, on separating from her he would make her a parting settlement so as to tide her over until she could find another 'protector'. With no lover, a mistress was out of 'work'. A small number of men gave an indefinite settlement. When the time came for Gabrielle to be rejected by Etienne, if she was lucky, she would pass on to one of his friends or acquaintances. But, as her looks faded, unless she had cleverly squirrelled away a tidy sum, her future would be one of increasing poverty.

Preoccupied with her sense of powerlessness, by 1908, Gabrielle's ambition to get to Paris was forming into a plan. She wondered aloud to Etienne what would happen to her. He teased her about being bourgeois and asked her whether she wasn't all right there at

Royallieu. Etienne worked hard, but his mistress had little with which to occupy herself and soon mentioned her future once again. Etienne gave the same response; and so it went on for several months.

Etienne's wealth meant that he could enter or reject society as he chose. While on the one hand benefiting from the privilege his wealth afforded him, on the other he was irritated by the social codes of his class, its obsession with security, family, property and honour handed down from father to son. Instead, Etienne focused on a particular kind of earthy impermanence. He loved risk: the transience of a horse race, the playing of juvenile games and pranks, a brief, intense affair or a sophisticated gamble begun one day and finished on the next. Gabrielle appears to have stirred in him something different.

No doubt spurred on by her talk about her future, Etienne was apparently moved to ask his shop-assistant mistress to marry him. In years to come, Gabrielle would say that Etienne's elder brother, Jacques, came twice to Royallieu and asked her to do so. (Etienne may have sought his brother's assistance here.) When Gabrielle protested, telling Jacques that she didn't love his brother, he replied that it wasn't important; she should marry Etienne anyway. With Etienne and Jacques's parents dead, perhaps Gabrielle's status as a kept woman with no background mattered less to the Balsan brothers. Gabrielle recalled Jacques's anger at her refusal, and that he told her she would end up with nothing. When she replied that she wanted to work, he retorted angrily that, as she didn't know anything about anything, what on earth did she think she was going to do?

Work indeed became Gabrielle's new conviction; it was her only possibility of escape from her position as a *demi-mondaine*. She would later recall how, as a mere twelve-year-old, she had realized that 'without money you are nothing, that with money you can do anything . . . I would say to myself over and over, money is the key to freedom.'[18] She told Etienne that, although she was good on a horse, she wouldn't be permitted to earn her living as a female jockey, so she would like to open a hat shop. One can imagine

Etienne's surprise. He knew she was unusual, but employment was not expected of a mistress.

He was probably only vaguely aware that, for some time, female visitors to Royallieu had asked Gabrielle where she found her hats. Almost beyond our comprehension today, it is worth remembering that, at that time, virtually everyone, however old or young, rich or poor, wore a hat. (In many early photographs, where we see men, women and children too poor to wear shoes, they are, nonetheless, almost without exception, wearing a hat.) And women's headgear was a highly significant aspect of dress. The fashionable woman's hat was a dramatic edifice intended to cause a stir, to be noticed for its beauty and its grandeur.

One of the few places Gabrielle had visited on her rare trips to Paris was the palatial department store Galeries Lafayette. Here, instead of leaving with a haul of the seductive luxuries on offer in this temple to the new consumer, Gabrielle bought a number of basic hat forms made of straw or felt. Back at Royallieu, she decorated them, minimally, often with little more than a ribbon around the crown, to which she might simply add a large hat pin.

As in all previous periods, the definition of elegance and fashion was still the beautiful and the refined. Beauty was associated in large part with adornment. And adornment, whether in the form of costly jewels, silks, satins, laces, furs or hugely complicated hats, was associated with luxury and wealth. (The poor quite simply couldn't afford these things, nor, therefore, fashion.) The frisson provoked by Gabrielle's hats thus lay in their great simplicity and *lack* of adornment. Being shocking wasn't then something associated with high fashion, but Gabrielle wasn't entirely alone. Some high fashion was beginning to practise the same thought, put forward by a few radical contemporary artists: to shock was the idea. And this, those unconventional female visitors to Royallieu were now keen to emulate.

6

Captive Mistress

Every autumn, Etienne was invited to the château at Pau, an old town in the foothills of the Pyrenees, where he and his friends rode, hunted and played polo. Years later, Gabrielle recalled the 'green pastures, the mountain streams rushing to the plains, the grass-covered jumps and the hunters in their red coats', in what she described as 'the best fox-hunting land in Europe'.[1] She remembered the horses, saddled up and impatient to be off; could still hear their clattering hooves on the cobblestones. That season at Pau, in 1908, was an intoxicating interlude for Gabrielle. It was here, she said, that she met Arthur Capel, a wealthy polo-playing Englishman; a playboy to outdo all the others.

Arthur Capel and Etienne were already acquainted, but this was apparently the first time Arthur and Gabrielle had met. The Englishman was a noted horseman. His manner was seductively nonchalant, he spoke fluent French and possessed an engaging wit. This didn't, though, entirely mask his sense of purpose. In Arthur Capel's eyes there was a hint of something steely, reflecting the difference Gabrielle would recognize between this man and Etienne's other friends. Instead of spending his inheritance, Arthur chose to work for his living. His dark good looks were enhanced by an air of inscrutability, and women found him irresistible. Gabrielle, too, was fascinated. Arthur was soon visiting Etienne's château.

Gabrielle's conversations with Etienne about setting up a hat shop had so far come to naught. Living with one's mistress was unconventional enough for an upper-class man in 1908, but for her to work was verging on the scandalous; it would signal that he didn't have the finances to support her. Gabrielle remonstrated with herself that she must do something, asking herself, 'Otherwise what will become of you?' She said later, 'The proud know only one supreme good: freedom!'[2]

Her efforts at persuasion at last bore fruit. Unwilling as Etienne was to finance a shop, why didn't she try out her idea from the *garçonnière* (bachelor apartment) he shared with his brother? Ironically, many an ex-*demi-mondaine* before her had followed Gabrielle's chosen occupation, and she now quietly launched herself as a milliner at her lover's Parisian apartment at 160 boulevard Malesherbes.

Arthur Capel's apartment, then also on boulevard Malesherbes, was close to Etienne's *garçonnière*, and he often dropped by to see the 'abandoned little sparrow', as he and Etienne called Gabrielle. If Etienne's support for Gabrielle's venture was rather half-hearted, Arthur's interest was balm to her ruffled sensibilities. Indeed he gave her the most enthusiastic encouragement she had so far received, and sent along his women friends to look at Gabrielle's hats. So did Etienne's friends. There was no doubt Gabrielle had talent. Arthur's visits became more frequent. While showing due consideration for his friend Etienne, in the most amicable way Arthur gradually made his intentions clear regarding Gabrielle.

It was probably at this point that Etienne proposed to her for the second time. It seems that Gabrielle may for a while have played a worldlier, more courtesan-like part than she would ever admit to in the future, and shared out her favours. Now, leaving Royallieu, she was put up by Arthur at the Ritz. While officially Etienne's mistress, she had several admirers. Miguel de Yturbe, Léon de Laborde and Arthur Capel were young men at the heart of Parisian society, and all were on hand to court her.

Yet, while Gabrielle may have had the looks, the wit, the character and intelligence, plus the necessary hard-headedness to become a fully fledged courtesan, she refused to foster some of those qualities that led, first, to a courtesan's success, and then to her survival. Besides, Gabrielle's insecure beginnings had left her too preoccupied with her future. Without quite knowing it, she had also caught the scent of change upon the air. She wanted influence, but she wanted it via a route that wasn't dependent upon her willingness to act the courtesan part of a possession. In other words, although she may have been making herself available to more than one lover, ultimately, Gabrielle wanted independence and didn't see the role of *professional* lover as her way to secure it.

Notwithstanding this reluctance, one notices how the trajectory of her life has a number of parallels with the lives of the most stellar *demi-mondaines*. First, she had imbibed from them the notion of continual inventiveness, and then, just as their inventiveness was translated into fashion, so Gabrielle would discover in herself their ability to remain just one step ahead of it. Balzac, in his brilliant description of the courtesan Valérie Marneffe, called these steps 'the supreme efforts, the Austerlitzes of coquetry or love', which are then transformed into what is 'fashionable in lower spheres, just when their happy creators are looking round for new ideas'.[3] We will see how, once Gabrielle had made something new, she was at once impatient to move on. And, in this way, she would perfect the courtesan's sometime role, indeed would make it her vocation. She would show first society women and then the rest how it was they should look for the new century.

We don't know when one or two amorous encounters with Arthur Capel developed into a full-blown affair. But, some time around 1909, Gabrielle told Etienne that her 'entanglement' with Arthur was becoming serious. Etienne was overcome, and set sail for Argentina. Gabrielle would say that he had been 'packed off . . . by his family'.[4] She also hinted that, on his return from the New World, nothing had been resolved, and her relationship with her two lovers became ever more fraught and confused. While Gabrielle ensured that the details of this triangular relationship are lost, it appears that, as far as Etienne was concerned, a dalliance with another man was acceptable, but the basic commitment was clear: Gabrielle was his. Arthur's interest in Gabrielle also reminded Etienne how much he wanted her. Whatever the games Gabrielle might have played, and the discord this provoked, there was never really much doubt: whatever previous liaisons she might have hidden from us, once Arthur had made his feelings clear, this particular young woman was his.

While Gabrielle frequently obscured her past with invention, in this case her claim that she and Etienne were never in love with one another may have been a salve for her conscience. What she meant here was that *she* was never in love with Etienne. The story has it that her passing from him to Arthur was, in the end, amicable. Etienne's family, meanwhile, remembered him describing Arthur at the time as 'an adventurer' – contemporary slang for 'lousy foreigner'. But, whatever Etienne's thoughts, his defences were to no avail; his friend, Arthur Capel, had carried off his mistress.

This mistress now found herself in a state of mind to which she was quite unaccustomed: she was content. We can only guess at what she may have revealed to Arthur about her origins and her miserable early life, but it did nothing to deter him. He wanted Gabrielle. And sharing his apartment just off the Champs-Elysées, for the first time in her life, Gabrielle basked in being loved; she felt cherished and encouraged.[5] As we saw earlier, Arthur was to act as the inspiration for the transformation of her life. But Gabrielle's path would not be an easy one, and personal misfortune would dog her along the way.

The year 1910 was to be momentous for her; it included the sudden death of her eldest sister. As Gabrielle's first childhood companion, Julia-Berthe was linked with her inescapably and, on hearing of her death, Gabrielle collapsed. The cause of her sister's death was said to be tuberculosis, but it now appears this was a fabrication. At the time, Gabrielle apparently demanded to know the truth and was secretly told that Julia-Berthe had in fact committed suicide.[6] The macabre family story had it that she rolled herself back and forth, back and forth, in snow and ice until she lost consciousness and was eventually found frozen to death.

This seems impossible; she died in early May. But either the winter ended very late that year or there was something particularly grim about the way Julia-Berthe killed herself. Such a story is otherwise unlikely to have been 'remembered'. Years later, Gabrielle herself would tell a friend[7] that her sister had fallen in love with an officer, who had quickly abandoned her. Gabrielle said she was struck by her sister's despair and had wanted to meet this man. On discovering him, she had 'fallen in love'; no doubt this is code for an affair. When her sister found out, she was driven to commit suicide. If this was true, was Gabrielle not only mourning her sister but feeling implicated too?

Gabrielle may have been sorrowful, but she was also in love and living with a man who represented everything she could want. For the moment, her ambition seemed unimportant, and she was luxuriating in being distracted. When she went to live with Arthur, at first Etienne hadn't wanted to see them. But he was a forgiving man, and his heart would recover. In time, the new couple were welcomed back to Royallieu and entered once more into the life of the château. We see Gabrielle, previously such a reluctant-looking photographic subject, seated at table with Arthur, Léon de Laborde and Etienne. A smile plays over her face, at once flirtatious and fulfilled.

In another photograph, guests at a Royallieu house party have been organized by Gabrielle into donning costume and play-acting a 'country wedding'. Two things stand out in the 'play' itself. While the sophisticated young people take a swipe at bumpkin country folk, they also satirize the idea of marriage, the grown-up institution effectively banished from Royallieu. The pretty little actress Jeanne Léry plays an adoring bride; the socialite Lucien Henraux is a smitten groom; Arthur is the goofy, buxom mother-of-the-bride; Léon de Laborde is a bonneted, dopey-looking baby; while the rising-star actress Gabrielle Dorziat takes the part of a slightly retarded, pigeon-toed, village-girl maid of honour, in a short dress and socks.

And then, we notice Gabrielle, who has taken the role of adolescent best man. She looks straight into the camera with that disconcerting seriousness. Dressed from the boys' section of a Parisian department store, she wears trousers that don't reach her ankles, pale socks, buttoned ankle-boots, a Peter Pan-collared shirt and a waistcoat set off by a little dark jacket. Despite the deliberately crumpled white shirt, the clumsy cravat and the pulled-down straw hat, to our contemporary eyes, Gabrielle is the one person who fails in her attempts to appear awkward. A century later, the way she has put together and wears the little 'suit' strikes us as having an insouciant, particularly modern kind of style. No matter how sophisticated and relaxed her friends might appear, they remain fixed in their own time, the early years of the twentieth century. It is Gabrielle alone who looks as if she might have been photographed just yesterday.

Describing herself as 'unlike anyone else; either physically or mentally',[8] Gabrielle was also ripe with contradiction and rich in paradox. All her life this would make her easy to misread. While craving solitude, she lacked serenity, and possessed an electric, pent-up energy. Without the voluptuous curves then most desirable in a woman, her taut body was more like an adolescent boy's. She was unusually forthright yet, at the same time, was subtle and seductive. Capable of easy-going light-heartedness, she was also provocative, and had a mordant wit. In her enigmatically beautiful face there was more than a hint of severity. This sprang from a deep seriousness, a profound quality given only to a few.

Gabrielle had developed an aversion to mere prettiness; she wanted beauty. She believed she had an unerring sense of what was 'fake, conventional or bad'; the implication being that the conventional is as objectionable as what is 'fake' or 'bad'. Her unusual ability, growing stronger with age, to intuit the essence of a person and a situation amounted to what a friend described as 'a kind of sixth sense'.[9] Yet, while Gabrielle was both unusually perceptive and knowing, in those early years Paris made her frightened. Painfully aware of her lack of sophistication in that most sophisticated of cities, she later recalled her ignorance of 'social nuances, of family histories, the scandals, the allusions, all the things that Paris knew about and which are not written down anywhere. And since I was much too proud to ask questions I remained in ignorance.'[10]

While Gabrielle would never entirely overcome her sense of social inadequacy, she possessed a quality having nothing to do with inadequacy: humility. Hers was the humility of the artist open to everything, and it complemented her underlying self-confidence and strength of personality. Someone who would know her well in the future would say, 'She was very elegant, but elegance is something natural, whereas being sophisticated . . . is a conscious choice . . . Elegance is something you're born with.'[11] To this innate elegance Gabrielle added her own singular femininity. For contemporary men attracted to strength as well as delicacy and mystery, Gabrielle Chanel held great appeal. Indeed, she had unsettled the glamorous Arthur Capel, stirring his emotions, and his yearnings, beyond sexual prowess and social prestige.

In 1924, the fashionable diplomat Paul Morand would write his first novel, *Lewis et Irène*. In the dedication of his book to Gabrielle, he referred to the similarities between Arthur Capel and his fictional hero, Lewis.[12] Morand was fascinated by Arthur, a man with whom he shared an addiction to speed, horses, cars and women. In time, Gabrielle would tell Morand much about her relationship with Arthur. Not only did Arthur become the inspiration for Morand's hero Lewis, so too the similarities between Irène and Gabrielle, and many aspects of the Chanel–Capel relationship, were widely recognized by their contemporaries. *Lewis et Irène* is in large part their story.[13]

Morand saw Arthur as the dashing exemplification of a new kind of man, and made Lewis out of the same mould. Their similarities began with Lewis's appearance. He had 'beautiful brown eyes, quick and hard, a strong jaw, thick, very black hair, in disarray, and a half-open hunting vest'.[14] Lewis was like Arthur in being determinedly modern and up to the minute, with his reading of Freud on sexuality, his scorning of much of the past and his air of always being in a hurry.

And while *Lewis et Irène* was in many ways a depiction of Gabrielle and Arthur's relationship, it was also the first French novel in which the heroine's unusual self-reliance enabled her to have a relationship in which she was an equal partner. At Irène's first entrance, in her black swimsuit, with her slim, muscled and bronzed limbs, she is clearly a modern woman. Lewis's admiration soon turns to something more, and in Irène he feels that his 'fate was absolutely mapped out'. He realizes that, without her, 'What coldness when she is gone . . . what boredom.'[15] Lewis tells Irène that he is learning how to be human, and that his first need is to adore her. She replies that her first need is to surrender to him, and that she doesn't have to 'regret my madness any more'.[16]

Gabrielle would recall that, during her first winter living with Arthur in 1910, their relationship was a very private one, and they invited few people to their apartment.[17] Morand said of Lewis and Irène that 'in the morning they stayed in bed. Lewis had kept a few racehorses. He telephoned . . . from his bed for news of their hooves, their teeth, their tendons.'[18] At first, the intimate world of lovers was enough for Gabrielle and Arthur. Gabrielle described how, initially, she 'distanced him from his friends'[19] but also how Arthur wanted her to 'remain the unsophisticated, untainted creature that he had discovered', believing that she would be 'damaged' by having friends.[20]

It was the beginning of their love affair and, for the moment, Gabrielle apparently accepted Arthur's judgement. Constantly surprised by his edgy brilliance, she said, 'He had a very strong and unusual character, and was a passionate and single-minded sort of man.'[21] Paul Morand wrote that Lewis lived his life at top speed, ate while driving his car, sat on the floor and slept very little.[22] Gabrielle recalled Arthur's stable of polo ponies, she talked of his refined yet eccentric manner, his cultivation and his 'dazzling social success'. Importantly, he was also the first person in her life who didn't 'demoralize' her.[23]

Arthur exemplified the personal superiority and distinction of those for whom the notion of elegance and good taste had changed; it was no longer based upon birth or wealth alone. Membership of this group largely hinged on a particular *savoir vivre* and a new, nonchalant brand of elegance based more upon individuality than membership of any particular group. Morand's description of Lewis rings true of Arthur yet again: 'To appear carelessly dressed in elegant places, because it pleased him to give an impression of strength and rudeness. That is why he readily dined in a sports jacket [rather than dinner jacket], among women in low-cut evening gowns.'[24]

Gabrielle was entranced by Arthur's English dandyism, which fulfilled the anglophile cultural ideal of '*le gentleman*'. Unaware that some of Arthur's compatriots from across the Channel mightn't always find him quite old school enough for their prejudices, Gabrielle was dazzled. She described him as 'more than handsome, he was magnificent'.[25] But her appreciation of Arthur went much further than his looks.

One of the sources of their intense mutual attraction lay in their recognition that the other was untypical. And, while they were both ambitious, Arthur was one of the only people in Gabrielle's life until then whose authority she was happy to accept. Her days as a *poseuse* at Moulins were well behind her, when her slenderness had been called 'thinness' and attributed to too much partying. (It had been rumoured that she would come to no good, and one of her nicknames at the time, La Famine aux Indes, was borrowed from the disturbing contemporary famine photographs from India.)[26]

But her life had changed beyond recognition since Moulins. Even though Gabrielle sometimes refused a trip to the dressmakers or a new pearl necklace, courtesy of Arthur, the bondage she had assumed was luxurious, and she was happy. She wore beautiful clothes, discovered that her slender grace was found increasingly alluring, and revelled in an unaccustomed happiness. Gabrielle's natural charm blossomed as never before, and an admirer was to remember, 'She had a roguish smile and delighted in mocking people with a tantalizing look of innocence.'[27]

Gabrielle's fascination for Arthur lay not only in her unusual beauty but in her intelligence, her striking directness and her capacity for silence. But while Morand's fictional Lewis was impressed by Irène's 'uncluttered and imperious mind', he was also intent on educating her out of what he saw as her abominable ignorance. In the habit of 'improving' his conquests, he set out to 'cultivate their minds'.[28] In like manner, Gabrielle recalled that, for all the luxury of Arthur's apartment, his outlook was in some ways a strict one. She said that 'in educating me, he did not spare me; he commented on my conduct: "You behaved badly . . . you lied . . . you were wrong."'[29] Gabrielle could accept this admonishment and his attempts to school her (including instruction in small details, such as the best years for champagne) because she didn't feel undermined by that 'gently authoritative manner of men who know women well, and who love them implicitly'.[30]

Her background and her desultory education had inspired in Gabrielle a reasonable idea of what she wanted. First was escape from the meanness of her upbringing. On moving out of the haberdasher's shop into her own lodgings, she was determined to make her own way. Like many shop assistants before her, she had possibly augmented her earnings in Moulins with modest prostitution, and was eventually partnered with Etienne Balsan. Later, in his château at Royallieu, she found something to which she could seriously apply herself: horseriding. Not only did she become a talented rider, Gabrielle was also well informed about the most significant racing fixtures, the best jockeys, the finest horses. Yet her social life was spent largely with sportsmen and their mistresses, aristocrats, courtesans and turf society. During her years at Royallieu, she may have had the privilege of grandeur and being waited upon but, clearly, Arthur didn't believe it had imbued her with much sophistication.

He was an established figure in the highest Parisian circles. Yet, although he had fallen in love with this unusual creature, his social standing impelled him to a certain caution regarding transgression of the status quo. As a result of this, Gabrielle was effectively forbidden access to the *haut monde*. That subtle and precise brutality practised by most elites, whose sense of exclusiveness functions with a hair-trigger sensitivity, meant that her lover didn't escort his live-in mistress around the capital's select salons, where he normally found his friends. And, no matter what the private indiscretions of the *haut monde*, that same society wasn't unconventional enough to visit a bachelor and his mistress at home. While at Royallieu, we remember, Etienne had no wish to receive society. This was just as well, because society would have been most unlikely to accept his invitations; his establishment was disreputable.

So Gabrielle and Arthur went out, and he introduced her to his more rakish friends, at fashionable public places such as the theatre or Maxim's, the Café de Paris, or the Pré Catalan restaurant on the Bois de Boulogne. At times, Gabrielle hankered after an obvious kind of respectability: she was in love with Arthur Capel and would have married him if he'd asked. But, unlike Etienne Balsan, for the moment, he did not.

Arthur's numerous female admirers – several of them ex-lovers – were unhappy at his co-habitation with his mistress. She, meanwhile, recalled an episode intended to demonstrate her hold over him to the *haut monde*. Arthur was due at an important gala at the ruthlessly fashionable Deauville casino. On a whim, Gabrielle insisted that he should dine there with her alone. All eyes were upon them. While Gabrielle may have felt diffident before the Parisian elite, the urge to stake her claim over her man publicly was a far from timid action. She remembered that her 'awkwardness, which contrasted with a wonderfully simple white dress, attracted people's attention. The beauties of the period, with that intuition women have for threats unknown, were alarmed; they forgot their lords and their maharajas; Boy's place at their table remained empty.'[31] ('Boy' was the nickname by which Arthur was commonly known.) Gabrielle's first moment of public triumph was not, however, based upon a conspicuous white dress and her connection to the glorious Arthur Capel alone. People remembered that evening and her memorable mix of engaging honesty, *hauteur* and charm. *Le tout* Paris had already whispered a good deal about the eligible Arthur Capel's new liaison, but this episode announced it with a megaphone.

Many of the details of Gabrielle's affair with Arthur remain obscure. And while, as we shall see, Arthur had reasons for keeping aspects of his own background mysterious, in the future, Gabrielle would maintain far greater secrecy about her own. As a result, the chronology of these years is very difficult to disentangle.

7

Arthur Capel

Gabrielle would admit that she hated 'to submit to anyone, to humiliate myself . . . to give in, not to have my own way', because 'pride is present in whatever I do.'[1] And yet Arthur Capel had so captured her heart and her imagination that, half a century later, she would still speak of him with a kind of awe. As we saw in the prologue to this book, Gabrielle believed he was 'the great stroke of luck in my life'. And, bearing in mind her different versions of her early life, she remained touchingly consistent in her descriptions of this man. Her conviction that he had shaped her, made her; that 'he was my father, my brother, my entire family', never changed. Arthur was everything to her.[2] Yet, despite his great renown at that time, and Gabrielle's feelings for him, today he is barely known.

The story told in all Gabrielle Chanel's previous biographies is that Arthur Capel inherited large interests in shipping and Newcastle coal from his distinguished Catholic family. In addition to his considerable wealth, he was a noted polo player and rake. But, while his origins were apparently a little mysterious – there were rumours about his paternity – and his drive to make money was untypical of the Parisian *haut monde*, nonetheless, Arthur was one of the elite.

Until now, very little further detail has been known: his background, his early life, his arrival in France, his movements between Britain and France, his urge to make money, his activities during the First World War and, afterwards, as a political secretary at the Versailles Conference. Finally, our knowledge of his affair with Gabrielle, his marriage and its aftermath, all have remained obscure.

Gabrielle's biographers and fashion journalists long ago turned Arthur into something of a caricature: a polo-playing, womanizing tycoon who had done important things in the First World War. Little more than an adornment in his role as consort to the icon Coco Chanel, the finer points of the real Arthur Capel and his story were lost, while his character was submerged in cliché as the improbable hero from one of Gabrielle's newspaper fictions. For more than half a century, the very elusiveness of Gabrielle's lover has added to the romance of his reputation. But if she so insistently credited this unreal figure with her very invention, we can reasonably assume that, in discovering more about him, we will understand more about Gabrielle.

In piecing together much new information about Arthur, it became clear that significant details were wrong, even his date of birth. Part of the problem has always been that one of the few sources of information about Arthur was Gabrielle and, while her comments are invaluable, she added to the confusion with unintentional inaccuracies.

After more than a year, research led me to Arthur's family. In the lengthening dusk of a winter's afternoon, we sat by a fire as they told me what little they knew. This, and the small cache of letters they gave me – hidden in a 'secret' book in a private library for more than half a century – were together, however, to become immensely significant. The letters were written by Arthur during the First World War. His generous handwriting, almost spilling over the small, forgotten pages, gave a clear sense of that voice sought for so long. With each letter, this elusive man emerged with more clarity from the shadow of his lover, Gabrielle.

What stood out in the letters, across the almost one hundred years that separated us, was the strong impression of a man who was confident, humorous and ironic. He was also commanding, thoughtful and touching in his intimacy. As one learns more about his and Gabrielle's story, one appreciates both why Arthur wanted to be with this young woman without background, and why he appeared, both to Gabrielle and to many others, as quite unforgettable. In discovering Arthur Capel, we do indeed discover more about Gabrielle herself.

★　★　★

Arthur Edward Capel was born in Brighton, on the southern English coast, in September 1881. This made him two years older than Gabrielle Chanel. His parents, Arthur Joseph (so as not to confuse father and son, I will refer to him as Joseph) and Berthe, already had three small daughters, Bertha (English spelling), Edith and Marie-Henriette. Their mother, a Parisian, had met Joseph while she was a boarder at a London school (most probably through Joseph's brother, Thomas, a prominent socialite Catholic priest). While Berthe's family, the Lorins, remain frustratingly mysterious (the relevant archives in Paris went up in flames in 1983), enough has come to light about Joseph to make some of the forces that drove his son, Arthur, more comprehensible.[3]

Joseph Capel's family was of very modest means – his father was a poor coastguard, his Roman Catholic mother, from Ireland, had been in service – but Joseph was industrious and ambitious and had quickly risen from a position as a clerk to prosper as a man of business. His talent as an entrepreneur then enabled him to move his family from London to a pretty house on Brighton's Marine Parade, where his only son, Arthur, was born.[4] Joseph commuted to London's hub of commerce, the Royal Exchange, while expanding his business portfolio still further. This included extending, for example, his contact with Europe by becoming the agent for several railway and shipping companies in France and Spain.[5] Work often took him abroad, and he now mixed in the upper circles of 'society'.[6]

Enterprising and adaptable, at thirty-seven, Joseph was a rich man and moved his family to Paris, where he was now able to live on his investments. While this move may have come about because Berthe wanted to return to her homeland, it might also have been precipitated by Joseph's priest brother Thomas's recent and dramatic fall from grace in the British Catholic community. A popular society priest, he had been chamberlain to Pope Pius IX, lectured at Oxford and was appointed by the distinguished Cardinal Manning as the President of Kensington University College, Britain's first Catholic university since the Reformation. Not only was Thomas

Capel responsible for this important venture ending in financial collapse, but amongst other misdemeanours, he was also brought to book over an alleged affair with one of his parishioners. Cardinal Manning exerted his far-reaching influence and Capel was forbidden to act as priest anywhere in the world, his reputation was ruined and he emigrated to America.[7]

In Paris, the Capels were removed from this shameful scandal. Their home, at 56 avenue d'Iéna, was previously one of the great Rochefoucauld family mansions. Situated in the sixteenth *arrondissement*, the tree-lined avenue d'Iéna, with its understated wealth and assiduous discretion, was particularly distinguished. The Capels' *haut bourgeois* neighbours included politicians and the odd aristocrat. Today, the avenue hosts a number of diplomatic missions; the Capels' mansion has become the Egyptian embassy.

After Arthur's junior period at the elite St Mary's in Paris, his parents chose for their son a distinguished English school. Beaumont College was at Old Windsor, in Berkshire, and was dubbed 'the Catholic Eton'.[8] And it was from here, throughout his adolescence, that Arthur travelled back and forth across the Channel, to holiday with his parents at avenue d'Iéna and fashionable French resorts. In 1897, at sixteen, his ordinary school studies over, Arthur moved to complete his education with an advanced course of study.

It has always been said, mistakenly, that he went on to Downside School, in the county of Somerset. However, a move from a Jesuit college (Beaumont) to a Benedictine one (Downside) would have been highly unlikely. Arthur in fact went on to one of England's most venerable Jesuit institutions, the college of Stonyhurst, in Lancashire.[9]

It was only recently that Catholics in England had been permitted to obtain degrees, in a handful of Catholic colleges such as Stonyhurst. In 1897, some years after Arthur's uncle's failure to make the London Catholic University prosper, Stonyhurst was the most important place of Catholic higher learning in Britain. And Arthur was duly welcomed into its small senior group, holding the illustrious title of 'Gentlemen Philosophers'. These young grandees' college lives were part country-house living, part finishing school and part Oxbridge college. They played much sport, rode, hunted and shot (keeping their own horses and dogs at the college); they also wore extravagant clothes 'and bore themselves with a careless dignity'.[10] The Gentlemen Philosophers were ferociously sociable; they acted, made music, debated fiercely, and conscientiously smoked and drank their way through their privileged college years.

Arthur was one of the youngest of the Gentlemen Philosophers but, more focused than many seventeen-year-olds, he flourished in this climate and took several academic prizes. Armed with Stonyhurst's excellent intellectual training and his battery of awards, at the end of 1899, following his eighteenth birthday, he left behind the safety of academia and went out into the world.

With the exception of a few tantalizingly brief references, after Stonyhurst, his trail all but disappears. Three years later, we find him bound for France on board ship from America.[11] Almost certainly, this was to see his ailing mother. Two months later, at only forty-six, she would die. It was 1902. Arthur was twenty-one. And then there is silence.

We know that Arthur completed a roving apprenticeship in his father's businesses, in London, Paris and America. Quite probably, he travelled further afield, to North Africa, Arabia and Persia, where other Capel interests were flourishing. Having progressed to fully fledged membership of his father's firm, Arthur reappears in 1909.[12] Now twenty-seven, he had bridged the complex social divides between the super-wealthy bourgeois of his father's acquaintance and the *haut monde* of ancient titles, great houses and estates, and had become a young Parisian of note.

Arthur Capel has often been described as a self-made man but, as we see, it was not Arthur but his father who rose so far above his origins to become a figure of considerable social standing. Compared to Gabrielle's upbringing, Arthur's was one of unimaginable privilege. Without the need to strive for more, once he had learnt the arcane rules of business, he turned it into a kind of sport – the sport of making money. Thus, in Morand's *Lewis et Irène*, Morand would have his hero, Lewis, say: 'I work for fun. Negotiating a loan entertains me more than sailing does; drawing up a company act more than playing poker. That is all.'[13]

Yet, for all the suavity his upbringing had conferred upon him, Arthur also concealed a seriousness beneath the amusement, and was motivated by an urgent ambition. This revealed itself in his transformation of money-making into a game, his love of competitive sport, at which he regularly beat his friends, and his serial conquest of women – sometimes, their women. (Did this come about in part because he was the favoured only son with several sisters?) Whatever its source, within Arthur, there existed a tension that women found compellingly attractive.

There were several, including Paul Morand, who explained Arthur's slightly mysterious past with a rumour. While never mentioning his mother, apparently, he was the bastard son of a descendant of Portuguese Jews, the great banker, Jacob Emile Pereire. Pereire died, it was said, shortly before Arthur had finished his studies. No one ever bothered to calculate that in fact he was dead before Arthur was even born. Meanwhile, it was said that the stigma of this illegitimacy was the clue to his ambition. Morand was, however, mistaken; though not entirely.

Arthur's ambition did arise out of his sense of inadequacy. However, it wasn't because of any illegitimacy but because his parentage was undistinguished. As much as anything, he was driven by the desire to move – as was Gabrielle, and his own father before him – beyond his origins. This brought about the urge to reach a still higher social position than the *haut bourgeois* one his father had created for his children to inhabit. The Capels had considerable riches, but neither a great name nor the land traditionally accompanying one. Later, we will see the tragic consequences for Gabrielle, and Arthur, to which this urge would eventually drive him.

In the meantime, Arthur played polo and socialized with society.[14] A close friend was Duc Armand de Gramont, Comte de Guiche, one of the most gifted and sympathetic personalities of his generation. Armand was a tall, dazzlingly handsome polo player whose family had managed to divert him from becoming a painter and steered him towards what they saw as the more serious pursuit of science. Here, Armand's considerable gifts would eventually help make his name far beyond the self-absorbed confines of the disintegrating *haut monde* from which he sprang. His and Arthur's impeccable connections had permitted them entry to the Jockey Club, that luxurious male preserve and organ of the ruling elite. In 1908, Marcel Proust was elated to be put forward as a member. The sponsors for Proust's promotion to another of the city's most distinguished clubs, the Paris Polo, were none other than the two young heart-throbs, Arthur Capel and Armand de Gramont. On 30 April, *Le Figaro* announced that 'Marcel Proust, presented by the Comte de Guiche and M. Arthur Capel, is received as permanent member of the Polo de Paris.'

In spite of Arthur's great worldly success, his drive and ambition were shot through with ambivalence. Although he liked the lustre of his friends' privileged lineages, an important aspect of his close friendship with men such as Armand de Gramont and Etienne Balsan was not their joining with him in the leisured man's love of high living, but their notable strength of purpose. While increasing his wealth and socializing with the *beau monde*, the young playboy was not fulfilled by money and power alone. Labouring under the philosophical and spiritual disquiet of many sophisticates at the dawn of the twentieth century, he questioned the Jesuit ethos under which he had been schooled. Searching, he had taken up one of the routes followed by a number of his contemporaries who felt restricted by the old religions. Maintaining a friendship with the popular spiritual guru Rabindranath Tagore, Arthur also joined the Theosophists, the recent religious movement whose declared objects chimed with his own leanings.[15]

Somehow, between his hectic schedule of work, socializing and grand sporting events, Arthur also found time to cultivate his affair with Gabrielle. Indeed, it was over the winter of 1909–10 that the problems regarding her relations with her two most significant lovers, Etienne and Arthur, reached a resolution: she moved into

Arthur's apartment on the avenue Gabriel. This was where we first met them, on that evening when Arthur shocked Gabrielle out of her fantasy by telling her she wasn't making any money.

In deciding to work at all, Gabrielle had made her position socially ambiguous. While in some ways resembling a courtesan who made money, Gabrielle was now an untypical rich man's mistress who did not. Part *grisette*, again, Gabrielle wasn't typical, in that the *grisette* was more often a man's lover than his live-in mistress.

Popularly seen as charming and 'all-powerful interpreters of fashion', *grisettes* were often highly artistic craftswomen. It had always been convenient to see their traditional poverty and appallingly long hours as 'dignified for wanting little'; something Gabrielle had experienced and left behind. Although the sporadic prostitution to which many of these 'all-powerful' women were forced to turn meant that they were seen as girls of easy virtue, their clients romanticized their hard-working lives and applauded their 'charming respectability'. Noted for frequenting bohemian artistic venues and forming relationships with artists or poets, as a rule men found it expedient to glamorize the *grisettes* as pretty, light-hearted things with hearts made of gold.[16]

When hats were still an indispensable element of any fashionable ensemble, pre-eminent amongst the *grisettes* were the milliners. With their clever modification of old styles and constant invention of new ones, they had always been seen as the acme of the working girls. The indefatigable commentator on Parisian women Octave Uzanne lovingly described them as 'the aristocracy of the workwomen of Paris; the most elegant and distinguished. They are artists. Their ingenuity in design seems limitless.'[17] A remarkably accurate description of Gabrielle's own credentials characterizes the *grisette* as 'a poor girl, perhaps an orphan too well raised to be a simple worker and too little instructed to be a teacher'.[18]

Meanwhile, in order to achieve real success in the fiercely competitive Parisian millinery trade, Gabrielle was going to need all her doggedness and determination. As she laboured, and slowly began to comprehend some of the essentials of running a business, her work began to satisfy her and fed her pride. The actresses and courtesans whom she knew from Royallieu had sometimes brought others to take a look at Gabrielle's hats at Etienne Balsan's *garçonnière* on the boulevard Malesherbes. The *demi-monde* and the stage had been curious to take a look at Etienne's mistress at work but, now that she lived with Arthur Capel, overcoming their prejudices, some of the more daring young society women, who were dressed by the great couturiers of the day, began to drop in too.

Whatever has been written about Gabrielle's meteoric rise to fame, in fact, she neither took Paris by storm once launched nor was she a born socialite only waiting to be scooped up and 'brought out' by someone sympathetic to her such as Arthur Capel. Notwithstanding Gabrielle's precociously advanced character, she did not possess a precocious ability for self-expression, nor was she quick to develop her innate abilities. Indeed, the period in which she learnt how to become a designer, a businesswoman and the person she wanted to be had a lengthy gestation. While her life at Royallieu had been her first major step, the time Gabrielle spent working in boulevard Malesherbes and her move to live with Arthur Capel were two of the crucial periods in which she was, effectively, serving her apprenticeship. Through Etienne Balsan and his friends at Royallieu, and then Arthur Capel and his connections, she was growing beyond the limitations of her background and assimilating much about the art of self-presentation. In keeping with the most renowned courtesans, however, Gabrielle would travel beyond these ideas and experiment with the more complex art of reinvention.

But while this young milliner was never short of ideas, as business grew, her ignorance of technique was beginning to hold her back, and when told by Etienne of someone who might help, she quickly made an approach. Young Lucienne Rabaté was a rising star who worked for one of Paris's most prestigious milliners, Maison Lewis. Seduced by the liveliness of the little Chanel salon, Lucienne brought with her two more of the Maison Lewis's best assistants.[19] Gabrielle's designs, her assistants' skill, and their word-of-mouth promotion meant that business continued gaining pace.

Gabrielle had remained close to her aunt Adrienne, who was still living quietly in Vichy with her lover, the Baron de Nexon. Adrienne was inclusive and generous spirited in her concerns for her family, and she now suggested the employment of Gabrielle's younger sister Antoinette to receive customers and look after the salon.

Antoinette had been first at Aubazine, then followed Julia-Berthe and Gabrielle to the convent at Moulins, and was now emulating her sister in trying her hand as a singer in Vichy. She was pretty and vivacious but had no voice and, like Gabrielle before her, was failing to find any work. As a result, Adrienne was supporting her. With some of her sister Gabrielle's boldness, plus a genuine charm, Antoinette became a decorative ambassador for Chanel Modes. With nothing like Gabrielle's intelligence or initiative, however, she was biddable and worked hard. Meanwhile, Gabrielle's salon had begun to outgrow its cramped quarters on the boulevard Malesherbes, and she turned to her lover for assistance. Would Arthur give her the finances to expand?

Arthur was businessman enough to recognize his mistress's intelligence and energy and, although she wasn't making great sums of money, he believed she had potential. As the entrepreneur in him thrived on risk, he agreed to fund the opening of Gabrielle's own shop. In this way, at the beginning of 1911, she took on the leasehold of some first-floor rooms on the rue Cambon, just off the fashionable rue de Rivoli.

The perceptive and witty diarist Elisabeth de Gramont, Duchesse de Clermont-Tonnerre, shines some light on the situation while also giving the impression that Gabrielle was at a loose end and without many ideas. Elisabeth de Gramont recalled an evening at her half-brother Armand de Gramont's house. Arthur was also present, and he and Elisabeth fell into conversation on the subject of his mistress, Gabrielle. He said, 'I am very attached to Coco and I am looking for an occupation for her.' Perhaps Arthur wished, here, to boost his own importance when implying that she didn't already have something to do:

I am a very busy man and I am not free in the afternoon; she is on her own, she gets bored, and this irritates me . . . Idleness can hang heavily on some women, especially when they are intelligent, and Coco is intelligent. You've got family, relatives, social obligations . . . She's got nothing; when she's through with polishing her nails, the time between two and eight is void . . . We don't always realize how important schedules are in people's emotional lives; we always speak of the heart, it is not that difficult to attune two hearts, but to synchronize two watches is a problem. I set her up in a little millinery shop, but it hasn't worked very well. However, she's energetic, she has the qualities of a businesswoman, and she is from Auvergne [meaning that she was determined and hard-working] . . . she would like to open a shop that sells knitwear and jerseys. Well, we will see.[20]

With a dressmaker already working at 21 rue Cambon, the law forbade Gabrielle to do the same thing. (Manufacturing knitwear and jerseys would get round this prohibition because they were not counted as dresses.) It is said that Gabrielle merely chanced upon this site, but our little milliner had in fact chosen it with great care, fully aware of its prime position. It was at the heart of that quarter encompassing the rue de la Paix, rue Royale, rue St-Honoré and the streets leading off and around the magnificent place Vendôme. For many years, this Parisian district had been the one where the most costly silks, jewels, furs, hats, perfumes and fashions were to be found.

8

Refashioning Paris

As a collective visual statement, fashion is about the appearance of the individual and of the group. It is at once about self-presentation and conformity. Like music, it is improvisation within a structure. As the human condition doesn't appear to respond well to too much repetition, fashion could be described as one of our antidotes to boredom. It must be new, but not too new; novel rather than radically different. A kind of planned spontaneity, it is *applied* art, making use of potentiality. Clothes can change more rapidly than other artefacts; although they are functional they are *statements* too. Fashion could be described as the cultural genome of clothes.

Writing on fashion appears almost universally to accept the idea that fashion follows power. At the courts of rulers and kings, this was undoubtedly the case. By the seventeenth century, Louis XIV of France had understood perfectly the connection between fashion and power. His dramatic self-presentation was about manipulating clothes as actual and symbolic reflections of the greatest power: in other words, his own. But the idea that fashion always follows power is far too simplistic and is only an approximation of what actually happens. In Gabrielle Chanel's case, the story is more complex and interesting than that.

Over time, the most fashionable rendezvous in Paris had been exclusive or semi-private. As the nineteenth century wore on, however, its sweeping changes were reflected in the fact that one of the most significant places to be 'seen' was now on the city's new boulevards – in public, on the streets. Here, the populace 'treated life as a spectacle . . . and intensely enjoyed their own and everyone else's performance'.[1]

Between 1830 and 1860 alone, Paris almost doubled its population, rising from 500,000 to almost a million, spreading ever further outwards. And still it grew, and the city's social problems multiplied. After years of division, plots, counter-plots, massacres and the raising and breaking down of the barricades, in 1851, the Machiavellian nephew of Napoléon I, Louis Napoléon, led a *coup d'état*. Having hoodwinked the nation, he was soon installed, by referendum, as Louis Napoléon III, absolute monarch of France.

Over the centuries, many had attempted to organize the chaos of Paris but, when Louis Napoléon took on as his assistant the engineer Georges-Eugène Haussmann, all was set to change. Louis and his accomplice were quintessential representatives of 'Industrial Progress' and saw the hundreds of streets in the city's busy, cramped, ancient quarters as a series of dreadful anachronisms. In an almost messianic urge to drag Paris into the modern, industrial world, the two men conceived an unprecedented urban renewal. Haussmann envisaged 'the Imperial Rome of our times', while Louis saw Paris as the modern capital of the world, and a monument to his power.

Beginning as they meant to go on, in one great onslaught, neither the monarch, nor Haussmann, calling himself the 'demolition artist', gave a jot about the Parisians' sense of their buildings, their neighbourhoods, or that the city's grandeur was found in the densely interwoven layers of its past. For years, as much as one fifth of Paris's workforce was occupied in making continual noise and dust, as buildings, streets, whole quarters were ruthlessly torn down and replaced by acres of large, uniform apartment blocks lining the wide, stately new boulevards. These were too expensive for the working classes, who were pushed to the jerry-built outer suburbs. There they were deprived of either the benefits of the age-old system or those of the new one.[2] In addition, the railways, bringing food from far and wide, squeezed out the traditional providers of much of the city's food and drink. The vineyards, market gardens and farms ringing the outskirts of the city for centuries gradually dwindled to a handful. Artisans, small-scale industrial enterprises, merchants large and small, the rich, the middling sort and the poor, had always lived and worked cheek by jowl in each of the city's quarters. For the first time, they were separated, as the new neighbourhoods became bound by class.

And, while Paris's great new inner boulevards, road junctions, squares and vistas were quite breathtaking in scale, this modern city par excellence had lost much of its previous intimacy. Many were troubled by the loss of 'old roots'. Not only were at least 350,000 displaced by the 'Haussmannization' of Paris, but one critic also complained that, for the first time, the city was physically divided in two: the rich and the poor. It was said that the continuous destruction of Paris had led to a destruction of its 'society' and, as a symptom of this loss, Parisians were more detached from one another. Paris had become superb, but it was also slightly chilling.[3]

But France was a world power and Paris was its capital. Emulating London's Great Exhibition, with the expositions of 1855 and 1867, Louis Napoléon succeeded in attracting millions. These trade fairs, celebrating the nineteenth-century cult of technology, were nowhere invested in so heavily nor used so impressively as in France. The Paris Expo of 1878, for example, launched the first experiments with electric street-lighting; 1889 saw the building of the Eiffel Tower. This masterpiece of technology, at first condemned by the literary and artistic establishment as 'the dishonour of Paris', soon became one of the most iconic city emblems in the world. With the Expo of 1900, the Paris underground network, the Métropolitain, was opened.

While these fairs dazzled on an enormous scale, another type of urban spectacle was locating itself in a new kind of marketplace: the department store – *le grand magasin*. As multi-storey temples to modernity, the department stores overflowed with goods never seen before under one roof. (At Le Bon Marché one could find fifty-four different types of crinoline.) Lined up along Haussmann's *grands boulevards*, these vast palaces of consumption became household names. They included: La Belle Jardinière and La Samaritaine, on the Right Bank by 1870; Le Bon Marché and the Galeries Lafayette, well established on the Left Bank by 1900. In ultra-modern settings, using the latest technology, the *grands magasins* displayed their myriad luxuries in fabulous interiors at a range of prices everyone could manage, 'from the duchess to the flirt and from the millionaire to the beggar'.[4] At least, that was the theory. In practice, the poor couldn't afford them.

If the better off had always had their dressmakers, many of the rest had bought much of their clothing from the wardrobe dealers selling cast-offs in markets around the town. Although this trade would continue, by the 1850s, it had also become possible to buy a variety of inexpensive new ready-to-wear clothing. While the invention and development of the sewing machine spurred on this democratization, it was the *grands magasins* that first introduced off-the-peg clothes to a bourgeois clientele in upmarket settings. In these Aladdin's caves, Parisians learnt to indulge themselves as never before and acquired the habit of mass consumption. The launch of mail-order catalogues extended further the *grands magasins'* influence, and thousands of women, such as Gabrielle's aunt Louise, living far away from Paris, longed to visit these great cathedrals to the new religion of commerce.

Many disliked the new city of inexhaustible pleasures, and writers, such as Zola, set out to record the particular conjunction of sexual and financial transaction seen as emblematic of Haussmann's newly corrupt Paris. Fashionable women of all sorts now rubbed shoulders in the *grands magasins*, and one observer wrote, 'One does not know, nowadays, if it's honest women who are dressed like whores, or whores who are dressed like honest women.'[5] Commerce became impersonal, and many of the small boutiques, relying on relatively local suppliers and serving regular customers, were overtaken by the department stores, who often bought from international sources and sold to people whom they had never met before.

Unlike old Paris, however, the new inner city did actually function. Despite the criticisms and the failure of 'all classes to mix', from the sanitation system to the department stores and the cafés, restaurants and theatres found on the *grands boulevards*, central Paris was indeed the epitome of modernity. Even those who disliked it were forced to admit that its thrusting energy and creative life gave the city a savage new kind of magnificence.

While the nineteenth century had witnessed the confident emergence of the bourgeois, at first considered philistines in all matters of taste, their rise and rise had left them a powerful force across society. The industrialization of France, the parallel exodus from the country and the growth in population had meant that the lives of huge numbers of people had changed more rapidly than their parents could ever have dreamed possible. As the bourgeois caste had grown, so its members were keen for guidance, and the proliferation of magazines for their women had grown proportionally.

In September 1909, that same year in which Gabrielle began living with Arthur Capel, a fashionable young actress, Lucienne Roger, was featured wearing one of Gabrielle's hats on the cover of one of these magazines, *Comoedia Illustré*. Inside the magazine were two more of Gabrielle's hats, bearing the commentary:

> I have just written a name which needs to be introduced to those of my readers for whom it should still be unknown. In this column we show two delightful models by the refined artist Gabrielle Chanel. First and foremost a lover of the line, her imagination is always . . . inspired and full of surprises, and always remains in good taste.

Comoedia Illustré was the recently launched weekly supplement to the French daily *Comoedia*. Run by Maurice de Brunhoff, scion of one of the most influential publishing families in France. *Comoedia Illustré* was devoted to coverage of the arts, and catered to an eclectic band of sophisticates whose social mix would have been virtually impossible a few decades earlier. De Brunhoff set his sights on these personalities and professionals who were representative of the social changes sweeping through large sections of French society. The financiers, industrialists, socialites, artists, writers, actors and *demi-mondaines* read such a magazine because it made them feel they were keeping abreast of the increasingly fragmenting artistic world and the radical changes emerging in all matters of style and taste.

Comoedia Illustré acted as cultural guide for its elite readership. Besides fashion, it presented photographs (very few magazines yet did this), illustrations, exhibition reviews and new, elite music as well as popular entertainment. And the magazine's largely youthful readership also identified with its undertow of rebellion. When Gabrielle had used her powers of persuasion on this, one of the city's most stylish magazines, her liaison with one of the most high-profile young men in Paris would not have gone unnoticed. With Lucienne Roger wearing Gabrielle's hat on *Comoedia*'s cover, Gabrielle had carried off a brilliant piece of self-promotion.

Maurice de Brunhoff's gamble on the newcomer paid off; the response to Gabrielle's hats was good. As a result, for the next month's issue, October 1909, Gabrielle herself modelled two of her designs. Whether large, or small and close to the head, her hats were very simple, with no more than a single flourish. They were described as having 'a style and harmony of lines that are unique to her' and, in November, Gabrielle once again got herself coverage, taking up a full page of the magazine. The December issue had another actress modelling another of Gabrielle Chanel's hats and, throughout the following year, coverage of her work continued, with comments such as: 'This design and those which surround it are of a rare distinction, and they honour Gabrielle Chanel, whose chosen and numerous clientele appreciates the assured and delicate taste more every day.'

The actresses and *demi-mondaines* of Gabrielle's acquaintance were regularly prevailed upon to help in her promotion. Thus, in January 1911, her friend the actress Jeanne Dirys appeared on a *Comoedia Illustré* cover in an illustration done by the precocious young artist Paul Iribe. By May that year, the same magazine is telling us that Gabrielle Chanel's distinguished work is now just as much sought after by beautiful women in town as in the theatre.

As so often in the past, under the influence of actresses and the *demi-monde*, society women were beginning to take note. In early

1912, Gabrielle's work was described as 'original', and she herself was hailed as 'this clear-sighted artist'. Meanwhile, Gabrielle Dorziat, Royallieu habitué and high-profile actress, modelled Gabrielle's hats for *Les Modes*, another influential magazine. Dorziat wore Gabrielle's daringly simple hats in an adaptation of Maupassant's *Bel Ami*; the press loved the actress, *and* her hats. Before the year was out, *Comoedia Illustré* declared that 'this young artist . . . [Gabrielle] is taking a dominant place in fashion at the moment.' Not only were her hats lauded for their 'unfailing stylishness and good taste', they were used to complement outfits by fashionable couturiers.

In all the commentary on Gabrielle the designer, one is told that it was her astounding simplicity that was so radical. However, while bearing in mind that our own perception of past fashion must differ from that of its contemporaries, looking through a cross-section of old magazines, Gabrielle's hats do *not* stand out as entirely radical. In the elite magazines, one comes across a handful of other designers who were *also* throwing out the complexity and grandiosity of much contemporary fashion in favour of simplicity. Gabrielle was not alone in thinking 'the women I saw at the races wore enormous loaves on their heads; constructions made of feathers and improved with fruits and plumes'.[6] The difference was that her designs were more conspicuous because they reflected her own unconventional lifestyle. The other designers were not the live-in mistress of one of the most up-to-date young men in Paris. Gabrielle would say, 'In the grandstands they were talking about my amazing, unusual hats, so neat and so austere, which were somehow a foretaste of things to come.'[7]

Meanwhile, she had stiff competition in quality from the big names in Parisian millinery. The atelier system involved apprentices slowly working their way up under the severe and demanding *premières*. These years of training equipped the best milliners with great craftsmanship, subtlety of design and an inside knowledge of the trade, none of which Gabrielle possessed. The ambitious young woman Gabrielle had filched from the Maison Lewis, Lucienne Rabaté, grew impatient with Gabrielle's refusal to take her advice (to make sure, for example, that a woman and her husband's mistress never met at the Chanel atelier). Instead, Gabrielle squandered attention on a famous courtesan, the kind of undesirable whom Lucienne disdained. Society clients were the prize. Perhaps Gabrielle wasn't so unaware of the nuances, and simply chose to ignore them. She was defiantly comfortable with the courtesans; she admired them, spoke the same language. At least they 'worked' for their living and were not out to make her feel socially inadequate.

Lucienne eventually left the Chanel atelier; a story to be repeated many times with Gabrielle's employees. No matter how much more knowledgeable than Gabrielle they might be, they accepted her way, or they left. Gabrielle's own unorthodox instincts were, however, to serve her very well. But her intense dislike of selling, or of ingratiating herself with her clients – 'The more people came to call on me the more I hid away . . . And I didn't know how to sell; I've never known how to sell. When a customer insisted on seeing me, I went and hid in a cupboard'[8] – led to her sister Antoinette assuming most of this role.

Combining disingenuousness and the capacity for searing truth, Gabrielle was always a bag of contradictions, including the possession of extraordinary confidence and driving fear. Knowing, for example, that if a client found a hat too expensive she might well reduce it, she kept herself in the background. Her most significant intuition here was the courtesan-like understanding that being enigmatic only made one more fascinating, and she coined the axiom: 'A customer seen is a customer surely lost.' Despite the numerous mistakes and the slowness of it all, Gabrielle's determination and growing sense of priorities were assuring her reputation.

There were also lighter moments. When the salon was empty of clients, for example, she and Antoinette could often be heard singing their hearts out in risqué numbers from the *café-concerts*. Business and its lighter moments weren't, however, the only things then on Gabrielle's mind. For the first time, she was truly in love. Not only did she love, she was loved in return, and experienced a rare sense of well-being.

Her lover, meanwhile, was, like her, possessed of tremendous energy; he was forever on the move. After the launch of Deauville's polo club by his friend Armand de Gramont, other grounds had sprung up in a small number of country estates and elite summer resorts and, with his friends, Arthur played them all. Thus, in January 1911, *The New York Times* announced he would play at Cannes, while another newspaper reported his arrival with his polo ponies on the Côte d'Azur. In May, he was taking part in a tournament at Compiègne, and in August he was back competing at Deauville. At Dieppe, and then Châteauroux, in August, Arthur and Etienne Balsan coursed their greyhounds, and then played more polo. The personification of the modern man, Arthur was either in a state of distraction or doing something at breakneck speed.

After the hunting, the galas and the balls, he even managed to find time to expand his fortune. Apparently, Gabrielle didn't feel neglected by her lover's tremendous pace; to a degree, it matched her own. She admired in him 'the mindset of a businessman . . . not hampered either by precedent or hierarchy', and she loved his 'eccentricity'. Yet, in the whirl of Arthur's life, how much of it included his mistress? A man in the vanguard of his times, he was, for example, a staunch believer in the emancipation of women. No doubt bearing Gabrielle in mind, in a political treatise he was soon to write he would say:

> The door to the future city is still closed to women. For centuries women have been considered by their masters as inferior creatures, as beasts of burden or of pleasure. The time has come to liberate them. Already they are liberating themselves . . . The education of women tends to teach them only the art of pleasing. In society as it is conceived, the woman who is incapable of pleasing falls into a state of dependency and inferiority. As the convent is no longer very much in fashion, one must choose between prostitution and work. The latter has shown that the inferiority of women was only an illusion of the other sex.[9]

However, with the customary tension between belief and practice, Arthur's actions weren't always quite consistent with his sentiments. It was common knowledge that he lived with his mistress but, where a liberal upper-class hostess might now welcome a bohemian artist, writer or musician into her salon, it was a rare one who yet dared do the same for a tradeswoman. But if attendance with one's mistress was out of bounds in the salons of the *haut monde*, obliging contemporary double standards enabled navigation around such prohibitions. In the theatre, in fashionable restaurants and bars, it wasn't only acceptable, it increased one's cachet to be seen out with one's mistress. And at private suppers where fellow diners were not all entirely 'respectable', Gabrielle felt at ease. These people, too, lived at the edge of society.

And yet, largely untrammelled by the constraints of family, Gabrielle had also been left rudderless by her dysfunctional upbringing. With the exception of Adrienne and Antoinette, she saw very little of her family. This was the great significance of her statement that Arthur was her brother, her father, her entire family. Meanwhile, Gabrielle's failure to become a singer in the *café-concerts* in Vichy had left her hankering after something other than hats, and her tremendous energy and rich inner life hadn't yet found an adequate outlet for expression. While Arthur was often away and understood Gabrielle's need for occupation, he now encouraged her in an activity which, although unrelated to her work, did have a bearing on her perception of herself as a modern woman.

Back in the 1870s, France had taken up 'physical culture' and, following Britain, sport for men was promoted as patriotic, and a healthy and moral outlet for the newly urban masses. Upper-class women, who had enjoyed croquet, archery and horseriding for some time, were now joined by their bourgeois sisters, who also took to the streets in outdoor clothing developed by the English companies Burberry and Aquascutum. Country walks became a favourite feminine pastime. A small fraction of women also took up 'physical culture' and other forms of exercise such as callisthenics and, in the early years of the twentieth century, the idea of exercise as a form of self-expression was developing.

In 1913, the American dancer Isadora Duncan was scandalizing Europe. Her uninhibitedly sensual emphasis upon the expression of emotion and physical improvisation was revolutionary, and deeply shocked many of her contemporaries, who were still convinced that the body was a shameful thing. Duncan believed intensely in the idea that we are mind *and* body; her body was not external to her, it *was* her. She rejected formal dancing, including ballet, with its strict rules of posture and formation, because they were 'ugly and against nature'. Her following was huge. Whatever Isadora Duncan's pretentiousness and however justified her critics, this woman had responded to the emotional and physical alienation emerging as a side-effect of life in the first machine age. She touched many of those who flocked to see her in revealing the very un-machine-like possibility of an unself-conscious relationship with one's body. When the Théâtre des Champs-Elysées was completed in 1913, Duncan's reputation was such that her likeness was carved by the sculptor Antoine Bourdelle over the entrance while, inside the theatre, Duncan appeared in Maurice Denis's murals of the nine muses.

Gabrielle was in search of a means to express something in herself as yet undefined, and now believed that she, too, wanted to be a dancer. Contriving an invitation with a friend to a private performance at Duncan's house, she was game enough to be unimpressed and would remain caustic in her criticism of the great muse. Rejecting such a distinguished teacher, she found instead Elise Toulemon (stage name Caryathis), an early devotee of the dance methods of Emile Jaques-Dalcroze.

In about 1905, while attempting to improve his music students' abilities, Jaques-Dalcroze had created a system of musical education. Naming his 'harmonious bodily movement as a form of artistic expression' Eurhythmics, his intention had neither been an end in itself nor a form of dance. However, the timing was propitious and his ideas had spread quickly across Europe. Suggesting as they did non-balletic dance techniques, the principles of Eurhythmics would

soon be used to develop radically new dance forms. At the same
time, by 1912, Eurhythmics as a form of dance-exercise had become
something of a Parisian fashion.

The health-giving aspects of sport, plus Isadora Duncan and
Jaques-Dalcroze's philosophies of self-expression, encouraged a
small number of young women to take up these ideas as a form of
self-development as well as a means of maintaining lithe and exercised bodies. Such attitudes were seen by most contemporaries as
distastefully anti-feminine, and the young women were regarded as
more or less outrageous. They themselves saw their exercising as a
kind of emancipation. Reacting against the flaccidness of middle-
aged women, made taut by nothing more taxing than a corset,
Gabrielle diverted herself with the unconventional idea that physical perfection could only be gained via exercise.

Her dance teacher Elise was most definitely unconventional.
Having escaped from a background as impoverished and defective
as Gabrielle's, Elise ended up in Montmartre, where her flamboyance had given her a wild reputation. Later, she would make a
tempestuous marriage to the troubled homosexual writer Marcel
Jouhandeau but, for now, she was one of the dancers at the Théâtre
des Arts. In the period when Gabrielle met her – about 1912–13 –
while Elise's talents as a dancer and choreographer were becoming
recognized, to make ends meet she also gave classes in expressive
dance. Her extrovert sensuality would be captured in the Russian
artist-designer Léon Bakst's poster for the composer Erik Satie's
'ballet', *La Belle Excentrique. La belle excentrique,* Elise, danced her
invention in a provocatively scanty outfit designed by a very young
poet-artist, Jean Cocteau. Renowned for her wit, her untamed and
extravagant personality and her numerous affairs, at the time she
and Gabrielle met, Elise was in the midst of a tumultuous relationship with Charles Dullin, the avant-garde actor-producer.

Day after day, Gabrielle climbed up to Elise's studio in Montmartre and then strove to convince her teacher that she *could*
become a dancer. Once again, however, she was to be disappointed;
after several months, Elise told her that she just wasn't right for the

stage. For all her noted grace, was it that some part of Gabrielle remained self-conscious, inhibiting her ability to abandon herself completely? Whatever the reasons for her failure, she was by now devoted to her expressive dance lessons (and her eccentric teacher), and continued with the classes. Convinced by the idea that a beautiful body was a slim and exercised one, for the rest of her life Gabrielle would work to keep hers that way. If she couldn't become a dancer, at least she would have a dancer's body.

The Rite of Spring

In 1913, some doubted whether France was still the cultural arbiter to the world, arguing that it had become more fascinated by foreign culture than by its own. While French artists and composers such as Renoir, Braque, Matisse, Ravel, Debussy and Fauré were being seen and heard, it was the innovation of the foreigners – Picasso, Chagall, Apollinaire, Sarah Bernhardt, Arthur Rubinstein, Rachmaninov and the Ballets Russes – that was attracting more animated attention. The foreigners seemed more thrusting in their search for liberation from past aesthetic and moral ideals, from authority and bourgeois conformity. They had travelled, physically and mentally, from the margins to Paris, which they saw as the place where revolution was fermented. The Polish-Italian Frenchman Guillaume Apollinaire understood that an essential element of the modern mentality was exile, the 'battle on the frontiers'. The French painter Jacques-Emile Blanche wrote that the French capital had become the central station of Europe, and that 'in Paris uncertainty rules.'[1]

One May evening in 1913, following much anticipation, the Russian impresario Sergei Diaghilev presented a new ballet at the avant-garde Théâtre des Champs-Elysées. This work embodied the rejection of everything in art and life that its creators regarded as outmoded, and was to become one of the seminal works of the modern era. In the audience on that historic occasion was Gabrielle Chanel, invited by her dance teacher Elise Toulemon. (Eurhythmics had become so influential that Diaghilev and his dancer-choreographer, the legendary Vaslav Nijinsky, had visited its founder, Jaques-Dalcroze, to ask for help with the dance movements for their ballet.)

Its composer, Igor Stravinsky, had named the ballet *Le Sacre du printemps* (*The Rite of Spring*). He said that 'it represents pagan Russia, and is unified by a single idea: the mystery surge of the creative power of Spring. The piece has no plot.'[2] Nijinsky, who was Diaghilev's lover, had written to Stravinsky: 'Now I know what *Le Sacre du printemps* will be when everything is as we both want it: new, beautiful and utterly different – but for the ordinary viewer a jolting and emotional experience.'[3]

Stravinsky told his mother not to be afraid if the response to the ballet was negative, saying that 'it is in the order of things.'[4] Meanwhile, Nijinsky's dancers complained that his ideas were incomprehensible and his style entirely without beauty. With Stravinsky and Nijinsky, Diaghilev was intent on confrontation; their united goal was to shock.

How had it come about that Sergei Diaghilev and his dance troupe, the Ballets Russes, had not only become an essential element of the Parisian avant-garde, but were central to the development of the modern movement?

A younger Diaghilev had described himself candidly to his beloved stepmother in a letter expressing his anxieties about his younger brothers: 'As for myself ... I am first a great charlatan, although one with great flair; second, I am a great charmer; third, I've a great nerve; fourth, I'm a man with a great deal of logic and few principles; and fifth, I think I lack talent; but if you like I think I've found my real calling – patronage of the arts.'[5] He had written that he felt a force in himself, and had come to realize 'that I for the devil am not an ordinary person'.

Sergei Diaghilev's father was a cultivated provincial aristocrat who had become a bankrupt. His son learnt to convert several vital elements – the collapse of his family, his sexuality and the loss of his homeland through revolution – into an evangelical blurring of all present boundaries. Diaghilev had early flaunted his homosexuality – then a dangerous thing to do in Russia – and established himself as a cosmopolitan dandy with deeply anti-establishment sentiments. If he lacked the essential talent to become an artist, nonetheless, Diaghilev's remarkable ability to innovate and transform the world of art itself would be carried out with an extraordinary degree of creativity. He loved the tension caused by all that was contradictory: 'He loved the friction, the struggle and the fire that was engendered by the new but not necessarily . . . for its own sake.'[6]

Diaghilev had founded an influential art journal in Russia, mounted highly successful exhibitions and gradually come to believe that only the ballet exemplified the ideal, which was that all art forms should be united into one. By 1909, he had formed his own company. The Ballets Russes de Diaghilev caused a sensation across Europe. The colours and boldness of the sets and costumes and the foreignness and exoticism of the company's Russian and oriental themes became all the rage. But while Diaghilev's aim was a totality of art, it was as much about liberation of all kinds, including sexuality. And sexuality became a vehicle of rebellion against bourgeois values and one of the central themes of the modern movement.

Audiences were awed by Diaghilev's lover, the extraordinary dancer Nijinsky, whom Debussy called 'a perverse genius . . . a young savage'. It had been Nijinsky's elemental faun simulating orgasm in Debussy's *L'Après-midi d'un faune* that broke all traditional rules of good taste and brought the underlying eroticism of much of the Ballets Russes's work blatantly to the fore. Women, and men, were left in a heightened erotic state; *Faune* had caught the imagination of a generation. Privately, homosexuality too was a powerful element of the rebellious theme pervading the Ballets Russes; Stravinsky noted that Diaghilev's entourage was 'a kind of homosexual Swiss Guard'. While each new success encouraged Diaghilev to blur yet more boundaries and become still more daring, any disquiet at his company's work was outweighed by the loud approval.

By 1912, Diaghilev had turned to more introspective and expressionistic music. Without any overarching philosophy of art, he was a master of a powerful strand in modern artistic thought. This was the belief that art delivered people from the constraints of morality and convention to recover a spontaneous life of the emotions. A man constrained by morality would never be free to create. In this way, art was seen as a life force greater than the individual and, eventually, a substitute for religion.

Thus it was only natural that Diaghilev should become one of the standard-bearers for this developing attitude to life and art. Emotions and intuition had just as much validity as all that was rational and objective, and an element of shock was necessary to provoke experience. Art would no longer teach. Its aim was to excite, provoke and inspire, to unlock experience. Diaghilev's Ballets Russes was a success because the spirit behind it was already in the air.

However, in 1913, at the first performance of *The Rite of Spring*, Diaghilev and his colleagues' daring was to unsettle even this audience that saw itself as in the vanguard of change. Rumour and counter-rumour had carefully been circulated by Diaghilev for weeks, and the air of anticipation was palpable. An observer wrote later that, in fact, the audience's 'role had been written for it'. This was that it should be scandalized.

As the very first mournful notes of the bassoon melody rose up, some in the audience began to whistle. But by the time the weirdly dressed dancers appeared, with their shivering and shaking and jumping up and down in ugly and angular poses, there were cries of disapproval. Stravinsky and Diaghilev's staunch followers loyally cheered, but many others booed at this 'grotesque caricature'. People began to argue: some apparently exchanged punches; a society woman spat in a man's face; and it is said that a duel was fought the next morning. It was reported that, in all, there was pandemonium.

Over the years, many told their memories of that heady night. Comparing several of the 'memories', however, one finds a mass of contradictions. It turns out that not only did almost everyone remember inaccurately, some of those who 'recalled' the hysteria of that night weren't even there. But, here, the audience had become as significant a part of the performance as the dancers and the musicians. They were part of its 'living elements', and their response was as important to the meaning of this art as the intentions of those who introduced it. This new art had indeed 'transcended reason, didacticism, and a moral purpose' and become 'provocation and event'.[7]

While Gabrielle would later admit that she hadn't understood much of *The Rite*'s first performance as a 'living element' of the ballet, as one of those who would contribute to the overthrow of much in life and art seen as outmoded, it seems most fitting that she was present.

Meanwhile, her own so far modest contribution to the avant-garde was about to become more prominent. For some time, Gabrielle had interspersed her wardrobe with her own designs but, by 1912, she was consolidating her style. This is reflected in the earliest known dress probably designed by her: an utterly simple sheath of dark velvet set off by a collar of delicate white petals. It was made in 1913 for Gabrielle's friend Suzanne Orlandi, mistress to Etienne Balsan's friend Baron Foy. Gabrielle would become fiercely protective of her reputation for originality and was neither to leave any record of her earliest ideas about clothes nor speak about her influences. What she did talk about was motivation, and she famously said, 'My work came about as a reaction to my times.' But while admitting her admiration for the designer Vionnet, Gabrielle would also play down the influence of another designer, Paul Poiret. Perhaps more even than the clothes, Gabrielle observed his example in self-presentation and the way one ran a business. Yet she would also understand her century better than Poiret and consequently go far beyond him.

In 1911, Poiret was a charismatic young couturier (just four years older than Gabrielle) who had provoked outrage with the introduction of his harem pants. Seen as a perilous development, they were thought to challenge male supremacy and encourage the Women's Movement. Nonetheless, by 1914, Poiret would hold sway as one of the most radical designers in Paris.

He had trained with the great Jacques Doucet, himself a product of the extravagant nineteenth-century Second Empire and a fierce advocate of taste and discrimination. Doucet's rue de la Paix atelier was only a few doors away from that of his own mentor, Charles Frederick Worth, the first couturier of them all and still the dominant figure in the fashion industry at the end of the nineteenth century. Like Worth, Doucet amassed a large library and works of art, including Picasso's *Les Demoiselles d'Avignon*, bought directly from the artist. Doucet believed the watchwords for couture were luxury and distinction rather than practicality and function. Young Poiret had set out to emulate his master.

At first, Poiret gained notoriety with dresses and costumes for famous actresses, including Sarah Bernhardt and the courtesan Réjane. Then he quickly outstripped Worth and Doucet to become the fashion guru of the moment. His greatest contribution towards the history of dress was in his outright rejection of a fundamental convention. This was the fierce division of a woman's body into two. Previously, the abdomen and ribcage were encased in armour-like corsets, while the lower half was swathed in voluminous skirts, plumping out the behind. (Proust said that women looked as if they were 'made up of different pieces that had been badly fitted together'.)[8] Instead, Poiret utterly shocked his contemporaries by doing away with this rigid division and making dresses that clung revealingly to the body in soft, fluid lines, from a high waist just below the bust. Provoking still further outrage, he insisted his clients must dispense with their armoured corsets. This gave the Poiret silhouette a particularly sinuous and alarmingly natural effect, driving furious critics such as Worth to denounce it as 'hideous and barbaric'. Worth thundered that Poiret's clothes were really 'only suitable for women of uncivilized tribes'.[9]

Fashion is a fabulously subjective pastime, and contemporaries were unable to see that Poiret's designs weren't really so outlandish. Above all, they were a reflection of fashion's frequent tendency to look over its shoulder to the past. Poiret's major inspiration was in fact the post-Revolutionary Directoire period, whose 'classical' understatement was in turn inspired by Ancient Greece and Rome. At the same time – largely under the influence of the Ballets Russes – all things exotic and oriental were then much in vogue, and Poiret's intense palette of colours, plus his layered dresses and turbans, earned him the description 'Pasha Paris'. In strong contrast to the Belle Epoque craze for embellishment, which was synonymous with haute couture since its beginnings, any ornament or elaboration in Poiret's dress, hairstyles or millinery was very spare. As with Gabrielle's hats, it was the very simplicity of Poiret's designs that some at first regarded as disturbing.

By 1913, *Vogue* announced that Poiret had become the 'prophet' of simplicity, and quoted his claim that 'it is what a woman leaves off, not what she puts on, that gives her cachet.' Poiret was interested in the underlying structure of clothing, saying that he rejected the confusion of richness with what is beautiful, and costliness with what is elegant. As the first truly modern designer, while his vision was an original one, Poiret found phenomenal success not only as a result of the design of his clothes.

In newly urbanized France, this young entrepreneur understood that a name needed constant airing; to appear in as many different guises as possible. And, in those rapidly changing times when many were unsure, Poiret *was* sure, and promoted his own way of life as an idealized lifestyle that his clients were able to purchase. The first designer-entrepreneur to use the now ubiquitous concept of the 'brand', Poiret not only put his name on perfumes but also on cosmetics and accessories. Indeed, his strategy of extending the designer's name far beyond the simple promotion of clothes would eventually become the financial pillar of almost every twentieth-century fashion house.

Meanwhile, as far as the traditionalist Worth was concerned, fashion had become a 'meaningless jangle, hopelessly out of tune'. And while this description synchronized with the growing restlessness of an age of fast motor cars and flying machines, several other couturiers were catching up with Poiret's simpler, unstructured shapes. Indeed, during the first decade or so of the century, high fashion was making a momentous move away from the Belle Epoque's leisure, consumption and waste, towards what was memorably described as 'conspicuous outrage'. Indeed, flouting traditional standards of 'good taste' was almost becoming the rule.[10] Gabrielle's unusually simple hats had already placed her in the category of unconventional and daring but, with her next step, she was to initiate a far more concerted attack upon the idea of the traditional.

A month or so after the *Rite of Spring*'s dramatic premiere, Arthur and Gabrielle left for Deauville, the 'elegant kingdom', with its world-renowned racecourse, France's first polo ground and a sumptuous casino. The resort's rail link with the capital had made it easily accessible for well-to-do Parisians, and its glamour and proximity to the English Channel proved attractive to the British *nouveau riche* and upper classes. This in turn meant that the British love of games and sports was catered for, with tennis courts and a golf course.

As a young man of distinction and a polo player of note, Arthur was one of the resort's darlings. And so its habitués looked on with interest as he arrived for the season with the woman rumoured to be his live-in mistress, and whose hats were becoming familiar to the *beau monde*. *Vogue* had recently given Deauville its stamp of approval as 'the summer capital of France', with the 'shortest, gayest, and most exciting season of any of the fashionable resorts on the continent'. Arthur now took a suite of rooms at one of the grandest hotels, the newly opened Normandy, which was connected by an underground passage to the opulent new casino.

While society dismissed the rumoured talk of war and flocked to the 'summer capital', Gabrielle was preparing to launch her new venture: with Arthur's financial backing, she was about to open a new shop. Having chosen with Arthur premises on the rue Gontaut-Biron, the smartest street in Deauville's select shopping quarter, Gabrielle had hired two country girls as seamstresses, organized the redesign of her shop, and begun putting out the word.

Like all resorts, Deauville's prestige was sustained by the theatricality of its daily life. All events and venues, from the restaurant to the parties and the polo ground, to the boardwalk by the beach, relied for their entertainment on the dress and behaviour of the visitors. Catering to a community of ever-changing, socially fluid personalities, the resort's entertainments were promenading, sports and parties. The changes of dress required for the morning promenade, the afternoon's races, polo, golf, evenings spent at the casino, dancing, or a party, called for large and varied wardrobes.

And it was aspects of resort lifestyle that had inspired Gabrielle's designs. Few women took part in any sports; they were observers dressed in immensely impractical clothes. But, for the small group of younger women like Gabrielle, who played tennis or golf or actually went to the beach to swim, what they now wanted was fashion with greater ease of movement.

In Gabrielle's boutique, with its striped awning proudly bearing the name 'Gabrielle Chanel', she offered clothes and hats based on simplified elements. There were open-collar blouses, simple sweaters, loose, belted jackets and long skirts for relaxed and outdoor living. Most famously, Gabrielle had taken familiar items of men's practical clothing and turned them to her advantage. The fisherman's shirts, turtle-necks and over-sized sweaters; the polo sweater, Arthur's having apparently been donned one day because Gabrielle was cold – all these she modified for women. The polo shirt, for example, became an open-necked, belted tunic with sleeves rolled up. Borrowing from those workaday wardrobes, she amazed and delighted her audience by demonstrating that the practical and the everyday could be the source of high style, until then invariably rooted in luxury and the exotic. In a place like Deauville, attuned to the slightest diversion in dress, Gabrielle's salon immediately set tongues wagging.

Adrienne was once again pressed into service, leaving the boutique several times a day to spend time around the town with friends, sporting one or other of Gabrielle's outfits. This proved so successful that Antoinette joined the ranks as mannequin, while Gabrielle and Arthur's circle was also drumming up interest. This first range of clothes was almost certainly ready-to-wear, Gabrielle's first couture collection coming later. At the beginning of September, the magazine *Femina* published a full-page illustration evoking the jolly atmosphere around Gabrielle, accompanied by the following puff:

> Every morning at the chic hour, groups form outside the fashionable shop. Sportsmen, noble foreigners and artists shout at one another and chat; some, friends of the house, harangue female passers-by, inviting them to come in . . . 'Come on, dear countess, a little hat, just one, only five Louis . . .!' And one goes in: people chat, they flirt, they show off amazing outfits . . . Outside it's a hubbub, the double rank of people sitting down who watch, contemplate and criticize: a non-stop double-stream, moving towards the sea.[11]

Femina showed Gabrielle with a client and some illustrious friends, including one of the most celebrated contemporary painters, Paul Helleu, and the aviator Alberto Santos-Dumont. Santos-Dumont was a Brazilian whose aeronautical feats had included the first European public aeroplane flight, making him one of the most famous men in the world.

We see Gabrielle in a casual white outfit on the boardwalk by the beach, with that length of dark hair caught up and setting off a loose, easy blouse and a long simple skirt. To this she has added an over-sized, open-necked cream tunic with large patch-pockets, and into her buttoned belt she has tucked a white flower. Pockets were as yet uncommon on the outside of stylish women's clothing, unless it was for sporting occasions. (British companies such as Burberry made fishing or walking coats with pockets.) Anyone other than the most forward-thinking observer would have regarded Gabrielle's hands, dug comfortably into her pockets, as audaciously unladylike. In another photograph, Adrienne poses in a wrap coat, and she and Gabrielle stand together smiling broadly in front of the boutique, its 'Gabrielle Chanel' awning wafting in the sea breeze.

Recently discovered photographs give a lively impression of the resort's street theatre. Arthur and his stylish friends lounge nonchalantly around the entrance to Gabrielle's salon. In another photograph, a group of celebrities passes the time of day on comfortable chairs in front of the salon. Paul Helleu and his friend Giovanni Boldini (also friend to Edgar Degas), probably then the most successful portrait painter in Paris, sit talking with another friend, Sem, pseudonym of Georges Goursat, the most notable French caricaturist of the day. His studio was near Gabrielle's boutique on rue Cambon in Paris, and he had been a friend and admirer for some time. Sem was a small man who dressed carefully and whose sardonic pen made those in the public eye fear him. In Jean Cocteau's characterization of Sem one senses Cocteau's defensiveness. Sem was 'a ferocious insect . . . progressively taking on the tics of his victims he pursued. His fingers, his stump of a pencil, his round glasses . . . his forelock, his umbrella, his dwarfish, stable-boy silhouette – all seemed to shrink into and concentrate upon his eagerness to sting.'[12]

That summer, Gabrielle captured Deauville's imagination. Her lover's social standing, Gabrielle's own striking appearance and personality and her cohort of admirers combined to help promote and accommodate this young woman of undistinguished background in this most elite of locations. Later, Gabrielle also recalled her own sense of conviction when she said: 'The age of extravagant dress, those dresses worn by heroines that I had dreamt about, was past.'[13]

Amongst her visitors on the rue Gontaut-Biron was the Baroness Diane 'Kitty' de Rothschild, who brought with her Cécile Sorel, one of the capital's leading actresses. A delicious piece of gossip going the rounds had it that Kitty Rothschild, a devoted client of Poiret's, had turned up one day at his salon with her retinue of male admirers. They had not only followed the baroness into the dressing room but also entertained themselves by making suggestive remarks to Poiret's young mannequins. Poiret was at the pinnacle of his career and gave vent to his anger by banishing the Rothschild retinue from his salon. Whether or not this ban was extended to Kitty Rothschild herself is uncertain. Nevertheless, the young socialite let it be known she was intent upon revenge.

Knowing full well that, as one of the most fashionable women in

Paris, her patronage was invaluable publicity, she shunned Poiret's salon, putting out the word that she now followed the exciting new designer, Gabrielle Chanel. Soon, other stylish young women, such as Princesse Baba de Faucigny-Lucinge, née Erlanger, Pauline de Saint-Sauveur and Antoinette, pretty wife to the fashionable playwright Henri-Adrien Bernstein, were to be seen in Gabrielle's salon. Gabrielle and her assistants were kept frantically busy into the new year of 1914.

In March, Gabrielle was given a sensational public endorsement when Sem parodied the foibles of high fashion in a famous series of satirical albums for the newspaper *L'Illustration*. Entitled 'True and False Chic', in them he compared the ostentatious pomposity of contemporary 'false chic' with the elegant lines of 'true chic', for him exemplified by the beautiful courtesan Forsane, whom he depicted in a svelte, fur-trimmed outfit by none other than Gabrielle Chanel. Sem soon followed this up with an even more notable cartoon in which Arthur Capel, drawn as a virile, polo-playing centaur, carried off Gabrielle in his arms. Arthur's polo mallet was the centaur's lance, on the end of which dangled a hat, while from Gabrielle's arm hung an unmistakable hat box inscribed with the word 'Coco'. The allusions were clear: the well-known playboy Arthur Capel was both lover and sponsor to Gabrielle Chanel, who was now an identifiable enough figure that she could also be caricatured.

The End of an Epoque

In the period preceding the First World War, there appears to have been a widespread unwillingness to face the likelihood of conflict. And the closer the impending catastrophe approached, the more a striking acceleration of luxury and high living could be observed. Paul Morand's fictional hero Lewis says to Irène, 'For myself I come with limited responsibility, and . . . I accept none out of pessimism.'[1] Irène replies that this is the easy way out, telling Lewis that 'we don't have any worries if we think the world is meaningless.'[2]

In an atmosphere heightened by foreboding, on 3 August 1914, the opulence of the grand style was overnight curtailed. The West was launched into a conflict that would leave it irrevocably altered. Germany had declared war upon France; the First World War had begun.

On the following day, Britain entered the fray by declaring war upon Germany. Twelve days later, Arthur Capel was commissioned as a second lieutenant in the Cavalry Division. The contrasting sentiments with Lewis's declaration above and the fortitude and commitment typifying Arthur's army service were both echoed in the words he would later write: 'Let us get the strong words of Guillaume le Taciturne set firmly in our mind: "One does not have to hope in order to undertake, nor does one have to succeed in order to persevere."'[3]

By 24 August, Arthur had joined the British Expeditionary Forces – under orders from General Allenby (Cavalry Division) – which were taking part in the retreat from the battle of Mons. Mons was the first major action by the British army against the Germans but, while a relatively minor battle in itself, its position meant that it took on considerable significance. Although initially planned as a simple tactical withdrawal, what came to be known as 'the long retreat' lasted two weeks and involved considerable loss of life, as a disciplined German army followed in relentless pursuit.

On 4 September, the French commander-in-chief, Joseph Joffre, recognized a major German tactical error and halted the retreating Franco-British armies at the river Marne, only thirteen miles from Paris. Rallying, they overcame the Germans in the first battle of the Marne. When the German commanding officer, General von Moltke, heard that his army might now be destroyed, he suffered a nervous breakdown and had to be relieved of his command. By 12 September, it was all over and the Allies had won the battle. This transformation of a virtual rout into a victory became known as the 'Miracle of the Marne'. But the casualties and deaths, in an onslaught where over two million men fought and almost one hundred thousand had died, were as nothing compared to the maiming, death and destruction that would follow in the events of this war. Meanwhile, this battle set the stage for four years of stalemate trench warfare along the length of the Western Front.

On enlisting, Arthur had been sent, with another Englishman, to join a small intelligence unit under George de Symons Barrow. Accompanying 'the long retreat', Arthur and his intelligence comrades went back and forth from the front line to their commanding officers, gleaning as much as they could about the relentless Germans advancing behind them. Intelligence work was difficult, often carried out at night, and frequently very dangerous, as revealed by the two anecdotes below. George Barrow wrote that, while retreating with the army:

> The division crossed the Oise at Compiègne [close to Etienne's château], and occupied high ground . . . We were assured that all the bridges . . . had been demolished. I went at night with Capel to make sure that no . . . Germans had got across in boats by other means.
>
> We were very hungry, and going into a baker's shop . . . got a newly baked loaf of bread . . . I found a room in a workman's cottage and Capel found one next door. It was 1 a.m. Very tired, I took off my belt,

haversack and sword and threw myself fully dressed on the bed. At 4 a.m. the owner . . . came to my room and said: 'The Prussians are in the village . . .' I replied: 'Impossible: all the bridges are broken'. He said, 'It's true, and I'm off' . . . I did not believe him, and was desperately in need of sleep . . . Then I thought, 'It's not good enough to run the risk . . .' and dragging myself off the bed went to the door. I heard some shots and bangings at doors . . . at the far end of the street. At the same moment, Capel rushed out. I got my belt and haversack, left my sword – a useless weapon – behind in my hurry and we jumped into the car, which was facing the wrong way. A thick mist had come up from the river and the engine was cold. It seemed like hours before Capel could start it. Then the car had to be turned in the narrow street. Meanwhile, the door bangings drew closer and closer. At last the car was got round the corner, a hundred yards or less away. One or two shots whizzed close over our heads before we were hidden in the mist.[4]

Before the great retreat finally came to an end, near Paris, Arthur and Barrow experienced another narrow escape when setting off one night in Arthur's car to discover the proximity of the enemy. As they drove out of a wood, to their horror a German brigade crossed the road only three hundred yards ahead of them and joined up with several regiments in the fields. Incredulous at not being spotted, Arthur backed stealthily into the wood and turned the car around. Barrow wrote:

I had my eyes fixed on the enemy during the process of reversing and turning and was equally astonished and relieved that not a single German looked in our direction. At last we got around and away to safety. Had we been half a minute earlier or the German brigade half a minute later, we must have met and Capel and I would have seen no more of the war.[5]

In fact, Arthur and Barrow would both live to see a good deal more of this war.

★ ★ ★

Behind the lines, forced as the revellers at Deauville had been to face this thing that so many of them had assiduously avoided, they panicked and left the resort. On the fourteenth day of that momentous August, normally the height of the season, Elisabeth de Gramont described how The Normandy, the hotel where Gabrielle and Arthur had stayed, was half closed and The Royal was going to become a hospital. Luxury shops were closing, rental agencies were empty and foreigners were disappearing: 'Cars are requisitioned, the price of petrol is going up, and horse-drawn cars demand a hundred francs to go up the hill . . . Some prudent people . . . are hiding little bags of gold in their corsets . . . others are buying petrol.'[6]

When Paris had almost been cut off by the encircling German army, Joseph Joffre was unable to ensure the safety of the capital and advised the government to retreat to Bordeaux. At that point, up to a third of Paris fled, too, and Deauville was once again packed with people as the *haut monde* flocked to the safety of the hotels and their villas. A number of country properties had been occupied or destroyed in the wake of the advancing German army. One of these was Etienne Balsan's château, Royallieu, occupied by German staff officers. Retaken during the battle of the Marne, the Royallieu barracks was then converted into a front-line hospital.

Before Arthur left for the Front, he had instructed Gabrielle to remain in Deauville; his instinct was that she should keep her boutique open. Meanwhile, luxury, extravagance, conspicuous consumption of any kind suddenly didn't seem appropriate, and practicality became the order of the day. A number of the socialites remaining in Deauville volunteered at the hospital, and a pared-down, unostentatious wardrobe became a practical necessity. Yet while many of the socialites claimed they had 'lost everything', they also spent that strange summer living a life as luxurious as the great resort was able to provide. Unaware that this season was the last of an epoque, intimations of change nonetheless led many a wealthy woman to Gabrielle's door, to equip herself with those unfussy clothes she had originally designed with sport and leisure in mind.

And, in spite of shortages of material, Gabrielle continued using her initiative and quickly reaped the rewards: her salon was always busy. Mustering her growing number of assistants, she had them sew and sew, and later said, 'I was in the right place, an opportunity beckoned. I took it ... What was needed was simplicity, comfort, neatness: unwittingly I offered all of that.'[7] Elisabeth de Gramont, whose stylish unconventionality made her one of Gabrielle's early devotees, remembered the tremendous activity in the boutique and the new sombreness of women's wardrobes. Gabrielle recalled the races, just before the war, and said she hadn't realized that:

> I was witnessing the death of luxury, the passing of the nineteenth century; the end of an era. An age of magnificence but of decadence, the last reflection of a baroque style in which the ornate had killed off the figure, in which over-embellishment had stifled the body's architecture ... woman was no more than a pretext for riches, for lace, for sable, for chinchilla, for materials that were too precious.[8]

She decried the Belle Epoque tendency to transform women into 'monuments of belated and flamboyant art', and deplored the trains of insipid pastel dresses dragging in the dust. Referring to the decadence of those years, she remembered how there was so much wealth that it had become 'as ordinary as poverty'. And that little had changed since the 1870s, 'with its frenzy of easy money, of habits of straying from one style to another, of romantically taking its inspiration from every country and all periods, for it lacked a way of expressing itself honestly'.[9]

One of those Gabrielle had in mind here was Paul Poiret. His hugely simplified designs had signalled a fundamental redirection of women's clothing, so that now it was cut along straight lines and constructed from rectangles of fabric. Nonetheless, there were significant aspects of Poiret's work that Gabrielle would resolutely eschew. First, Poiret looked with nostalgia to the past. Second, he was seduced by the romance of the exotic, at that moment involving the fantasy of Russia, central to the vogue for all things oriental.

Gabrielle recognized that what both these strands of thought – the exotic and indulgence in the past – were doing was hiding from aspects of the present. While Poiret had embraced his radical times and believed he was intent upon liberating women, in his costume 'fantasies', they still played out a version of the old stereotype – woman subjugated and presented as more ideal than real. His harem pants were a perfect case in point.

In the realm of clothing at least, Gabrielle was no longer interested in fantasy. Embracing what she saw as the reality of her times, she not only gave women practical, stylish clothes but also made them fashionable. And at the end of that hectically busy summer at Deauville, the first of the war, Gabrielle had earned the huge sum of 200,000 gold francs. (In today's currency, this is worth approximately £560,000.)

Arthur rushed back from the Front when he could, to maintain his business interests and visit Gabrielle and his friends. But life was entirely altered. The majority were paring down their lives and feeling diminished by the war. To begin with, aside from the old men and boys, much of the male population had been packed off to fight. Paris felt unrecognizable:

> Rid of its bad ferments, [it] had become popular, fraternal again: we were humble little things at the mercy of events: the stock exchange was closed, theatres were shut, the Parliament was away, luxury cars were in Bordeaux . . . the streets of Paris have become great village streets again, where one communicates from door to door.[10]

But Gabrielle and Arthur's entrepreneurial spirit – some would call it opportunism – made what they had to offer very saleable, and their response to their times united them still further. While Gabrielle sold her simple, stylish and appropriately sober clothes, Arthur used his fleet of ships to become one of France's major providers of coal, then one of the most crucial resources in the running of a country and a war.

★ ★ ★

By the end of November 1914, Arthur was based in Flanders with his fellow officers at the Château de la Motte au Bois. Its châtelaine, the Baroness Clémentine de la Grange, noted how appropriate Arthur's first billet, with two lady milliners, had been, saying that it was 'not for the first time . . . that millinery has played a part in his life'. As a close friend of the baroness's nephew, another intelligence officer, Odon de Lubersac, Arthur was invited to stay at the château.

Shortly before Christmas, Arthur's commander, General Allenby, offered to have her driven to visit her other son at Reims. She later recorded:

> I started in Captain Capel's car, driven by a Parisian ex-jeweller, his chauffeur. Captain Capel and Lieutenant Pinto asked permission to accompany me to Paris. When passing through the village of Croisettes . . . I stopped a few minutes to see my nephew, Renauld. As I went back to the car I saw a crowd round it. Boy Capel was already seated by the chauffeur, smoking his pipe, with an expression on his face that aroused my suspicions. Lieutenant Pinto and I, before getting into the car, tried to fathom the reason for the villagers' curiosity. At last we discovered on the back of the car, which was thick with dust, that the wretched Boy had written with his finger, 'Honeymoon!' I was the joke of the village!
>
> Capel, though of a most solemn and serious appearance, cannot resist a joke, good or bad.[11]

Meanwhile, along with many of the Deauville *beau monde*, Gabrielle returned to the capital with Antoinette, leaving a saleswoman in charge of the salon. While the war hadn't reached the rapid conclusion that had been predicted, people realized that, for the moment, Paris wasn't going to be overrun.

In the meantime, Adrienne had returned to Vichy, apprehensive for the safety of her lover, de Nexon, now fighting at the Front; many had already lost loved ones. Two more deaths, while probably leaving Gabrielle relatively unmoved, nonetheless bore a significant connection to her past. Her grandparents had come to their final rest: Adrienne's mother, Angélina, had died a year earlier, and now Adrienne had her father, Henri-Adrien, buried beside her at Vichy.

In those months following the initiation of hostilities, with Gabrielle's greater financial autonomy, she took on the responsibility for her little nephew, André Palasse, whose mother, Julia-Berthe, had committed suicide so gruesomely. Gabrielle would always feel a particular tenderness for André and, while spending Christmas with Arthur, they decided to send the boy away to school in England. At Arthur's suggestion, Gabrielle chose his old prep school, Beaumont, so as to teach André English and to begin equipping him with the manners and the bearing of a gentleman.

Following another six months of war, with vast numbers of casualties, there was still no progress along the Western Front. It has often been suggested that it was the appalling experience of trench warfare that forced the various armies to move almost overnight into the age of technological warfare. By 1915, planes were flying for reconnaissance, and flame-throwers, hand grenades and the terrifying poison gas were regularly being used. What Gabrielle called the 'age of iron' had well and truly begun.

Early in the summer of 1915, on a brief respite from the Front, Arthur took Gabrielle for a few days to St-Jean-de-Luz, just south of Biarritz and close to the Spanish border. Originally a fishing port, St-Jean-de-Luz had been transformed into a seaside retreat for the wealthy. For those satiated with the large-scale glamour of the more substantial luxury playground Biarritz, there was the culturally more select St-Jean-de-Luz. It received an eclectic mix of artistic, aristocratic and literary visitors. Here, embracing a moment of ordinary tranquillity in extra-ordinary times, Gabrielle and Arthur were to be found one day, picnicking on the beach with friends.

Gabrielle wore her hair caught back in a headband and a dark bathing costume. Unrecognizable as a swimsuit today, it looks more than anything like a touchingly modest above-the-knee dress. In

1915, however, there was no question: a young woman wearing one of these outfits was rather risqué. Sea-bathing had become an important pastime for the French upper classes in the first decade or so of the century, but it was still only intrepid women who took part in this activity.

There are very few images of Gabrielle and Arthur together but, in a handful of recently discovered photographs from that day on the beach, we catch a glimpse of their convivial picnic on the sand. In one, they are with the heir to a sugar-refining fortune, Constant Say. In another, a young woman, lying with her face upturned to the sun, is Constant Say's mistress, the rising-star opera-singer Marthe Davelli. Davelli's artistic success, and the depth of her lover's purse, meant that a holiday villa was being built for her nearby. In 1915, suntanned skin was the lot of the poor, forced to work in the sun, and sunbathing was regarded as outrageous. Although it is often stated that Gabrielle was the first woman to make a suntan fashionable, in these photographs, we see that her friend Marthe Davelli had already taken to it with enthusiasm. Another of the picnickers is the ageing novelist and playwright Pierre Decourcelle, whose suggestive novels Gabrielle had been caught reading in her days at the Aubazine convent.

Early the following year, when Arthur was again back in Paris from the Front, the society painter Jacques-Emile Blanche recorded meeting Gabrielle and Arthur at a dinner party. The guests comprised an exalted cast, and Gabrielle's presence is revealing of society's awareness of her increased status in changing times. She wasn't simply the striking mistress of the dazzling 'Boy' Capel but was also acquiring her own reputation as a trendsetting woman of means.

Amongst those at the dinner were Philippe Berthelot, the suave Director of Political Affairs at the Ministry of Foreign Affairs; the political essayist Henri-Adrien Massis; the smoulderingly beautiful Comtesse Anna de Noailles, thought by many (first amongst whom was herself) to be the reigning poet-queen of the literary salons; the Abbé Mugnier, diarist, indefatigable socializer and profoundly unjudgemental confessor to the *haut monde*; and the opium-smoking, lesbian princess Violette Murat, who loved nothing better than a night out in the downbeat cafés and nightclubs of Montparnasse and Montmartre. Violette Murat was already one of Gabrielle's clients. While there was to be more than a whiff of snobbery about a dressmaker in society circles for some time to come, Gabrielle emanated character and quietly held her own. Indeed, she would come to count as friends several of those present on that evening.

During the war, the resort of Biarritz remained one of the favoured destinations of European royalty. And, for all those whom war prevented from reaching the resort, there were just as many who were happy to replace them. They came from across the social spectrum – including black-marketeers and those newly rich from speculation – and from countries that were neutral. They were unflagging in their desire to escape from thoughts of war, and Biarritz's elegant attraction soothed their lurking fear.

II

Master of Her Art

Perhaps it was while Arthur and Gabrielle were nearby at St-Jean-de-Luz that they came to the conclusion it was the right moment for Gabrielle to open another salon. This time, in Biarritz. Whenever the decision was made, before Arthur returned to the Front he had already put up the finances for a venture on a far larger scale than Gabrielle's salon at Deauville. The site she chose was one of the grander private buildings in Biarritz, the Villa Larralde, on the rue Gardères. A faux castle, its situation was perfect: facing the casino, it was en route to the promenade and the beach. Gabrielle was preparing to launch not only her first *maison de couture* but also the first couture house in Biarritz.

During that same summer of 1915, one of the earliest mentions of Gabrielle's dresses appeared in the influential American magazine *Women's Wear Daily*, and showed how the reputation she was already forging was to act as foundation for her latest venture in Biarritz:

Deauville, July 14

Everything points to a brilliant season here. Already quite a few of the villa colony have opened their homes and the leading hotels . . . are well filled . . . An interesting feature of life at Deauville for the fair sex is shopping, and the most fascinating shops to be found anywhere in the world are situated principally on the rue Gontaut-Biron and the rue de Casino. These shops are branches of well-known Paris houses. The Maison Chanel has re-opened for the season. This house, by the way, was the first to employ Rodier's golfine and last season launched here the sport coat made of that material. At once golfine became the craze. One wonders what novelty M. Chanel is holding back to launch this year.

The following day it was reported that:

Gabrielle Chanel has . . . some extremely interesting sweaters which embrace new features. The material . . . is wool jersey in most attractive colouring as pale blue, pink, brick red and yellow. Striped jersey . . . in black and white or navy and white, is also employed. These sweaters . . . slip on the head, opening at the neck for about six inches and are finished with jersey-covered buttons . . . A great success is predicted for these sweaters.

This would prove to be something of an understatement. Using all her ingenuity, Gabrielle had quickly turned the grim wartime circumstances to her advantage. Both tenacity of purpose and ingenuity were required to overcome the shortages of textiles and accessories needed to maintain any dress shop, let alone the possibility of three exclusive salons. Gabrielle drew in Etienne Balsan's brothers, Jacques and Robert, who worked for the family textile firm, to help obtain broadcloth and to put her in touch with the silk manufacturers of Lyon. In addition, Arthur sought out for her the best woollen weavers and dyers that Scotland could provide.

However, the fabric whose possibilities Gabrielle was to utilize in entirely new ways, and which was the source of as much attention, indeed amazement, as any of the other unusual things she made in her first years as a designer, was the textile mentioned above: jersey, or *djersabure*. Clothes made from knitted materials – silk or wool jersey – had become fashionable some years earlier, and heavier hand-knitted jumpers were often worn with linen or flannel for tennis, golf and beachwear. However, un-dyed jersey had never before been used for women and was seen as one of the most humble of materials.

There are several versions of how Gabrielle came to use it, but the gist of the story is that she had met a textile manufacturer named Jean Rodier, who showed her some material he'd had made up as an experiment before the war. He had intended his machine-made knit for use as underwear for sportsmen, but they found it too scratchy. A machine knit was just what Gabrielle had been looking for and, to Rodier's surprise, she bought the lot. It was its very soberness, which had not drawn others to it, that Gabrielle found attractive, and she asked Rodier to make her up another lot as well as the one she was already buying.

He refused, saying he was doubtful she would ever sell it. And with the war making raw materials difficult to obtain, he was unwilling to run the risk of wasting a consignment. Why didn't she make it up and, if her outfits sold, come back to him for more? Gabrielle's insistence was useless: Rodier was adamant. His reluctance to weave for this woman – who wanted to make into outerwear for her wealthy customers this humble material that had even failed to sell for use as underwear – was reasonable. Of course, with hindsight, we know that Gabrielle proved Rodier wrong.

At first, she used Rodier's natural cream and grey jersey then, when he saw that she really could sell it, they collaborated to create some beautiful new colours, as noted above. They also developed corals, Madonna blue, what was described as 'old-blue', and various greys. By 1916, when *Women's Wear Daily* heralded the fact that Gabrielle was 'the one to bring jersey into prominence', *Vogue* described her salon as 'The Jersey House'. (Gabrielle wasn't the only designer to use the fabric, but she was undoubtedly the most innovative, and the one who transformed it into a high-fashion textile.) War shortages and high prices meant that, through Gabrielle's triumphant lead, jersey would overtake more familiar materials such as twill-woven serge, now in great demand for the armed forces' uniforms. In the summer of 1916, *Vogue* revealed Gabrielle's growing influence when describing the promenade of one of the most distinguished streets in the world:

The Avenue of the Bois de Boulogne presents a rather animated appearance. There is the brilliancy of all the Allied uniforms, starred with decorations of all kinds, and there is the measured clank of swords . . . There is the sprinkling of the new frocks . . . against the background of neutral-tinted garments which are affected just now. There is the subdued woolen glow of jersey cloth . . . the liking for jersey has . . . developed into a passion – a veritable craze. Everyone goes clad in jersey; in palest gray, in beige, in white, and in all shades of blue. Bordeaux jersey is smart . . . and for young girls there is a red . . . the modish jersey frock is exceedingly simple in line . . . [jersey] is cool looking and indescribably chic.

Although jersey was to be the material Gabrielle used most commonly during the war for day clothes, she would also make inspired use of a small number of other fabrics, such as suede for hats, as well as coats and jackets, sometimes embroidered with decorative bands. For afternoon and evening, she created dresses of satin, velvet and tulle. On occasion, these were embroidered with cotton, silks or beads. At their best, her clothes were astonishingly beautiful in their masterly unification of fabric, simplicity of design and decoration. In November 1916, *Vogue* gave a hint of impatience that Gabrielle's apparently limitless capacity to design using the previously downmarket jersey was clearly not shared by the readers, when it informed them that 'it has been rumoured lately that women were growing tired of jersey, but Chanel is master of her art, and her jersey frocks are as complete and as daintily finished as frocks of more thoroughly patrician stuffs.'

In another report, *Vogue* described Gabrielle's decoration of her thoroughly un-patrician jersey, in a 'cloak of this thick warm tissue, in yellow, trimmed with grey rabbit'. Here, Gabrielle had once again launched one of her remarkable reversals of tradition. For fashionable women, fur had always been one of the accepted means of demonstrating luxury; and the more rare and expensive the better. Not only had Gabrielle been promoting a textile that in other hands was regarded as entirely downmarket, she now turned another notion on its head: she attached rabbit, that most plebeian of furs, to many of her outfits. And rich and fashionable women flocked to buy them. Gabrielle had the excuse of the war, but selling these downmarket fabrics at upmarket prices, her motivation was complex. She would say:

> I had decided to replace expensive furs with the humblest hides. Chinchilla no longer arrived from South America, or sable from the Russia of the czars. I used rabbit. In this way I made poor people . . . and small retailers wealthy; the large stores have never forgiven me . . . Like Lycurgus I disapproved of expensive materials. [This is an exaggeration, but the essence is correct.] A fine fabric is beautiful in itself, but the more lavish a dress is, the poorer it becomes.

And then she made one of those singular Chanel remarks: 'People confuse poverty with simplicity.'[1] Nowadays we immediately comprehend this notion in dress, but it was Gabrielle above all others who would teach us to understand it.

Bearing this idea in mind, the clothes she made with jersey were perhaps the first Gabrielle created that were truly original. And while, as the century progressed, she was to go on and initiate many of the crucial elements in the modern woman's wardrobe, her influence was to become more far-reaching than simply being first. By the end of the First World War, it would be Gabrielle more than other designer who had revolutionized women's dress. But concentration on a length, a style or a type of material is not always the most significant aspect of her originality. What women wore was only the most visible aspect of more profound changes Gabrielle would help to bring about. Through her own extraordinary and unconventional example, she was to become instrumental in forging the very idea of modern woman.

Gabrielle always understood fundamentals and would say, 'Eccentricity was dying out; I hope . . . that I helped kill it off. Paul Poiret, a most inventive couturier, dressed women in costumes.' And she went on to describe the varieties of make-believe she thought that people indulged in, so that 'the most modest tea party looked like something from the Baghdad of the Caliphs. The last courtesans . . . would come by, to the sound of the tango, wearing bell-shaped dresses, with greyhounds and cheetahs at their side.' She said this was all very pleasant but warned against 'originality in dressmaking, you immediately descend to disguise and decoration, you lapse into stage design'.[2]

She concentrated on the silhouette, the structure and architecture of clothes. In making it clear that she believed simplicity of line counted above all and that decoration and ornamentation were the secondary elements of what one wore, Gabrielle had a more accurate finger on the pulse of her times than many of her competitors. Understanding better than most what those times were about – Poiret had very daringly revealed the foot! – it was Gabrielle more than anyone else who was responsible for lifting the hemline above the ankle. Already she was loosening the waistline; in time, she would drop it below the waist.

She had done away with the decoration that life in the past could support; the details that had become obsolete. But, in doing this, as in her own life, Gabrielle was also attempting to clear away the games and the pretences about women. In making clothes fit for the women of a new and mechanical age, she declared, 'I had rediscovered honesty, and in my own way, I made fashion honest.'[3]

Meanwhile, in that summer of 1915, with some reservations, Antoinette arrived in Biarritz to help her prospering sister. She was now twenty-eight, and unmarried, and worried that living and working far from Paris would make finding a husband even more difficult. As for Adrienne, Gabrielle's stalwart, this time, she remained obdurate: she could not come to Gabrielle's aid just yet. She was on tenterhooks, awaiting permission to visit her lover at the Front. When finally that permission came, apparently the demure Adrienne was shocked, on being asked by the soldier checking her visitor's pass, if she was Baron de Nexon's wife. Embarrassed, she admitted that she wasn't, upon which the soldier waved her through, telling her that the colonel didn't like wives, they made a man soft. Girlfriends, they were a different matter!

In Biarritz, where the balmy weather made the season pretty well continuous, and where sports and youthful activities had not long since become the order of the day, Gabrielle saw her clothes fulfilling a hitherto unrecognized need. She also sensed that time was of the essence and, for the first time, pushed on without Adrienne.

When the frantic preparations were at an end and Gabrielle threw open her sumptuous *maison de couture*, she was taken aback at the enthusiasm that greeted her new business. The highly priced accessories and chic day clothes for tennis, golf or swimming; the ensembles for the casino, or the races; and the new evening dresses she had designed for the resort's hectic nightlife, all dazzled her excited clients.

What Gabrielle offered was quite different from the overt luxury and opulence hitherto expected of an upmarket boutique. What her clients now found was what Gabrielle's head of workrooms, Marie-Louise Delay, later described as the 'sensational quality of unparalleled simplicity and chic'. This, Marie-Louise said, was 'so different from Poiret and Madeleine Vionnet'. The Maison Chanel, with Antoinette greeting the clients, was overwhelmed by orders. They came from Bilbao, San Sebastián, Biarritz, Madrid, Paris, other French cities, and also further afield. Europeans, bored by the dullness of war, could afford to ease their tedium in one of the last outposts where luxury remained the highest priority.

While Gabrielle and Marie-Louise Delay were organizing the seamstresses to work as fast as they could, Antoinette returned from Paris with several others she had brought back from the boutique in rue Cambon, itself already busy. From the outset, Gabrielle used as much cotton and jersey in Biarritz as she was now using at the salon in Paris. While her lease in rue Cambon forbade her to make dresses, jersey was considered such a lowly material, not previously used for them that, apparently, it didn't count.[4]

Gabrielle called in her acquaintances and friends: Marthe Davelli became a devoted client, and brought along other singers and actresses, while the powerful socialite Kitty Rothschild kept up her influence on French women staying at Biarritz. Some of the most significant clients for Gabrielle's luxurious new shop came, however, from just across the border in Spain. Both the Spanish aristocracy and several members of the royal family were much taken with her stylish clothes. Indeed, in that year, 1915, the American magazine *Harper's Bazaar* stated that 'the woman who doesn't have at least one Chanel is hopelessly out of the running.'[5] In February 1916, the authoritative *Women's Wear Daily* reported that, in France, 'It is not unusual for smart women to place orders for three or four [Chanel] jersey costumes in different colours at one time.'

While Gabrielle was kept tremendously busy with her most ambitious undertaking so far, Arthur was once again back at Baroness de la Grange's château, experiencing the vicissitudes of war. In the first days of August 1915, a wretched experience badly unsettled him, giving a small insight into the strain of life near the Front. The baroness would record that:

> A car driven by Captain Capel skidded . . . and was hurled against a peasant's cart. The shaft struck poor Hamilton-Grace full in the chest and flung him out on the road. [It] was not fully realized for a moment, and when they ran back to help him he was already dying. Captain Capel was nearly out of his mind with despair. Luckily, my nephew, Odon de Lubersac, his friend . . . prevented another misfortune . . .
>
> The coffin was borne by the men . . . and the heavy tread of spurred boots rang like a knell on the paved road . . . That same evening the Cavalry Corps left here. After nine months together, we have become great friends . . . and my adieux were full of regret.[6]

When the baroness wrote that her nephew had 'prevented another misfortune', she meant that Arthur was in such distress that if, at that moment, he hadn't been prevented, he might well have shot himself. One wonders whether he confided this sad episode to Gabrielle. Or had the war, which kept so many couples apart, already inculcated the need for a new kind of emotional self-sufficiency? While we will never know how much Arthur confided his troubles to Gabrielle, we do know that, notwithstanding their separation, she gained immeasurably from Arthur's support and confidence in her abilities.

In spite of Arthur's inherited wealth, as we saw, he chose to make money. He told Gabrielle that it wasn't out of greed. At first he had been driven to do it but, in these times, it was becoming something he did for his country. At the same time, his own instinct for business was remarkable and, in the previous couple of years, Arthur had shown himself to be an entrepreneur of genius. (This included his advice to Gabrielle.) His fleet of ships carried coal to France at such a rate for vital manufacture and heating that soon he was dubbed 'King Coal'.

Distance, perforce, may have made conversations rare between Arthur and Gabrielle about how and where to proceed next, but those conversations they were able to have were of great import. Gabrielle's lover encouraged her entrepreneurial spirit and confirmed his faith in her by continuing to contribute to the large finances necessary to make that spirit flourish.

Gabrielle was fully conscious that Etienne Balsan had enabled her to leave behind her background and make the first significant steps towards her redefinition. She also knew perfectly well that, without Arthur's backing and connections, she could have achieved little more. However, while she never forgot that her great self-belief was fostered in these early years more than anything by the support of a remarkable and powerful man, no amount of support would have helped if she hadn't possessed exceptional gifts and an extraordinary dedication to work. In years to come, she would say, 'To begin with you long for money. Then you develop a liking for work. Work has a much stronger flavour than money. Ultimately, money is nothing more than the symbol of independence.'[7]

Meanwhile, the orders flew in and Gabrielle sent her *première*, Marie-Louise Delay, to Paris, where she was in charge of an atelier in which sixty people worked, making Chanel couture for Spain. The Spanish court 'bought dresses by the dozen. Soon I was one of five forewomen,' said Marie-Louise.[8] With five workrooms working for her, Gabrielle still chose everything herself: 'laces, ornaments, colours. She always chose the most beautiful tones among the different pastel shades that the Lyon and Scottish dyers could produce in silk and wool. Our workrooms were like a fairyland, a veritable rainbow.'[9]

By late 1916, Gabrielle's arch-rival, Poiret, had directed his efforts towards the army and successfully redesigned its greatcoats to reduce their cost. Whatever Poiret's patriotic labours, Gabrielle had, meanwhile, effectively lost her rival and now appeared unstoppable in the field of wartime fashion. At this point, she had over three hundred people working under her command.

Clear-headed and decisive, Gabrielle had already arrived at her own working methods. Marie-Louise recalled how she 'never set foot in the workrooms. She would call us together to tell us what she wanted after she had chosen the fabrics.' While admiring Gabrielle's ability to evoke and describe what she wanted, her *première* also believed that her lack of technique sometimes created misunderstandings. When this happened and they made something Gabrielle didn't like, she didn't hide her frustration.

Although Marie-Louise believed that Gabrielle's lack of technique led her to compensate with an unsettling need to demonstrate her authority, Marie-Louise was in awe of what she described as 'her innate taste'. Whatever the *première*'s criticisms, she remained impressed by her employer's 'audacity and incredible nerve, especially since she was a milliner and knew little about dressmaking'.[10] She would add that Gabrielle's method 'must have had something good in it, since we made such admirable things'. As for Gabrielle herself, Marie-Louise found her 'extraordinarily chic. You should have seen her, getting out of her Rolls-Royce in front of the firm on the stroke of noon, for she had . . . acquired a Rolls with a chauffeur and footman. She was a queen!'[11]

This 'queen' remained at the salon until two or three o'clock, depending upon the importance of her customers. And then, 'She retired to her drawing room, where she entertained a great deal.'[12] The impression this gives – that Gabrielle didn't work hard – was just what she intended, and is also entirely inaccurate. And one remembers her famous remark, made years later: 'It is through work that one achieves. Manna didn't fall on me from heaven; I moulded it with my own hands . . . The secret of this success is that I have worked terribly hard . . . Nothing can replace work; not securities, or nerve, or luck.'[13]

At the same time, as we have seen, Gabrielle had insisted on remaining in the background when she sold hats from Etienne Balsan's *garçonnière*, sending her assistants out to deal with the customers rather than meeting them herself. And, over the preceding few years, as she had become familiar with people and surroundings of the highest sophistication, the impression that would sometimes be given, that Gabrielle didn't do much work, signalled something significant in her present thinking. She had recognized that, in order to acquire a greater reputation than her fellow designers, she would be wise to cultivate the impression that she didn't need to work hard; that, by implication, she was the equal of her clients. Having had her nose rubbed in her social inferiority throughout her life, as Gabrielle grew more successful, she felt less and less a sense of personal inadequacy before those more socially exalted than herself.

Under Arthur's watchful eye, at first using her contacts and the press to promote her hats, Gabrielle's keen instincts had begun telling her she needed something more all-encompassing than the old-fashioned virtue of a well-known name. However consciously, we will never know, but Gabrielle began fostering something on a grander scale.

Even her *première*, who knew Gabrielle's working methods and something of her complex personality, was convinced enough by her projection of status to call Gabrielle 'a queen', and misinterpreted her entertaining as no more than that – entertainment. As Gabrielle's innate self-belief began to flourish, she was also drawing the outlines of a persona. She was cultivating around her name something that can only thrive on any real scale in the modern world through an ongoing relationship with the press: a public image.

The War Bans the Bizarre

Even during the war, the upper echelons of French society, with whom Arthur had always passed his time, still dedicated much of theirs to leisure. The nobility was no different from other classes in being made up of various elements – including intermarriage with the *grande bourgeoisie* – and was neither an assimilated nor a homogenous group. Yet, while no longer retaining much power, they nonetheless retained much of their old sense of exclusiveness, and still enjoyed great status. Conferring prestige and receiving deference from those around them, they confirmed the existence of a social hierarchy at whose apex they had remained.

Arthur was an *haut bourgeois* imbued with the idea that work was commendable. However, with no need of money, and having transformed his work ethic into an almost existential need for experience, he was also one of the few from the upper classes unconventional enough to live with his mistress. He was also sufficiently forward thinking that he found subservience in a lover ultimately unrewarding. Gabrielle was compellingly unsubservient. And, despite her lack of education (perhaps 'cultivation' is a better word, as there were so few women in this period who had much of a formal education to speak of), her outstanding natural intelligence was clearly a match for Arthur's. Gabrielle was the only woman he had ever met who appeared to be his equal. And yet, however strong his love and admiration for her, these feelings had done little to curb his prodigious appetite for women.

In the first flush of their affair, Arthur's need for conquest was temporarily held in check, but it wasn't long before his compulsion had asserted itself once again. As for Gabrielle, she apparently felt reassured in the belief that she was Arthur's only real love. Saying she felt no jealousy, she even asked him who his other lovers might be. But Arthur's tastes ranged wide, and he laughed and told Gabrielle that her knowing would only make his life more complicated than he had already made it.[1]

In addition to these private 'complications', Gabrielle's lover managed his fleet of ships, his now enormous coal interests and a ceaseless shuttling between the Front, Paris and London. Yet, whatever his work-related absences or the brief spells in other women's arms, Arthur always returned to Gabrielle, his most significant companion.

By the beginning of 1916, when the war showed no sign of ending, Arthur's experiences had stimulated his interest in a more political role. Accordingly, in March, he requested permission to resign his intelligence service commission in the hope of being taken on as a liaison officer instead. He had made it his business to become acquainted with both politicians and senior commanders in the French and British armies. Perhaps with a nudge from someone high up, the British War Office wrote to the commander-in-chief of the British army in France saying that Arthur wished 'to go to Paris in order to carry out his ordinary business. It is probable that this . . . may involve his participation in French political affairs. In these circumstances it would be very inadvisable for him to retain his . . . commission and the status of a "British Officer on leave".'[2] It appears that there were also more personal reasons for Arthur's resignation of his commission. Working in such a stressful occupation near the battlefields of the Front – plus the death of his friend Hamilton-Grace, for which he held himself responsible – had reduced him to a state of emotional exhaustion. 'His health broke down and he had to resign his interpretership in the field' was how a commentator would put it.[3] Either Arthur himself, or a doctor, had recognized that, in order to recover, he must take a job away from the Front.

Arthur's chaotic times and privileged background had made him a worldly sceptic who, until the war, had pretty much done what he wanted. He had, after all, described himself to Gabrielle as a cheerful pessimist, whose dictum 'One does not have to hope in order to undertake' had enabled him to sign up for active service without much conviction. Yet the appalling suffering and loss of life he had witnessed had not reduced Arthur to a state of bitterness and demoralization. Instead, his religious faith had provoked in him a renewed sense of hope. Ironically, this change was to set in motion a series of grievous results.

For the moment, however, Arthur did believe in a future and, in utopian spirit, away from the Front, he set out to write a book. He often showed Gabrielle what he was writing.

By the end of that year, 1916, Gabrielle was becoming more self-reliant. Her business was so prosperous she chose to return all of the 300,000 francs Arthur had invested in her salon at Biarritz. And, if his frequent absences were not only on war business, Gabrielle by no means languished at home. If her comment, made later in conversation with Morand, 'I was my own master, and I depended on myself alone,' was made with some defensiveness in relation to Arthur's absences, it was also increasingly the case. There was no question of Gabrielle's sincerity when she declared that Arthur 'was well aware that he didn't control me'. This, of course, was part of her attraction for him. And yet, with regard to supporting her ventures, this was the point at which Arthur made that melancholy statement to Gabrielle referred to in the prologue to this book. Characterizing the problems men and women faced when trying to devise new ways of relating to one another, he said: 'I thought I'd given you a plaything, I gave you your freedom.'[4]

The year 1916 saw the twin disasters of Verdun and the Somme. Verdun, the longest battle of the war, gained no advantage for either side and was responsible for over half a million casualties. The battle of the Somme was notorious for its first-day British casualties of 58,000, one third of whom lost their lives. One liaison officer, for whom the romance of war had long since disappeared, felt it was nothing more than 'a dreary massacre, a stupefying alternation of boredom, fatigue and fear'.[5] In February 1917, Jacques-Emile Blanche said to his friend the writer André Gide:

> Huge portentous things are happening above our heads, through the branches of the trees in my garden which fall under Olivier's axe, and will replace coal in the winter 1917–18. Boy [Arthur] Capel, our friend, the great coal importer, mobilized by England and France at St Dominique Street [the Ministry of Defence], the man our tomorrow depends on . . . said to Rose, 'Have your cook come up, I will make her understand her duty. From next month onwards things will be very difficult. Stock up. Do without what is not absolutely necessary. Around June, it will be almost famine. As for next winter, even if peace is signed, you will have to stay in bed and suck your thumb.'[6]

The effects of the Russian Revolution were now playing out their relentless course; on 15 March 1917, Tsar Nicholas II abdicated. In early April, to the great relief of the Allies, America at last entered the war and, on 26 April, Lenin arrived in Russia to agitate more unrest. Then, with the second October Revolution, Russia withdraw from the conflict. Meanwhile, the French commander-in-chief, Nivelle, had argued for a massive onslaught on the German lines, which was to bring about a French victory in forty-eight hours. Many high-ranking officials disagreed, but the prime minister insisted.

The massive attack on the German positions was eventually supposed to link up with the Allied forces. From the beginning, the plan was dogged by delay and information leaks and, by the time the battle was launched, the Germans had had plenty of time to prepare their defences. The offensive was an unmitigated disaster for the French, who suffered 187,000 casualties. On the Western Front, the slaughter was appalling. Thousands died every day, and the people of France were in a poor state of morale.

Arthur had been appointed to the new Allied War Coal Commission, but he was also unofficially liaising between the British and

French politicians and the military. In addition, by the spring of 1917, when the Allied position had never been more in doubt, he published *Reflections on Victory*, in which he was confident of just that. To many, this looked misguided. While respecting the move towards democracy, Arthur abhorred the centralizing state. In its place he proposed a 'Europe-wide Federation, giving full autonomy to every corporate body, region, people and race'. This federation could be seen as a forerunner to the present-day European Union and indeed was recognized as such by one of those later to become one of its architects.[7]

Reflections on Victory was reviewed in serious journals and, despite Arthur's anti-federal critics, the book broadened his reputation within the circles of power. Those who had only known him as a rich playboy-businessman – made even richer by the war – now looked at him with more discernment.

Few, however, shared Arthur's optimism. The war had become a crushing burden, leaving many incapable of enthusiasm for anything. Even with the long-awaited arrival of the American troops in Paris, 'the crowd, especially the women, were weary, every spark gone; wanting only the quickest possible end to this dreadful war.'[8] The catastrophic failure of the Nivelle offensive proved the last straw for some, and French soldiers now mutinied, refusing any longer to go over the top to certain death. The mutinies weren't quelled till the end of May, by the new commander-in-chief, Marshal Philippe Pétain.

While the slaughter continued at the Front, in Paris in that May of 1917, the Ballets Russes gave the premiere of a new work, *Parade*, in aid of war victims. It was the only Ballets Russes work put on in Paris during the conflict and was by invitation only. Diaghilev's carefully chosen audience consisted of a selection of society figures, prominent experimental musicians and artists, plus a good number of the bourgeoisie, who he knew liked the frisson of dabbling in the avant-garde. Diaghilev also invited Gabrielle.

However much bolstering and covering up had been necessary

during the growth of industrialism in France, pre-war Belle Epoque society had muddled along, shoring up the old social structures and attitudes. The Belle Epoque had clung on to its belief in the value of permanence and tradition, which in turn depended upon an over-riding belief in the idea of authorities. For years before the war, a number of artists had reacted to this hypocrisy by searching for a language to express their sense of alienation from the modern world. Now, as the war dragged on, the initial belief of the popula-tion that a secure world would survive the hostilities was physically and metaphorically being smashed to smithereens. Diaghilev's new ballet mirrored aspects of this instability, and was to strike yet one more blow at the certainties of the past.

The ballet was young Jean Cocteau's brainchild, and he provided the scenario and libretto. Léonide Massine was choreographer; the ungovernable and cheerfully eccentric Erik Satie, initially distrustful of Diaghilev – 'Will he try to screw me? Probably'[9] – was persuaded to write the music; and Picasso, already the most famous modernist painter, agreed to create the sets. These became a Cubist cityscape with high-rise blocks of flats. But the most radical element was two figures (a French and an American manager) costumed as over-lifesize Cubist sculptures.

While the audience's response was nothing like the first night of *The Rite of Spring*, it was still shocked, and became raucous in its disapproval. In part this was because, aware of what was going on at the Front, the audience expected something soothing and patri-otic. Instead what they got was an unconventional experiment. To many, it was an exercise in 'banality and superficiality',[10] and some of the audience made its way towards the stage, yelling for the cur-tain to be lowered. A horse appeared wearing a Cubist mask, cavorted about, then danced, knelt down and bowed. 'The audience clearly thought the dancers were mocking their protests and com-pletely lost their heads; they yelled, "Death to the Russians!", "Picasso's a Boche!", "The Russians are Boches!"'[11]

This was the first ballet ever to be set in the present. In addition, its witty and apparently light-hearted romp through popular culture – the circus, the music hall and the ephemera of everyday life, including fashion, advertising and the cinema – had never before been used as the subject matter for ballet. However, under the guise of frivolity, *Parade*'s aim was in fact a serious one: an attack on the old authorities.[12] Those in the audience who were already embracing avant-garde fashion, popular music and a wider social range of people, believing they were just as worthwhile as the traditional elites and high culture of their parents, understood the ballet's subversion and applauded.

Parade wasn't a great ballet, but it was a seminal artistic work. As the first to push modernism to centre stage, it made it part of mainstream artistic culture. *Parade*'s creators were not only intent on dragging art down from its high-culture pedestal; they believed they had revealed the essential, simple artistic beauty of the mundane and the everyday.[13]

Once again, Gabrielle's presence at an avant-garde event was appropriate: Cocteau's ballet was at one with her own path. (Their friendship was almost inevitable.) Borrowing from workaday wardrobes and using modest materials, Gabrielle was the designer then showing that a democratization of fashion was possible. And, while her daring hints at classlessness were at first only taken up by a wealthy clientele, as time went on, her simple designs and 'modest' materials would be transferred from the salons to the streets. All over France, and abroad, women would be able to copy Gabrielle's styles, allowing more of them than ever before to take part in the game of fashion.

Remember that you're a woman

A few days after the premiere of *Parade*, the woman then regarded as France's finest classical actress, Cécile Sorel, gave a dinner to celebrate the ballet, and to which she invited a novel mix of guests. This included Arthur and Gabrielle. Cécile Sorel understood that, while Arthur was one of Paris's most eligible bachelors, Gabrielle's presence as an 'avant-garde' designer gave her evening greater cachet.

Sorel's dinner party would be long forgotten if it hadn't been recorded by that urbane future novelist, the diplomat Paul Morand, who made it his business to attend the numerous Parisian social events during those strange war years. Sorel's unorthodox guest list included Morand's boss, Philippe Berthelot, one of the highest ranking French diplomats; a fashionable artist, the immensely rich and mad Spanish painter José Maria Sert; Sert's twice-divorced and most unconventional mistress, the Slav patroness and artist's muse Misia Edwards; the literary gadfly and artist Jean Cocteau; a playboy businessman, Arthur Capel; and his mistress, Gabrielle, a lower-class couturier.

While Morand's snobberies had him imply he wasn't at the dinner and refer to Sorel's unconventional social mix as 'preposterous', he also noted with interest Gabrielle's presence. Her achievement of a most unusual thing – the advancement of a couturier from 'mere' dress-designer status to the drawing rooms of the Parisian elite – fascinated the novelist in Morand. And, while he noted that Gabrielle was the least socially significant person at that dinner, he referred to her as 'Coco Chanel, who is definitely becoming quite a personage'.

The second matter of note about that evening at Cécile Sorel's recorded by Morand was that both Cécile and Gabrielle had done an outrageous thing: they had cut off their hair. 'In the last few days it has become the fashion for women to wear their hair short. They're all doing it, Madame Letellier [a mistress to the late Edward VII] and Coco Chanel in the lead, then Madeleine de Foucault, Jeanne de Salverte, etc.'[1]

Jean Cocteau told Morand that 'this fashion was launched for charitable purposes – that all the cut hair is put together . . . and sold for the benefit of the wounded.' One can only say that this reveals nothing more than how far removed Cocteau was from what these women were thinking. (This we will come to in a later chapter.)

It has always been said that it was at Sorel's dinner, in mid-1917, that Gabrielle first met Misia Edwards.[2] The two women had actually met a year *earlier*, in 1916. This meeting would develop into a life-long friendship, becoming infamously rich in complexity and conflict.

Misia Edwards is traditionally credited as the person who culti-vated Gabrielle; the person who expanded her horizons beyond sportsmen and business. This, however, underestimates Gabrielle herself and the position she had already come to inhabit as the mis-tress of a cultivated man. First, with so little known about Arthur until now, it has been impossible to appreciate the full extent of his influence upon Gabrielle. Second, as Gabrielle would obscure so much detail of this period in her life, a source used repeatedly for information on her meetings with figures of any cultural note is Misia Edwards's memoir.[3] Misia Edwards was an extraordinary woman of remarkable cultural influence, but she was also a breath-takingly self-absorbed one, and her late-life memoir was written as much as anything with a view to signalling her own part in the development and advancement of numerous twentieth-century artists' careers.

While Misia was completely sincere in her belief that Gabrielle's role in their times was a highly significant one, she also believed that, without her, Misia, the world would not have recognized

Gabrielle's gifts, society would not have welcomed her and she would not have become involved with the artists who were making those feverishly creative times. Misia wrote, 'One could say that it is easy to help a beautiful diamond to shine. Still, it was my privilege to help it emerge from its rough state, and – in my heart – to be the first person dazzled by its brilliance.'[4]

Although Misia was *not* the first to introduce Gabrielle to any kind of culture, what she *was* the first to do was introduce her to the core of the Parisian avant-garde. Having said that, these artists were inverted snobs of a high order, and even an introduction by the famed Misia Edwards – muse and patron to so many of them – would not have been enough to gain Gabrielle admittance to their circles. Her own personality and originality would almost certainly have led her to them anyway. Unlike Misia, who was invaluable as a muse and patron, Gabrielle had the *character* of an artist. Her acceptance within the spectrum of the avant-garde came about, above all, because she was recognized as a kindred spirit.

Recalling that evening, in 1916, when she first met Gabrielle, Misia would say:

> My attention was immediately drawn to a very dark young woman . . . She radiated a charm I found irresistible . . . She seemed . . . gifted with an infinite grace and when, as we were saying goodnight, I admired her ravishing fur-trimmed red velvet coat, she took it off at once and put it on my shoulders, saying with charming spontaneity that she would be only too happy to give it to me . . . Her gesture had been so pretty that I found it bewitching and thought of nothing but her.
>
> The next day I could hardly wait to see her in the rue Cambon . . . When I arrived, two women were talking about her, calling her 'Coco'. I don't know . . . but my heart sank . . . Why trick out someone so exceptional with so vulgar a name?
>
> Magically the hours sped by . . . even though . . . she hardly spoke . . . That same evening Sert and I went to dine at her apartment . . . There, amidst countless Coromandel screens we found Boy Capel

. . . Sert was really scandalized by the astonishing infatuation I felt for my new friend . . . And I myself was rather surprised that a woman I had met the night before could already fill such a place in my thoughts.[5]

Misia's description is borne out in Morand's novel *Lewis et Irène* – where Irène bears such a resemblance to Gabrielle – when Morand describes the singular character of his heroine:

Irène proved very popular. Paris had plenty of businesswomen, but they were talented dressmakers, lucky actresses . . . who were only looking at generating profits, to establish themselves, to be accepted, to deal with famous men, thus showing the limit of their ambitions . . . Irène was liked because of her grace, her absence of . . . pretensions, her direct manners, her simple and imperious mind. She was courted. Lewis was not jealous.[6]

★ ★ ★

When Arthur's political profile was in the ascendant with the men prosecuting the war, his encouragement and financial backing also continued being a source of stimulation to Gabrielle. But they were also often apart. Arthur was unable to remain faithful, and Gabrielle was becoming more self-reliant.

Arthur was, like so many, apprehensive about the conflict causing the disintegration of social cohesion, and at this point he felt driven to begin his second book. One of the central planks of this work was the new position of women, and he heralded women's changed lives, rejoicing that their inferiority had only been an 'illusion of the other sex'. His own mistress was acquiring a name as a working woman and, with her growing 'equality', she was the perfect example of just what Arthur was espousing.

Taking into consideration Gabrielle's later confidences to Morand about her relationship with Arthur, Morand's description of Lewis sometimes being unsettled by his mistress Irène's drive and self-reliance seems understandable:

He wondered how she could manage to be so self-sufficient. She was never late, received visitors, wrote notes . . . and it never looked like it cost her anything. Irène's desk was always clean, tidied up at the end of each morning . . . Irène left nothing to chance; she used everything.[7]

For all Arthur's energetic open-mindedness and forward thinking, believing a thing and acting upon it with any consistency are all too often different. And, living with a New Woman was no doubt far harder than writing about one. In practice, Gabrielle's equality may sometimes have been too challenging.

In her post-Second World War conversations with Paul Morand, she would quote Arthur's advice to her: 'Remember that you're a woman,' and would add, 'All too often I forgot that.'[8] Arthur's plea was that Gabrielle be less driven and less cerebral. And Morand has his heroine, Irène, say to Lewis, 'Giving up working? You saw, I tried, I cannot remain idle . . . I am an island . . . something simple, isolated, where you cannot live . . . Can we go on living like this? It will tear us apart.'[9] Although concealing any vulnerability she might feel, Gabrielle had also blossomed and was luxuriating in her new power. Arthur's words urging her to remember she was a woman would, therefore, have little effect upon her progress. Arthur's own progress, however, was now to take an unexpected turn. His affairs with other women did not usually unsettle his emotions, but he was about to become absorbed by someone who never forgot for a moment that she was a woman.

The Hon. Diana Wyndham (née Lister) was the youngest daughter of Thomas Lister, 4th Baron Ribblesdale, who so perfectly exemplified the Edwardian aristocrat in his portrait by John Singer Sargent. Ribblesdale was a soldier, landowner and courtier, and his impenetrably nonchalant style was reflected in his unmistakable hauteur. This was born of confidence in a world that had in fact been under threat for some time. The agrarian wealth of the Ribblesdales and their kind had been undermined by the industrial

1. (*top*) The vast chestnut forests seen from Ponteils, the mountainous Cevennes hamlet where Gabrielle's paternal ancestors lived.

2. (*middle*) Gabrielle's great-grandfather's inn, 'the Chanel'. Today, the shutters firmly shut, its stony bulk has an air of neglect.

3. (*bottom*) The Aubazine convent-orphanage where Gabrielle lived for many years.

4. The earliest known photograph of Gabrielle, with Adrienne at Vichy *c.* 1904.

5. Etienne Balsan on military service, *c.* 1903, around the time Gabrielle met him.

6. Gabrielle, *c.* 1909. Tastes were changing; her angular 'modern' beauty had become desirable.

7. The famed courtesan, Emilienne d'Alençon, Etienne Balsan's lover when Gabrielle appeared on the scene.

8. Royallieu, where Gabrielle lived with Etienne as his mistress.

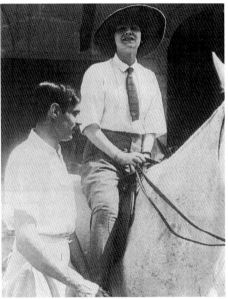

10. Arthur Capel and Gabrielle.
Jodhpurs and sitting astride were
unconventional for a
horsewoman in 1910.

9. Arthur 'Boy' Capel,
c. 1910, who was to transform
Gabrielle's life.

11. Arthur Capel was
a noted horseman and
excelled at polo.

12. (*top left and right*) Gabrielle in her own hats, seen in *Comoedia Illustré*, 1910.

13. (*middle left*) The actress Gabrielle Dorziat 1910, in 'Marie-Louise' hats, almost indistinguishable from Gabrielle's own designs.

14. (*left*) Gabrielle Dorziat in a Chanel hat for the play *Bel Ami*, 1912.

15. (*right*) Gabrielle Dorziat in another Chanel hat, 1912.

16. (*top left*) Outside Gabrielle's boutique with Adrienne (*left*) in Deauville, 1913. Note the awning reading 'Gabrielle Chanel'.

17. (*top right*) By 1913 Gabrielle was becoming known, and Sem caricatured her with her immensely eligible lover Arthur Capel. .

18. Gabrielle at her Deauville shop doorway. Previously unrecognized, on her right is Capel; furthest right is Balsan, still a friend. (There are only a handful of known photos of Gabrielle and Capel together.)

19. Gabrielle was in the minority of women who took to playing sports. At Deauville, *c.* 1913.

20. Gabrielle, Capel and Constant Say at St-Jean-de-Luz in a moment of calm during the First World War.

21. The Picassos in front of Pablo's Ballets Russes poster, 1917. Olga's outfit, including her handbag, are Chanel.

riches of a new and metropolitan aristocracy, which included families such as Arthur Capel's. In turn, this metropolitan aristocracy would soon open up its ranks to an even newer variant, in the person of Gabrielle Chanel.

The children of the traditional upper classes would be the last to grow up in the old world. And many of the generation now being slaughtered in the war appreciated, however incoherently, that great change was in the air. To give a minor example, Lord Ribblesdale's privileged daughter, Diana Wyndham, was a volunteer ambulance driver, close to the front lines of battle.

Diana was a tall, slim, blue-eyed girl whose delicate candour was matched by what someone who knew her well described recently as 'a kind of naiveté. She was a very sweet person; most feminine until her dying day.'[10] Great loss had revealed early Diana's self-possession. Her mother had died when Diana was thirteen, then she was widowed in the first month of the war – only seventeen months after her marriage to the Hon. Percy Wyndham – and, by 1915, she had also lost both her brothers.

So unlike Gabrielle, this young woman, with her uncomplicated femininity, brought out the gallant in Arthur Capel, and he had soon visited her near the Front. Any discomfort Arthur felt at Gabrielle's increasing success and independence must have made the delightful young Englishwoman appear all the more seductive.

Arthur's attraction to Diana Wyndham has characteristically been portrayed as one generated by social ambition alone: his 'new' money in union with tradition. The one thing Arthur, or his mistress Gabrielle, could never achieve was Diana Wyndham's noble heritage. But in Arthur's long-hidden and recently discovered letters to Diana[11] we see that both his sincerity of feeling and his transparency about his doubts are considerably more subtle than pure ambition. In that period of great flux, Arthur longed, like so many others, for some kind of certainty. However obscurely, he saw it in the rootedness Diana and her well-established family appeared to represent.

If, by chance, Diana hadn't heard of Arthur Capel before they met, she would soon have got wind of his longstanding affair with the ultra-fashionable Coco Chanel. Arthur didn't hide from Diana that, at thirty-five, he sometimes felt himself world weary. Yet, while he confessed to her that she had reawakened his dormant heart and he no longer wished to stray, a strand of lingering doubt is evident in these letters. He writes:

> I re-read your letters in which you say things that are very true – it is a bore to love too many people. It has in fact been the principal bore of my life, in fact poisoned the butterfly's honey, but now I don't long any more to explore new countries, unless it be to see the setting sun in your blue eyes.[12]

And then, almost in spite of himself, Arthur displays that note of ambivalence: 'Perhaps this is only a mood & will get stale, perhaps it won't.'[13] Other letters reveal not only Arthur's but also Diana's doubts, and were to become typical of their affair. Above all, for months, Arthur was endlessly torn between Diana and Gabrielle.

He knew Gabrielle was one of the most unusual women he would ever meet. But, moving in the most urbane of French circles, Arthur was captivated by Diana's simplicity. And she, while herself moving easily in London society, where her friends were among the most polished in England, felt more comfortable on an English country estate than mixing with the arch-sophisticates of Paris. She was wary of the great differences between her own life and Arthur's,[14] and her uncertainty was confirmed by friends telling her that Arthur was sometimes seen with Gabrielle when she, Diana, was not in Paris. If our knowledge of Gabrielle's feelings during this period is limited, we do know that Arthur and Diana's mutual doubts led them several times to call off their liaison. In one particularly poignant letter, he tells her:

I stepped into hell the morning we parted . . . & only just kept my head. Yesterday morning the reaction came. I saw my life as it used to be before I met you & resolved to take up its threads again and carry out its obligations . . . Fate as usual stepped in and I put my resolution into execution yesterday. Then for 24 hours I found peace at last from all these perishing doubts & hesitations. This morning comes your letter one day too late. It would be long & useless to explain but the position is that now I cannot marry.

. . . feel quite sure that we could not be happy with so little confidence in ourselves . . . Put the whole thing out of your mind for the time being, let me work out my salvation (or the other thing) & I shall go on loving you just the same, although I know now that it is no use trying to build our house upon sand.

Au revoir mon petit Buggins . . . I want no more of it . . .

Boy[15]

While Arthur had returned to Gabrielle and clearly felt unable to renege on whatever promises he had made her, this sad episode was not to be the conclusion of his affair with Diana, and they would return yet again to their see-sawing indecision. In the letter perhaps most revealing of Arthur's philosophy, he wrote:

I've slid down every cursed slope and the hills. I hate the main road & the crowd. The world I know is of my own making, the other makes me sick. Their morals, their convictions, their ambitions mean nothing to me. Fancy, sympathy & illusion have ever been my bed mates & I would never change them for Consideration, Position or Power, except perhaps the Position where two make one – blush my sunbeam . . .

All this, my 'blonde', is very complicated and I don't give a damn about knowing why I love your lips and your big blue eyes and your brave smile when your soul gives me the illusion that it's talking to my soul . . .

Be happy and I will be too.

Boy the Wanderer[16]

And while Arthur wished that what he suspected was the 'illusion' of his and Diana's love would be real, Gabrielle was to say to Paul Morand that she'd been having so much fun she had 'forgotten about love'. Yet by the time she came to her senses and halted her incessant round of activity for a moment, her intuition told her that something was very wrong. Arthur, meanwhile, rushing from meetings with the military and politicians in France then on to their counterparts in London, made no mention (any more than he normally would have) of his assignations and letters to Gabrielle's English competitor.

The French president, Poincaré, had asked Georges Clemenceau, who was then seventy-six, to take over as prime minister, in November 1917. Irritable and recklessly brave, Clemenceau had already been prime minister between 1906 and 1909. While disliked by the Right and the Left, he insisted upon unity, above all. Temporarily surmounting political differences, he succeeded, as no one else had, in re-enthusing his compatriots with the will to fight and win the war.[17] Upon Clemenceau's appointment, Arthur immediately sought an audience with him, offering to place his fleet at the service of the French government and to supply the country with coal. Clemenceau accepted Arthur's offer, their friendship blossomed and Arthur was increasingly called upon to liaise at a high level between the British and the French. Having already gained considerable respect as liaison officer to General Allenby's Cavalry Corps, alongside Edward Spears he now became (formally) one of the two most important officers liaising between the French and the British governments.

In Paris, in the spring of 1918, we find Arthur's favourite sister, the exuberant and capricious Bertha, watching the showing of Gabrielle's new season's clothes, upstairs in the gold-trimmed salon at rue Cambon. (Gabrielle was one of the first couturiers to have live models walking back and forth, wearing her collections in a floor show.) On 1 April, *Vogue* would describe the collection as ingenious, admiring the knitted-jersey dresses' 'silken suppleness, clinging so closely to the body'. Citing the society women wearing Chanel, such as the Princess Radziwill, *Vogue* said that 'many well-dressed women' were wearing versions of Gabrielle's grey silk jersey 'costume' embroidered in grey cotton, and that Mlle Saint-Sauveur had sported one, this time embroidered in gold, 'just a few days ago at a lunch at the Ritz'. At the same lunch, the Princess Violette Murat showed off one of Gabrielle's embroidered dresses 'of blue silk jersey', while a Mrs Hyde and a Mlle d'Hinnisdal also wore dresses by Gabrielle.

As the floor show got under way, without warning Bertha Capel and her fellow guests were shocked out of their state of self-absorption by the sudden thump of an explosion that blew in windows and rocked the buildings nearby.

Paris was under fire from one of the huge long-range German cannons (nicknamed 'Big Bertha'), the like of which had never been seen before. Shells followed one another twenty minutes on twenty minutes. A friend of Bertha's at Gabrielle's show remembered that, at the first cannon shot, 'the little emaciated models continued their walk, impassive. "It is a rather extraordinary thing," she [Bertha] says, "to watch the show of a mellow spring collection, during which the rhythm of the bombings sets the pace for the models' presentation."'[18] The cannons launched their shells on the city from as far away as seventy-five miles. Arriving without warning, the German bombardment could continue for several days at a time. On a particularly successful day, as many as twenty shells might reach Paris. From March to August 1918, they were responsible for the deaths of over two hundred people and injuries to hundreds more. Their prime objective, however, was psychological. The aim was to weaken Parisian morale. Meanwhile, the British ambassador, Lord Derby, irritably confided to his diary:

. . . of all the stupid things today the War Office telephoned here to know exactly where the shells from Big Bertha had fallen . . . as it is the one thing you are not allowed to talk about and . . . can be of no possible use to the Cabinet – unless it means they are frightened to come here – I told Capel . . . that he had better not send any reply.[19]

Several of the women then staying at the Ritz came over to Chanel on the rue Cambon – situated just across the way from the hotel's rear entrance – in search of something appropriate to wear should the shelling take place at night. Taking sudden shelter down in the Ritz's cellars, what could Gabrielle substitute for their delicate nightgowns? The enterprising Gabrielle brought up and offered the rich refugees a consignment of men's scarlet pyjamas. The dashing young couturier decreed that these were not only acceptable, they were also stylish. She was soon reproducing them in coarse pale silk, and her more bold clients were delighted. 'It was very chic, very daring and very new, as pyjamas would only really become popular three or four years later, on the Lido at Venice.'[20]

By the summer of 1918, the Germans had concluded that their only remaining chance of victory was to defeat the Allies before the overwhelming resources of the United States forces could be deployed against them. Meanwhile, Old Tiger, as Clemenceau was now known, travelled from one headquarters at the Front to another, haranguing the generals and endearing himself to the troops by hobbling down into trench after trench to rouse and inspire them. He threw out the French commander-in-chief, Philippe Pétain, and replaced him with Ferdinand Foch. Paris was now bombarded from the air; the distant cannons continued hurling shells into the city, and, once more, the fighting had almost reached the capital. Again, there was an exodus. Those who could went by car, while the rest squeezed on to crowded trains and any other transport they could find.

And, while Arthur and Diana vacillated about their feelings for one another, Gabrielle was at the mercy of their uncertainty. Arthur may have gone for periods without seeing Gabrielle, but he found it impossible to give her up.

Between the strenuously hard work and the heartache, Arthur

somehow made good progress on his new book. Here, complaining of a neglect of the art of maternity, and the prevalent system of marriages of convenience, he asked, when mothers married off their daughters for wealth, 'What becomes of love and virtue in these barters of gold and beauty?' He believed that the natural result of this prison for women was that they turned to adultery, and 'discretion replaces virtue'.[21] Arthur believed that 'this conception of marriage is a crime; a dreadful crime against the woman . . . Intelligence, beauty and virtue are the most precious gifts of a race. They all depend on motherhood.'[22] The war was turning Arthur's thoughts towards the regeneration of society, and thus he was being led to a new estimation of motherhood. And he must, at least partly, have had Diana in mind when he went on to say that 'the English aristocracy . . . does not give a dowry to its daughters and leaves it to love to unite its children . . . the future role of women consists of making a Utopia a reality by giving birth to a generation that will be capable of thriving in it.'[23]

At last, in that spring of 1918, Arthur and Diana came to a final decision. Somehow, Arthur broke the news to Gabrielle: he had found someone else and he had asked her to marry him. Perhaps Gabrielle had no longer been able to bear what she sensed already and had initiated this confession. But no matter how much she might have suspected, or indeed prepared herself for it over the last months, Arthur's words left her devastated.

She had never been an ordinary mistress, for whom the hackneyed old explanations would have to suffice. And, while her growing success seemed only to increase her allure, one commentator, imagining that this bold 'queen of fashion' must have 'some corners of vulgarity where one could detect the common extraction', found that 'yet she is a charming and graceful being. Neither pushing nor servile . . . a cultured and subtle mind.'[24] Had the very thing attracting Arthur to Gabrielle in the first place – her difference – become too challenging for him to manage?

In making herself financially independent, even wealthy, Gabrielle had apparently made herself free – and also exposed herself to hurt. And we recall again Arthur's prophesy to her – 'You're proud, you'll suffer' – and his realization that, thinking he'd given her a plaything, he had in fact given her freedom.[25]

14

Alone

Arthur's intention to marry left Gabrielle feeling weak and abandoned. She had lost, perhaps forsaken, the only man she had ever really loved. In company with the courtesans and the mistresses whose lives she had struggled to transcend, it appeared she still wasn't good enough to marry. More than any other person, it was Arthur who had helped Gabrielle to become the person she wanted to be. But it now seemed as if the independence she had so striven for had been earned at the cost of her heart. With an awful resignation, Morand's Irène tells Lewis that she believed she had been wrong to work so much. But she also recognized that, now, she could not turn back:

> It is not a game one is free to take up or abandon. Laziness is an ornamental art, and it makes one lighter. Labour is a heavy law, with grave consequences I'm only beginning to make out today . . . everything that is happening is my fault . . . I will explain to you what you don't dare tell me: that you [were with me] to be happy, at peace, and not to turn your house into a trading post.[1]

Gabrielle was unable to alter what she had become. But if her intuition had prepared her for Arthur's news, so that she was able to conceal from him the depth of her feelings, when his rejection finally came, it broke her heart. Unforeseeably, the war had changed Arthur's notion of commitment and he had felt honour bound to make a choice.

Once he had broken the news of his impending marriage to Gabrielle, she could no longer remain at the apartment they lived in together. Then, while the Germans approached Paris and those thousands were fleeing the embattled city, Misia Edwards came to her rescue. She knew of a beautiful apartment hastily abandoned by a friend and told Gabrielle she really must take it on. The large ground-floor windows at 46 quai Debilly overlook the Seine on one side and the Trocadéro on the other. While mirrors lined the walls of the entrance hall and more filled an alcove, the ceiling shone with fine black lacquer. A huge Buddha dominated the low-level furniture and a slight scent of cocoa hung upon the air. The recent occupant was a devoted opium smoker and had been fearful that remaining in a fallen city would leave him without sources for his habit. Gabrielle was for the first time in an apartment paid for out of her own purse. She set about arranging it exactly to her liking.

In addition to finding Gabrielle a place of refuge, Misia 'sent' a couple to look after her: Joseph Leclerc, and his wife, Marie. These two were to prove Gabrielle's devoted servants. In the same way, in 1913, Arthur had sent a woman, named Mme Aubert, to Gabrielle at rue Cambon. Her real name was Mademoiselle de Saint-Pons, and it was she whom Gabrielle would give credit for 'advising me and guiding me'.[2] Despite Mme Aubert's flaming-red hair, she remained discreetly in the background. Invisible to the public, she helped everything at rue Cambon to run smoothly and was indispensable to Gabrielle, even more so in difficult times. Her discretion was such that Gabrielle's great-niece would later say, 'Hardly anyone knew her'; she would remain as Gabrielle's amanuensis until the Second World War.

Meanwhile, Arthur wrote to Diana one of those letters in which he both strived for her and tried to be realistic about their difficulties: 'Don't bother about your qualms, they are fully justified . . . but what does it matter if we love one another – my Buggins?'[3]

Having finally made her decision to marry, Diana wrote to tell her friend, the diplomat Duff Cooper. All the same, she was defensive and gave the impression that there were those who disapproved. The fact that Arthur was 'half French and not fond of country life' was, for example, in her aunt's eyes, indeed a black mark against him. Diana did, however, find support from her father and sisters. Family opinion has it that her sister, Lady Laura Lovat, was an extremely competent, even controlling young woman, who would never have 'permitted' her younger sister to wed someone of whom she did not approve. Meanwhile, Diana said to Duff Cooper: 'I've been ill, we've nearly lost the war, and I think I'm going to marry Capel after all . . . I look for nothing but abuse from the world, but I prefer this sort of marriage to the . . . mariage de convenance and feel quite certain that this one is fraught with great possibilities & charm.'[4]

She implored him to write to her 'and say you're pleased about it. And that you like my "darkie", I adore him.'[5] In preparation for this married life, Arthur had found a grand apartment on the avenue du Bois. He then asked his sister Bertha to live with him as a kind of chaperone, by way of announcing to the world that he no longer lived with Gabrielle.

The bloody battle to repulse the German army from Paris had begun, and Arthur was kept very busy in his role as Assistant Political Secretary. Owing to the extraordinary circumstances, all leave was cancelled, and preparations for his and Diana's wedding, at her sister and brother-in-law's Scottish estate, Beaufort Castle, were held up.

It has been traditional to place the date for the Capel marriage in October. In fact, despite their prevarication, Arthur and Diana were actually married considerably earlier than this, on 3 August 1918[6] in the Lovat family chapel, with Diana's brother-in-law Lord Lovat as chief witness. Arthur must have been required back on duty without delay, because by the following Saturday (10 August), the British ambassador, Lord Derby, recorded in his diary that several people coming to lunch with him in Paris had missed their train after the ferry crossing, 'but the Capels (late Diana Wyndham) motored them from Havre'. The following day, the newlyweds were Lord Derby's guests with several others, and Diana confided in him that their delayed wedding had been her fault because of her indecision. The ambassador thought that 'the marriage will be a success, as he is a real good fellow, though a little rough, but that is just what she will correct. She became a Roman Catholic either the morning of her marriage or the day before and I expect really it was making the change that made her undecided.'[7]

Little did Lord Derby know how mistaken he was as to one of the most significant reasons for Diana's doubts: Gabrielle. But what of this third side of the triangle, forced to remain in the shadows for these past weeks and months?

As the date of Arthur's marriage drew nearer, the strain had told upon Gabrielle so badly that, shortly before the nuptials, she had suffered an emotional collapse. Unaware of this, a friend, Antoinette Bernstein, wife of the playwright Henri Bernstein, had written to reprimand her for some negligence or other. Gabrielle's stoic yet poignant reply conveys the suffering she was then trying to contain. She was telling herself, as much as Antoinette, that she would recover; one sees the effort necessary to overcome her emotional exhaustion.

> *My dear friend*
>
> *Do not accuse me; pity me for I have just spent three very bad weeks! As things always work themselves out in the end my health is much better. I still have a thousand worries. I fully intend to leave them here [in Paris]. So if you will still have me I can leave at the end of next week. Write soon.*
>
> *Much love*
>
> *Coco*[8]

Another letter, sent by Gabrielle's secretary, and regarding the renting of her house, refers to the fact that 'Mademoiselle Chanel has been unwell lately and was not able to reply right away.'[9]

By 18 August, one week after Arthur's return with his bride to Paris, we find that Gabrielle had fled the city, in an attempt to leave behind her 'thousand worries'. She had gone to find comfort with her friends Henri and Antoinette Bernstein, as promised, at a spa town, Uriage, in the Alps. And here Gabrielle was to spend the rest of that summer. Ostensibly, she was part of the grand annual exodus from the capital's August heat. In fact, she was taking a spa cure to help restore and thereby 'cure' herself of Arthur. As it turned out, for much of Gabrielle's stay, Antoinette Bernstein was summering by the sea at Deauville with her mother. But, shortly after Gabrielle's arrival, Antoinette brought her and Henri's small daughter, Georges, to see her father at the villa that Gabrielle and he were sharing while taking their 'methodical and prolonged cure'. Antoinette stayed for about a week before returning to Deauville. In Paris, meanwhile, the British ambassador was noting in his diary that:

> Capel is an invaluable . . . link with Clemenceau, but I am very anx-ious about his health. He is very neurasthenic [the contemporary term for nervous instability, which sounds close to a breakdown], and I am certain he himself thinks he is going off his head . . . Though he talks freely with me, they tell me that when he is alone at home he sits for hours without saying a word and you cannot get him to buckle down to any work. I am sending him away for a fort-night's holiday.[10]

The huge stresses of Arthur's war work would have reduced many to an emotional crisis of some kind. In addition, he had been living for many months under the strain of conducting his romance with Diana with a divided heart. He had never been able to push the source of that division – Gabrielle – very far from his mind. He had not entered into the sacrament of marriage lightly, and the enormity of his action had overcome Arthur and reduced him to a state of emo-tional collapse. Unbeknown to one another, he and Gabrielle were suffering a simultaneous crisis.

As Gabrielle made her own attempt at recuperation, also far from Paris, a young observer, Simone de Caillavet, recorded that she was mystified by the relationship between Gabrielle, Henri Bernstein and his wife. She found Antoinette and Gabrielle 'equally emaci-ated' and commented on their 'vehement friendship for one another'. Simone was unable to fathom 'what bonds link the three units of this enigmatic trio'.[11] Henri Bernstein was an incorrigible philanderer and a man possessed of a rather intense and melodramatic personality, rather like the heightened endings of his plays about love, which were so successful at the time. Gabrielle had arrived in the mountains overcome by a sense of rejection and loss, and temporary forgetfulness in seduction by this older man may have given her a welcome respite from her secretly desperate state of mind.

Gabrielle and Henri Bernstein did not, however, spend all their time alone. There were visitors to the villa. Adrienne came to stay, bringing a friend, a former dancer. Photographs show the women, and Henri, walking and picnicking in the summer mountain pastures. The women are all dressed in variations of a Chanel jersey skirt and loose belted jacket. In another photograph, they wear Gabrielle's linen outfits. Her followers had become women of fashion who, for the first time, were prepared to look very similar. Previously, a couturier had to make endless tiny modifications to a style, because one of a woman's greatest fears was to find herself in the same outfit as someone else.

In other photographs, Gabrielle appears as a dazzling representation of 'modernity', with her bobbed hair and in her outfit of coarse silk pyjamas – that same style she had recently made the height of chic in the bomb-shelter basement of the Ritz. Even Henri Bernstein was wearing these 'outrageous' pyjamas. In one photograph with a number of visitors, Antoinette is the only person not smiling. Young Nadine Rothschild was convinced that Antoinette 'ignored the affair between her husband and Gabrielle because she had a "costly passion" for fashionable clothes and found "sufficient compensation" in being dressed for free by Gabrielle in many of her "sensational designs"'.[12]

Then finally, this appalling war, waged at the cost of so many lives, was at an end. On 29 September 1918, the German Supreme Command informed Kaiser Wilhelm II that the military situation was hopeless. With no choice but to take his command's recommendation, the

Kaiser then asked the Allies for an immediate ceasefire. The negotiations that followed dragged on, and on, and the social deterioration of Europe grew worse than it might otherwise have been. This included a revolution in Germany, the abdication of the Kaiser and the proclamation of a German Republic on 9 November. Finally, on 11 November, the armistice was signed, famously, in Marshall Foch's private train carriage, in that same forest of Compiègne where Gabrielle had ridden so many times with Etienne Balsan and their friends. During the course of the war, 11 per cent of France's population, approximately 6 per cent of Great Britain's, and 9 per cent of Germany's was killed or wounded. The number was almost unimaginable; in all, approximately nine and a half million men had lost their lives.

While the armistice ended the fighting, it took another six months of negotiation at the Paris Peace Conference for the Allied victors to set peace terms for Germany and the other defeated nations. During those six months, Paris effectively became the seat of world government, as the negotiators brought to a close the reign of bankrupt empires and redrew the world map. As new countries were created, the infamously punitive peace treaty with Germany declared it must bear full guilt, and the Allies required reparations be paid to them. Many thought this excessive. As Assistant Political Secretary to the British Delegation, Arthur was kept very busy for many months to come. Notoriously, if the aim had been to pacify, conciliate or permanently weaken Germany, it had failed; the Paris Peace Treaty would prove fertile ground for the roots of the Second World War.

If Arthur's marriage had driven Gabrielle to leave the city, she now continued outside it in a villa she rented in the leafy outlying suburb of Garches. Here, with a view out over Paris, she returned after long days of work, for peace and the company of her dogs, to whom she had become very attached in recent years. If Gabrielle entertained any doubts about whether, at thirty-five, she could still be found attractive, she need not have worried. Henri Bernstein took her to meet his ex-lover, the beautiful ex-courtesan Liane de Pougy – now the Princess Ghika. Writing of Gabrielle and Bernstein's visit, de Pougy said, 'Bernstein . . . brought . . . the dressmaker, Gabrielle Chanel – the taste of a fairy, the eyes and voice of a woman, the hair-cut and figure of an urchin.'[13] Gabrielle had no shortage of admirers. When the armistice had at last been signed, Paris went mad and Gabrielle was to be seen at the festivities with a new lover, another handsome playboy, Paul Eduardo Martínez de Hoz. De Hoz was a member of the Jockey Club and scion of one of Argentina's wealthiest families.

King George V came to Paris to celebrate the armistice, and a large and distinguished party met at the Capels' apartment to watch the procession from their balcony. The English socialite and diplomat's wife, Lady Helen d'Abernon, later one of Gabrielle's clients, recorded that:

> It was a wet day and the entry was far from imposing, although guns fired and the streets were lined with troops and with spectators the whole way to the Elysée . . .
>
> I passed most of the morning in the company of monsieur Bondy, a quiet but charming writer, and at intervals 'Boy' Capel came and sat down beside us. The *jeune ménage* – his and Diana's – appears oddly assorted. Capel is a curious, rather strange-looking man, more French than English. He has had an eclectic and not unromantic past, yet he is interested – and successfully interested – in big financial affairs. Diana is very pretty and has the charm of all the Listers, but she seems a half-assimilated, exotic little figure amongst these brilliant, vociferous, scintillating French people. They appear metallic, yet I do not think that they are fundamentally hard – sensitive rather, in an unsentimental, slightly animal way. I like them and admire them, while realizing that they are as different from the Anglo Saxons as it is possible to be.[14]

In hinting at the chasm of difference between the French and the Anglo-Saxons, in noticing how French Arthur was, and how only 'half-assimilated' Diana seemed amongst this gathering of 'brilliant' people, Helen d'Abernon's comments were unwittingly astute. Yet, in addition to their great cultural differences co-existed Arthur's 'not unromantic past', in the form of Gabrielle. Try as he might, he could not banish her from his mind.

Nevertheless, the Capel family was to grow and, in April 1919, while Diana was staying in Scotland with her sister Lady Lovat, she was delivered of a baby girl. Christened Ann Diana France Ayesha Capel, she was a most welcome addition to Arthur's life.

Yet, though he and his blue-eyed English wife socialized a good deal, she was not proving as docile and compliant as Arthur might have imagined, when he chose her over the extraordinary and characterful Gabrielle Chanel. As the months wore on, time was not tempering the wedded couple's differences.

For example, previously, Arthur had seen nothing unusual in buying clothes for Diana from Gabrielle's salon in Biarritz but, once married, Diana began to object. Arthur overruled her. Why should she not be dressed by the most exciting designer in Paris? The long-standing tradition in Diana's family has it that she disliked Gabrielle.[15]

Meanwhile, Arthur had come to the decision that he was no longer able to live without Gabrielle, and made his way back to her, in her villa out of town. If Arthur didn't actually tell Diana, she soon guessed it anyway, and found the negotiation of the age-old triangle in the ensuing period most painful to accept. She spent Easter 1919 alone and weeping. While Arthur's guilt weighed upon him, any objections Diana might have raised were ignored, and his visits to Gabrielle grew more frequent.

There were few in Paris in whom Diana could confide, but she learnt to lean a little on an elderly English friend, Lady Portarlington, who would come and keep her company when Diana knew that Arthur must be with Gabrielle. Keeping a mistress was so commonplace that Paris would have been more surprised at its causing disagreement than at its actually happening. And, anyway, Arthur was almost universally liked. Diana's unhappiness at accepting what

Bertha told her – that her brother 'just cannot give Gabrielle up' – made the young foreigner loath to remain in Paris.[16] Thus, she took to spending more time in England, where her presence was easily explained: Arthur was very busy, and Diana was visiting friends and family. She also took up her flirtation with her old friend Duff Cooper once more. Even so, while Cooper's recent marriage, to the beautiful socialite Lady Diana Manners was never to inhibit his activities, his and Diana Capel's enjoyable flirtation did not develop into a full-blown affair.[17]

At the anniversary Victory Ball of November 1919, Cooper talked with Diana, who was 'looking very well in gold trousers'.[18] (It was still most unusual for a woman to wear trousers, and these were almost certainly from Chanel.) One wonders if Diana and Cooper spoke of Gabrielle. When, earlier that same day, Arthur had once again absented himself from home, he probably didn't tell Diana that he was to act as a witness at the marriage of Gabrielle's sister Antoinette.

Having failed to find a Frenchman who would marry her, Antoinette had fallen in love with a Canadian airman ten years her junior. To Oscar Fleming, the son of a wealthy but strict Protestant Ontarian, Antoinette appeared exciting and sophisticated. Whatever Gabrielle's opinion of this whirlwind romance, the beautiful lace wedding dress she had in her collection for that season was very likely designed for Antoinette.

Not long after the newlyweds' arrival in Canada, with Antoinette's maid and many trunks of clothes, Antoinette began sending plaintive letters to Gabrielle and Adrienne, begging for a passage home. Little is known about Antoinette's time in Canada but, apparently, Oscar's father insisted his son finish his training as a lawyer in Toronto, and said he would work better if he studied there alone. Antoinette's maid soon left her, but Antoinette was obliged to remain alone in Ontario with her in-laws. She spoke almost no English and was desperately unhappy. The replies to her letters that came from Paris exhorted her to persevere. Could she not try out her Chanel clothes from her trousseau on the stores in Detroit? All that is known of how Antoinette went about this is that she was unsuccessful.[19]

Two days before Christmas 1919, Diana telephoned Duff Cooper to say she had just arrived in London. Arthur had, meanwhile, started for the south of France, and she was to join him in a fortnight.[20]

Diana lunched with Duff Cooper and her friend Lady Rosslyn, then flirted with Cooper as their taxi crawled through the London traffic. Cooper had dropped Diana back at Asprey's for tea with Lady Rosslyn, but noticed that Diana had forgotten her book. Turning back and finding her still standing outside Asprey's with her friend, Cooper returned the book and drove off. Reading the paper the following morning, he realized why, standing there on the pavement, Lady Rosslyn had looked so awful. She was about to give Diana a terrible piece of news Lord Rosslyn had cabled her, and for which there was no good way to prepare Diana.

The details were sketchy but, a few hours earlier, as Arthur was driving to the south of France, it appeared that one of his tyres had burst. The car was flung upside down, it exploded into flames, and he had died in the blaze. While the car was burnt, almost to a shell, Arthur's mechanic, Mansfield, was badly injured but had managed to escape. Duff Cooper wrote: 'December 24, 1919. The first thing I saw in the Daily Express this morning was the death of Boy Capel, Diana's husband, who was killed in a motor accident in the south of France on Monday [22 December]. I was very shocked.' Arthur had almost certainly spent the night before that fateful day with Gabrielle.[21] Then he had set out with Mansfield to make the 620-mile journey south.

Some weeks later, when Lady Rosslyn told Duff Cooper how dreadful it had been breaking the news of Arthur's death to Diana, she added a bleak insight into the workings of their marriage. She said 'how impossible Diana's relations with Capel were becoming, how he had entirely ceased to live with her and hardly ever spoke to her. That he confessed she had got on his nerves and he could barely stand her presence.'[22]

It seems odd, under these circumstances, that Arthur and Diana had been planning to meet up in a fortnight. Was he going to attempt another beginning with his wife, in which case he may well have formally broken off his affair with Gabrielle before driving south? Or had Arthur simply said goodbye to Gabrielle at Garches with the intention of ending his marriage when he met up with his wife in the south of France after Christmas? Whichever of these conclusions Arthur had made, one is left with the mournful understanding that, while the resolution of this state of affairs had to end sadly for at least one of these three, instead it became a tragedy.

Whatever confused thoughts had filled Arthur's head as he sped south to Cannes for Christmas with his sister Bertha – rather than spending it with his wife and baby girl – we will never know. But, in the very early hours of the following morning, Arthur and Gabrielle's companion from Royallieu days, Comte Léon de Laborde, at one time most likely Gabrielle's lover, was ringing at the door. He knocked, he broke the silence of the quiet enclave and shouted. No one came. De Laborde refused to give up and, finally, Gabrielle's butler, Joseph, was there at the door. He was very reluctant to tell Mademoiselle and wanted to wait until morning. But Léon insisted that Gabrielle *must* know. At last she came down the stairs. In white pyjamas, her short hair tousled, she looked to him 'the silhouette of a youth in white satin'.[23]

Léon told Gabrielle all that he knew. It had been late last evening, on the road between St-Raphaël and Cannes, when Arthur and Mansfield had almost reached their destination. Léon said that Arthur must have been very tired.

As he spoke, Gabrielle's face was tortured, but she did not cry; only sat there, utterly still.

After a few minutes, still without a word, she walked back up the stairs. Returning, she had dressed and now carried an overnight bag. No, she would not wait; she wanted Léon to take her south, immediately. As they set off in his car, the dawn light was spreading over Paris.

Gabrielle refused Léon's pleas with her to rest on the arduous journey south, and they reached Cannes the following evening.

Although it was late, Léon went from hotel to hotel, asking did they have a Lady Michelham (Arthur's sister) staying there with them. He made some calls. At last, he found her. Bertha was distraught. Gabrielle's bid to see Arthur before he was buried made her refuse rest on the journey, but her wish was not to be granted. Apparently, Arthur had been so badly burnt that the coffin had already been sealed up.

Bertha insisted that the travellers must stay in her suite of rooms. They did, but Gabrielle refused a bedroom, sitting up on a chaise for the remainder of that night. The next day, she would not accompany Bertha and Léon to the first office in Arthur's honour, at which he was given military honours, nearby at Fréjus cathedral. Instead, Gabrielle requested that Bertha's chauffeur take her to the place where Arthur had died.

This man later told Bertha that, at the spot where the captain's car still lay, burnt out like a blackened skeleton on the edge of the road, he stood back. He watched as Gabrielle walked around the car; touching it, as if she were blind. Then she sat down on a milestone beside it. And, at last, the heartbroken woman bent her head and sobbed. When Arthur had married, Gabrielle had 'lost' him. Yet while he was alive there had always been hope, and he had returned. Each time he left her, there was the possibility he would come back. This time, there was none. To the chauffeur, standing discreetly at a distance, it seemed as if Gabrielle wept for hours.

On 28 December 1919, *Le Gaulois* reported that 'the body of Captain Arthur Capel, Knight of the Légion d'Honneur, Mons Star, killed in a car accident, arrived yesterday morning [in Paris] and was laid in S.-Honoré d'Eylau, in the church's vaults.' On 2 January, the newspaper announced that 'the funeral of Captain Arthur Capel, Companion British Empire . . . will take place tomorrow, Saturday 3 January at midday.'

A good portion of Parisian society congregated in the church filled to capacity that day.[24] So, too, did a large English contingent, led by the British ambassador, Lord Derby, plus a deputation of Arthur's fellow British officers. Diana's sisters and husbands were present, but Diana herself, and Arthur's mistress, Gabrielle Chanel, were both absent. Afterwards, Arthur was laid to rest in the cemetery of Montmartre, where a large tomb was later raised. In keeping with the ultimate elusiveness of this extraordinary man, it was marked with neither name, date, nor epitaph. It reads simply:

FAMILLE CAPEL

In letters of condolence to Diana, friends described Arthur's importance to them, and how much he was loved.[25] One of Diana's sisters talked of his 'pilgrim's soul', saying that 'he never seemed to be very securely anchored' to this world. 'His country was unexplored, don't you agree?' One friend wrote: 'He was such a strange, exceptional, attractive human being. And for you this must seem like the end of the world ... Everyone here [in Paris] is shocked beyond words and I hear on all sides appreciation and regret.'[26] Clemenceau said, 'He was much too good to remain among us,' while a friend wrote that 'Boy was the best, the most loyal, and the most devoted friend one could have, and we loved him like a brother ... Every day will make us realize more the huge loss.'[27]

Many years later, Gabrielle would add her own mournful and definitive elegy: 'His death was a terrible blow to me ... I lost everything when I lost Capel. He left a void in me that the years have not filled.'[28] For Gabrielle, Arthur's death did indeed 'seem like the end of the world', and for the moment she struggled to survive.

If she took any time away from her work, it can only have been a few days, for she had discovered what distracted her better than anything else: this was work. It was fortunate that Gabrielle's reputation was in the ascendant and that her salon in rue Cambon was rarely still.

Beginning Again

Three months before Arthur's death, Gabrielle had signed a contract. While keeping number 21 rue Cambon, she was to move
her salon and personal apartment to much larger premises, just
down the street at number 31. At this address, she was registered
for the first time in Paris as a couturier. The five floors of 31 rue
Cambon were where Gabrielle was to design, meet clients and
promote her business. By no means the largest Chanel salon, to
this day, number 31 has remained the most important in the
Chanel empire.

During the first months after Arthur's death, on Saturdays,
Gabrielle's chauffeur drove her back to her villa retreat out at
Garches. There, relieved of the need to pretend, she gave herself up
to grief. At times, her faithful butler and housekeeper, Joseph and
Marie Leclerc, became concerned. Gabrielle had her bedroom and
everything in it done out in black. Grief had not, however, entirely
obscured her good sense and robust physical and mental health.
Having retired for her first night in her tomb-like black bedroom,
Gabrielle was overcome by its melancholy and reappeared, begging
Marie to make her up a bed somewhere else.

In February 1920, Arthur's will was published in the London
Times. The executors in Britain were Diana's father and brother-in-
law, Lords Ribblesdale and Lovat respectively. In Paris, Arthur had
chosen his friends the banker Evelyn Toulmin and Armand de Gramont, Duc de Guiche.

To Arthur's sisters, Henriette and Edith, he bequeathed £20,000.
To his favourite, Bertha, he left nothing, knowing that she was well
taken care of. (In early 1919, Bertha had entered into an arranged

marriage with Herman Stern, son of the extremely wealthy art collector, Lord Michelham. Herman was rather retarded, and he and his wife never lived together. But this had apparently been the deal with Bertha and her scheming mother-in-law, who wanted her son to inherit the majority of the family fortune. Bertha kept her promise to have no children by Herman and in return was made financially independent for life. It appears that Arthur was an integral part of the negotiations, which had ensured his rather dotty sister's future.)[1]

For Gabrielle Chanel, and someone called Yvonne Viggiano, Comtesse de Beauchamp, there was £40,000. Having dispensed his fortune with the freedom from constraint sometimes accompanying thoughts of death, Arthur had made no attempt to hide this hitherto unknown aspect of his life. Yvonne Viggiano was a young, recently widowed Italian countess with whom he must have had an important relationship. We know nothing more, except that she had a son.

For the remainder, Arthur left his estate upon trust to Diana, 'for life, and then for our child'. Before the other bequests were taken out, the total sum was well over £700,000 (equivalent to approximately £10 million in today's currency). *The Times* noted that Arthur had disposed of his great assets in a mere one hundred words.

Regarding the emotional complications of Arthur's short life – he was thirty-seven when he died – and his regret at having given up Gabrielle, his comment to Elisabeth de Gramont springs to mind: 'It is easier . . . to organize the trade of coal than one's private life.'[2]

The few who cared to look behind Gabrielle's professional demeanour would see that, three months after Arthur's death, she had not begun to pull herself out of the misery into which it had plunged her. Her mourning was now to play itself out in a dark and complex fashion.

Early that spring, she would move, with her two German Shepherd dogs, Soleil and Lune, their three puppies, the two terriers, Pepita and Popee (her last present from Arthur), Joseph, Marie Leclerc and their little daughter, Suzanne, to a large art nouveau villa, Bel Respiro, just a short walk from La Milanaise, the one Gabrielle had rented for the previous year. It has always been said that she bought Bel Respiro.[3] Gabrielle did indeed buy Bel Respiro, but not for a whole year after her move there. This was because, at first, the owner only permitted her to rent it. To all intents and purposes, this move was to help Gabrielle make a fresh start, with her friends Henri and Antoinette Bernstein as next-but-one neighbours. The real story of Gabrielle's move was, however, much stranger than that, and until now has not been known.

On moving to Bel Respiro, she had the shutters painted an intense black. This was strongly disapproved of by her neighbours, but Gabrielle was not in a fit state to care. Indeed, those black shutters were the first indication that Bel Respiro was to be both her refuge and a kind of mausoleum for her memories. And in fact, it wasn't the proximity of her friends but her memories that were the most significant reason for Gabrielle's move here.

Extraordinarily, it turns out that Bel Respiro belonged to *Arthur* – it was the very house he had bought for himself and Diana the previous year.[4]

This explains the mystery of a letter from Diana to Duff Cooper, written not long after Arthur's death and headed 'Bel Respiro'. Diana had told Cooper that 'I have been and still am, & I suppose I shall go on being, so terribly, desperately unhappy . . . I can't write more because there is nothing to say . . . I have to lead the life of a recluse, otherwise I can't sleep . . . I suppose I shall leave here soon and return to England.'[5]

Diana did indeed soon leave France, and almost never visited it again.

Meanwhile, Gabrielle was not only aware that Bel Respiro was Arthur and Diana's house, this was *exactly* why she wanted it. How better to immerse herself in Arthur than by living in his home? It didn't concern Gabrielle that Diana had only recently left, or that she knew it was Gabrielle who took up the lease. (Diana must have been beyond caring that the new tenant was to be her husband's old lover.) Gabrielle cared only that by being there, in some strange way she would be 'living' with Arthur. In addition, her presence in *his* house would erase Diana from his life, and Gabrielle would gradually 'replace' her.

For several months, she lived out this half-cracked existence at Bel Respiro with no one, beside Joseph and Marie, really aware of what she was doing. In her state of semi-breakdown, Gabrielle, who could always move from reality to fantasy in one bound, now did so more readily. At the same time, each day, she was driven into Paris to the salon, and business prospered. Although she was a wreck and often close to tears, work really was the only thing that kept her from collapse. One wonders how she responded to the news that Diana Capel had given birth to another baby girl, in June of that year, 1920. Named June, the baby had been conceived only three months before her father's death.

It was Misia Edwards's marriage that August, to José Maria Sert, her lover of twelve years, that would finally initiate Gabrielle's recovery.

Misia's efforts to lift Gabrielle out of her blackness had so far failed. So, after the wedding, she instructed her to get out of Paris and come away with them to Venice. Tempted by the prospect of distraction, of possible relief from a state which had become a kind of madness, Gabrielle accepted Misia's invitation to leave Paris behind her. From now on, the Serts would become two of her closest friends.

As a young woman, Misia had acquired a salon and become one of the undeniable queens of Paris. Paul Morand described her then as 'a beautiful panther, imperious, bloodthirsty and frivolous'. He also said that she was 'brilliant in perfidy, and refined in cruelty'.[6]

Misia Godebska had grown up in the world of *haute bohème*, where artists and society met. Musically gifted, she had married at twenty-one, to Thadée Natanson, founder of the *Revue Blanche*, then, in order to clear her husband's debts, had married the fabulously wealthy newspaper magnate the monstrous Alfred Edwards. Full of perverse nonchalance, Misia cared little about discretion or the scandal her behaviour provoked.

Misia's stormy friendship with Sergei Diaghilev had been forged at their first meeting when, after hours of talking, Diaghilev recognized the quality of Misia's musical and artistic appreciation. Diaghilev and his impresario, Gabriel Astruc, knew that in order to succeed on any scale, they needed the patronage of the self-absorbed world of artistic fashion. Astruc called these patrons '*mes chers* snobs' and cultivated them with great flair. Like these 'snobs', Misia Sert was wealthy. However, her feeling for art ran far deeper than snobbery or fashion. Her generosity to the financially incompetent artistic genius Diaghilev was interspersed with endless disputes, reconciliations and Slavic declarations of affection. Without Misia, much of Diaghilev's work might never have reached the stage.

Paul Morand said that Misia was a 'harvester of geniuses, all of them in love with her – Vuillard, Bonnard, Renoir, Picasso'; the list also included Toulouse-Lautrec, Ravel and Debussy, as well as poets such as Verlaine, Mallarmé and Apollinaire. Having divorced, when Misia began living with José Maria Sert, a master voluptuary, he revealed her own as yet unfulfilled sensuality to her. In Sert, Misia had finally discovered her life's companion. Misia's impromptu and bohemian entertaining had an infectious and exciting quality, reflecting the newer Paris rather than the 'studied grandeur' of the older *haut monde*. As for Sert's serial infidelities, the new bride had for long schooled herself to ignore them, even treating them with a 'grudging admiration'.

En route for Venice, the Serts and Gabrielle stopped off at Padua, where Gabrielle went with Misia to the basilica of St Anthony. Misia insisted it would dissolve Gabrielle's despair: St Anthony would give her peace. Gabrielle was reluctant but, constantly close to tears, she had obliged. Where Donatello's high-altar masterpiece still stands, Gabrielle found herself before his statue of the saint.

Asking for help to recover from her ceaseless mourning, she saw before her a man, resting his forehead on the stone floor: 'He had such a sad and beautiful face, there was so much rigidity and pain in him, and his exhausted head touched the ground with such weariness that a miracle took place within me.' All at once, Gabrielle felt shameful. 'How could I compare my sorrow ... with someone in this distress? Energy flowed through me. I took new heart and decided that I would live.'[7] Gabrielle believed she wasn't alone, that the man she had loved was near her 'on the *other* side, and wouldn't leave me'. She now told herself that, as long as she felt Arthur was waiting for her, she had no right to weep. 'It doesn't matter that you're alone *on this side* still, for a while.'[8] Gabrielle later told a friend how the woman 'who had turned into a shadow, came out of that church transformed'.[9]

In Venice, the reborn Gabrielle understood better Misia's fascination with Sert, the Spanish painter of grandiosity. Intense, short and vibrant, José Maria Sert was full of impassioned self-assurance, and also possessed a cruel streak. He was obsessed with art, enjoyed a consuming passion for women and, aided by an alcohol and morphine habit, lived in a world absurdly full of fantasy, high drama and adventure. The abandon of his parties was legendary.

Even the artists of Montmartre and Montparnasse, snobbish about Sert's abilities as an artist, gave him credit for his creation of atmosphere with his striking choices and juxtaposition of objects and works of art. In Venice, Sert spoke about works of art with an erudition that 'generated endless connections' for Gabrielle, and she marvelled. He took her to museums and churches and showed her the mournful splendour of the city's buildings. Fascinated and amazed, she absorbed it all like an intelligent, wondering child. Like so many before and since, Gabrielle fell under the sway of that melancholy, watery paradise *La Serenissima*, and returned to it regularly for the rest of her life.

In the end, though, it wasn't history that motivated Gabrielle. With the mind of an artist, she intuited that, by nurturing in oneself a certain savage disregard for the past, one was better able to make things for the present. Without denigrating the past, Gabrielle could say, with Misia, 'Oh, to hell with these Botticellis and da Vincis,' and they would go off to rummage around, unearthing unlikely treasures in some backstreet junk shop, or move from the city's restaurants to the luxury of a fashionable salon. This was the Venice where Gabrielle saw works of art in the palaces for which they were made; where she socialized with the Serts' friends, international and Venetian society keen to live the life of the present as much as dwelling upon the illustrious past of their ancestors.

By chance, the three travellers came upon Diaghilev, in a tête-à-tête with a mutual friend, the Grand Duchess Maria Pavlovna (the elder), and they stayed on to lunch. The Grand Duchess herself had been left with little, but was gracious, and grateful that she and her children had escaped the ravages of the Revolution. While they talked, Diaghilev spoke of his perennial financial problems. His choreographer, Massine, was rehearsing a new production of *The Rite of Spring* for performance in Paris; the cost would be prohibitive. As much as anything, this was because Diaghilev insisted on a vast orchestra. (In struggling to resuscitate the post-war fortunes of the Ballets Russes, he faced the problem that ballet audiences had changed, and both his French and Russian patrons' sources of wealth had collapsed.)

It is said that Diaghilev paid no attention to Gabrielle on this occasion, or several others when they met while in Venice.[10] But we know that not only had Gabrielle been at the original performance of *The Rite of Spring*, the premiere of *Parade* in 1917, and the parties afterwards, she had also been at the Parisian premiere of the first post-war Diaghilev–Stravinsky ballet, *Pulcinella*, in May of that year, 1920. And yet, this woman, whom Morand had described as 'quite a personality', was apparently meek and silent on these occasions. As we have seen, Misia would have the world believe that Gabrielle trailed round as her shadow in these early years of their friendship. The implication is always that the bohemian types with whom Gabrielle would socialize – and, on occasion, have affairs – liked her for nothing more than her money. The most significant reason for their friendship with her, however, was Gabrielle herself. As to her subdued manner in this period, it was more a result of her state of mourning than because she was meek and self-effacing.

From Venice, the ever-restless Serts took Gabrielle down to Rome.

'We arrived weary and drained, and were obliged to visit the city, by moonlight, until we were exhausted. At the Coliseum he [Sert] remembered the recollections of Thomas de Quincey, and said some wonderful things about architecture and about the parties that might be given amongst these ruins.'[11] Recalling Sert's gargantuan appetites and his inability to do anything on a small scale, Gabrielle said, 'he was as munificent and as immoral as a Renaissance man.' His perennial good humour, his erudition and encyclopaedic knowledge of the oddest things made him, for Gabrielle, the perfect travelling companion. She said that this 'huge, hairy monkey, with his tinted beard, his humped back, his enormous tortoiseshell spectacles – veritable wheels – loved everything colossal.'[12] He led her through the museums of Venice, explaining everything, and found in her an 'attentive ignorance . . . that he preferred to all his erudition.'[13] Gabrielle thought Sert resembled 'some enormous gnome who carried gold as well as rubbish inside his hump like a magic sack. He had extremely poor taste and exquisite judgement, the priceless and the disgusting, diamonds and crap, kindness and sadism, virtues and vices on a staggering scale.'[14]

Returning to Paris, Gabrielle appeared to have emerged from her emotional retreat, and the Serts pronounced her cured. Gabrielle would never be entirely cured of Arthur's loss, bearing forever its scars. Nonetheless, her powerful urge to life and growth was too strong to lie dormant in her for more than a certain amount of time. Exhilarated by the two Serts' mad adventures, she had decided 'to live'.

One of the first signs of this more positive frame of mind was that Gabrielle now made a dramatic move. There are several versions of this story. One has it that she appeared at Diaghilev's hotel and asked if she might see him. Another, which subtly alters the balance of power, has it that she asked him to come and see *her*. One suspects it was the latter, and that her description is correct:

I understand that there is a great tragedy. He has fled London because he could not pay his debts . . . 'I live at the Ritz hotel, come

and see me, say nothing to Misia.' He came to my apartment . . . I
gave him a cheque . . . I think he didn't think it was real . . . He never
wrote to me, he never compromised himself by a word.[15]

The astonished impresario, who had hoped Misia Sert would bail
him out, had instead been given a very large sum by Gabrielle to
relaunch *The Rite of Spring*. Her request that he tell no one was to
no avail; Diaghilev thrived on indiscretion almost as much as his
boon companion, Misia, and in no time at all she knew. The customary explanation for Gabrielle's gesture of munificence is that
she was flexing her cultural muscles: it wasn't only Misia who could
make things happen. Unlike Misia, however, for whom the cultivation of a salon was almost a *raison d'être*, the artist in Gabrielle
meant that she was only moderately interested in one with herself
at its centre. (As we have already seen, her interest in power was not
for its own sake, it was above all as a means to an *end*; usually, freedom to do her work, and thereby maintain her independence.)
Gabrielle never failed to fall under the spell of creativity, and what
primarily interested her in Diaghilev's case was the fact of his being
another artist at work. Anything made well, however modest, never
ceased to enchant her. There was, however, nothing modest about
Diaghilev's Ballets Russes.

The maestro, Sergei Diaghilev, was an extraordinary creature, an
incongruous, distracted mix of impulse and caprice, generosity and
meanness, combined with a breathtaking ability to manipulate. He
had no qualms whatsoever about a ruthless dedication to his object-
ives, which were devoted almost exclusively to his art. As someone
remarked of him, 'It was not easy to resist Diaghilev's pressure. He
would wear out his opponent, not by the logic of his arguments,
but by the sheer stress of his own will.'[16] His single-mindedness
made him arrogantly selective about his companions, and perhaps
it was only in Venice that he first registered Gabrielle properly. Perhaps it was in Venice, too, that Gabrielle understood something
better about Diaghilev himself. Certainly, she found his exotic foreignness most attractive. Later, she would describe him as 'the most

delightful of friends. I loved his zest for life, his passions, his scruffiness, so different from the sumptuous figure of legend.'[17]

Meeting once again this powerful and charismatic figure, three of whose ballets she had now seen brought to the stage, Gabrielle was keen to be a catalyst for the return of the most scandalous of them so far: *The Rite of Spring*.

The war had not been kind to Igor Stravinsky. Little of his music had been played, and he was eking out an existence with his family in neutral Switzerland. With the successful launch of his ballet *Pulcinella*, however, enhanced by Picasso's stage sets and costumes, all was set to change. Stravinsky both reclaimed his position at the centre of the Ballets Russes and was re-launched as the musical darling of the most elevated Parisian salons.

For many years, with the cream of Europe's elite, *le tout* Paris had revelled in the ritual of Venice's Rabelaisian *Carnevale* festivities, and a series of glittering balls was followed assiduously by the journals of style. *Vogue* was so enamoured of *Carnevale* that it became the sole subject of each February's issue. The mid-winter trip to Venice broke the tedium of the cold season and, in the emotionally chaotic post-war years, the sloughing off of inhibitions as a prelude to the privations of Lent was indulged in with particular abandon. For those unable to get to Venice, a round of parties was held in Paris, in private ballrooms. Fancy dress was already popular and, as many of the young now believed that life was pretty worthless, they sought escape in partying with a kind of nihilistic fervour. While reflecting the association of this attitude with the dark undertones of *Carnevale*, Stravinsky's *Pulcinella* brought the fashion for fancy dress out on to the theatrical stage.

If Diaghilev hadn't vetoed it, Picasso would probably have put the female dancers into contemporary dress. And, here, the strong connection between contemporary art and fashion would have been made more explicit. Picasso's new wife, the Ballets Russes dancer Olga Khokhlova, 'had many new robes from Chanel to show', as Stravinsky would report.[18] Olga Khokhlova was already a devotee of Gabrielle's clothes before her marriage to Picasso in 1918 but, as his reputation began to soar, she was far less constrained by cost. And, while Picasso indulged his insatiable appetite for sexual encounters outside marriage, he also indulged his beautiful bourgeois wife's passion for avant-garde fashion, which included much Coco Chanel.

After the premiere of *Pulcinella*, a legendary costume party was thrown for the *beau monde* by the affable and extravagant young Prince Firouz of Persia, then a favourite of Parisian society. (He died not long afterwards, probably at the hand of an assassin.) The relay of party-goers' cars was directed out of Paris by men flashing electric torches at crossroads towards a bogus castle rented by an ex-convict friend of Cocteau's. (The ex-convict's business was illicit nightclubs, and he regularly had to escape capture by the police.)

On this occasion, 'Vast quantities of champagne were drunk. Stravinsky got tight, he went up to the bedrooms and, collecting all the feather pillows, counterpanes and bolsters, hurled them over the banisters into the great hall.'[19] The ensuing pillow-fight was so enthusiastic that the party went on until three the next morning. It was at this party that Gabrielle met Stravinsky once again. Afterwards, he left for the provinces.

Still in festive spirit, Misia and Picasso's friend the 'fiendish social tyrant' Count Etienne de Beaumont gave one of his magnificent entertainments, a regular highlight of the Parisian spring calendar. From early May to the end of June, this included a series of events which took place across the city as the *beau monde* disported itself before its peers, all aching to outdo one another in the outlandishness of their costumes and their behaviour.

Etienne de Beaumont and his wife, Edith, were then at the apex of the Parisian elite. After the war, the young couple had quickly become two of the city's most significant hosts, and events at their spectacular *hôtel particulier*, at the heart of the fashionable seventh *arrondissement*, were noted for their edgy flavour of modernity. *Vogue* cooed, talking of 'dinners and balls without ceasing', and did its part to keep the de Beaumonts in the forefront of everyone's minds. Their friendships and patronage of artists of all kinds, including Picasso, Braque, Satie, Cocteau and Massine, and their reputation for daring and exhibitionism, were heralded at an evening in 1918 at which American jazz was played by black performers, arguably for the first time in France.[20]

The height of each year's entertainment was the de Beaumonts' spring costume ball, a melding of seventeenth-century court masques and the most radical avant-garde. These spectaculars always had a theme, and the one for 1919 was that guests 'leave exposed that part of one's body one finds the most interesting'.[21] No matter how incredible de Beaumont's guests' costumes, he always strove to upstage them, with one extraordinarily androgynous outfit after another, and always designed by him. Etienne de Beaumont liked men; his wife, Edith, liked women; they also had a great fondness for one another.

Gabrielle was asked by de Beaumont to help design some of the costumes for his 1919 spring ball. De Beaumont loved nothing better than accentuating his power through manipulating his friends, and typically kept everyone in suspense about their invitation. He made a point of leaving off two or three who expected one, plus anyone 'in trade'. When Misia discovered, to her embarrassment, that her friend Gabrielle Chanel had not been invited, she protested by refusing to take up her own invitation. Instead, on the night of the ball, she collected up Gabrielle, 'with Sert and Picasso as our escorts . . . and mingled with the chauffeurs crowded in front of the house, to watch the costumed guests make their entrance'. They must have made an odd quartet: Picasso, known to several of the guests, Misia and Sert, well known to most of them, and then Gabrielle, unknown to a great many but recognizable as an immensely stylish woman.

Misia said they had an uproarious time sending up the guests. No matter how up-to-date the upper class's attitudes to the arts, to Bohemia, they still appeared mired in the suffocating and ancient habits of social superiority. Indeed, Etienne de Beaumont had no qualms about using Gabrielle's skills while rejecting her as a guest. It wouldn't be long, however, before he and his wife comprehended

Gabrielle's growing significance and were then all too keen to include her in their suave set.

It is commonly said that, once Gabrielle gained power, she made it her business to subject the *haut monde* to the same condescension she had suffered at their hands. But Gabrielle was a more complex and ambivalent creature than that.

The strangest and most brilliant years[1]

In 1921, after several months at a small Breton seaside resort, Stravinsky had been driven to distraction for lack of stimulation and returned to Paris in search of a house for his chronically ill wife and four children. His financial position was precarious. Recognizing his difficulties, Gabrielle suggested Stravinsky bring his family to stay at Bel Respiro. She had spared no expense in the creation of a beautiful and consoling retreat and, by late September that year, the Stravinsky entourage, including extended family and various domestic and childcare staff, had settled themselves into Bel Respiro's luxury.

Writing to an old friend, Stravinsky sounded tense. Apologizing for the brevity of his letter, he said his nerves were 'in a poor condition'; possibly a reference to the emotional complications developing at the villa.[2] Stravinsky had fallen for Gabrielle. When she voiced concern for Stravinsky's wife, Catherine, his 'very Russian' response was: 'She knows I love you. To whom else, if not her, could I confide something so important?'[3]

Stravinsky took to absenting himself from Bel Respiro and visiting Gabrielle at the Ritz, where she had taken a suite while his family were staying at her house. The composer's originality as a musician was augmented by his brilliant, intense and highly ambitious nature. He was not handsome, but his memorably strong features were an interesting contrast to his notably dandyish appearance. His aloofness added an attractive element to a complex personality. Gabrielle said, 'I liked him . . . because he was very kind, because he often went out with me, and it's very pleasant to learn . . . from people like that.'[4] They went out to clubs, to parties and, once, with Misia and Sert, to the Paris fair. This is borne out by the passport-type photograph they had taken of themselves to commemorate the event.

Gabrielle had little knowledge of music, but Stravinsky set out to teach her. Unsurprisingly, she proved an able pupil. In the process, she developed a passion for Stravinsky's compositions. He, in turn, developed a passion for Gabrielle, and it wasn't long before they were launched into an affair. Gabrielle had been seduced once more by that Slavic cast of mind she seems to have found so irresistible: first Misia, then Diaghilev, and now Igor Stravinsky.

If the composer's nerves were strained by the management of his liaison, his stay at Bel Respiro was, at the same time, very creative. Not only did he finish the brilliant *Concertino for String Quartet*, he also completed *Les Noces villageoises*, a ballet he had struggled with for several years. This was first heard, in 1923, at the magnificent townhouse of Winnaretta Singer, the Princesse de Polignac, and heiress to the vast Singer sewing-machine fortune. Winaretta's highly dedicated musical salon was one of the most powerful in Paris and, on that evening, Stravinsky, Diaghilev, the whole of the Ballets Russes and a number of other guests were present. The princess, who had by then become one of Gabrielle's clients, was asked, 'Why do you not ask Chanel?' and, in her famously imperious manner she answered, 'I don't entertain my trades people.'[5] Winnaretta Singer admired hard-working, self-made women, and her refusal to associate with Gabrielle may well have been partly out of jealousy; she was one of Stravinsky's most important patrons.

We know little of the details but, during Stravinsky's affair with Gabrielle, he was able to complete his memorial tribute to Claude Debussy, *Symphonies d'instruments à vent*, recognized as his most important work of that decade. Its spare and urbane quality has been related to the way post-war reconstruction became an important aspect of all Parisian artistic endeavour. The *Symphonies* are seen as a new departure in Stravinsky's music, for which no label yet existed, and which was at the heart of the modern sensibility.[6] There is no doubt that this brief but intense period at Bel Respiro saw Stravinsky liberated to resolve several longstanding musical problems.

The composer and his lover may have been worlds apart, but one can appreciate the attraction this now quintessentially modern woman had for a man whose musical power had already acted as a force blasting away the last of musical Romanticism. With the end of the war, the intellectual climate had been transformed by a sense of the futility, the sheer irrelevance of so much that had gone before. A fellow composer, Pierre Boulez, would say in the future that 'something radically new, even foreign to Western tradition, had to be found for music to survive, and to enter our contemporary era. The glory of Stravinsky was to have belonged to this extremely gifted generation and to be one of the most creative of them all.'

Seven years after *The Rite of Spring*'s composition, Stravinsky made significant changes in preparation for its new staging. One of the Stravinsky children recalled how the house was often filled with 'the echoes of the piano', resounding with 'music so powerful that it scared us'.[7] In this new version of the great ballet's score, Stravinsky was delineating the outlines of a more urban, cosmopolitan modernism than in its earlier, more folkloric incarnation. This was exactly the atmosphere emanating from Bel Respiro, and from Gabrielle herself. Stravinsky's artistic imagination cannot but have been stimulated by having an affair with a woman who exemplified that very sense of modernity which the composer now incorporated into *The Rite of Spring*.

While the ballet was re-launched by Diaghilev on 15 December 1920, *The Rite*'s scandalous reputation had gone before it. And the air of anticipation was so intense that success was almost inevitable. One admiring critic wrote that audiences had simply needed time to catch up with the modernity of the composer's great work. Gabrielle, whose sponsorship made it possible, would later say, 'I loved the Ballets Russes very much . . . when Diaghilev would tell me, "but it will be very expensive to put this on" . . . I didn't care at all.'[8] Declaring that money was an 'accursed thing' and, because of that, 'it should be squandered,' Gabrielle used her patronage to put into practice her professed belief that the only real point of wealth was its ability 'to make us free'. She not only 'squandered' it on Stravinsky's *Rite of Spring*, she was to become, albeit as discreetly as possible, one of Diaghilev and Stravinsky's major patrons for several years to come.

From its first night, this *Rite of Spring* was heralded as a classic, and Gabrielle was present at the grand supper party Diaghilev gave to celebrate the launch of the new season. Among the guests were the principal dancers, the Picassos, Stravinsky, Misia and the choreographer and principal dancer, Léonide Massine. Massine became overwrought, made himself completely drunk and apparently burned 'Picasso's hand with a cigarette (Picasso never moved)'.[9] Diaghilev had just discovered that Massine, his present lover, was having an affair with one of the female dancers.

Diaghilev's fantastic possessiveness made him incapable of forgiving Massine. And, although his reaction to Massine's affair would drive Diaghilev to an emotional collapse, he was obdurate that his gifted friend would no longer work with the Ballets Russes.

While this episode was particularly dramatic, emotional dramas of one kind or another were not only constantly being played out behind the scenes in the Ballets Russes, they were integral to its existence. Somehow, Diaghilev and his troupe created an ongoing atmosphere of chaos, out of which they made their extraordinary ballets. Picasso's own kind of creative chaos had a very different rhythm, however, and he had vowed he wouldn't work with those mad Russians again. Diaghilev's notoriously unscrupulous passion and conviction were, nevertheless, so persuasive that he had succeeded in luring back the painter, normally intractable once his mind had been made up. Even Diaghilev's fellow Russian, Stravinsky, obviously familiar with the vagaries of the Russian temperament, once declared:

> It is almost impossible to describe the perversity of Diaghilev's entourage . . . I remember a rehearsal in Monaco, at which our pianist suddenly began looking very intensely beyond the music stand.

I followed his gaze to a Monegasque soldier in a tricorne and then asked what the matter was. He answered 'I long to surrender myself to him.'[10]

When Misia had got wind of Gabrielle's philanthropy towards Diaghilev, she felt her role as the sole source of invention, especially if it had to do with Diaghilev and the Ballets Russes, had been subverted. Extraordinarily, she complained to Gabrielle about giving Diaghilev the finances to mount *The Rite*. Then, on hearing of Gabrielle's further generosity, she said, 'I am overcome with sorrow when I think that Stravinsky has accepted money from you.'[11]

Misia was fascinated by Gabrielle, and would remain so for the rest of her life. She understood, with that uncanny intuition, that Gabrielle was different; in her own way, completely original. But she felt that the great Diaghilev was her 'property'. Now that Gabrielle's own philanthropic acts had intruded on Misia's territory, she was incensed.

Gabrielle's creative success and distinctive persona were enlarging her position in Parisian society. While only the most up to date of the *haut monde* was prepared to socialize with this 'dressmaker', she was now meeting some of the most significant musicians, artists and writers then in Paris. With both the *haut monde* and Bohemia curious about her, Gabrielle had allowed herself to be seduced, not by another wealthy socialite, but by an artist. This particular artist, Stravinsky, was no ordinary struggling composer, and Gabrielle's affair with this towering figure was an intriguing and thought-provoking interlude. While sometimes denying the affair, she also said what was clearly closer to the truth for her: that 'he was marvellous.' This relationship confirmed Gabrielle's unusual ability to inhabit those two worlds which are, in many ways, mutually exclusive: the world of society, the *haut monde*, and the world of the artist.

This ability involved a tension at the heart of Gabrielle's creativity, and something she would have to negotiate for the rest of her life. Like all true artists, Gabrielle was obsessed with reality and functionality and, in turn, the peculiar relation of these to beauty. This was the unique position she was forging for herself in fashion: an unobtrusive functionality.

The artist in Gabrielle intuited that, if an artist associates too much with power, the creative spirit can be sterilized. And yet luxury, which was an essential part of what she was promoting, is about exclusivity, itself inextricably associated with power. As a couturier, Gabrielle was dressing the rich and powerful, who used their luxury to exhibit their wealth and power. As an artist of simplicity and minimalism, Gabrielle was running into implicit conflict and confrontation all the time. She worked in the midst of a paradox. Yet, unlike many of her artist friends, Gabrielle was not a rebel whose actions were based on destruction. Her fascination, even obsession, with youth and youthfulness emerged from a different motivation. For Gabrielle, youth was a vital, creative force, *not* a destructive one. In dressing the rich as if they were poor – in frustration, Poiret described this as her *pauvre de luxe* – she was forever walking a tightrope. A tightrope from which, nonetheless, she didn't fall, because, unlike the rebel, Gabrielle was not *attacking* culture.

An image of her has grown up over the years, originating in this period. It evokes a picture of an ignorant, socially meek woman whose powerful personality helped her rise to prominence as a designer, because she had an instinct for the right clothes. Apparently, through Misia Sert's tutelage and introductions, Gabrielle was able to meet and understand how to communicate with the artistic community. This picture is the one painted by Misia Sert for her own aggrandizement. It is an image perpetuated by all subsequent writers on Gabrielle. And it is nonsense. It implies that Gabrielle's association with artists was simply a diverting pastime. In fact, her friendship with these people was crucial both to who she was and to the cultural influence she was already wielding.

Gabrielle did not become a person of artistic significance because Misia made her one. Misia wanted to know Gabrielle because Misia's unerring sense of the creative possibilities in other people picked up on something in Gabrielle that was already *there*; something whose great force Misia described in her memoirs. The image of a slightly pathetic Gabrielle is one based on a veiled snobbery which subtly discounts both her tremendous intelligence and her remarkable character. With that unsettling capacity for self-knowledge, Gabrielle herself signalled how it was that her qualities had made her quite equal to the challenge of formidable success: 'I was self-taught; I learned badly, haphazardly. And yet, when life put me in touch with those who were the most delightful and brilliant people of my age, a Stravinsky, or a Picasso, I neither felt stupid, nor embarrassed.'[12] She went on to say that this was because 'I had worked out on my own that which cannot be taught . . . It is with this that one succeeds.'[13]

When Stravinsky met Gabrielle, she already had achievements behind her that, for the times, must have appeared astounding. Although her modernity was expressed with great finesse, it would, nonetheless, have been seen by many as quite shocking. With a very few exceptions, the only women who were financially independent were those with inherited wealth. Amongst the most prominent of these exceptions were the courtesans and the actresses, who had made their own money – but at what long-term cost? As we have seen, the ability of these women to act with real independence was severely curtailed by a series of powerful social constraints. One of the outstanding contemporary exceptions, regarded as an exciting stimulant, and a very dangerous one at that, was the writer-actress Colette. Colette had flaunted her outrageous difference for several years (as a bisexual who had lived with her female lover, performed semi-nude and in provocative female embrace on stage), had transformed herself, through tremendous hard work, from being an entirely dependent woman to one who was financially independent.

One of the ways Gabrielle expressed her independence was in establishing friendships with the coterie of artists, writers and musicians that was making Paris the seat of modernist art. She felt most at ease with these people, whose work inevitably made them outsiders. For Gabrielle, the artists' lives, and the way they were perceived, were not so very different from the courtesan's, living, as they did, both at the centre and at the edges of society.

As far as we can make out, the day before New Year's Eve 1920, Gabrielle and Stravinsky, and a number of these artists, were present at a party later recorded by Paul Morand. He tells how it 'started again at Chanel's' at rue Cambon. A buffet was laid out in the fitting rooms. A good proportion of upper Bohemia was present; several were to become Gabrielle's lifelong friends. These included Diaghilev's chief dancer Serge Lifar, Satie, the painter André de Segonzac, the sculptor Jacques Lipchitz, who in 1922 would sculpt a bust of Gabrielle, Picasso's fellow founder of Cubism Georges Braque, Picasso himself, the painter Luc-Albert Moreau, Jean Cocteau, his sulky teenage boyfriend Raymond Radiguet, the literary prodigy of the moment, Misia and José Maria Sert, Elise Toulemon (Caryathis), the outrageously modernist writer Blaise Cendrars, and several young composers, who came to be known as Les Six:

> The presence of the Russians gave rise to a rather beautiful party . . . Auric [one of the members of Les Six] cracked his fingers on the piano and there was blood running down the keyboard. Jean [Cocteau] contorted, was initiating the Duchesse de Gramont in a broken Cancan . . . Drieu and Larianoff were shoring up the walls of an attic, Chanel, her legs in the air, was snoring on a sofa. Stravinsky was drinking his ammonia. J.M.S. [José Maria Sert] was taking a swimming lesson in the knocked over overcoats. Massine was doing things in the middle of the parquet floor, very quickly, on his own, then fell like a mass, and Rehbinder . . . was taking vodka for the Volga. Ansermet [Diaghilev's conductor], whose beard Misia wanted to cut, had wrapped a towel around his head, and yours truly went home in the morning with no hat and no tie.[14]

Gabrielle's personal involvement in the great cultural shifts taking place in these years made her a most interesting woman. As someone also involved in the forging of a new world, irrespective of whether he spoke about it or not, Stravinsky cannot have failed to recognize, and find stimulating, this difference in Gabrielle. In years to come, Gabrielle's undignified inclination to represent Stravinsky as younger and less sophisticated than he was may have come about in reaction to her virtual omission from future discussion of this period in his life.

While snobbery was at the heart of the musical establishment's motivation here, jealousy of Gabrielle may well have motivated the woman who would take charge of constructing Stravinsky's legacy. This was Vera Soudeikine, who began her own affair with him shortly after he was rejected by Gabrielle, and who would eventually become Stravinsky's second wife.

Meanwhile, fascinated as Misia was by Gabrielle and Stravinsky, she was also piqued at their affair and, when an opportunity arose, she strove to bring about its ruin. While Gabrielle and Stravinsky's mutual friends could see how deeply he was affected by her, Stravinsky's wife, Catherine, accepted his neglect with almost superhuman grace, concerned above all for his own and her children's welfare.

Misia now put it about that she was horrified lest Stravinsky should divorce his poor wife, so as to marry Gabrielle. Sert next took it upon himself to 'talk' to Stravinsky, informing him that Capel had 'entrusted [Gabrielle] to me; and a man like you . . . is known as a shit'.[15] While Sert 'cultivated the anguish' Stravinsky was suffering, Misia heightened the emotional atmosphere by telling Gabrielle that Stravinsky was distraught, and wanted to know if she would marry him. Having stirred up this drama, the Serts were then highly amused by Stravinsky's distress and spread the story amongst their friends, including Picasso. At last, Gabrielle begged for the drama to stop and for Stravinsky to 'come back'. He did, every day. If Gabrielle did not feel the depth of passion that her Russian lover felt for her, her mind, her emotions and her intelligence had nonetheless become engaged in a new way. Apart from anything else, the compliment of having an intelligent and highly creative man in love with her must have been restorative after her tormented months of mourning.

Stravinsky's very Russian soul was, in itself, an escape for Gabrielle from herself into an exciting mental and emotional landscape. Indeed, she would say, 'Russians fascinated me. Inside everyone from the Auvergne [the place she sometimes chose to claim as her own] there is an Oriental one doesn't realize is there: the Russians revealed the Orient to me.'[16] Gabrielle said that she found 'all Slavs . . . naturally refined'. She must also, in Stravinsky, have identified with the deep seriousness central to the artist's life. For a woman who said, 'Nothing interested me any more . . . nothing at all, only esoteric things,'[17] her love affair with Stravinsky had helped her, secretly still mourning, to feel herself more grounded and alive.

It had also brought a measure of humour, albeit a mad Russian version, back into her life. Someone who was not close enough to be sure about the affair would later write that:

> There were rumors of a great flirtation between her and Stravinsky; nobody knows how far it went. All I know is that once, after one of her large dinner parties in the garden of the Ritz, she asked for a glass of water and Stravinsky, in a playful mood, or maybe in a fit of jealousy, filled a large glass with vodka and brought it to her. Coco drank the strong alcohol practically in one gulp, stood up, and fell on the floor. She had to be carried to her bedroom.[18]

Finally, when the Ballets Russes was leaving for a tour of Spain, Stravinsky asked Gabrielle to come with him. She said she would follow soon. Whether Gabrielle really intended going is uncertain, because she allowed herself to be waylaid by circumstance, and Stravinsky was to wait for her in vain.

Dmitri Pavlovich

On 9 February 1921, not long after Stravinsky had left Paris with Diaghilev and the Ballets Russes, a young man recorded an evening with Gabrielle at the singer Marthe Davelli's, with whom Gabrielle and Arthur had picnicked on the beach at St-Jean-de-Luz in 1915. Our diarist said of Gabrielle that he 'hadn't seen her for ten years'. Commenting that she 'didn't say a word about Boy Capel', he said she was a most agreeable companion and was almost unchanged in looks. Gabrielle drove him back home, 'and we suddenly found ourselves on an amazingly friendly footing.'[1]

The diarist was Grand Duke Dmitri Pavlovich, grandson to Tsar Alexander II and cousin to the Tsar Nicholas. No previous biographer of Gabrielle has had access to Dmitri Pavlovich's diaries. But, with them, not only has it been possible to revise important aspects of their ensuing relationship but also to trace the course of a famed yet mysterious trip they made together not long after their meeting.

At thirty, Dmitri Pavlovich had already experienced a life of great upheaval. His mother had died at his birth and his father's remarriage, eleven years later, had led to his banishment, so that Dmitri and his sister Marie were placed with their aunt and uncle. Grand Duke Sergei loved his young charges, but the relationship became strained as they grew older. When this uncle was assassinated by an anarchist's bomb in 1905, Dmitri was sent to a military academy; he was fourteen. The men he loved – his educational supervisor, his father and the tsar – through personality or circumstance were all to thwart Dmitri's need for a man he could unreservedly admire. As an intelligent young patriot, he combined traditionalism with what he saw as open-mindedness. Although wishing to serve his country in some significant way, Dmitri also felt inadequate to the task through a lack of self-assurance.

In 1916, he was one of those involved in the conspiracy to murder the 'holy man' Grigori Rasputin, whose hold over the tsarina had become deplorable. After hours of black farce, the assassins rolled Rasputin up in a curtain, tied it with rope and then dumped him in the river Neva through a hole in the ice. When discovered, Rasputin had survived poisoning and gunshot wounds, finally to die by drowning. Dmitri's efforts at improving the situation in his country were largely frustrated. Camouflaging his shyness and any depth of character behind his good looks and the persona of a charming playboy, he always found it difficult to be taken seriously.

Rasputin's murder led to Dmitri's exile to an army unit on the Persian front. Thus, when most of the Russian royal family – including his father, brother and aunt – was murdered by the Bolsheviks in 1918, Dmitri was one of those few who escaped the slaughter. Throughout his life, great privilege had served him ill in his loss of every figure of significance, save his sister, Grand Duchess Marie. A life already filled with such loss may have inhibited Dmitri in the formation of close attachments aside from his sister.

Making his way to Britain from Tehran at the end of the war, Dmitri was permitted to take up residence. Here, he studied, in preparation for his possible future role as tsar. He also continued socializing; with a noted predilection for actresses and ballerinas. Dmitri's sister described his life before the Revolution:

He had had a large fortune with very few responsibilities . . . unusually good looks coupled with great charm, and he also had been the recognized favourite of the Tsar . . . there was no young prince in Europe more socially conspicuous than he was, both in his own country and abroad. He walked a golden path . . . His destiny was almost too dazzling.[2]

Dmitri's breathtakingly privileged and yet isolating upbringing had left him badly equipped to make the changes necessary for a successful new life in the West. Like most of his fellow Russian aristocrats, Dmitri had not only lost virtually his entire wealth in the Revolution, he had also lost caste, to a devastating degree.

Marie described the aristocratic émigrés' social lives: 'the atmosphere that settled down around us had almost nothing to do with the people or the interests of the country we were living in; we led an existence apart.'[3] All had lost family, and narrowly avoided death. And, while they had usually been reduced to near-poverty, they didn't speak of their losses or 'the harrowing tales of our escape from Russia. Everyone tried to make the best of his present situation . . . We managed even to be gay in a detached, inconsequential sort of way.'[4]

While Dmitri appeared to have adjusted to his new life, it was as if the energy involved in escaping (and losing) one's country had left him, like many fellow émigrés, so emotionally reduced that he was unable, really, to begin his life again. Although many were still young, they had effectively withdrawn, living an impoverished version of their old lives. A few even allowed their transformation into celebrity pastiches of their previous selves: modelling clothes for couturiers or film acting, their noble blood touted as the draw. Only recently, Dmitri Pavlovich had turned down a lucrative film contract with Hollywood.

Meanwhile, in 1919, he had arrived in Paris from England, where he had pursued the beautiful 42-year-old American heiress Consuelo Vanderbilt, ex-wife to the Duke of Marlborough. Consuelo Vanderbilt described Dmitri as 'an exceptionally handsome man, fair and sleek with long blue eyes in a narrow face, he had fine features, and the stealthy walk of a wild animal, moving with the same balanced grace'.[5] But Consuelo quickly thought better of this briefest of liaisons and made a happy marriage to Jacques Balsan. Balsan was the famed aviator elder brother of Etienne, Gabrielle's lover from Royallieu days.

For many years, it has been said that Gabrielle met Dmitri

Pavlovich through Marthe Davelli, at Biarritz, in 1920. Thanks to Dmitri's diaries,[6] we now know that, while Gabrielle and Dmitri did indeed meet through Marthe Davelli, it was in 1921 and in Paris, not Biarritz; and also, Marthe Davelli's 1921 dinner was not their first meeting. As Dmitri's diary records, they had met ten years earlier, in 1911. No doubt this was on one of Dmitri's periodic visits to his father, Grand Duke Paul, living at St-Cloud, outside Paris.

Dmitri's lineage, his gracious manner and fine looks had given him an immediate entrée to the *haut monde* and, at twenty – in 1911 – he was already known for his sympathetic and carefree personality. He and Gabrielle would have met through Arthur's connections. As a fine horseman – Dmitri represented Russia in the 1912 Olympics – he may also have ridden to polo with Arthur and Etienne when in France.

The most significant aspect of Dmitri's diaries, however, is its revision of Gabrielle's relationship with him. What little has been known derives from the older Gabrielle's fairly jaundiced comments to Paul Morand and others, implying that it was no more than her allowing this handsome young nobleman to bed her. Gabrielle's comments have successfully concealed from us what Dmitri's diary reveals: how vulnerable she was at the beginning of their affair.

The day after their meeting at Marthe Davelli's dinner, Dmitri bumped into Gabrielle and Marthe once again, with what he called 'all the old crowd'.[7] Following 'an amazingly boring dinner' at the Ritz, Dmitri spied Gabrielle dining there, and invited her back to his apartment, where 'she remained until four a.m.'[8] The next morning, Dmitri's tennis suffered as a result, then the couple lunched together again. Seeing them together on several occasions, the gossips set to work putting around word of their trysts.

Misia and Diaghilev 'adored gossip and had talents for intrigue that were to blossom alarmingly'.[9] Misia had rapidly discovered the identity of Gabrielle's new lover and fired off a spiteful telegram to Diaghilev and Stravinsky in Spain. 'Coco is a little shop girl who prefers Grand Dukes to artists,' it read, and Diaghilev famously sent it back by return to Gabrielle, saying that under *no* circumstances should she now appear in Spain, because Stravinsky wanted to kill her. Gabrielle was incensed at Misia's telegram, refused to believe her protestations of innocence, and didn't speak to her for weeks. This episode signalled, definitively, the end of Gabrielle and Stravinsky's affair.

Gabrielle's chance meeting with the young duke was thus the unexpected route by which she stepped back from Stravinsky's emotional fervour. Their affair had been stimulating and life affirming for her, but it had also become something of a burden. Gabrielle's well-concealed yet underlying state of mourning left her unable, or unwilling, to be involved at Stravinsky's level of intensity. His jealous rage at her rejection must have been compounded by the knowledge that he had not only been thrown over for a younger fellow Russian, but also by a member of the royal family.

Meanwhile, Gabrielle and Dmitri continued their daily assignations, until a week later, when he 'stopped by the Ritz to say goodbye', en route for a few weeks' stay with friends in Copenhagen. Sir Charles and Lady Lucia Marling had been the ambassadorial couple in Tehran who had looked after Dmitri there in exile. Sir Charles was now British ambassador to Denmark.

After this pleasant trip, Dmitri went to Berlin. There he met with ex-tsarist officers and aristocrats, who hailed him as the tsar-in-waiting of a new imperial Russia. Dmitri was rather ambivalent about accepting this role, and claimed that he was taken aback at his reception. He was evidently not a particularly adept tactician, for on returning to Paris he was left berating himself for having co-operated in any way: the Russian press in France and Britain were lambasting him for having put himself forward as pretender to the throne.

One of Dmitri's relatives, the Grand Duchess Victoria, even travelled to the French capital to inform him that it was her husband, Cyril, who was the rightful tsar, and that Dmitri should be 'shot as a traitor for having presumed to play such a role'.[10] Dmitri was appalled at the vehemence of this faction within the Parisian Russian community, so from this point on he did indeed give up any pretensions to the Russian throne. The episode left him very low, and it was in this state of emotional exhaustion that he met Gabrielle once again.

Always reluctant to reveal his feelings, Dmitri appears to have found it easier to confide in women than in men. He confessed some of his strains to Gabrielle and said that, until things calmed down, the best thing would be for him to take a trip to London. His diary records that 'as a result of ardent persuasion' from Gabrielle, however, he decided instead to go to 'Menton [in the south of France] or Monte Carlo and bask with her in the sun'.[11] Gabrielle insisted 'so sweetly and touchingly' that she would be making the trip because it would be good for Dmitri. Although he was not entirely without finances, it sat badly with the young man's conscience that he knew Gabrielle would be the one largely funding this holiday. In the end, however, he allowed himself to be persuaded.

Gabrielle decided she would buy a new car for their expedition. And one is reminded of how her considerable wealth could now guide her decisions. She went with Dmitri to one of the city's most select car showrooms and after a very brief inspection bought a Rolls-Royce convertible, a Silver Cloud. With Dmitri delighting in how 'splendidly' the car drove, they took a trial run to Rouen, stayed the night and returned the next day. They parted but, later that day, Dmitri called in at the Ritz to see Gabrielle and was embarrassed when people thought his face was red because he was drunk. He was sunburnt from the open-topped-car drive. Dmitri was not impervious to gossip, or the fact that a compatriot, who had got wind of his plans, tried to dissuade him from leaving with Gabrielle for the Riviera.

Nevertheless, in somewhat defiant mood, they secretly set off. This clandestine atmosphere set the tone for the following three weeks. It also dictated the lovers' initial plan, to stay at Menton, where it was unlikely they would meet anyone they knew. As it turned out, the hotel fell well below their expectations, Gabrielle had 'horrible nightmares' and they made for the Riviera Palace at

Monte Carlo, one of the most luxurious hotels on the Riviera. Gabrielle's personal maid and Dmitri's valet now arrived. The kindly giant Piotr had been Dmitri's servant for years, serving him devotedly throughout his insecure childhood and youth and then following him into exile in Persia.

Gabrielle and Dmitri soon settled into a routine, where Gabrielle rose late, Dmitri played morning golf, they joined each other for lunch and then took scenic tours in the open-topped Rolls. En route they often discovered some little church or ancient village, such as the tiny and beautiful Coaraze, high up in the hills above Nice. At first they ate in their suite of rooms but, growing less wary of being spotted, they graduated to the hotel dining room and then to a couple of restaurants. Gabrielle and Dmitri were both discerning about food, and one of their favourite restaurants was the eminently fashionable Ciro's, situated in the only part of Monte Carlo as yet regarded as sufficiently fashionable for society. This quarter was within a hundred yards or so of the central Galerie Charles III and the casino, where Gabrielle and Dmitri could be found most evenings; Dmitri was an inveterate gambler, winning – and losing – large sums.

He described how Gabrielle did 'everything she could' to draw him out, anxious in case this tranquil life should bore him. To the contrary, the calm rhythms of their routine combined with Gabrielle's 'rare goodness' soothed Dmitri and revived his state of mind. Although admitting to himself that their relationship was 'as strange as can be', he delighted in Gabrielle's cheerful companionship, appreciating her 'good spirits' and 'surprising sweetness'. And, during several weeks in each other's company, Gabrielle helped Dmitri to pull himself together with such success that he wrote, 'It would have been impossible to choose a better friend for that moment in time than dearest Coco.'

Dmitri wrote that he was not in love with Gabrielle and that they never discussed anything to do with their future, but he became devoted to her, and was touched by her loving treatment of him. In this way, his diary entries act as a powerful correction to the typical portrayal of this relationship, where Dmitri is the lovesick young nobleman mooning around Gabrielle, the predatory Amazon.

Dmitri's diary for this period displays a noticeable preoccupation with 'discovery' by his peers. And, while concerned lest Gabrielle, whom he found 'surprisingly observant', should be troubled by this preoccupation, he consoled himself with the thought that she felt the same way. Despite the greater likelihood of Dmitri's reputation being compromised than Gabrielle's, there was also nothing new in a grand duke spending time with his lover. Above all, Dmitri's reluctance to be spotted with Gabrielle stems from his concern not to be seen as a kept man. Gabrielle's wealth was now common knowledge, but so, also, was the impoverishment of Russian royalty. The greater mystery is why Gabrielle herself should have feared gossip and 'the gaze of acquaintances'.

Gabrielle's new-found wealth was in part predicated upon the creation of a reputation as a public figure. But, while she would never let gossip have any effect upon her affairs, her coyness about being seen with Dmitri may have been related to her very recent lover, Stravinsky, finding out more details of her new liaison. Another explanation for Gabrielle's apprehension about being spotted with Dmitri could well have been related to her new status. She had become a figure whose life was lived – increasingly, like Dmitri's – under regular public scrutiny. The last months had left her emotionally exhausted, and the interlude on the Riviera was a moment in which she tried, temporarily, to recapture a life that was private.

When Arthur Capel had told Gabrielle of his plans to marry, it had both reduced her emotionally while also obliging her to move out of his apartment and live alone. Since then, however, she had been schooling herself in the ways of the modern woman, one best described as emancipated. Under the circumstances in which Gabrielle found herself with Dmitri, she was luxuriating in the ability to dictate her own life, enjoying a kind of autonomy that the vast majority of contemporary women couldn't possibly have contemplated. While remaining an outsider, Gabrielle was now able, if she chose, to live with the freedom of the *haut monde*, yet without some of its burdens. She had achieved the autonomy of the successful courtesans, but with one crucial difference: Gabrielle was now financing herself from work unrelated to whosoever was her present lover. She had achieved her goal: she was now genuinely independent.

Notwithstanding the vein of sadness coursing through Gabrielle's life, her natural optimism and vitality were, in the end, unquenchable. Not only did these qualities come to the fore in this interlude with Dmitri Pavlovich but, for the first time, one also notices something else. However vulnerable she might feel and whatever the sensitivity with which she behaved, Gabrielle also had the upper hand. This is not to say that, in the past, she had simply been a passive female, subject to male whims. Gabrielle's story in relation to men was never as simple as that. Indeed, when she chose to reveal her charm and charisma, many a man was seduced by it. With all her force of character, Gabrielle remained a very feminine woman, who did not, in theory, want to rule any man.

Whatever Dmitri and Gabrielle's private concerns, their leisurely weeks on the Riviera had been a refuge of order and tranquillity for Dmitri, and balm to Gabrielle's much-troubled spirit. Their holiday had passed off without mishap, with the exception of one dramatic event as they drove back to Paris.

When the time came to leave the south, they decided to break up their journey en route to Paris by stopping along the way. With the Rolls-Royce re-tuned, they planned to drive along the Riviera, turn inland after Marseille and then follow the old road on up to Paris. Dmitri was keeping an eye on the calendar, because he wanted to be in the capital in time for his beloved sister's birthday. Up early on 27 April, the travellers were met by unpleasant weather: it was cold and wet and, as they left Monte Carlo, the road was very slippery. Taking the 'low road' to Nice and Cannes, Dmitri drove slowly and with great care.

As a result of what he called a 'wretched misunderstanding', they found themselves driving right past the place where Arthur had been killed a year and a half earlier. Dmitri described seeing a cross marking the spot where the accident had taken place. (It has only recently become known that this was erected by Gabrielle.) Dmitri was mortified at this most unfortunate incident, and recorded its dreadful effect upon Gabrielle. She became very quiet, 'frightfully melancholy', and they drove on through the driving rain in complete silence. Meanwhile, as a driver of some experience, Dmitri couldn't help but find the apparent cause of Arthur's accident mysterious, noting to himself that not only was the road at that point completely level, there were no ditches alongside it either. Although Dmitri and Gabrielle tried to push the misery of this episode aside, it hung heavily upon them for the rest of the day. On reaching Marseille, they retired for the night very early.

The strength of Gabrielle's reaction, on seeing once again the place where Arthur had died, reveals how little she had recovered from his loss. As few of us are prepared to expend more than a minimal amount of imagination on the thoughts and feelings of others, taking what they offer us pretty much at face value, almost everyone had chosen to be convinced by Gabrielle's pose. Her real feelings were hidden behind that great vitality. Long ago, in her miserable childhood, her intelligence and defiance had taught her the habit of self-protection, of revealing herself to almost no one.

Bearing this guardedness in mind, while most had believed her relationship with Arthur was rather insecure, amongst their inner circle there was an implicit understanding that their union was a profound one. Captivated by Gabrielle's allure, her knowingness, her intelligence and gaiety, Arthur had also been struck by her seriousness and her sheer, breathtaking force; qualities all leavened by her great femininity. But it was that very force, which was making her so successful, that had led to Arthur's loss of courage and rejection of her. He made, he believed, a simpler choice: Diana – and came to regret it.

Was that the ultimate cause of Arthur's accident, as he had driven along the Cannes road towards a Christmas with his sister? There was no satisfactory resolution to his dilemma: staying with Diana, or going to Gabrielle. Had Arthur's tiredness at the end of that long journey south been the last factor heightening his overwrought state of mind, so that he brought about his own death? The possibility of his suicide must have occurred to Gabrielle when she had sat weeping beside the wreck of her dead lover's car.

The following day, Gabrielle and Dmitri left old Marseille behind them. Marvelling at Aix-en-Provence, Avignon and Orange, they drove on, reaching Lyon for the night. Next morning, they altered their proposed route, making a long detour to Vichy. The subsequent entries in Dmitri's diary show that, while *he* was unaware of it, there was actually nothing random about this next leg of their journey. Gabrielle was giving the impression of leaving things to chance; in reality, she had made a plan.

As they left Lyon, the sun shone, and they drove with the Silver Cloud's roof rolled down. After lunch, they abandoned the major road and drove out 'across country'. With the Rolls impressively negotiating the winding road through high and remote terrain, Dmitri noted their frequent stops to admire the drama of the Auvergne landscape, where the peaks are often snow covered. On reaching Vichy, he was less impressed, finding it flat and unattractive. The weather had turned, and the resort was mournful in its dearth of tourists. Thanks to the low season, Dmitri was grateful that they met no one there they knew. On a desultory walk around the town, little could Dmitri have known that his companion had a clear agenda: she was secretly reliving her youth. As far as we know, Gabrielle hadn't returned to Vichy since her failed bid for the stage over fifteen years earlier. How her life had changed.

The next day, she suggested a trip to Thiers, the centre of the French cutlery trade since the fifteenth century. She must have had to sell this detour to Dmitri with some enthusiasm, for Thiers is almost twenty-five miles in the opposite direction from their final destination, Paris. But Gabrielle was now in earnest; she was intent on travelling through the terrain of her childhood.

While Dmitri innocently noted Thiers's reputation, Gabrielle was re-living her memories of her father buying his scissors and knives there, for re-sale throughout the Midi. Dmitri recorded that, after a bad meal they 'made a little excursion around the area'.[12] First navigating the tortuous mountainous roads through the chestnut and pine forests, in their 'little excursion' Gabrielle *must* next have suggested they follow the river Dore just six miles further south to Courpière, her mother's birthplace.

How strange it must have been to see the place where Gabrielle's mother had left her and her siblings in search of her renegade husband; the place where Gabrielle had played those lonely childhood games in the churchyard. Gabrielle gave away nothing to Dmitri about the significance of this remote Auvergne backwater, but her thoughts must have been brimful of the past. Driving in one of the world's most luxurious cars and supporting herself as one of the world's most avant-garde designers, she was the personification of female modernity. She was being sought out by the Parisian elite, could name among her friends some of the most famous artists, writers and musicians of the day, and now her travelling companion was a grand duke. Did Gabrielle feel triumphant, remembering those Courpière relations who had said she was useless, and who had pitied 'poor Jeanne' for following that no good Albert Chanel around? Jeanne, the woman her daughter defended with the comment: 'Hadn't she at least married the man she loved?'

Gabrielle had not only travelled way beyond that humiliation, she had also outgrown the mindset burdening her with those judgements. And while, from her origins, she drew her stubborn and forthright tenacity, for the rest, Gabrielle Chanel had long since outgrown her roots. Ironically, it was that inherited capacity for endurance that had permitted her to make the leap from a fantasized self-transformation to one sustained by reality and hard work. These were the two opposing yet complementary aspects of Gabrielle's nature. Like any artist of calibre, she possessed an outlandish imagination, which had allowed her to reinvent first herself, and then the wardrobes of the female population; she also possessed the essential counterpart of a vivid imagination: practicality.

Gabrielle would say, 'People say I'm an Auvergnat. There's nothing of the Auvergnat in me. Nothing, nothing! My mother was one. In that part of the world . . . I was thoroughly unhappy . . . I fed on sorrow and horror, and regularly thought of dying.'[13] How Gabrielle had hated her childhood. Meanwhile, on that very day, 2 May 1921, while she chose her secret return to the distant places of her childhood, on the other side of the world, one of her closest childhood companions reached a mournful conclusion.

From Canada, Gabrielle's sister, Antoinette, had continued sending despairing letters to Gabrielle and Adrienne, and they had continued urging her to persevere. But Antoinette was entirely unsuited to her new life. In response, Gabrielle had recently dispatched a young Argentinian with a letter of recommendation to Antoinette's father-in-law. The reasons are lost with the letter, but he may have been an emissary, sent to discover the extent of Antoinette's plight. Antoinette found the young man entertaining and, within days of his departure for Buenos Aires, she had fled her in-laws' household, leaving everything behind her.

Whatever precipitated her departure, once Antoinette arrived in Buenos Aires, her movements are a mystery. All we know is that any hopes she might have had of beginning again were disappointed, because, on 2 May, she gave up the struggle and took her own life. This was almost certainly with an overdose of drugs. Until the recent discovery of Antoinette's death certificate,[14] the story has usually been told that she had already died, a year earlier, in 1920, a casualty of the post-war Spanish flu epidemic.[15] Gabrielle and Adrienne possibly never knew the real cause of Antoinette's death. On the other hand, they might have fabricated the Spanish flu story, so as to conceal her despairing end and avoid the stigma of another family suicide.

Gabrielle's response to her sister's suicide is nowhere recorded.

But Antoinette had been part of Gabrielle and Adrienne's under-taking to transform their lives, and she had worked hard for her older sister. She had benefited, but, in reality, Antoinette had only taken on the trappings of their new lives. She hadn't possessed Adrienne's prudence, which would finally lead to her marriage to the man she loved. Nor did Antoinette have the inspired, rule-breaking originality of her sister, Gabrielle. In the end, poor Antoinette lacked their tenacity and force of personality. She nei-ther succeeded in marrying 'above herself' nor in making herself into a truly New Woman, dependent upon no one but herself. Perhaps there was no connection, but for many years Gabrielle didn't present a wedding dress at the end of her show, a tradition all the couture houses followed.

Gabrielle saw Adrienne, and occasionally her brothers, who peri-odically called on her in rue Cambon. She regularly sent one of them a cheque, and looked after André, her dead sister Julia-Berthe's son, mostly away at boarding school. Aside from this, Gabrielle now had very little to do with her extended family. With Antoinette's death, one more connection with her childhood was lost, and she was a little more alone. Years later, in referring to her relations, Gabrielle would say that no one in her family grew old: 'I don't know how I escaped the slaughter.'[16]

As Gabrielle made her secret journey through her past with Dmitri, their sojourn was concluding. Dmitri would write that Gabrielle was 'sad that tomorrow our trip comes to an end'. With many miles ahead of them, on the final morning they were up early and drove through rain, then thick snow, until eventually halting for coffee to warm up. Setting off again, Dmitri wrote that 'the highway was covered in snow, and the countryside looked Russian. It was rather sad and moving.'[17] The weary travellers finally reached Paris, where Dmitri would again ask his diary why it was they had made that detour around Vichy.

Laughing off rumours of marriage to Gabrielle during his 'adven-ture', Dmitri was less sanguine about the rumour put around in their absence that she was keeping him. He did nonetheless go and see her the following evening. Moved by her inability to conceal 'her sadness that our excursion had come to an end', Dmitri didn't leave her suite until two the next morning. The following afternoon, 'She had cheered up but was nonetheless very touching.'[18]

The Lucky N°5

Work for Gabrielle had long since become a refuge and the place where she could put her feelings aside. She would say that work gave her energy. She had endured the emotional torments of the last two years or so and her creativity seemed unstoppable. The countesses Rehbinder, de Castries, Sjorza, de Noailles, Doubazow and Moustiers, the princesses Radziwill and Murat, Mme Miguel Yturbe (wife of one of Gabrielle's earlier admirers), the Hon. Mrs Anthony Henley, Mlle Gabrielle Davelli, Mlle Cécile Sorel, Mlle Gabrielle Dorziat and Misia Sert were only a selection of the society women and celebrities making their way to Gabrielle's salon door.

In autumn 1920, *Vogue* had enthused over Gabrielle's 'perfect taste . . . and her extraordinary perception of the woman of today', and discussed the variety of Gabrielle's offerings. A particular cape, then the thing, was 'a very smart affair of conservative lines but elaborated with a design in quilting which covers most of its surface . . . this is both warm and decorative'; then there were 'evening wraps, enveloping capes, superb manteaux of rich-toned velvets embroidered with gold and enriched with otter or sable, very simple in line', and gowns of lace and tulle, and 'sheath frocks': 'The embroideries which she uses are all designed for her, and her laces are unusual and distinctive.'

Over and again throughout these years, the magazines advised that, because at Chanel there was what *Vogue* described as an 'avoidance of extremes, each model at this house suits an amazing variety of types'. Saying that, while Gabrielle followed principles that could at first be thought uninteresting – practicality and simplicity – the magazine admired her unerring ability to create 'many new effects each season'.[1]

Speaking of 'eminently wearable and well-designed costumes', there were 'tailored suits in black, beige or grey'. And here we note the colours that were to become Chanel trademarks establishing their place in her canon. In addition to the tailored suit, there was 'the coat-frock, where the frocks cling without side-seams and close at the sides with embroidery or buttons'. Other frocks had loose backs 'combined with a closely fitting front which follows the lines of the figure and emphasizes the absence of the corset'.

It was Poiret, not Gabrielle (as is often said), who first attempted to dispense with the corset. While apparently representing greater freedom, Gabrielle's much straighter, shape-revealing twenties chemises, often made in diaphanous materials, would have been unthinkable for most women without a corset of some kind. Gabrielle may have been fairly ruthless in her attitudes to women who weren't as slim as her, but she was also business minded enough to realize that not everyone had her girlish figure. Consequently, she sold corsets. For Gabrielle, they had the dual purpose of not only pulling in any 'excess' plumpness but also flattening the bust. She had set out to design because she thought contemporary dress unsuitable for the new times; her clothes were in essence made for herself. Thus Gabrielle's designs looked far the best on androgynous figures like her own.

Gabrielle's vacation with Dmitri Pavlovich had helped her still unsteady sense of equilibrium and, in this improved state, she was better able to put into effect one of the most important undertakings of her life. At some point between the previous autumn, and now, the spring of 1921, Gabrielle had met another young man. His name was Ernest Beaux. Beaux was not to become her lover. Instead, with Gabrielle, he would create Chanel N°5, destined to become the most famous perfume in the world. While so much about the first half of Gabrielle's life is cloaked in uncertainty, the story of this most iconic of all perfumes – created at around this time – is a major factor in the construction of her myth. A myth, of course, is not the same thing as history, and the *history* of Chanel N°5 proves stubbornly resistant to reconstruction.

Yet N°5's appearance is also typical of an enduring element in the allure of all great perfumes: the secrecy surrounding its ingredients and the manner of its creation. The provenance of any fine perfume is better thought of with reference to the old alchemists, who, in the manner of all secret societies, ensured the idea of exclusivity by keeping their 'knowledge' hidden. The alchemist's exalted claims were never made by the perfumers, but there were parallels. Certainly, the perfumers understood that they dealt in an art where, while their methods were practical ones, the process and its results were often intangible.

Whatever has been written or said to the contrary, it is not actually known how or when Gabrielle Chanel met the gifted young perfumer Ernest Beaux. Even more significantly, no one really knows exactly when Chanel N°5 was created. In fact, from its two creators' first meeting to the perfume's inception, its production and its very first sales, Chanel N°5 is shrouded in mystery. But the main reason for this is because, from the outset, Gabrielle and Beaux understood that this was crucial.

The story has traditionally been told in the following way. Gabrielle had decided she wanted to have a perfume as an accompaniment to her clothes and, during the summer of 1920, Dmitri Pavlovich introduced her to Ernest Beaux, whom he had known through Beaux's connection with the Russian court. Together, Gabrielle and Beaux now set out to create Gabrielle's perfume. By early 1921, Chanel N°5 was in production and being launched. The month is often given as May. However, remembering that Dmitri's diary tells us it wasn't until a year later – February 1921 – that he himself met Gabrielle, it is almost impossible that Gabrielle and Beaux could have made, packaged and launched their perfume between, approximately, February and May of that year. Either Dmitri did not introduce Chanel to Beaux or, if he did, the perfume had to have been launched later.

While Chanel has become one of the world's most famous 'brands', without N°5's high profile, most of us might barely have heard of Coco Chanel, or her part in revolutionizing women's lives. Although Gabrielle had already begun to formulate elements of her myth by 1921, it was in turn furthered by the creation of Chanel N°5. Both have been perpetuated by the Chanel Company. With N°5's given date of creation – 1921 – mired in uncertainty, who was Ernest Beaux, the man who helped make the first Chanel perfume such an outstanding success?

Beaux's father was one of the directors of the French perfume company Alphonse Rallet & Co., purveyors of fragrance to the Russian court. Ernest joined the company, worked under its enlightened perfumery director and was encouraged to explore both new ingredients for perfume, and contemporary art and culture. He was already celebrated as a perfumer when the Revolution drove him and his colleagues to leave Russia.

The Rallet Company based itself outside Grasse, in the south of France, and Beaux arrived in late 1919 – having lost everything – to begin his life again. Beaux was noted for his experimentation with synthetic components, including synthetic aldehydes. (Aldehydes are those organic compounds present in various natural materials, for example, rose oil and citrus essence.) His famed early fragrance, Bouquet de Catherine, probably created in 1913, most likely used synthetic aldehydes, which would be essential in the development of Chanel N°5. Between 1919 and 1920, Beaux further experimented on the Bouquet de Catherine formula.

In 1946, he would give a lecture in which he described his own contribution to Chanel N°5. Questioned about its creation, he said it was 'in 1920 exactly, upon my return from the war'. We remember that, in fact, he returned from the war in 1919. Beaux then said that N°5 was launched 'at the time of the Cannes Conference'; but this was held in early January 1922. So he has now told us that Chanel N°5 was launched in both 1921 *and* 1922. In the end, all we know is that, at some point in 1920, or 1921, Beaux was introduced to Gabrielle, and they began developing the new fragrance. Like

Gabrielle herself, the true provenance of N°5 has been converted into a myth.

Despite Misia Sert's urge to take credit for the triumphs of her 'protégée' Gabrielle, the following story is, however, plausible. Lucien Daudet, secretary to the Empress Eugénie, wife to Napoléon III, had brought Misia an astonishing beauty formula he had unearthed in the papers of the empress. From the hand of the perfume maker to the sixteenth-century Queen Catherine de Médicis, consort to Henri II of France, was the recipe for the renowned toilet water, The Secret of the Medici. Neither exactly a perfume nor a normal cosmetic cream, this was an essence said miraculously to repel the signs of ageing. Misia's claim that she saw the formula's possibilities, immediately took it to Gabrielle and proposed that she launch a toilet water based upon the recipe is probably correct. As Gabrielle's name 'was then on everyone's lips, it was in itself a guarantee of success'.[2]

Gabrielle liked Misia's idea, bought the formula and, according to Misia, they set to work, 'painstakingly experimenting with a very severe bottle, ultra-simple, almost pharmaceutical, but in the Chanel style and with the elegant touch she gave to everything'.[3] Here, of course, we are meant to see Misia's hand in the earliest version of the unmistakable Chanel N°5 bottle.

Misia said that, within weeks, Gabrielle had launched L'Eau de Chanel, and that 'it succeeded far beyond our wildest hopes. It was unbelievable.'[4] Her story is borne out by a document – in the Chanel archives – for a skincare product called L'Eau de Chanel signed and dated by Misia: July 1919. This Eau de Chanel may well have been a crucial step on the road to N°5.

Gabrielle had a preoccupation with cleanliness amounting almost to a neurosis, and she loathed it when someone didn't 'smell good'. Her admiration for the *grandes cocottes* in part stemmed from their pleasant fragrance. By contrast, speaking of society women, Gabrielle would say, 'Ah yes, those women dressed in ball gowns, whose photographs we contemplate with a touch of nostalgia, were dirty . . . They were dirty. Are you surprised? But that's the way it was.'[5] While all society women were not, of course, unwashed, Gabrielle's sense of smell *was* hypersensitive. Decrying this 'unwashed' upper class, she also abhorred the simple flower fragrances she said were used to camouflage their bad habits.

She would say:

> I, who love woman, wanted to give her clothes in which she could be comfortable, in which she could drive a car, yet at the same time clothes that emphasized her femininity, clothes that flowed with her body. A woman is closest to being naked when she is well dressed. I wanted to give her a perfume, but an artificial perfume . . . I don't want rose or lily of the valley; I want a perfume that is *compound*.[6]

Gabrielle wanted a perfume that scented a clean female body, a fragrance that through its subtle olfactory message completed her picture of a young, forward-looking woman who was independent, fashionable and desirable. Importantly, she also wanted a scent that would last.

With very few exceptions, fragrance had been the province of the perfumers, who also sold them. One rare exception, Paul Poiret, had long since developed a beauty and perfume business in tandem with his couture. But, while he had been well in advance of his times, Poiret now lagged behind, and it was Gabrielle's star that was in the ascendant. She was a master at capitalizing on her own and others' intuitions, and the practical sources of her success would always derive from combining her singular creative abilities with her talents as an entrepreneur. This always involved having around her a small group, usually invisible to the public, who supported and inspired her. This group of people was fairly fluid, but a handful remained with Gabrielle for many years. In this instance, the person acting as a catalyst for her latest project was the inspired perfumer Ernest Beaux.

It might at first appear that Gabrielle's introduction of clothes that were costly and simple was the exact opposite of what she now sought in a perfume: a composite refinement. But, for Gabrielle, these two ideas were entirely complementary. She was never in any doubt that her 'simple' clothes were actually artificial, and would say 'A dress is artificial, fabricated.' In the same way, she believed a perfume shouldn't try and emulate nature, it should be a *synthesis* of the natural. Thus her perfume would be a distillation of complex elements in a bottle of refined simplicity.

Misia said that Gabrielle had 'the genius' to see their Eau de Chanel as the beginning of something, and that its success gave her the idea to go beyond a cosmetic and make perfumes too. Gabrielle is normally given the credit for the original concept for Chanel N°5: a synthesis of fragrances. She is famously supposed to have described this to Beaux, who then set about putting it into practice.

There are various claims involving the originality of Chanel N°5; for instance, it is often said that it was the first synthetic perfume. It wasn't. It was, however, the first synthetic fragrance created in the twenties. The first 'modern' perfume we know of featuring any synthetic components was Fougère Royale, created by Paul Parquet for Houbigant, way back in 1882. (Another early 'modern' perfume using synthetics was Jicky, made by Aimé Guerlain in 1889.)

However, as one of the earliest perfumers who understood the significance of aldehydes, Beaux's brilliance lay in his ability to blend perfectly the natural and the chemical elements in such a way that the chemicals reinforced the natural. Of almost equal importance was his understanding that the aldehydes kept the perfume stable, thereby making it last far longer once sprayed from its bottle. The use of these chemicals was to revolutionize luxury perfumes.

When Beaux met Gabrielle, he was experimenting further on Bouquet de Catherine, which contained a pronounced aldehyde element. Early in the recent war, aware of possible sensitivities about the perfume's namesake, Catherine the Great, the perfume had been renamed. Interestingly, it was now simply a number: Rallet N°1. Almost certainly, Beaux's researches on Rallet N°1 were what he now brought to Gabrielle. In his lecture, he would say, 'I came to present my creations, two series: numbers 1–5 and 20–24. She chose a few, one of which was N°5.' Beaux remembered asking

Gabrielle, 'What should it be called?' She said that she was presenting her dress collection 'on 5 May, the fifth (month) of the year; let's leave the name N°5'.[7]

Gabrielle was superstitious, and it is said that a gypsy had told her that five would be her lucky number. Her zodiac symbol, Leo, is the fifth sign, and she may well have known that five – signifying the cosmos for the old alchemists – was the quintessential number. The story that she never forgot the five-sided star, laid out in the floor mosaic at the convent at Aubazine, may be wishful thinking on the part of Gabrielle's more recent followers. Whatever the true source of her superstition, she believed with a passion that the number five brought her luck.

Gabrielle and Beaux had discovered in each other the perfect partner. Beaux's awareness of the cultural and artistic changes taking place around him had undoubtedly fed into his creation. Meanwhile, Gabrielle was asking for exactly what Beaux achieved: an exclusive synthesis of nature. Nevertheless, even if the story that her questing intelligence enabled her to make a suggestion here or there is true – she would later comment, 'How I annoyed him' – in the end it is Beaux who must take by far the greater credit for creating Gabrielle's perfume. This perfume has acquired such status in the Chanel Company that today it is referred to as their 'treasure'.

Gabrielle and Beaux's relationship was, though, complementary. Faced as we are with the myth constructed so carefully around N°5, we will never know if it was Gabrielle or Beaux who initiated the idea at the heart of the perfume's mystique: a fragrance that smelt of a synthesis of 'woman'. For Gabrielle, this meant a perfume symbolizing modern woman: in other words, herself. When Beaux told her that the perfume's large number of rare ingredients, especially the jasmine, would make it 'very expensive', she is supposed to have said, 'In that case, add more of it. I would like to create the most costly perfume in the world.'[8]

With Gabrielle's sensitivity to her times, her instincts had told her years ago that the manner in which she presented what she sold would be essential to its success. And, by 1922, Gabrielle herself had undoubtedly become a crucial part of her message. Her edgily fashionable clothes, her short hair (in 1921, still seen by many as outrageous), her possessions, her lovers, her independence; in all this Gabrielle was in the vanguard of her times. In short, while the private lives of the rich and famous were respected infinitely more than today, Gabrielle was nonetheless becoming fascinating to those who had never met her. In the style journals, 'Gabrielle Chanel' had previously been mentioned as the name of the designer who had made this or that highly sought-after dress or hat. Now she was unique amongst the couturiers in that she was in the society pages as much for herself. She was becoming as newsworthy as her illustrious clients. In the magazine *Femina*'s October 1921 issue, for example, we see Gabrielle in a photograph with Countess Doubazow, being filmed in 'a beautiful garden in the environs of Biarritz'.

Gabrielle had pushed at the old boundaries of acceptability and forged new ones. If appearance is about communicating – and implicit in Gabrielle's work was her ability to communicate – she was attempting to show women how best they could accommodate themselves to life in this radically altered modern world. What was the kind of appearance that would facilitate their handling of their new society? As Gabrielle said, she was developing her style according to her own needs and, implicitly, the needs of her fellow sex. If fashion articulates and illuminates the moment, Gabrielle did this to a radical degree. For rather than simply following and reflecting what was happening around her, she was ahead, articulating it.

Continually refining who she wanted to be, while never interested in being a revolutionary, Gabrielle was undoubtedly one of the first 'modern women'. But when she said, 'One day in 1919 I woke up famous,'[9] she was being disingenuous. Gabrielle had achieved notice through years of hard work and careful management of her image. En route she had understood, like the best courtesans, that her image was something she must nurture. With this in mind, we find in a small and very rare black and beige catalogue not only the select array of perfumes and cosmetics that, in two years' time – by 1924 – Gabrielle would have developed for her clients, but also a document revealing the essential promotional psychology of the House of Chanel.[10]

From the very first sentence of the little catalogue's preface, we are introduced to the idea not only of outstanding luxury, but also that it is something only properly understood by the cognoscenti. Gabrielle draws in her followers by flattering them with the thought that they are the select few, who possess a secret 'knowledge':

> Luxury fragrance: it is an expression that has lost much of its value through excessive and improper use ... The Chanel fragrances, created exclusively for a clientele of connoisseurs devoted to the idea of ... an original fragrance, different from all the others ... Mademoiselle Chanel has succeeded in producing ... fragrances that so eloquently evoke the Chanel style they rank among her finest creations. For an elite clientele price is a secondary consideration. Mademoiselle understands this ... These ingredients are combined in the test tubes of a master perfumer ...
>
> The pride of Mademoiselle Chanel is to offer to a well-informed clientele, in simple bottles and cases adorned solely by their whiteness, precious drops of perfume ...
>
> It was never imagined that they could become luxury fragrances for the general public ... They must remain exclusive ... chosen by an exclusive public with refined tastes.[11]

As with the alchemists, the Chanel client is enjoined to become part of a select, semi-secret society, membership of which makes her exclusive. In the twenties, luxury perfumes were sold in bottles that were glassblowers' 'triumphs' of excess. Intended to signal the promise of the contents, they were in the shape of cupids, suggestive female figures, or were richly exotic, associating the perfume with the seductive mystery of the East.

The designer of the unmistakable Chanel N°5 'simple bottles and cases adorned solely by their whiteness' is yet another mystery. In

1973, Gabrielle's lawyer of many years, Robert Chaillet, said that she designed the bottle herself: 'As soon as she had found her perfume . . . She designed something supremely simple and therefore supremely sophisticated . . . The bottle has never changed. There is total recognition. We can run a full-page advert in the most fashionable magazines simply by photographing the bottle. We need no explanatory text.'[12]

What would twenty-first-century advertisers give for this level of brand recognition? Another story tells how the first bottles were made by a company called Brosse, and that they were a copy of one of Arthur Capel's toiletry containers. A third story has it that, in 1924, when Gabrielle would make a deal securing distribution of her perfumes, the bottle was designed by Jean, the son of the fashionable artist Paul Helleu. This story may be the correct one, for we know that Jean Helleu began working for Gabrielle in the twenties, and remained with the Chanel Company for the rest of his working life.

According to Gabrielle's lawyer, following her choice from Beaux's samples, that evening Gabrielle dined with friends in the largest restaurant in Cannes. With an atomizer of Chanel N°5 on the table, she sprayed each person who walked past. 'The effect was amazing. All the women who passed the table stopped, sniffing the air. We pretended not to notice.'[13]

Asking Beaux to bottle up samples for her, Gabrielle is said to have returned to Paris with a hundred in her luggage. When clients were in the fitting rooms, her assistants sprayed the perfume around. Particularly privileged clients were given a little sample bottle of N°5 as a present and, when Gabrielle was asked where it might be bought, she said she had just come upon it while away; she forgot where. Meanwhile, she prodded Beaux for delivery of the larger quantities she had ordered, and was told that production could not be hurried. (To reiterate the beginning of this chapter: it is almost impossible that Dmitri introduced Gabrielle to Beaux in early 1921 and a few months later the perfume was in production.) Eventually, Beaux was ready. Gabrielle had by now cleverly drummed up sufficient interest among her clients that it appeared she was simply following their requests. In this way, Gabrielle now began selling small quantities of her perfume in all three of her salons, in Deauville, Biarritz and Paris.

A crucial element in the signature design of the Chanel N°5 bottle is the small black letter 'C' within a black circle set as the seal at the neck. On the top of the lid are two more 'C's, intertwined back to back. We know from the little Chanel catalogue mentioned above that, from at least 1924, the N°5 bottles sported the unmistakable logo. While we can't be certain who designed the minimalist art deco bottles for the perfume, the equally inspired piece of graphic design, the black letters 'CC', definitely originated with Gabrielle. It is of course correct that these two 'C's refer to Gabrielle – in other words, Coco Chanel herself, and would become the logo of the House of Chanel. But a discovery we made gives a possible additional meaning to these intertwined 'C's.

Gabrielle was fascinated by symbols and surrounded herself with objects ripe with meaning. (She apparently also read Tarot cards.) Wheat, for example, traditional symbol of prosperity, is a recurrent theme. Then there are the lions – symbol of Gabrielle's astrological sign, Leo – in wood, silver, bronze and alabaster. (Gabrielle also used the lion as a signature symbol on her buttons.) In 1921, she had Baccarat make her a stately crystal chandelier, incorporating several numbers and letters. This magnificent sculptural object, now in Gabrielle's apartment on rue Cambon, includes amongst its great glass pendants of fruit and flowers in crystal and semi-precious stones repeated metal figures of five (Gabrielle's 'lucky' number), 'B' for Boy (Arthur) Capel, and several double 'C's for Coco Chanel.

At the Paris Polo Club, where Arthur had played so often, there is a large silver trophy inscribed 'Arthur Capel Cup'. This was donated by his sister, Bertha, in Arthur's memory, almost certainly in collaboration with Gabrielle. The top of the cup sports what is a most unusual form of decoration on a polo trophy for the period, a relief band of intertwined circles, or back-to-back 'C's. The cup was first presented to a player in August 1922, only nine months after Arthur's death. These 'C's may represent Arthur and Gabrielle's surnames. With Arthur still uppermost in Gabrielle's mind, it could well have occurred to her to suggest this decoration to Bertha. Representing Arthur's and her own name: Capel and Chanel. If not in actuality, in a symbolic fantasy Gabrielle and Arthur would be conjoined.

As for the perfume's name, the claim that N°5 was the first perfume to be named simply by a number, rather than the descriptive titles then in vogue, is not correct. As we have seen, Ernest Beaux had already set the precedent several years earlier, when renaming his Bouquet de Catherine with a number: Rallet N°1. Yet, while Rallet N°1 would drop from the perfume repertoire, the apparently indeterminate name Chanel N°5 would acquire its own very modern kind of romance. This would help sustain N°5's developing myth, in turn assisted by one of the longest and most sophisticated advertising campaigns of the century. The very first image was created by Gabrielle's friend the caricaturist Sem. Here, a slim short-haired girl in a slight blue dress, the same as the ones Gabrielle then wore, ecstatically holds up her hands to a huge bottle of Chanel N°5.

Whatever the real chronology of the development and launch of Chanel N°5, shortly after Gabrielle and Dmitri's return from the south of France, in late spring 1921, Gabrielle invited Dmitri (accompanied by his faithful servant Piotr) to stay with her at Bel Respiro, Arthur's former house. For a while, this elegant house on the edge of Paris became a rendezvous for Dmitri's émigré comrades and Gabrielle's avant-garde artist friends. Then, when Paris closed its doors for the summer vacation, Gabrielle hired a house on the Bay of Biscay, not far from the flourishing southern resort of Arcachon.

Parts of this dramatic Atlantic coastline were frequented in summer by a sprinkling of artists and writers – both those who eschewed the more developed resorts, and those with deeper purses who preferred to be more remote in their villas. With the surf breaking against the garden wall of their white villa, the lovers were taken care of by Piotr, and Gabrielle's faithful Joseph and Marie. In the two months they spent by the sea, the days merged quietly one into the other, with swimming and walking on the beach or through the pine woods close by. While a handful of friends had villas nearby, there were not many visitors. But it seems to have pleased Gabrielle and Dmitri to live quietly like this for a while.

Once the summer was over, Gabrielle launched herself into a venture she had already instituted back in Paris. For some time, she had used her rooms at the Ritz for overnight stays. But shortly before her holiday she had left behind her quiet retreat, Bel Respiro, and took up residence in a distinguished eighteenth-century *hôtel particulier* on the Faubourg St-Honoré.

Gabrielle believed that in losing Arthur she had lost her life's companion, and this had left her essentially lonely. In some sense, it also released her and would drive her forward even further. Yet, in releasing her from some of the private constraints accompanying real dependence upon a man, it also left Gabrielle without an emotional anchor.

In 1921, Gabrielle was thirty-eight but looked almost ten years younger. She was extremely attractive, in possession of considerable wealth, much experience and growing social prestige. However, her emotional hardships, combined with her growing power, had brought about a certain disillusion. During the twenties, a change would take place in Gabrielle: it was now she who might well initiate a relationship. Meanwhile, in combination with her pride in herself and her achievements, the genuine modesty that went hand in hand with Gabrielle's self-assurance was sometimes obscured by her great force of character. And her subtlety could go unnoticed by all but those few who knew her well.

Beginning with Stravinsky, for the next ten years and more, Gabrielle was to have a series of high-profile affairs, sometimes simultaneously. She would later say, 'My love life got very disorganized, because the person I loved had died.'[14] At the same time, in the years after Arthur's death, Gabrielle was to apply herself professionally with such initiative and vigour that her name would become known far beyond the shores of France. Later, she went on to become more famous still, and even wealthier, but in this period her life took on a kind of emotional and artistic fervour in which she would become not only a discreet artistic patron but would also create the closest she ever came to a salon, where her palatial home became one of the artistic nuclei of Paris.

These years could fairly be described as the highpoint of Gabrielle's life. The increase (one might say the confirmation) of her status was inseparable from the life she lived, itself reflected in her clothes. She was the absolute personification of modern woman. Indeed, during Gabrielle's years at Faubourg St-Honoré, she was to become one of the most glamorous figures in the world.

Entirely in white and covered in pearls

The Hôtel de Lauzan, at 29 Faubourg St-Honoré, was built in 1719 for the Duchesse de Rohan-Montbazon, with very large formal gardens running all the way down to the avenue Gabriel. Perhaps it was no coincidence that its new occupant had chosen this address. It was on the avenue Gabriel that she had spent her happiest years with Arthur Capel, before the appearance of Diana Wyndham.

Gabrielle had taken the magnificent ground-floor rooms of the Hôtel de Lauzan, while the owner, Comte Pillet-Will, remained on the floor above. When Gabrielle said that 'the interior of a home is the natural projection of a soul,' adding that 'Balzac was right to attach as much importance to it as he did to clothing,' she effectively gave both her creed and her statement of intent. Her immediate response to the Faubourg St-Honoré was the enjoyment of acknowledging its grandeur. The main rooms had last been altered in the previous century, and Gabrielle hated the greenish, gilded panelled walls she was not permitted to change. It is said that she asked the Serts to redecorate and furnish her new home.

We know that Gabrielle was impressed by José Maria's taste but, in the context of her future houses, including her apartment at rue Cambon, and the house she would later build for herself, this is not convincing. The Serts may well have made suggestions but, by this stage in Gabrielle's life, it is difficult to imagine that she hadn't arrived at a pretty confident style of her own. All style was in a general state of flux in the early twenties, and for her interiors Gabrielle gravitated, like a number of those in her circle, towards a type of modern baroque. This open-ended style accommodated quite different personalities, who loosely mixed old and new with juxtapositions sometimes intentionally startling. The result was that one looked at things with more care.

In several rooms, Gabrielle covered the gilded walls with mirror glass from floor to ceiling, and then added Louis XIV furniture, combined with an underlying oriental theme. This took the form of numerous Coromandel folding screens, which became a signature element of Gabrielle's interiors, and which she first lived with in Arthur's apartment. In one of the salons, she had a huge Regency sofa covered in orange velvet and set in front of one of these enormous Chinese figured screens. On the side tables were lamps made of large crystal balls set one upon the other, with lampshades made of parchment. (These same elegant lamps are now in Gabrielle's apartment in the rue Cambon, as are a number of the Coromandel screens.) A small library, with natural, pale woodwork, had fine old carpets, with furniture and curtains, all in beige. This colour may sound unappealing, but Gabrielle made it work with such success it was to become one of her trademarks.

A fine classical marble torso was reflected in a mantelpiece mirror, both bought on that recent trip to Italy with the Serts, and now also in the rue Cambon. In Gabrielle's bedroom were floor-to-ceiling mirror panels covering one wall, while her bed was spread with a dark fur coverlet enclosed by cream silk curtains falling from a wooden baldachin. Coromandel screens stood behind another velvet-covered sofa, a huge crystal chandelier hung above a small silver table, while hanging on the mirror wall panels was an enormous Venetian mirror decorated all around the edge with crystal flowers. This astounding piece of craftsmanship, today in Gabrielle's apartment, was bought from the sale of the recently bankrupt and legendarily stylish narcissist, the Marchesa Luisa Casati. That Gabrielle would keep several of these outstanding pieces of furniture confirms one's sense that the grammar of her decorative style was already well established.

Gabrielle loved gold, and the colours beige and black. Like Misia, she also loved crystal. However, as for Misia's own taste, Gabrielle later described her apartment before her marriage to

Sert as 'all that pile of objects'. Misia's very busy interior had at first led Gabrielle and Arthur to the conclusion that Misia must be an antique dealer. And Arthur had unashamedly asked, 'Is it all for sale?' Gabrielle loathed what she called 'the doctrine of clutter'. Speaking of Misia's, she said, 'It wends its way along walls, piles up underneath tables, proliferates on the stairs, the cupboards no longer shut.'[1] Nevertheless, Paul Morand, a man of most particular and snobbish tastes, described Misia's apartment's 'crystal, its lacquer, its general air of exquisite rococo', without criticism. No doubt Gabrielle did owe something to Misia and Sert's aesthetic, but she now practised a doctrine of luxury, size and space whose elements were her own.

Into the magnificent setting of the Faubourg St-Honoré she transported Joseph Leclerc, now chamberlain to a bevy of servants looking after his mistress and her steady stream of visitors. By day, Gabrielle perfected and sold the clothes which were making her so quintessentially modern and, by night, she was establishing herself as a sought-after Parisian figure. Preferring, on the whole, the company of artists, it was in this period she became close to Jean Cocteau. If Cocteau's following, or 'school', is hard to define, while both loved and reviled, he had, nonetheless, positioned himself as a spokesman for modernist art. His famous personal charm and dazzling conversation were evanescent but almost impossible to replicate, and even Cocteau-haters thought 'his life was his masterpiece' and that 'his talk was the best part of him.' For his detractors, he was full of gimmickry, artifice and vacuity. He, meanwhile, said, 'A poet owes it to himself to be a very serious man, and yet, out of politeness, to appear the opposite.'[2] For over fifty years, Gabrielle would oscillate between love and dislike of Cocteau.

After the recent war, artists had continued arguing back and forth: what should their subject now be, and how should it be presented? A savage, nihilistic atmosphere, emerging from the brutalities of the war, meant that many artistic and cultural values were now unceremoniously hurled out, until the artists arrived at the anarchy of Dada. One of its founders, Gabrielle's friend Tristan Tzara, said that Dada meant nothing and this was the point: *nothing*. Dada was to be 'an inventory of the ruins of art and society left by the void of war'. While Gabrielle was in one sense party to these sentiments, she was also more interested in asking herself what she could do to move *with* her chaotic times. And, at the centre of events, she made her own definitive contribution. She lived an unusually progressive and un-bourgeois life, her independence and sexually liberated attitudes reflected in Gabrielle's short hair and ruthlessly simple clothes.

At the Faubourg St-Honoré, she threw herself into what became the most expansively sociable period of her life, and one of her first undertakings was to have a fine piano brought in and placed in an otherwise empty room. Seldom relinquishing the luxury of friendship with a former lover, by this stage Gabrielle and Stravinsky were once again on close terms. And Stravinsky now came to the Faubourg St-Honoré, along with society and artists. These included Diaghilev, his lovers, Ballets Russes dancers, Misia and José Maria Sert, Erik Satie, and a series of other performers and composers, including Les Six, who in turn included Georges Auric, Darius Milhaud and Francis Poulenc. The musicians played, and partied with Gabrielle's society and artist friends, including the likes of Braque, Modigliani, Juan Gris and Francis Picabia, long into the night.

On the upper floor, meanwhile, the Comte Pillet-Will found the clamour of their contemporary music unendurable, and he and his tenant came to an amicable accommodation. She would pay handsomely for the rest of his vast residence, and the count would take himself elsewhere.

Jean Cocteau's offering for that year, 1921, was *Les Mariés de la Tour Eiffel*, a parody of a Parisian wedding, again with the anarchic high spirits of his ballet *Parade*. Olga Picasso had insisted that she and her husband take a villa outside Paris for the first months of their baby son's life. Picasso was now invited to join Misia's box as Gabrielle's escort for the ballet's premiere. Picasso was always in two minds about Cocteau, whom he infuriated by teasing him. But he and Gabrielle enjoyed Cocteau's verbal sparkle, his spiteful tongue and his urgent and shamelessly insincere need of the friendship of the *haut monde*. Had Picasso and Gabrielle seen Cocteau's diary, they would have revelled in his remark about 'the actresses without theatre that are society women'.[3]

By this point, Gabrielle had known Picasso for some time. Indeed, she was one of the small group of guests at his wedding in 1918, when Olga wore a Chanel dress and Cocteau had written, 'Olga in white satin, tricot and tulle – very Biarritz.'[4] When Picasso became claustrophobic in his villa and came into town in search of his friends, he wouldn't stay alone at night in his and Olga's apartment. He was apparently terrified by the prospect of loneliness. So, Gabrielle had one of her light, airy rooms at the Faubourg St-Honoré made permanently available to him. She saw a good deal of Picasso at this time and was, in her own words:

> . . . seized by a passion for [him]. He was wicked. He fascinated me the way a hawk would; he filled me with a fear. I could feel it when he came in: something would curl up in me; he'd arrived. I couldn't see him yet, but already I knew he was in the room. And then I saw him. He had a way of looking at me . . . I trembled.[5]

Misia had observed this attraction between her two friends, and did her best to foil any real intimacy developing between them. But any control she might previously have exerted over Gabrielle had evaporated when Gabrielle wrote the cheque for Diaghilev's *Rite of Spring*. Characteristically, Gabrielle was not particularly concerned by the idea of Picasso's wife in the background, and saw Picasso at his apartment on the rue de la Boétie. Developing her 'passion', they spent the odd night – perhaps more – together at the Faubourg St-Honoré. But with Picasso always quick to demand sexual and emotional subservience from his women, and Gabrielle being in many ways just as intense and formidable a character as he was, this affair could only ever have been a brief one.

In 1921, when *Vogue* commented that 'the couturiers are still embroidering their way to success,' Dmitri Pavlovich's sister, Grand Duchess Marie Pavlovna, took advantage of the trend. Marie Pavlovna was short of funds – like all the Russian émigrés – and on the spur of the moment suggested to Gabrielle that she could make the embroidery for her clothes at a better price. Gabrielle was surprised at the suggestion but agreed that Marie should try. Despite Marie's personal hardship and losses, her attempts at adapting to her fate were impressive. Describing the Russian nobility's plight, she said they had been 'torn out of our brilliant setting . . . still dressed in our fantastic costumes. We had to take them off . . . make ourselves other, everyday clothes, and above all learn how to wear them.'

In only three months, Marie Pavlovna had set up what became a highly successful wholesale workshop, Kitmir, with Russian women machine-embroidering clothes for couture houses and, in particular, the House of Chanel. Marie designed many of the embroideries herself, basing them on her memories from art school; a number of Russian motifs and new research.

It has been customary to say that Gabrielle began embroidering her clothing under the influence of her Russian lover, Grand Duke Dmitri Pavlovich. This is quite wrong. Gabrielle had come under the influence of the Russians – Diaghilev, the Ballets Russes and Stravinsky – before her affair with Dmitri; she had been decorating her clothes with embroidery since at least 1917. In addition, from contemporary descriptions, we see that it wasn't only Gabrielle who used embroidery to decorate her clothing, so were some of her fellow couturiers.

While Marie Pavlovna marvelled at seeing her embroideries worn by Gabrielle's clients, sadly, there are very few examples of them still around. What is left to us from Marie, however, is one of the very best descriptions of Gabrielle at work. As Marie evokes the scene, we see how Gabrielle's method of creating, first described by

Marie-Louise Delay, in Biarritz, has remained quite unchanged. Gabrielle's cutting, pinning and sculpting of a material on a real woman's body would, much later – in an age of male couturiers, designing by making drawings alone – become famous for its singularity. This had in fact been the traditional dressmakers' accustomed method of working.

After Gabrielle had draped her mannequin with a fabric, in order to see its fall and movement, she would then work in another material, such as a fine calico, until she was satisfied with her design on the girl's body. From this first model, called a toile, the real material would be cut out by the *premières* and made into the final garment. In Marie Pavlovna's description, we see how a real and beautiful female body was and would always remain an essential part of Gabrielle's inspiration. The girl's shape and colouring were all part of the inspiration for her transformation of a piece of material into something that could be worn. (She insisted that her mannequins were very slim, and almost all were dark haired, like her.) Marie Pavlovna described her fascination with the way her embroidered materials were transformed into clothes:

> For several years to come I watched Chanel's creative genius . . . She never designed anything on paper and would make a dress either according to an idea already in her head or as she proceeded. I can still see her sitting on her stool . . . with a log fire burning . . . she would be dressed in a . . . dark skirt and a sweater, with the sleeves pushed up above her elbows . . .
>
> The models would be called in one by one from the landing outside . . . sometimes for hours in various stages of undress . . . A girl would walk into the room and up to Mlle Chanel, who sat . . . with a pair of scissors in her hand.
>
> 'Bonjour Mademoiselle.'
>
> 'Bonjour Jeanne.'
>
> This was the only moment when Chanel would look up at the model's face . . . As the girl approached, Chanel, with her head slightly bent to one side, would take in the first impression. Then the

fitting began . . . The fitter standing beside her handed her the pins. No one spoke except Chanel, who kept up a steady monologue. Sometimes she would be giving instructions, or explaining some detail. Sometimes she would criticize and undo the work . . . already done. The old fitter listened to all, in silence, her face impenetrable . . . Chanel, intent on her work . . . talked on without taking notice of anybody.

I had seen people occupying great offices . . . had listened to orders being given by those whose birth or position gave them the right to command. I had never yet met with a person whose every word was obeyed and whose authority had been established by her own self, out of nothing.

At about five o'clock, coffee was brought in, sometimes with sandwiches. If the day's work was complete, Gabrielle stood up, stretched, and the models, condemned to wait outside, were finally permitted to leave. If the pressure was on, Gabrielle gulped down her coffee then took up her work once more. One or two 'obsequious executives and an occasional friend sat around on the carpet' while Gabrielle held forth indefatigably. 'Discussing everything and everybody with immense assurance, she dispensed strong opinions on people and events; these opinions could just as quickly be reversed. Forging on, her power of persuasion was amazing.'[6]

Maurice Sachs was an ambitious young conman, who sometimes acted as Cocteau's secretary got himself small writing commissions and, later in the decade, became an astute chronicler of his times. In his portrait of Gabrielle, he said that she 'created a feminine personage that Paris had not known before'. He was surprised at 'how small she was. She was very slim; the line of thick black hair was low, her eyebrows met over the nose and when she laughed her eyes [were] hard and sparkling.' Commenting that she 'almost always' wore simple black clothes, he said:

She put her hands in her pockets [then still an unusual thing for a woman to do] and began to speak. The flow of her words was extraordinarily fast, rushing forward, but she laid out clearly what she had in mind. She had none of the circumlocution, and fabricated asides that so often make a woman halt at incidental subjects and never reach the target of their conversation. Her train of thought was utterly clear . . . She had great practical sense; she liked to manage, to organize, to put in order and to be in charge.[7]

Gabrielle had a redeeming contradictory trait, and one particularly rare in people who are controlling. An old employee would say that 'she hated things which were planned. She didn't have this notion of organization like we do.' And Jean Cocteau once said, 'She has, by a kind of miracle, worked in fashion according to rules that would seem to have value only for artists.'[8]

At the same time, Sachs believed that in giving her orders with such certainty and authority, Gabrielle 'was a general: one of those young generals of the Empire in whom the spirit of conquest dominates'. Gabrielle shared another trait with military men: 'a shyness which overcame her as soon as she left the battlefield'.[9]

As each of the biannual collections approached, the atmosphere at Chanel heightened and Gabrielle grew more nervous. Like many an artist working under pressure, it was these tense conditions that often provoked her most successful pieces. Marie Pavlovna was repeatedly amazed at how the chaos in the days prior to a show was miraculously transformed into a collection just in the nick of time. On the eve of a show at rue Cambon, Gabrielle had a 'dress rehearsal' for herself and her personnel, in the salon below her studio. Anything considered unfit was 'banished altogether' or else sent back, somehow to be redone before the morrow. Marie was intrigued by the 'language of the dresses'; how their different characteristics and appeal were so familiar to Gabrielle, and how it was this unified set of relationships she was most concerned with at this final stage. 'Not one single detail escaped her notice. She was so concentrated upon the study that . . . she forgot even to talk.'

And, all the while, a 'religious and respectful silence hung over the salon, around which the saleswomen sat in a row along the walls', nodding, and no more than lifting their eyebrows by way of approval. Gabrielle's fashion shows were becoming extremely popular and, each season, the rue Cambon entrance was besieged by a crowd of indignant buyers. Only those with invitations were admitted. The largest (important foreign houses; above all, the US), were invited first, and only then did smaller and native firms receive an invitation. This very exclusiveness, of course, made them clamour still more for admittance. In future years, the detachment of police posted to guard the front door of Chanel at rue Cambon was an imposing sight.

When Marie Pavlovna's embroideries were first shown – probably in the spring of 1922 – she joined Gabrielle and a group of her friends in what were the most uncomfortable, yet most privileged 'seats . . . on the upper steps of the staircase, from where we could see what was going on'. (The mirror-panelled walls of this staircase were part of a modernist refurbishment Gabrielle would have installed at some point during the early twenties.) Until the end of her life, this ritual spot was where she placed herself to survey her collection below.

This now-famous staircase has remained intact. The salon below, while updated, is decorated in the same colour scheme to this day: carpeted in beige with white walls and the distinctive black cast-iron banisters. Gabrielle commented once, 'I spent my life on stairs.' The mirrored staircase was the spine of her house; everything that happened at rue Cambon could be observed from it. But Gabrielle was also making oblique reference to that other staircase, central to her youth and in the convent at Aubazine. Here, the orphan girls trudged up and down the great stone steps several times each day.

The show including Marie Pavlovna's embroideries lasted a full three hours – this was not untypical – but from Gabrielle's eyrie at the top of the stairs, Marie was amazed at the speed with which she had absorbed and gauged the audience's interest. Long before the concluding piece, Gabrielle told the dazed young Russian duchess that her work was a success.

The biggest orders for these embroideries – indeed, all Chanel clothes – came from America, a tendency that would become the norm. It was the sophisticated yet pervasively casual and sportive element of American society that had appreciated Gabrielle's 'language' as quickly as France, and possibly more so.

Marie learnt much from Gabrielle, not least the example of her worldliness. While, at first, the young aristocrat found the way clients were referred to 'behind the scenes' quite shocking, she eventually came to the conclusion that, in fact, 'any noble sentiments were wasted' on the customers of haute couture: 'Mlle Chanel did much to give me more practical views on life. A number of my illusions were destroyed in the process.'

Gabrielle, with her 'usual outspokenness', also steered Dmitri's sister away from the puritanical belief that taking trouble with one's appearance was unseemly. She told Marie that it was 'a great mistake to go round looking like a refugee . . . people will end by avoiding you. If you wish to do business, the first thing is to look prosperous.'

Gabrielle's abhorrence of amateurism impressed her employee. In this same spirit, Marie was taught how to use make-up and instructed to lose weight. Still despairing of Marie's long hair, one day, Gabrielle declared, 'No, I really cannot see you any longer with that unattractive bun . . . it will have to come off.' Deftly removing Marie's hairpins, she 'snatched up a pair of scissors and was cutting off my hair by the handful'. While subsequently having this 'cut' improved, from that day, Marie Pavlovna was more modish and wore her hair short.[10]

In early 1920, Cocteau had invited Gabrielle to a 'spectacle concert' of art, music and popular entertainment called *Le Boeuf sur le toit* (*The Ox on the Roof*). Financed by Comte Etienne de Beaumont, the show was Cocteau's, music was by Darius Milhaud, of Les Six, and sets were by the painter-designer Raoul Dufy. *Le Boeuf sur le toit* reflected the fascination with all things American and proved a great success with its avant-garde audience. In January 1922, when the patron of a bar called The Gaya – a focal point for artistic Parisian gatherings – launched his enlarged restaurant-bar on the rue Boissy d'Anglas, he had been given permission to call it, after Cocteau's spectacle, Le Boeuf sur le Toit. Often known to English enthusiasts as The Nothing Doing Bar, overnight, Le Boeuf sur le Toit became one of the most fashionable meeting places for artists and their cronies. Quickly rivalling the reputation of the Moulin Rouge or Maxim's, Le Boeuf was noisy, smart and 'amusing'; it was *the* place to be seen. And, with her artist and society friends, Gabrielle soon became one of its regulars.

Le Boeuf was one of the first bars hosting what came to be known as 'café society', both leading and reflecting a new kind of salon – a public one. Here, sexual preferences were openly indulged, and Le Boeuf appeared to be for everyone. As well as beautiful women and men, and beautiful boys, and boys dressed as girls, and girls dressed as boys, there were the poets, painters, musicians, actors, dancers, the titled, the rich and the famous. Anyone could speak to anyone. They talked, they danced, and the atmosphere was alive with possibility.

Opium, morphine and cocaine were acquiring a certain ubiquity at the time. And, while it wasn't only the social and artistic elite who regularly used one or more of these preferred narcotics, a good many became hopelessly addicted. Just three of the more famous examples would be Jean Cocteau, the lesbian Princess Violette Murat, hostess to a salon of prominent artists and musicians, and another of Gabrielle's friends, Misia Sert. Confirmed opium smoker that Cocteau would become, he, like the Princess Murat, also used cocaine, while Misia Sert's need for morphine was to get the better of her in the end. Despite Diaghilev's absolute veto of any drug use in his company, it has been said that he was a cocaine user himself.[11]

Le Boeuf sur le Toit aficionados soon read like a list of the contemporary avant-garde, combined with the fashionable elite of Europe. On any night of the week, one might come across André Gide swathed in a black cape; the *wunderkind* writer Raymond Radiguet; Jean Cocteau; and Max Jacob, the brilliant semi-alcoholic, semi-tramp, homosexual Jewish Catholic-convert poet. Then there were the 'non-painters': the Cuban Dadaist Francis Picabia, Dada's Hungarian founder Tristan Tzara, any number of musicians and composers, including Francis Poulenc and Georges Auric, Marie Laurencin, painter-printmaker and future illustrator for the Surrealists, another painter, Valentine Hugo, Misia and José Maria Sert, whose booming voice could always be heard above the hubbub, Stravinsky the dandy, with his 'mustard-yellow trousers, black jacket, blue shirt, yellow shoes, clean-shaven and with slicked-down blonde hair',[12] more Russians, and Erik Satie, the 'faun with the little beard and cracked laugh'. Then there might be Diaghilev and his entourage; the proto-Surrealist André Breton and his cronies; Maurice Sachs, with some beautiful boy, or girl, in tow; and then numbers of now-forgotten minor luminaries and colourful unknowns.

Le Boeuf came to represent not only the turmoil, disenchantment and excesses of the period, it also reflected every aspect of the intense, almost febrile creative atmosphere of those inter-war years in Paris. In those same years, Gabrielle and Cocteau's friendship was cemented. While Cocteau was accused of having no path of his own and of walking along everyone else's, in writing about his spectacle *Le Boeuf sur le toit* he also epitomized the mood of the times when he said, 'Here, I avoid subject and symbol. Nothing happens, or what does happen is so crude, is so ridiculous, that it is as though nothing happens.'[13] Cocteau's dizzyingly varied artistic activity antagonized many, yet it was the ever-perceptive English poet W. H. Auden who captured what Cocteau had to offer and saw that it was important. Here, one sees how modern Cocteau was, and also why Gabrielle had so much time for him:

> Now and then an artist appears . . . who works in a number of media and whose productions in any one of them are so varied that it is difficult to perceive any unity of pattern or development . . . Both the public and the critics feel aggrieved . . . His fellow artists . . . are equally suspicious and jealous of a man who works in several [media]. His first concern is for the nature of the medium and its

hidden possibilities . . . a person who is open to the outside world, so little concerned with 'self-expression', is naturally responsive to the present moment and liable, therefore, to incur the charge of wanting, at all costs, to be chic. To this one can only answer that to be 'timely' is not in itself a disgrace: Cocteau has never followed fashion though he has sometimes made it.[14]

★ ★ ★

In 1919, Cocteau had met and fallen for the precocious sixteen-year-old writer Raymond Radiguet, whose 'cool insolence, now spontaneous, now calculating', people found either repulsive or alluring. His quite remarkable callousness aside, Radiguet's astounding precocity and association with the great socializer Cocteau meant that he not only became known, he made it his business to know all Paris. This included frequently being present at Gabrielle's table.

Radiguet periodically resisted his clamorous lover-mentor Cocteau and would disappear to indulge in one, or all, of his escape routes: alcohol, opium and women. A Madame Warkowska, frequenter of Le Boeuf sur le Toit, introduced him to opium. Her effortlessly modish judgement on the prevalence of the drug was: 'Opium? Why make such a fuss? I smoked at my first communion in Shanghai.'[15] When Radiguet wasn't fulfilling Max Jacob's injunction 'You have to *do* things,' the boy wrote hard. Cocteau said, 'He wrote the way Beau Brummel dressed. No tics, no patina, but a special gift . . . of making the new look as though it had been seen before.' Referring to Diaghilev's famous command to Cocteau – 'Astonish me' – Radiguet subsequently countered with the remarkably adult 'Elegance consists in *not* astounding.'[16] These two injunctions –'making the new look as though it had been seen before' and 'Elegance consists in *not* astounding' – so exactly characterized Gabrielle's philosophy, they could have been her motto.

In the autumn of 1922, Cocteau asked Gabrielle if she would design the costumes for his modernized version of Sophocles' *Antigone*. The play's theme – defiance of the establishment – was then a most attractive one. With scenery by Picasso and music by Arthur Honegger of Les Six, the actor Charles Dullin played Creon. (This was the same Charles Dullin who had accompanied Gabrielle to the first night of *The Rite of Spring*, in 1913; his lover Caryathis had wanted to attend the performance with her *other* lover.)

Cocteau said, 'To costume my princesses I wanted Mlle Chanel, because she is our leading dressmaker, and I cannot imagine Oedipus's daughters patronizing a "little dressmaker" . . . I chose some heavy Scotch woollens, and Mlle Chanel's designs were so masterly, so instinctively right.'[17] Indeed, Gabrielle's costumes were powerful and convincing, and *Vogue* said they looked like 'antique garments discovered after centuries'. However, in an angry moment during a rehearsal, when Gabrielle felt her contribution wasn't being appreciated, she grabbed a strand of the heroine's hand-knitted coat and pulled it so far undone that there was no time to re-knit it; the heroine wore one of Gabrielle's own coats.

Charles Dullin said, 'Many society people came to the performances because of Chanel, Picasso and Cocteau.' The play was a success and, while the likes of André Gide and the poet Ezra Pound spoke in its favour, in the end, it was Gabrielle who was commended, for her costumes, rather more than her collaborators.

By March 1923, elite magazines such as *Vogue* were writing that 'Gabrielle Chanel is now famous for her treatment of the youthful short-skirted silhouette which innumerable smart women have achieved.' While a leader of fashion, at the same time, Gabrielle was almost 'outside' it. Thus, *Vogue* wrote, 'She doesn't concern herself with fashion but with *her* fashion, she improvises dresses which . . . do not age.'

The following month, the magazine stated, 'There is not only a Chanel Collection, there is a Chanel "style" made of youth, suppleness . . . [Its] somewhat sporty, yet very feminine look, met the needs of our time so well that women adopted it with enthusiasm as soon as it appeared.' Gabrielle herself was always the best advert for her fashions, and *Vogue* wrote, 'Mlle Chanel . . . wears the designs

her clients love with so much chic herself . . . that her daring pro-
vokes admiration; her success applause!' And, in August, about a
Diaghilev gala, the magazine cooed, 'Snobs would have given anything to be there that night! Just think: the Marquise de Ludres is on
the right . . . the Comtesse de Beaumont . . . the Duchesse de Gramont . . . Comtesse de Requena, Mme Sert, Grande Duchesse
Marie, the Comtesse de Chevigné.' (All, except de Requena, were
dressed by Gabrielle.) *Vogue* continued, 'And there is Gabrielle Chanel, dressed entirely in white, and covered in pearls.'

Three more of that summer's grand events give a flavour of
Gabrielle's entertainment: the de Beaumonts' fabulous annual
fancy-dress ball; Diaghilev's premiere party for Stravinsky's ballet
Les Noces, at Le Boeuf sur le Toit, and a now-fabled party for Stravin-
sky, given by the wealthy expatriate American socialites Sara and
Gerald Murphy, and said to be the inspiration for Scott Fitzgerald's
Nicole and Dick Diver in *Tender is the Night.*

Gabrielle could not only be found more than once a week at Le
Boeuf, she went to other restaurants and clubs, and also entertained regularly at the Faubourg St-Honoré. One marvels at her
energy and how she fitted any work into her punishing social
schedule. Unsurprisingly, one finds references to her constant lack
of time. A terse note to Etienne de Beaumont refers to a meeting
that 'wasn't worth the trouble'; another tells him she can't make an
event: 'I am sorry but not free tonight'; and yet another turns down
an invitation because, finally, she admits, 'I am too tired, forgive
me.'[18]

Gabrielle's chief competitors had been the couturiers Lanvin,
Paquin, Cheruit, Patou and Poiret, but, increasingly, she had edged
her way out in front. Somehow, between the socializing, Gabrielle
not only found the time to work, but was also dedicated to it. The
result of this intense application was a couture that received more
plaudits with every season. Over and again, the magazines put their
seal of approval on what *Vogue* described as her 'unvarying Short
and Slender Silhouette'. It trumpeted the fact that Gabrielle made
outfits 'the modern woman of today likes best, the type which is

best adapted to her life. The clothes made by this designer are simple, becoming, and above all youthful.'

The commentators were intrigued by Gabrielle's capacity to be 'beguiling and consistent without being monotonous. Witness her endless variety within narrow limits.' There were reports of long, straight coats of light wool or silk crepe, lined, for example, with a printed crepe used again for the simple frock underneath. (This was one of Gabrielle's clever methods of simplification and would become a Chanel trademark.) Another detail that became a signature element was Gabrielle's introduction of the camellia flower, probably first used in 1922 embroidered on a blouse.

The flower had both exotic and forbidden associations. Alexander Dumas's passionate story *La Dame aux camélias* was a favourite of Gabrielle's, and wearing a camellia had been widely recognized as a signal that a woman was available for seduction. Proust had worn a camellia in homage to Verdi's *La Traviata*, itself inspired by Dumas's novel, and this may in turn have inspired Gabrielle. The camellia has the added advantage of being without scent, and hence would not compete with Gabrielle's perfumes. By 1924, material renderings of the flower were often added to her clothes.

Meanwhile, *Vogue* described 'straight taffeta evening coats . . . gorgeous with all-over embroidery and fur collars. The slender frocks worn under them are often beaded. They have a new, deep, oval décolletage in the back.' (That deep décolletage at the back, and the short, beaded and fringed dresses which became so representative of the twenties are all innovations said to have originated with Gabrielle.)

Showing that she was eminently capable of using precious materials such as silk, crepe, satin, chiffon, lace and beading, Gabrielle also continued with her innovative use of jersey, including the most novel introduction of Scottish Fair Isle tricot. Indeed, she took up this comfortable knitted fabric, smooth on one side, with greater texture on the reverse, more than any other designer. Her almost austere elegance suited perfectly the fluid movement of this material, and her use of plain and patterned tricots was most instrumental in the belief that Gabrielle's particular kind of casualness was tremendously chic. The great push towards more 'active' clothes for women was not hers alone, but she was undoubtedly one of its first and most important proponents. (As early as 1921, Gabrielle had set up a 'Sports' workshop.)

Gabrielle herself was never anything but slim, but even she apparently devoted a good deal of time and trouble to ensuring that was how she remained. Thus she joined wholeheartedly in the custom of visiting health spas, for reducing and cleansing 'cures'. From one of these establishments, Gabrielle wrote to Antoinette Bernstein that she was 'tired of resting . . . I think only of fighting against Fat. I feel completely stupefied,' and hoped to 'profit' by her self-imposed ordeal.[19]

It is said that, in the summer of 1923, Gerald and Sara Murphy persuaded the Hôtel du Cap at Antibes to remain open for the summer months. Gabrielle and her artist friends, such as Picasso, the audacious, and sociable Polish painter Moise Kisling, and Cocteau, had discovered as yet unspoiled fishing villages, including St Tropez, some time ago, but the opening of the Hôtel du Cap during the summer is supposed to have set the precedent for change on a much more significant scale. Until then, the luxurious hotels and villas on the Riviera had their main season in winter and spring. In high summer, all the seaside resorts traditionally closed their doors upon the heat. We remember that Gabrielle went south with Dmitri Pavlovich in March, and the hotel they stayed at was closing down in May. With the advent of a high-summer season by the sea, sunbathing now became high style. Gabrielle was certainly one of the first to sport a tan (although, as we saw, her friend Marthe Davelli, for example, had already taken to it during the First World War).

Gabrielle is so often credited with initiating something, such as cutting her hair short, or introducing short skirts, because she had become the quintessence of high fashion. She had an unerring instinct for the moment, and what she did was now noticed and emulated. When, as long ago as 1908, the dancer with the wild private life, Caryathis, had chopped off her hair in a fit of pique, most had thought her outrageous and unattractively eccentric. But when Gabrielle cut her hair several years later, in 1917, her timing, as always, was exactly right, and everyone followed suit. By the twenties, what Gabrielle wore, where she went, what sport she took up, how she entertained herself, was of interest to the fashionable rich. This included sunbathing. From St-Jean-de-Luz, by the sea, Gabrielle wrote to a friend, 'I was ill at first but I think it is because I ate too much which is quite disgusting! We've had terrible heat and my poor women [her seamstresses] were in a lamentable state, with sunburns which makes them rather ugly. I looked like a crayfish myself.'[20] Eventually, thousands would follow.

In December 1923, the Parisian avant-garde was rattled when its prodigy Raymond Radiguet suddenly died. The boy's book *The Devil in the Flesh* had become so popular it was even sold on street corners and at stations, until it had made him famous. Reading France had fallen in love with Radiguet, and was appalled at the speed and premature nature of his demise. He had contracted typhoid when by the sea with friends, then, back in Paris, had once again fled Cocteau to a hotel across town. Here he picked up a girl and lived with her intermittently while revising his second book, *Count d'Orgel's Ball*. Radiguet became wracked with chills, and the doctor diagnosed pneumonia. Cocteau was sceptical and called Gabrielle, who immediately sent her own doctor to the patient. He saw at once that it was typhoid and also that it was too late; he sent Radiguet to hospital all the same. Radiguet's mother misguidedly left his bedside for the night and in her absence he died, alone. Cocteau neither spent that last night with him, nor would he see him dead, or even attend the funeral.

As always, opinion was divided over Cocteau. Did he behave like 'a self-indulgent queen', or was he so devastated it was best that he kept away? Gabrielle had paid for the doctor, and now she also arranged and paid for the entire funeral, described as 'most wonderfully done'. Artistic Paris turned out in force. Valentine Hugo wrote, 'We were in utter despair,' watching the white coffin, white hearse and white flowers, with just one bunch of red roses. It was all to Gabrielle's design. The mourners followed in a long procession down the boulevard towards Père-Lachaise, the cemetery already harbouring so many fellow writers.

Meanwhile, for several months past, Gabrielle had been spending time with another writer.

Reverdy

The date is lost but, at some point around 1922, Gabrielle had begun another affair, this time with Picasso's old friend, the poet Pierre Reverdy.

Reverdy was friend to many of the painters and poets of pre-war Montmartre, on its hilltop in northern Paris. When they joined the post-war artistic exodus for Montparnasse, the new Montmartre in the southern part of the city, Reverdy stayed behind. With Max Jacob and the wild modernist poet Guillaume Apollinaire, in 1916 Reverdy had founded one of the most progressive and significant literary magazines of its day, the short-lived *Nord–Sud*. The name referred to the Metro line linking those two artistic Parisian domains, whose inhabitants had fought over modernity within the covers of Reverdy's magazine.

His great friend Georges Braque believed that, while almost no French poets had understood the first thing about modern art, Reverdy was 'almost the only exception'. Indeed, Reverdy's publication on Picasso was one of the few that the artist himself admired. Reverdy was both attracted and repelled by the smart snobberies of the *haut monde*, famously saying that he preferred the company of artists, and that 'life in society is one huge adventure in piracy and cannot be successful without a great deal of conniving.'

By contrast, Gabrielle was less ambivalent about having the *haut monde* as her friend, although none among them in the end would become as longstanding a companion as the supreme Misia Sert. Gabrielle was more emotionally resilient, more earthed than Reverdy, using her acerbic wit as a jousting tool with which to defend herself and keep mentally in trim. Describing society as

22. John Singer Sargent's drawing of Diana Wyndham, the young Englishwoman who would usurp Gabrielle.

23. Deauville Polo Club's Arthur Capel trophy, given by his sister, Berthe, possibly in conjunction with Gabrielle.

24. Sergei Diaghilev (*left*) and Igor Stravinsky, *c*. 1920, with whom Gabrielle became intimately associated.

25. Clockwise from top left: Stravinsky, José Maria Sert, Gabrielle and the inimitable Misia Sert.

26. (*right*) Grand Duke Dmitri Pavlovich.

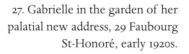

27. Gabrielle in the garden of her palatial new address, 29 Faubourg St-Honoré, early 1920s.

28. Dmitri Pavlovich.
with Gabrielle, 1920.

29. The earliest depiction
of Chanel N°5, by Sem,
c. 1921–2.

30. (*top left*) Gabrielle's costumes for *Le Train bleu*, 1922, were crucial to its up-to-the-minute air. Lydia Sokolova, Anton Dolin, Jean Cocteau, Leon Woizikovsky, Bronislava Nijinska.

31. (*top right*) Lydia Sokolova, Anton Dolin, Bronislava Nijinska and Leon Woizikovsky in *Le Train bleu*.

32. Lubov Tchernicheva as Calliope in *Apollon musagète*, 1929, her tricot tunic bound with neckties from Charvet, a classically simple Chanel touch.

33. (*top*) The poet Pierre Reverdy, whom Gabrielle lost to his religion.

34. (*right*) Paul Morand, man of letters, who took Gabrielle's memoir.

35. Bend'Or, 2nd Duke of Westminster.

36. The Duke of Westminster's Cheshire home, Eaton Hall.

37. Gabrielle with Winston and Randolph Churchill, boar-hunting on Bend'Or's French estate, 1928.

38. (*above*) Marion Moorhouse in a signature 'little black dress' by Gabrielle, 1926.

39. At Biarritz, 1928, in her trademark jersey, two-tone shoes and imitation jewellery.

40. Gabrielle on the Venice Lido, *c.* 1930, with Misia Sert
and Madame Berthelot. José Maria Sert is behind.

'irresistibly dishonest', she said, 'They amuse me more than the others. They make me laugh.'[1] Gabrielle's famed poise, mistakenly and patronizingly described as having been instilled in her by the Serts, was something she possessed naturally, and in abundance, long before she met them. Thus the confident and graceful Gabrielle felt quite equal to associating with the *haut monde*. Reverdy failed on pretty well all of these counts. So why had they become lovers?

However much Gabrielle might have found herself at the centre of fashionable society, she also remained an unconventional outsider. And, despite Pierre Reverdy's mulish stubbornness, and sense of pride that outdid even Gabrielle's, perhaps she fell in love with him precisely because he *wasn't* society. He represented something that, for her, was immeasurably greater. Almost half a century later, after he had died, she would say wistfully, 'He isn't dead. Poets . . . you know, they're not like us: they don't die at all.' This was the immortality Gabrielle herself longed for, and could not then know she would achieve.[2]

Gabrielle and Reverdy had known one another for some time before they began their affair, introduced by Picasso or Misia in the period after Arthur's death and when Reverdy had given up *Nord–Sud*. At the time, Gabrielle's heart and mind were entirely occupied with Arthur, but her suffering now made her more sympathetic to Reverdy's 'tormented and disquieting lyricism'.

Gabrielle was a deeply practical and pragmatic woman, yet an equally significant part of her lived wholeheartedly and unpragmatically in her imagination. This was a place quite other than the deeply absorbing craftsman's space she inhabited in her work. At the same time, she continued to believe, as had Arthur Capel and the Theosophists, in 'the fourth, fifth and sixth dimensions', and in tolerating and trying to understand religions 'other than one's own'. She found much solace in the idea that 'death is nothing; that one simply changes dimension.' Reassured by the thought that 'one never loses everything and that something happens on the other side,' she said, 'I believe in the unreal, I believe in everything that's full of mystery,' adding, 'But I don't believe in Spiritualism.'[3] These convictions helped Gabrielle empathize with Reverdy's blackness of temperament. Her beliefs also added to her sense of Reverdy drawing down something greater, and beyond, with which she identified. This humbled her, and was central to what would become a kind of reverence in which she was to hold Reverdy in the future.

Such thoughts and beliefs would lead Gabrielle to champion this strange and increasingly reclusive man's work. She would agree with the Surrealist André Breton's overstatement that Reverdy was 'the greatest poet of our time'. Since Gabrielle's first meeting with him, she had become more fully herself. Her defiance, never very far below the surface, was reflected in her love for Reverdy, itself an inevitable confrontation with the establishment. Gabrielle didn't really give a damn about the establishment. Demonstrating her accustomed capacity for paradox, while she may have acquired for herself one of the smartest addresses in Paris, and mixed with the *haut monde*, she cared little that she had also acquired a lover who was a poet, who eked out an existence as proofreader on an evening paper and was often virtually penniless.

A man proud of his forebears – freethinking craftsmen from the Bas Languedoc, at the southernmost part of the Cévennes – with southern roots like Gabrielle, Reverdy enjoyed, with her, the sensual, earthy pleasures of food and wine. His sombre, intense looks were just as dark as his lover's and, while he was passionately voluble, Reverdy was just as capable as she was of silence. Gabrielle identified with his childhood suffering, and one senses that she must have told this fellow southerner about her own youthful miseries and her punishing incarceration in the convent at Aubazine.

Reverdy had a devoted wife, Henriette, a seamstress back in Montmartre, who was admired by painter friends such as Modigliani, Gris and Braque. They wanted to paint her for her simplicity and her beauty. When Reverdy's failure to make a living from his writing meant that he and Henriette were on the verge of destitution, she took in sewing to help support them. Meanwhile, her husband was almost more adept at making enemies than he was at making friends. Cocteau rather spitefully described him as 'a false, uncultured, irascible, unjust mind',[4] but had to admit that, in his writing, he was absolutely the reverse.

The poet Louis Aragon, Dadaist and founding member of Surrealism, observed in Reverdy's eyes 'that fire of anger unlike any I ever saw'. Unlike Gabrielle, Reverdy was unable to use his towering pride as a spur. But, like Gabrielle, he was a character of great paradox, and, while exhibiting that overweening pride, he was also deeply modest. Finding balance almost impossible, he oscillated between indulgence and extreme ascetic abstinence. He was a brilliant talker, but his silences could be deadly, and everything was done by extremes: eating, drinking, smoking and women. Having over-indulged in all these, he was led by turns from revulsion to an inexorable sense of self-loathing. Yet these tendencies and their corresponding darkness did nothing to reduce Reverdy's ability to love women; no matter that afterwards he was overcome by remorse. It wasn't remorse alone, however, that periodically made him flee Gabrielle and the Faubourg St-Honoré and return to his wife in Montmartre. Gabrielle brought out in him a dread at the thought of being tied.

While Reverdy's vacillation between an obsession with Gabrielle and resisting her must have been emotionally taxing for both of them, she was prepared to suffer his erratic behaviour and ferocious rages. One day, Gabrielle was entertaining at the Hôtel de Lauzan. Amongst her guests was Aimé Maeght, art dealer and friend to most of the significant artists of the period, including Braque and Giacometti. Reverdy appeared with a basket on his arm. Completely ignoring Gabrielle and her guests, he walked down the steps on to the lawn, and calmly proceeded to collect snails and place them in his basket.

His disquiet about good living and wealth put Gabrielle right at the centre of Reverdy's doubts. But his love for her emerged from somewhere far more significant than her exemplification of refinement. There are a good many who make an art out of living and, while this is an undeniably important contribution to life, it should not be confused with art. But what drew Reverdy back to Gabrielle more than the lifestyle she represented was her strength, her *joie de vivre*, her imagination and her creativity. Reverdy also understood that an essential part of her was just as austere as he was.

Gabrielle accused him of masochistically refusing even fleeting possibilities of happiness, telling him he made his unhappiness into a 'principle'. But Reverdy's sense of isolation was almost impregnable; he believed that our most durable links with one another are the very barriers between us. He asked, 'What would become of dreams if people were happy in their real lives?' It wasn't that Gabrielle herself had ever been a particular devotee of the notion of happiness. Indeed, as time went on, she grew exasperated at the growing belief that one had a right to it. Nonetheless, she had a great urge towards life, and the positive, creative forces that this implied. More firmly grounded than Reverdy, she was not tempted by the mysticism gaining a hold over her poet. Battling to nurture him and nullify his remorse, Gabrielle tried to keep Reverdy by her, to tether him more firmly to this earth.

Offering her strength and capabilities as support, she helped him with great tact and generosity, made visits to his publishers, paid them grants to pass on to him, and also bought his manuscripts. It was Gabrielle who financed his first major book of poems, *Cravates de chanvre* (the hempen rope used for hangings). And all this she did in secret, so as to save his terrible pride. Reverdy alienated a growing number of his friends, including the Surrealists who had idolized him, and sometimes Gabrielle tried to mediate. Eventually, there were few left who would support his dreadful rages: Picasso, Gris, Braque, Max Jacob – friends Reverdy and Gabrielle had in common. One senses, too, that Gabrielle and Reverdy must have each caused the other emotional torment.

Gradually, his periods of absence from her home grew longer, until, some time in 1924, he left, no more to return. Finally, to his friends' amazement, Reverdy would withdraw from the world completely. Accompanied by his ever-faithful Henriette, he placed himself in a small house beside the Benedictine abbey of Solesmes, out in the Pays de la Loire.

For Gabrielle to trust a man was most unusual. But, over the years, whatever the tumult of her relationship with Reverdy, she never ceased admiring him and remained devoted to his poetry. It was immaterial that Reverdy was married, or that their love affair was turbulent. In turn, until his death, Reverdy would send copies of all he wrote to Gabrielle, with touching dedications:

Dear Coco
The time that passes
The weather outside
The time that flies
Of my obscure life I had lost the trace
Here it is found again darker than the night
But what remains clear is that with all my heart I give you my love
And all that follows doesn't matter.[5]

Despite all Gabrielle's best efforts, she had lost yet another man and, with Reverdy's final departure, she was left wretched. While outsiders had little comprehension of this relationship, they could yet see that, between this strange pair, there was a deep rapport. Some time later, that inveterate old commentator on the Parisian comedy of manners the Abbé Mugnier wrote, correctly, that Gabrielle's affection encouraged Reverdy to write and that she herself was not the same as she had been before their affair.

Cocteau's mother's comment on the relationship as 'the return of a peasant woman to a peasant', albeit said in snobbery, went some way towards understanding Gabrielle and Reverdy. It wasn't exactly that they were peasants – they had both travelled way beyond those roots, and neither of them could have either lived with or been accepted by their kin – it was the residual element of their inherited connections to the earth and tradition. Despite the strains of their relationship, in Reverdy Gabrielle had discovered someone whose significance, while not replacing Arthur's, reconnected her with the pastoral nature of her roots, giving her emotional and spiritual nourishment. Reverdy had written to her, 'You know well that whatever happens, and God knows how much has already happened, you cannot render yourself anything other than infinitely precious to me, for ever.'

With Reverdy's departure, Gabrielle's heart had been dealt a ferocious blow. But her habit of concealing the depth of her feelings was not so difficult to achieve, since the worlds in which she moved were noted for their particular egotism and self-regard. All the same, one suspects that, in her entire life, there may only have been a handful of people who understood this highly intelligent, paradoxical and defensive woman with anything like the emotional imagination necessary to do so.

In that same year, 1924, Gabrielle was once again asked by Cocteau to design the costumes for a new Ballets Russes production, *Le Train bleu*, whose inception arose out of a Diaghilev fit of pique. Following the death of Radiguet, Cocteau had gone to Monte Carlo to find distraction with his musical friends Stravinsky, Poulenc and Auric. Whatever the histrionics, Cocteau was genuinely prostrate at the death of his youthful *amour* and would take years to recover from it.

In Monte Carlo was the music critic Louis Laloy, a man of great cultivation, who was also addicted to opium. In 1913, his notorious *Le Livre de la fumée*, a history and manual of opium smoking, was credited with the great popularity of its practice in post-war Europe. Cocteau would write, 'My nervous suffering became so great, so overwhelming, that Laloy at Monte Carlo suggested I relieve it in this way,'[6] and so, with Poulenc, Auric and Laloy, he began smoking in earnest. By the time he left Monte Carlo a few weeks later, he was hooked, and would at times be reduced to an appalling state by his addiction in the future. While Gabrielle would complain about Cocteau, she also remained his supporter, paying on several occasions for his rehabilitation. It is worth bearing in mind here the opinion of a present-day expert in drug addiction: 'Addiction beginning in one's mid-thirties [Cocteau's age], or thereafter, is not a search for excitement or pleasure, as in the very young.' Cocteau was not out for kicks, he was desperate to escape the depths of his depression.

The ballet *Le Train bleu* came about initially as compensation for Cocteau's involvement in a contretemps between Diaghilev and the ambitious and flirtatious Ukrainian dancer Serge Lifar, who had stepped out of line. The ballet was set at a resort and became a vehicle for the extraordinary gymnastic antics of Diaghilev's present lover, a young Irishman named Anton Dolin (real name, Patrick Kay). Cocteau's thin storyline had Dolin impressing a troupe of golf and tennis players and featured beach belles of both sexes who were all in search of adventure.

With a score from Darius Milhaud, choreography was to be by Nijinsky's dour but gifted sister, Bronislava Nijinska; set designs were by the Cubist sculptor Henri Laurens, and costumes were by Gabrielle. Laurens's Riviera beach set of sloping Cubist planes and lopsided beach huts was in natural hues, dramatically setting off Gabrielle's costumes, in bright dynamic colours.

Diaghilev didn't like Laurens's front curtain. And, remembering that, in Picasso's chaotic studio, he had seen a canvas of the now-famous giant women, hand in hand, bare breasted and running across a beach, he set out to acquire it. Diaghilev loved the earthy abandon of these women, and his majestic powers of persuasion overcame even the wily and stubborn Picasso. Diaghilev was so pleased with this painting that a brilliantly enlarged version – painted by the Russian émigré Prince Shervashidze – was used as the Ballets Russes front cloth from then on.

The Blue Train to which the ballet refers was then the ultimate in chic. Launched only two years earlier, it carried the wealthy between Calais and the French Riviera in exclusively first-class carriages. Leaving Paris in the evening, and renowned for its cuisine, the train made three stops before arriving at Marseille the following morning. Then it called in at the most important resort towns along the Riviera, finally halting close to the Italian border. Named by its wealthy passengers for its beautiful dark-blue carriages, speeding south in search of pleasure and escape, the train had an image of up-to-the-minute sophistication and romance. Each of its sleeping cars had only ten compartments, with an attendant for every car. Early passengers included the Prince of Wales, Charlie Chaplin, F. Scott Fitzgerald, Evelyn Waugh, J. M. Barrie, Somerset Maugham and Gabrielle Chanel. In the years between the two world wars, the Blue Train carried almost everyone who was anyone travelling to the south of France.

In Gabrielle's utterly fashionable beachwear, Cocteau's undesirable passengers – gigolos, good-time girls and chancers of one sort or another – were 'hardhearted modern youth that pushes us around with impertinent contempt ... Those superb girls who stride past swearing, with tennis racquets under their arm, and get between us and the sun'.[7] Cocteau was commenting on the radical change in the way the young felt empowered to behave in the post-war years. They revealed the tendency to disdain authority, already flourishing in those small groups of artists in the early years of the century, and now sufficiently widespread that Cocteau could characterize it in a ballet.

A good fraction of Gabrielle's clients were young women in this category: tomboys with short hair who wished for emancipation. Their wealth and privilege made them appear liberated, but a few recognized that there was more to independence than pretending to it by simply taking their father's, their spouse's or their lover's money.

Gabrielle was present at many of the rehearsals for *Le Train bleu*, and was by now well versed in the infighting and tensions ever present during the making of a Diaghilev production. With the Ballets Russes, Diaghilev had created around him, as he always did, a kind of loose extended-family atmosphere where, whatever their differences, ultimately, they pulled together. Again generated by Diaghilev, an edginess and energy arising out of experiment was what his company of 'sacred monsters' thrived upon, often spilling over into near-chaos. While finding them all infuriating, Gabrielle, like her friend Cocteau, was also stimulated by the Russians' very un-French way of going about things. Logistics, money, the sets, the music, the fanatical dedication, the love affairs, treachery, high artistry and rampant emotion – all elements, of course, with their own creative and destructive possibilities in any kind of production. But Diaghilev and the Ballets Russes took them to the limit. The Russians were so entirely different from the cultivated, artistically minded French bourgeoisie and aristocrats. At a certain level, they were simply more interesting; more exotic, authentic and richer in possibility than the immensely self-conscious refinement found in the Parisian salons.

Diaghilev, a formidable despot, was whimsical, sarcastic and vindictive. Practising outrageous favouritism, he was also endowed with extraordinary artistic flair. The company might sometimes have grown tetchy at his despotism, but they understood it, and wouldn't have continued working for him if they hadn't recognized his great talent. Typically working up close to catastrophe meant that it was never quite certain until the last moments whether a Diaghilev production would actually take its bow in front of a first-night audience. And *Le Train bleu* was no exception.

At the dress rehearsal, almost everything was wrong. In Gabrielle's case, this meant half the costumes. Serge Lifar would later say, 'They were not costumes conceived for dancing.' Gabrielle simply hadn't appreciated the necessity of adapting her clothes to encompass the choreography. Unable to try them before the dress rehearsal, the dancers discovered it was impossible to move in them properly. The female lead, Lydia Sokolova, wore Gabrielle's bright pink knitted swimsuit, but it was loosely fitted and made it difficult for her partner to get a hold on her in the various throws and catches. (Sokolova – real name, Hilda Munnings – became the first English member of the Ballets Russes in 1913, dancing the demanding female lead in the 1920 revival of *The Rite of Spring*.) Sokolova's fake-pearl stud earrings – to become one of *the* fashion accessories of the twenties – were so heavy that, apparently, she could barely hear the music. And the head-hugging bathing cap Gabrielle had her wear soon became a must for any fashionable swimmer.

Diaghilev would also ask Gabrielle to step in on a number of productions to update the dancers' costumes. This included bringing right up to date the fashionable hostess in Diaghilev and Poulenc's *Les Biches* (1924) and redesigning the three muses' costumes for *Apollon musagète* (1929). These were beautifully simple tricot tunics, with neck-ties from the House of Charvet winding around the dancers' bodies. In these productions, for the most part, Gabrielle was uninterested in personal glory and became just as involved as the rest of the company in contributing to their success.

The problems with *Le Train bleu*'s dress rehearsal appeared insurmountable to Diaghilev, and he had fled up to the last row of the balcony, asking what on earth they could put on that evening instead. However, all the dancers and the stagehands, plus Diaghilev, Nijinska, Cocteau, Gabrielle and the dressers, stayed on in the theatre that afternoon and effectively remade the ballet. Amongst the radical changes, Gabrielle pulled apart and redesigned half of her modish beach clothes. These were then re-sewn by the dressers in a very few hours. Somehow, everything was done, the curtain went up and, on that evening of 13 June 1924, *Le Train bleu* was judged as 'distinctly new and modern', and a great success.

With *le tout* Paris and a good number of artists in the audience, Cocteau and Diaghilev had brought off a mix of theatre, dance, music, pantomime and satire. It fell way outside any classical definition of ballet, whose traditional siting had been in the unreal worlds of myth or fairy tale. It wasn't simply that these two *agents provocateurs*, Diaghilev and Cocteau, had freed ballet and produced a spectacle based on 'the powerful charm of the pavement'. As in *Parade*, they had once again created a new and entirely modern kind of theatrical performance. They had made another firm step in the development of modernist art, based above all on aspects of contemporary life. In this context, it was entirely appropriate that the couturier Coco Chanel, who was synonymous with modernity, should be the person who designed the ballet's costumes.

Integral to Diaghilev's obsession with every aspect of his company's performances was his fierce perfectionism about his dancers' costumes. As a result, during the twenties, Gabrielle and Misia Sert became his extra 'eyes'. Acting in a sense as superintendents of taste, they had the last word on the 'correctness' of colours, lengths, decoration and the general design of the costumes. And, following Gabrielle's first mistakes, most importantly, they asked the question, did the costumes 'work' in movement?

Between 1922 and 1937, Gabrielle designed the costumes for several more Cocteau productions, including *Orpheus*, *Oedipus Rex* and *The Knights of the Round Table*. She was also invited to make the costumes for several films, such as Jean Renoir's famed *La Règle du jeu* (*The Rules of the Game*) in 1939. Renoir's biting satire of French upper-class society, evoking the country's disjointedness in the lead-up to the Second World War, is regarded by many as one of the greatest films ever made. Gabrielle could present herself as opinionated in the extreme, yet she spoke very little of the work she carried out for the theatre and films. Over the years, interviewers would ask about some of the remarkable performances for which she had made the costumes, an activity so different from her accustomed working life. But Gabrielle remained frustratingly unforthcoming, hardly referring to the illustrious company present at opening nights, or to her involvement in these important works of art. When asked later about the first night of *Le Train bleu*, for example, she wanted only to recall the artists. By implication, when it came to art, for Gabrielle, high society didn't matter.

At the Centre

For Gabrielle there was an absolute distinction between the skills and technique of the artisan, as opposed to the workings of an artist. While she herself was always staunchly opposed to calling herself an artist, one also remembers she was a woman of paradox.

As the twentieth century wore on and the distinction between artist and craftsman became ever more blurred, Gabrielle found this mistaken and pretentious, insisting ever more vehemently she was only an artisan, a dressmaker and *not* an artist. She declared that fashion should be discussed 'without poetry, without literature. A dress is neither a tragedy, nor a painting; it is a charming and ephemeral creation, not an everlasting work of art.'[1] She insisted that while couture may have an awareness of art, it is only a technique, a business. Whatever the success of their creations, Gabrielle believed that did not 'justify couturiers persuading themselves or thinking of themselves – or dressing or posing – as artists'.[2]

She drew a clear distinction between craft and art. And while, paradoxically, Gabrielle had a good deal of the artist in her, she singled out the couturier's instinct for their times:

Creation is an artistic gift, a collaboration of the couturier with his or her own times . . . It is not by learning to make dresses that they become successful (making dresses and creating fashion are different things); fashion does not exist only in dresses; fashion is in the air, it is borne on the wind, you can sense it, you can breathe it, it's in the sky and on the highway, it's everywhere, it has to do with ideas, with social mores, with events . . .

Fashion should express the place, the moment. This is where the commercial adage 'the client is always right' gets its precise and clear meaning; that meaning demonstrates that fashion, like opportunity, is something that has to be grabbed by the hair.[3]

She would add that 'fashion roams around the streets, unaware that it exists, up to the moment that I, in my own way, may have expressed it. Fashion, like landscape, is a state of mind, by which I mean my own.'[4]

If one is searching for what made Gabrielle stand out from her contemporaries, the source of her originality won't be found by looking for any one particular thing. It lay in a combination of elements, at the heart of which was Gabrielle's profound instinct for her own period. Her powers of observation, her intuitiveness, her inherited shrewdness as the trader's daughter; these gave her an unusually alert sense of 'what was in the air'. In combination with her intelligence, these qualities made her a remarkable adept at interpreting and presenting their own epoch to her contemporaries.

Gabrielle's great gift lay in paying ruthless attention to the texture of the moment. If fashion can be said to illuminate or articulate that, then that was Gabrielle. Acting as a barometer, she gave her world what it wanted, just before it recognized the need. Her work was always just that one step ahead, because she intuited her times better than most of those around her.

For Gabrielle, the genius of the couturier lay in that quality that kept *her* so vibrantly alive. This was the ability to anticipate: 'More than a great statesman the great couturier is a man who has the future in his mind . . . Fashion is not an art, it is a job. If art makes use of fashion, then that is sufficient praise.' And then she justifies the necessity to follow fashion, the necessity to follow one's own times: 'It's best to follow fashion, even if it is ugly. To detach oneself from it is immediately to become a comical character, which is terrifying. No one is powerful enough to be more powerful than fashion.'[5]

These intelligent pronouncements, some of the best ever made about fashion, also reveal much about Gabrielle's motivation. They arose from a certain modesty about her own work, and a deep respect for what she believed was the work of the real artist. At the same time, she was never in awe of the great artists of her day. Associating happily with them, she was correct in her belief that, in some important sense, she was their peer.

Gabrielle's sense of invention now led her to develop a rich new seam of creativity. In 1924, she set up her own jewellery workshops, and Comte Etienne de Beaumont – who for some time had had jewellery made to his design by the best artisans, as presents for friends – became her manager. Gabrielle also asked François Hugo, already the director of her jersey factory at Asnières, to make her some jewellery designs. As there was already an extensive demand for replica jewellery, Gabrielle could turn to a wide range of highly skilled artisans, such as Madame Gripoix and her husband, famous costume jewellers, originally for Poiret. Gabrielle's inspiration was diverse. For all her austerity of design, she loved the exotic, and was also fascinated by Renaissance and Byzantine designs. During the twenties, she added many strings of fake pearls – and great coloured stones in the form of necklaces, brooches and pendants – to her understated clothes. And, in the late twenties, she even sparked off a fashion for asymmetrical earrings: one black and one white pearl. (One of the ways she signalled that her jewellery was imitation was by the unnatural size of some of her stones.)

Carmel Snow, who would become the highly influential editor of *Harper's Bazaar*, wrote of her sister Christine's return from Paris in that decade. When she showed the female members of the family her Parisian wardrobe, her mother was appalled at the Chanel dress made of jersey and decorated with some dubious fur:

> Worse than that, Christine festooned her dress with ropes and ropes of artificial pearls. In the first place, no lady wore anything but a single strand of pearls before eight o'clock in the evening. In the second place, they were real. Christine admitted that Coco Chanel

herself wore fabulous jewels with her own jersey dresses and sweaters, but that everyone in Paris who couldn't afford such a display was now wearing Chanel's imitation jewellery.[6]

But Gabrielle also wore this imitation jewellery. Indeed, she famously made a habit of mixing it with her own fabulous jewels, many of them received as gifts from her lovers. Imitation jewellery had been made for the less well off for thousands of years. But where these jewels had traditionally copied the 'real thing', Gabrielle's oversized jewellery was different in that it was ostentatiously fake. And her prestige was such that her clients followed her; women who usually owned valuable collections of precious *real* jewels wanted Gabrielle's imitations. She believed that:

> Expensive jewellery does not improve the woman who wears it . . . if she looks plain she will remain so . . . the mania to want to dazzle disgusts me; jewellery is not meant to arouse envy; still less astonishment. It should remain an ornament and an amusement . . . Jewellery from jewellery shops bores me; I had the idea of getting François Hugo to design clip-on earrings, brooches . . .[7]

In order to look right, it had to be imitation. Typical of Gabrielle's capacity for paradox, she believed that too much money killed luxury. She also had many of her priceless gems dismantled and re-ordered to her own designs. Later, the renowned jeweller Robert Goossens would say, 'I took apart a lot of Mademoiselle's jewels. I don't know if they were Grand Duke Dmitri's or the Duke of Westminster's, but I remember a ruby necklace . . . from Cartier, out of which I made earrings. Mademoiselle would give them away as presents . . . They were unique pieces.'[8]

During the daytime, Gabrielle often wore a mass of jewellery, while in the evening she might wear none at all. She had a more sophisticated understanding of luxury than many of the wealthy, and said, 'Jewellery should be looked on innocently, naively, rather as one enjoys the sight of an apple tree in blossom by the side of the road as one speeds by in a motor car. This is how ordinary people perceive it; for them jewellery denotes social standing.'[9] So it does for many of the rich. While Gabrielle was at pains to turn the snobbery of jewellery on its head, she was also ahead of her time in challenging the idea of what is 'real'.

Gabrielle worked extremely hard, turning out her two large collections every year, and the orders only grew. In 1924, when she had something like three thousand workers, her perfume, Chanel N°5, had been selling steadily from her salons in Paris, Deauville and Biarritz. Exactly how much demand there was for more perfume is unclear, but Gabrielle wanted to sell more. She was now advised by an acquaintance of some years, Théophile Bader, the owner of the largest Paris department store, Galeries Lafayette. He said he wouldn't sell Gabrielle's perfume until she had a much larger quantity than Ernest Beaux was presently making down in Grasse. Bader said he knew just the people Gabrielle should meet. These were two young brothers, Pierre and Paul Wertheimer. Intelligent, hard-headed businessmen, the Wertheimers owned Bourjois Perfumeries, the largest cosmetics and fragrance company in France, and were intent upon building on their father's considerable success. Apparently, the Wertheimers and Gabrielle met at the Longchamp racetrack, and there they struck a deal.

While Paul was a more retiring personality, Pierre's charm made his handsomeness almost irresistible. He loved horses, women and collecting and, in business, was said to be ruthless. Like the Rothschilds, the Wertheimers were a long-Gallicized Jewish family, who traced their roots back to Germany. They were also diligently discreet about the extent of their financial empire – a discretion that would, over the years, manifest itself in the manner of their control over Gabrielle's empire.

For over half a century, Pierre Wertheimer and Gabrielle were to carry on a tempestuous and complex relationship, in which they alternately needed and loathed one another but were never able to part. Battling out their differences in a sometimes bitter struggle, they each tried tirelessly to wrest an atom of respect from their partner-opponent, whom they loved but also hated. Almost in the same breath, Gabrielle would be able to refer to Pierre Wertheimer as 'that crook who cheated me' and 'dear Pierre'.

During their early meetings, Gabrielle apparently wasn't really interested in the details of the transaction. She would later say of herself, 'I've conducted business without being a businesswoman,' and that it bored her to death to think about such things as sheets of figures. It wasn't that she wasn't capable of counting money in the till at the end of the day, but her capacity to make vast sums was more instinctive than that. Gabrielle's money-making ability derived from her wily peasant ancestors and her mad urge to create. She could say, rightly, that 'I am not in the least frivolous, I have a boss's soul,' but that same soul was also deeply creative and questing. She was not an artist, but her manner of invention was, more often than not, in the spirit of one.

The woman of whom Picasso would say she was 'the most practical in the world' would herself say, 'Order is a subjective phenomenon.' This was the reaction of the creator who understood perfectly Apollinaire's words: 'Bringing forth order from chaos, that's what creation is all about.'

When Gabrielle was informed by the Wertheimers that, if she wanted them to distribute her perfumes, they would have to form a company, she is supposed to have said, 'Form a company if you like, but I'm not interested in getting involved in your business . . . I'll be content with 10 per cent of the stock.' Over time, this statement would be the cause of much disagreement. Gabrielle had meant 10 per cent of the perfume's profits, but the Wertheimers interpreted it differently. In future years, Gabrielle's lawyer, Réné de Chambrun, would become convinced that it was fear of losing control over her couture house that motivated her to sign away her perfume for 10 per cent of her already large business.

The partnership set up between the Wertheimers and Gabrielle in 1924 would be characterized by bickering, antipathy and a large number of lawsuits. But their relationship also came to include both mutual respect and real friendship, albeit often grudging. Nevertheless, Gabrielle's leitmotif for the following half a century was to be: 'I signed something in 1924; I let myself be swindled.' Certainly, there would be examples of injustices perpetrated upon her by her partners but, on discovering that, for example, on introducing her to the Wertheimers, Bader had received 20 per cent of the partnership (not uncommon in business), Gabrielle felt this was patronizing in the extreme. All the same, she was forever machinating against the Wertheimers and over the years gave just as good as she got. Quite possibly, Gabrielle had been 'swindled', but she was also unwilling to acknowledge the snares involved in the bargain she had agreed to when initiating her relationship with her middlemen, the Wertheimers.

In all likelihood, notwithstanding Gabrielle's instinct for her times, she didn't quite comprehend the ways in which this was a novel relationship; one that would gradually make her part of a new kind of company. The complexity of her business relations with the Wertheimers went way beyond that between the market trader and his suppliers. Its ramifications were more complex than any of the biggest international enterprises of the past, where a merchant and his agents might have travelled to the furthest corners of the earth in caravans of horses or camels, or on board ship, armed with their negotiating skills, their contacts and their ability to strike a bargain with their suppliers.

Gabrielle's new partnership was a twentieth-century corporation in embryo, and the commodity being sold was, essentially, Gabrielle. But while on the one hand proud of it, on the other, she would also remain ambivalent about being one of the founders of the twentieth century and all that its democratic, mechanized and merchandising possibilities eventually brought about. As the woman who, more than any other, would make fashion possible for millions of other women across the world, Gabrielle experienced the dilemma of being deeply individualistic in the first age of mass culture and mass consumption.

How could the skilled craftsmen and women who had made buttons, braids, ribbons and lace, woven beautiful textiles of all kinds by hand, and Gabrielle's *premières*, who used these things in their painstaking handiwork, compete with the speed and the cheapness of the mechanization of almost every conceivable task? Gabrielle's was an empire which, by the time she died, would have become a corporate one, and which, in the years since her death, has developed into something representative of truly modern times: a global corporation. Gabrielle's name has become a corporate identity.

In the course of 1924, Ernest Beaux developed another perfume for Gabrielle. They called it Cuir de Russie. Two years later, this was followed by Bois des Îles and, in 1927, another one, Gardénia, was being promoted. Yet, despite the Wertheimers' publicity department promotions, the success of these perfumes would be nothing compared to Chanel N°5. Even taking into account the fact that the lion's share of the profits went to the Wertheimers, by far the largest part of Gabrielle's wealth would soon depend upon this one perfume. Over the years, the company the Wertheimers named Les Parfums Chanel would promote Gabrielle's perfume with a publicity campaign of increasing sophistication. Here, like Gabrielle, the prodigy Raymond Radiguet had shown his flair for the spirit of the age when he prophesied, 'I speak of advertising ... In publicity, more than anywhere else, I see the future of the sublime, so threatened in modern poetry.'

During the war, the material damage sustained by France had been staggering. But, afterwards, while there wasn't an economic revolution, new activities, such as car production, helped boost the economy and, during the twenties, life for many carried on improving. At the same time, the structure of mainstream French society, and its attitudes, remained effectively the same. What need to change? There was a boom. And as part of post-war 'reconstruction', a traditionalist and government drive called for the preservation of home and hearth, and for women to have more babies.

The New Woman, however, was becoming more conspicuous,

spent less time by the French hearth and was producing alarmingly fewer babies. Not only was she infiltrating previously male preserves, by the mid-twenties, at least, she was also wearing versions of Gabrielle's straight-up-and-down dresses, camouflaging bosom and hips and cutting off her hair. This way, she earned for herself the sobriquet *la garçonne*; in the English-speaking world, she became the 'flapper'.

In 1922, Victor Margueritte's racy, best-selling novel *La Garçonne* – from which the above name derived – introduced a modern young woman, personifying the social, intellectual and technological changes now beginning to shape bourgeois urban life. Projected in the mass media leading an entirely altered life, the 'emancipated' woman drove motor cars, flew planes and was a dashing young thing entirely in control of her life. Attractive, self-assured, often quite aggressive, she was also independent and out for adventure. Always on the move, she travelled unescorted and succeeded in some newly invented career. Slicking down her short hair, she smoked, wore trousers, and even men's suits. And, while ambiguity of all kinds became a highly visible aspect of society, the majority of those women dressing in confrontational ways were actually only practising a 'visual language of liberation' rather than the real thing.

For most, 'emancipation' meant little more than what they did with their appearance. It was only a small number of women, like Gabrielle, whose lives really were entirely altered. In Paris, these included Colette; the fashionable bisexual painter Tara de Lempicka, who sniffed her cocaine with the likes of André Gide; the shipping-line heiress Nancy Cunard, who knew Gabrielle, wore Chanel and outraged her class, not by the drugs she used but by her cropped hair, her men's suits and her co-habitation with a black lover. Then there was the bisexual Russian dancer Ida Rubenstein, and the black American dancer Josephine Baker, whose erotic and challenging female persona took Paris by storm in 1925.

If, in reality, however, the scope for most French women had expanded little, in essence, what they wore was announcing to their menfolk, 'I am your equal.' A popular song from the twenties articulates well the anxieties these loosened boundaries were provoking:

> Hey, hey, women are going mad today;
> Hey, hey, fellers are just as bad, I'll say.
> Masculine women, feminine men,
> Which is the rooster, which is the hen?
> It's hard to tell 'em apart today, hey, hey.

Victor Margueritte described the heroine of his *La Garçonne*, Monique Lerbier, as the incarnation of 'woman's right to sexual equality in love', and her premarital erotic encounters, including those with women, provoked a public outcry. Margueritte saw bobbed hair as 'a symbol of independence, if not power'.[10] Antoine, the Parisian hairdresser who was a pioneer of the short haircut, meanwhile joked that, in creating the bob, he had avenged Samson by depriving Delilah of her hair and hence her power to charm men. Discussion and argument raged back and forth, fathers disowned short-haired daughters, and there was more than one case of murder. The socialite Boni de Castellane complained that 'women no longer exist; all that's left are the boys created by Chanel.'

Yet, in this age of confusion, Gabrielle herself believed she was in less doubt about what it was she was doing. Confident in her femininity, she didn't feel she was in competition with men. What she wanted was *scope* to act equally. This of course involved competition but, for her, it didn't mean trying to become the same. In years to come, she would make one of her breathtakingly dismissive statements reinforcing this attitude: 'Women who want to look like men, men who want to look like women are both failures.'

The stereotype of the 'flapper' was that of an apolitical consumer, hell bent on having a good time. A number of recent historians have seen Gabrielle and her kind as part of an emergent modern consumerism exploiting women in the pursuit of profit.[11] Although this is far too simplistic, 'emancipation' was indeed at times rather illusory.[12] In 1923, *Vogue* described the hours 'one poor woman' spent at the gym and the masseuse, and the pills and 'rub-ber girdles' used to attain 'an ideal shape'. Another article would say 'how seductive is the straight line of our winter dresses, how reveal-ing of the sveltnesse of the female silhouette,' but then admitted that this was pretty well impossible to acquire without some kind of corset: 'There was no other way of achieving the desired silhou-ette.'

One honest contemporary writer declared that there was a 'tyr-anny of liberty in current fashion', because of the desperate measures to which women were driven, and that 'the effect of extreme elegance . . . hardly leads someone to suspect it took two hours to achieve, so much is dependent on the triumphant appear-ance of simplicity.' This could well be a description of the amount of time we know Gabrielle took over her own preparations to dress. Our commentator did, however, also say that, if contemporary dress was an 'illusion of freedom', freedom was in fact the *objective* of the new look. But if a woman's bobbed hair and short dresses were not as 'liberating' as they were made out to be, and many women's lives were most unliberated, why did young women take to these fashions with such enthusiasm?

Perhaps the answer lies in the idea that in *appearing* liberated through what one wore, it gradually became a genuine aspect of personal emancipation. Wearing short hair and short dresses, women were able to project a fantasy of their ideal, liberated selves moving freely in society. Appearing thus liberated, they gave the idea a certain political power and did provoke a public outcry. The *appearance* of the 'flapper' represented a visual image of personal freedom. Wearing the clothes promoted by Gabrielle, women embraced what had become part of the meaning of fashion, throw-ing off their previous constraints.

Wearing the new fashions – copies of Gabrielle's fashions – kept the idea of female identity in the forefront of people's minds. While the debate in France was intensely political, women's short hair and short dresses became central to the cultural mythology of the whole era. Provoking outrage, frustration, envy and admiration, the way Gabrielle and her followers looked provided a powerful visual language for the upheaval and change that everyone saw around them.[13] And while, for most women, their clothes were as yet a fantasy of liberation, fashion itself was a powerful language of signs, heralding the arrival of a new world.

While Gabrielle's dresses may have been decorated, they were also not much more than sheaths, where any sign of the waist was long gone. Hips and busts were effectively banished, and those corsets must indeed have been in demand. Waists were firmly tethered to the hip, at the most women's designs were only semi-fitted, and Gabrielle's particularly versatile sporty looks were ever more popular and much copied. *Vogue* would write that her 'dresses, which met the needs of the time so well and which made those who were wearing them look so young, earned their creator worldwide fame'.[14]

Perhaps the most legendary of Gabrielle's designs was the one known as the 'little black dress'. It was described as 'little' because discreet. Quite how it came about is unclear, but Gabrielle's own version of events was told later. One evening in 1920, she was at the theatre. Looking at the women all around her in their flashy, gaudy colours, she said she was driven to say to her companion, 'These colours are impossible. These women, I'm bloody well going to dress them in black! So I imposed black . . . Black wipes out everything else around it. I used to tolerate colours, but I treated them as monochrome masses. The French don't have a sense of blocks of colour.'[15]

Forestalling the criticism of these ideas, Gabrielle said that it was wrong to think that dressing women in black removed all originality from them. Rather, she believed that apparently dressing alike helped reveal women's individuality. While wearing black earlier herself, in her 1926 collections Gabrielle introduced a number of utterly simple day dresses, all in black. A colour traditionally used for uniforms of various kinds, or during periods of mourning, black was on the whole considered unseemly if worn by women on other occasions. But Gabrielle had already made long and beautiful black evening dresses at least as early as 1917.

Now, she reinterpreted and restyled the colour in the most elegantly spare shapes. She was the first to show black dresses to be worn at any time of day or night, and later said, 'Before me no one would have dared to dress in black.' For daytime, the dresses were in wool or Moroccan crepe; for evening, they were in luxurious materials, such as silk crepe, satin and velvet. While their basic structure remained deceptively simple, they were counterbalanced by decoration, such as jewelled and rhinestone-decorated belts, or white collars, cuffs and much jewellery. Sometimes, Gabrielle used the striking flourish of a white camellia – made from various materials – pinned against a black dress. (Eventually, she loved to have them pinned in the hair.)

While Gabrielle's black designs were to become universally adopted, the initial response to their elegant economy of line was not unanimously positive. American *Vogue*, however, correctly predicted that the little black dress would become 'a sort of uniform for all modern women of taste'. Its very 'simplicity' would overcome the fear women had hitherto laboured under, of being seen in the same dress as another woman, reflecting an essential element of Gabrielle's whole outlook: a woman in a black dress draws attention as much to herself as to her dress. American *Vogue* had immediately grasped Gabrielle's message and, in the editorial, made the famous comment that these dresses were like the black, mass-produced Ford motor cars. By implication, they would become standard wear for the masses. A detail of that season was Gabrielle's addition of cloche hats. They may at first have been criticized by the likes of her friend Sem – 'They are nothing but plain tea strainers in soft felt, into which women plunge their heads . . . everything disappears, swallowed up by that elastic pocket' – but these 'tea strainers' quickly became the rage.

Gabrielle would say that women had previously thought 'of every colour, except the absence of colour'. And, though declaring that 'nothing is more difficult to make than a little black dress,' and that the tricks of the exotic are much easier, she was the first in her day to fully recognize that black and white have what she described as an 'absolute beauty . . . dress women in white or black at a ball: they are the only ones you see.'[16]

While Gabrielle has a reputation for having resented the upper classes, from the twenties onwards, she also began to employ them. In the future, she would say, 'I have employed society people, not to indulge my vanity, or to humiliate them (I would take other forms of revenge should I be seeking that), but . . . because they were useful to me.'[17] She maintained that, through the rich seam of contacts available to families with any lineage, she was kept abreast of things without having to be present at every social event. From observation and hard personal experience, Gabrielle had become tougher and did indeed have little respect for a good many of those with great privilege. And, to be sure, her aristocratic employees were useful to her, as emissaries and ambassadors for Chanel. Tapping into the prevalence for snobbery, especially among her clients, Gabrielle was well aware that the presence of the old European aristocracy as her employees added to the air of exclusiveness in her salons. This would have been virtually impossible before the war, when a couturier was not 'received' in society. But times had changed and many were obliged to work who had previously hardly known the meaning of the word.

In tough mode, Gabrielle said, 'When I took smart friends on a trip, I always paid, because society people become amusing and delightful when they are certain they won't have to pay for their pleasure. I purchased, in short, their good humour.' At the same time, she said she found them 'irresistibly dishonest' and, in her idiosyncratic way, had a genuine sympathy for their impoverished gentility. Gabrielle's bravado act often omitted the fact that she not only helped a number of those with distinguished lineages, but also found them sympathetic.

Although Gabrielle was born a peasant, her own nature was in many ways a patrician one, and she identified with certain traits associated with the upper classes: 'Yes, society people amuse me more than the others. They have wit, tact, a charming disloyalty, a well-bred nonchalance, and an arrogance that is very specific, very caustic, always on the alert; they know how to arrive at the right time and to leave when necessary.'[18] (Whatever ambivalence Gabrielle might have felt about this section of society was far outweighed by her deep antipathy to the bourgeoisie. She regarded their traditional small-mindedness as loathsome.)

The many aristocratic Russian émigrés, as well as Eastern Europeans and the odd upper-class French and Anglo-Saxon employed by Gabrielle, were people virtually unemployable elsewhere, and the Chanel salons became a refuge for a good number of them. Here, if the well born were prepared to turn their hand to commerce, they could also maintain their dignity. In Gabrielle's own way, she esteemed them; in particular, the Russians. The pianist Arthur Rubinstein recalled the sad story of a grand Russian woman fallen on hard times; part of her family had been shot by the Bolsheviks. She desperately needed work, and Gabrielle employed her.[19] An old retainer at Gabrielle's nephew's château remembered Gabrielle taking in a bankrupt elderly Russian countess: 'Mademoiselle had told us to . . . put back in the old lady's little box the cents she had saved with great effort, and which she would give to us as tips. We had been ordered to let the countess believe that we kept the money in order not to hurt her feelings.'[20]

Now that some of the most distinguished and trendsetting European and American women were Gabrielle's clients, the socially prominent, utterly fashionable and supremely self-important writer Princess Marthe Bibesco was regularly to be seen wearing Chanel couture. She even had Gabrielle design a wardrobe especially for her aeroplane travel. Gabrielle may have 'worked' for Marthe Bibesco, but her own renown was now such that Bibesco gave a thinly veiled portrait of Gabrielle – albeit ironic and patronizing – in one of her fashionable novels. The couturier became Tote, an autocrat of fashion who:

drains the wealth of about ten capitals and of at least three contin-
ents ... All the women who wear Tote sweaters, her flower [the
gardenia], her dress or her striped scarf, have twins and would recognize their lookalikes in New York, London, Rome or Buenos Aires
... Tote's bicolour scarf had made them coreligionists ...

One could say that civilization starts and ends with Tote's customers. Isn't the product that she exchanges for the most solid
currencies in the world quite simply her intelligence? The precious
matter, the imponderable, inexhaustible, and forever renewed, with
which she floods the world's markets every six months.[21]

Gabrielle was a master of the developing art of advertising, and
she capitalized on an updated form of self-promotion, initiated by
the sharper couturiers before the war. The great courtesans and
actresses, then the leaders of fashion, had sported both their charms
and the couturiers' new clothes at the races, that most prominent
of social platforms. But, with the demise of the great courtesans,
society women were now fashion's foremost promoters.

Once again bearing in mind the inordinate vanity of most of her
clients, Gabrielle presented a dress here, another one there, to a
financially reduced young woman of good family. This publicity
was multiplied when Gabrielle invited some of these same young
women to act as her mannequins. At one time or another, a number
of Gabrielle's friends – for example, Misia Sert – were also to be
found on the list of employees at the rue Cambon. Amongst her
other duties, Misia was a saleswoman – Gabrielle had often witnessed her formidable efforts as agent on her husband's behalf.
Misia was also sometimes a Chanel model, her name good for publicity.

While Cocteau's conman friend Maurice Sachs would never
work in Gabrielle's salon, she gave him ample funds to assemble her
a library at the Hôtel de Lauzan. Sachs misused the large monthly
sum she paid him, took a hotel suite, a secretary, a chauffeur, and
launched himself on a spree of dissipation. At the same time, he
bought less than first-class examples of all that Gabrielle should

read. For someone as astute as Gabrielle was, untypically, she had allowed herself to be duped by this charming and insinuating young parasite.

Europe appeared as if it was moving towards ever more frenzied escape, and the voices of protest were drowned out by those intent on experiencing, at all costs, every possible personal 'adventure'. In the vanguard, Paris had the first black jazz musicians; it was in Paris that the blues first became the rage; impromptu parties and clubs were the vogue, and revellers energetically flung themselves into narcotic euphoria and the ecstasy of vigorous dancing until they could barely stand up. And at the heart of Paris was the shimmering Coco Chanel. Georges Auric of Les Six recalled that 'of course she led a luxurious life, the kind it is difficult to imagine today. There was nothing but the best with her. She received a great deal and lavishly, and went out much, too. She liked to surround herself with brilliant people.'[22] Maurice Sachs described her as 'holding court and open table and dispensing privileges and pensions' – 'the pensions of the Grande Mademoiselle', the publisher Bernard Grasset called them. Sachs would write that 'the pulse of the world was beating perceptibly in Paris,' and added that Gabrielle was close to its centre.

Yet, while Gabrielle now lived on a grand scale, she was about to meet someone who lived on one almost unimaginably more so.

Bend'Or

In the summer of 1924, Gabrielle had been holidaying in southern France with Dmitri Pavlovich, her impoverished on-off lover of the last three years. (Like several others, the painter Marie Laurencin was convinced that she had secretly married him.) Meanwhile, the Duke of Westminster, known as Bend'Or, possibly the richest man in England, had recently separated from his wife.

Gabrielle's social prestige was now unquestioned. She was assiduously promoted in both the fashion press and the society pages; she was interviewed and photographed for *Harper's Bazaar* by the all-powerful society photographer Baron de Meyer. De Meyer had married Olga Caracciolo, reputedly the illegitimate daughter of King Edward VII. Despite de Meyer's Jewish heritage, his wife's connections and his own artistry and social finesses had enabled him to move into society. In London, he and Olga hosted one of the city's most powerful salons. (The de Meyers' union, a long and happy one, was a *mariage blanc*; each of them preferred partners of their own sex. One of Olga's most famous affairs was with the music patroness Winnaretta Singer.) De Meyer's article on Gabrielle was entitled 'Mlle Chanel tells Baron de Meyer her Opinions on Good Taste'.

Meanwhile, the American magazine *Women's Wear Daily* reported that 'the Prince of Wales terminated a delightfully informal visit to Paris by lunching quietly with some friends . . . at the Ritz . . . In his party was Mrs Vera Bate, who is . . . well known in English hunting circles. She was wearing one of Chanel's attractive [knitted] coats in a length that came half-way to the knee.' It was possibly Vera Bate's great friend Comte Léon de Laborde, Gabrielle's admirer from

Royallieu days, who introduced Vera Bate and Gabrielle. (The English woman's origins were mysterious. It was rumoured she was the
illegitimate daughter of the German Duke of Teck, who had re-
nounced his German titles during the war and been given an English
one, Earl of Athlone.)

Vera Bate's connection to royalty apparently explained her easy
familiarity with members of the set around the raffish Prince of
Wales. Vera was repeatedly described as having a 'great appetite
for life', which she coupled with a keen sense of dress. She also
appears to have been regularly short of cash. Thus, in a newly
discovered list of employees at Chanel at rue Cambon, we find
that Vera Bate had been employed by Gabrielle, in the 'advertising
department', since 1921; her social contacts made her invaluable
for Chanel public relations. Her hasty marriage to Frederick Bate,
at the end of the war, had resulted in a baby girl and a divorce not
long afterwards. Whatever Vera's true background, she moved in
some of the most fashionable circles in England. Wearing clothes
as well as she did, she was given the run of Gabrielle's salon.
Dressed only in Chanel, she was an important ambassadress for
Gabrielle with the British. Among Vera's friends, she included
Winston Churchill, and Churchill's great friend, the Duke of
Westminster.

Gabrielle had invited Vera to stay with her at the Hôtel de Paris,
in Monte Carlo, for the Christmas–New Year holiday. The Duke of
Westminster's vast yacht *Flying Cloud* was moored in the harbour,
and he had begged Vera to persuade Gabrielle to join him for supper on board. Apparently, Gabrielle was reluctant but, after
considerable persuasion from Vera, she agreed. Then, Dmitri Pavlovich telegrammed announcing his arrival in Monte Carlo, and
Gabrielle promptly cancelled her dinner engagement with Westminster. Dmitri said that he would rather like to see the famous
yacht, so Bend'Or telephoned and asked the young Russian duke to
come along too. Gabrielle told Dmitri this wasn't right: 'Fate
shouldn't be forced.' But the evening aboard ship went well, and the
conversation flowed. They all went ashore after supper to dance

and play at the casino. In years to come, Cocteau would say of Bend'Or, 'I saw him put down stakes on every table, where he would have forgotten them were it not for the respectful fear croupiers feel towards dukes and billionaires.'[1]

Bend'Or asked to see Gabrielle again. Again she hesitated. Her hotel suite was then swamped with flowers, which continued arriving on her return to Paris. A stream of letters, orchids and baskets of fruit was delivered all the way from Bend'Or's home in England, Eaton Hall, in Cheshire. Salmon caught by his own hand arrived in Paris by plane. The duke was in Paris at Easter, apparently to accompany his friend the Prince of Wales. He enlisted Vera Bate and the prince to help him charm Gabrielle, and then he personally delivered a huge bouquet of flowers to her at the Hôtel de Lauzan. Finally, she weakened and accepted an invitation to another dinner aboard ship, this time for a hundred guests in the harbour at Bayonne, near Biarritz. As the evening ended and the guests all left, Bend'Or performed one of his habitual tricks: he had his crew weigh anchor and set sail along the coast. His incredible persistence and particular brand of romance had finally paid off. He had won Gabrielle over.

A friend's commentary on this relationship is interesting, but how accurate it is we don't know: 'With Westminster Coco behaved like a little girl, timid and docile. She followed him everywhere. Her life was a fairy tale. Their love was not sensual.' Meanwhile, Gabrielle would say, 'If I hadn't met Westminster I'd have gone crazy. I had too much emotion, too much excitement. I lived out my novels but so badly! With too much intensity, always torn between this and that, between this man and that, with that business [the House of Chanel] on my back . . . I left for England in a daze.'[2]

Although the undercurrents of change were already at work in England, after the First World War, life for a number of the aristocracy appeared to go on as before. The Duke of Westminster was a man even richer than his monarch, and Eaton Hall, an enormous country house – he liked to describe it as 'St Pancras station' – continued functioning along much the same lines it had in the previous century. With a huge number of staff, as late as 1931, there were still ten housemaids and thirty-eight gardeners, with other offices in the house retaining a similar quota of staff. In that year, 1924, Bend'Or's second marriage, to Violet Rowley, had ended after only four years. While Violet was a woman of great personality and energy, she had failed to provide the male heir the duke so desperately wanted, and her 'decided character made life difficult. It was a marriage that needed at least one emollient partner.'[3] The duke's first wife, Shelagh West, and her relations, had spent years bleeding him of funds. This experience had gradually turned him from being a trusting and generous man into one very wary of being used.

In the present day, when many find large assets and great privilege distasteful, Bend'Or is usually portrayed as unrelentingly monstrous, and caricatured by his vast wealth, yachts, houses, affairs and the number of his wives (there would be four). Yet we frequently make the mistake of judging the past by the same standards as our own. L. P. Hartley's statement in *The Go-between* is apt here: 'The past is a foreign country; they do things differently there.'

Undoubtedly, the Duke of Westminster had many limitations and faults, but it is difficult to view this man and his strange life with real perspective without taking his times into account. In paying Bend'Or tribute, one of his most distinguished employees wrote of those who worked for him at Eaton Hall:

> Everyone enjoyed the distinction of working in one of the greatest of great houses, where everything was of the best and the standards were of the highest. The long hours were repaid by the highest conditions of service and the excitement of the great occasions ... Times have changed and much of the traditions of service have changed and become commercialized. While they were still maintained they were, at their best, a dignified and rewarding framework of human relations.[4]

This same man insisted that Bend'Or was 'uniformly loved and admired by all of those who worked for him'.[5]

The duke's parents had both conducted extramarital relationships but had stuck to the conventions of their day and remained partners in marriage. Although in many ways a Victorian, their son loathed private dishonesty and public hypocrisy and was less prepared to compromise. In his private life, this combination was unfortunate. Bend'Or's undoubted qualities of decisiveness, courage and leadership, admirably displayed in war, were not qualities he understood how to demonstrate with much efficacy in peacetime. His other great handicap, which has led to his being described, in effect, as a dumb ox, was Bend'Or's difficulty in explaining himself with much fluency.

Only on occasion was he moved to put his views forward (vehemently) and then, apparently, his comments were germane. With an aristocratic English lineage, wherein reticence about one's feelings was a prerequisite of acceptance as a gentleman, Bend'Or's schooling, plus the army, had compounded what must have begun as shyness and ended as the tendency to express himself inadequately. Depending upon one's viewpoint, the Duke of Westminster can either be seen as an inflexible, bombastic prude, or a flawed man of honour who was unable to negotiate well with his times, especially when they were peaceful. (In this, he resembled somewhat Winston Churchill.)

By the time Bend'Or met Gabrielle, he had become an edgier, more restless man, whose temper could flare up without warning. Although someone whose forte was action, rather than lengthy discourse or theorizing, there was, however, more to him than this. Apart from anything else, the caricature descriptions of Bend'Or the monster are demeaning to Gabrielle. Why would she have associated herself with someone who was utterly obnoxious? As a fiercely independent woman, she had great wealth of her own at her disposal. It was nothing by comparison with Westminster's, but her aspirations were not of that order. She had no need, really, of Westminster's incredible riches.

Marie Laurencin told the diarist Abbé Mugnier that 'Mlle Chanel and Misia Sert are bored women, the latter out of satiety.' Referring to the emptiness of much of Parisian society, the Abbé wrote that Gabrielle was 'a queen in a desert'. Was this in part why she allowed herself to be seduced by the Duke of Westminster, a man whose fabulous riches had made him, like her, a kind of exalted outsider?

Gabrielle now joined Bend'Or whenever she was able. He was a tall bear of a man, noted for his inability to do anything on a small scale and, although sixty for a weekend at Eaton Hall was not uncommon, Bend'Or increasingly preferred a smaller number of what he called 'real people'. Of an obdurate stubbornness, he was both easily bored and easily pleased. He was, really, a simple man. Gabrielle often met him at one of his various country estates, where she showed considerable prowess at hunting, fishing and entertaining the duke's friends. His Scottish estate, Reay Forest, 'a wild tract of eight hundred square miles' in the Highlands, included one of the most famous salmon rivers and some of the best deer-stalking country in Scotland. It was from here, in October 1927, that Winston Churchill wrote to his wife, Clementine:

> Here I am in the North Pole! Last night the fishing was unexpectedly vy good . . . Coco is here in place of Violet [the duchess]. She fishes from morn till night, & in two months has killed 50 salmon. She is vy agreeable – really a gt & strong being fit to rule a man or an Empire. Bennie vy well & I think extremely happy to be mated with an equal – her ability balancing his power. We are only three on the river.[6]

Gabrielle also travelled frequently to Bend'Or's other favoured spot, Mimizan, in the Landes, in south-west France, where they hunted wild boar. Both the estate in Scotland and Mimizan were difficult to reach by road, so the duke often used his second huge yacht, the *Cutty Sark* – built originally as a reserve destroyer – as his mode of travel from Scotland to France. This got him there with great speed. But, while Gabrielle's fearlessness as a sailor was another mark in her favour in Bend'Or's eyes, in truth, she was bored by the sea. Nonetheless, she was often to be found accompanying him in his restless shuttling from one property to another. Aside from Scotland and the Landes, other houses included a château near Deauville, and the townhouse in London. Gabrielle grew accustomed to the ritual of Westminster train travel, when two Pullman cars and four baggage cars were taken up for the luggage and the dogs.

Winston Churchill enjoyed the boar hunting in the Landes and, earlier in the year, had written to Clementine of his admiration for Gabrielle:

The famous Coco turned up & I took a great fancy to her – a most capable & agreeable woman – much the strongest personality Bennie has yet been up against. She hunted vigorously all day, motored to Paris after dinner & is today engaged in passing and improving dresses on endless streams of mannequins. Altogether 200 models have been settled in almost 3 weeks. Some have been altered ten times. She does it with her own fingers, pinning, cutting, looping, etc. With her – Vera Bate, née Arkwright. Yr Chief of staff? No, one of your lieutenants?[7]

Churchill's wife replied, saying that she enjoyed his description of a hair-raising boar-hunt, 'but more exciting . . . is your account of "Coco". I must say I should like to know her. She must be a genius.'

This 'genius' would say of Bend'Or, whom she described as 'a last king', that 'the greatest pleasure he gave me was to watch him live.' Several of his friends felt the same. Beneath Bend'Or's clumsy exterior he was a skilful hunter. Having said that 'a man would have to be skilful to hang on to me,' Gabrielle described their years together as 'living very lovingly and very amicably'. To her, Bend'Or was 'courtesy itself, kindness personified. He . . . belongs to a generation of well-brought-up men . . . He is simplicity made man; he has the shyness of kings, of people who are isolated through their circumstances and through their wealth.'[8]

This wealth allowed Bend'Or to indulge his fascination with jewels, which he lavished upon Gabrielle at every opportunity. She had already been given some tremendous gems by Dmitri Pavlovich but, with Bend'Or, her collection became quite fabulous. For Gabrielle, Westminster was 'elegance itself, he never has anything new; I was obliged to go and buy him some shoes, and he's been wearing the same jackets for twenty-five years.' Telling how he was the richest man in England, she said, 'Nobody knows this, not even him, especially not him.' She said she mentioned this:

> because at such a level wealth is no longer vulgar, it is located well beyond envy and it assumes catastrophic proportions; but I mention it above all because it makes Westminster the last offspring of a vanished civilization . . . Showing me over the luxurious surroundings of Eaton Hall . . . Lord Lonsdale said to me, 'Once the owner is no more, what we are seeing here will be finished' . . . his intelligence lies in his keen sensitivity. He abounds in delightful absurdities. He does harbour a few grudges, petty, elephant-like grudges.[9]

In 1927, Gabrielle opened a boutique on Davies Street in London's Mayfair, lent to her by Bend'Or; his own house was nearby. She was soon dressing the Duchess of York and other stars of the London firmament: Daisy Fellowes, niece to Winnaretta Singer; Juliet Duff, daughter of Lady Ripon; Baba d'Erlanger, who had grown up in Byron's home; Paula Gellibrand, the Marquise de Casa Maury; Lady Mary Davies; Duff Cooper's wife, Diana; Lady Northcliffe, wife of the newspaper magnate, Alfred; Olga de Meyer; and Mrs William Arbuthnot-Leslie. British *Vogue* reported that:

> Looks designed for sports graduate to country day-dressing and then arrive in town, and Chanel's country tweeds have just completed the course . . . She pins a white pique gardenia to the neck. Her lingerie touches are copied everywhere – piping, bands of contrasts, ruffles and jabots. She initiates fake jewellery, to be worn everywhere, even on the beach.

When Gabrielle was asked why Westminster liked her, she believed it was because she was French. She 'had not tried to lure him'. As a result of her experience of – largely aristocratic – English women, her opinion was that they 'think only of luring men, all men'. Declaring that she had no interest in doing this, Gabrielle came to the interesting conclusion that English women were 'either pure spirits ("souls") or grooms. But in both cases they are huntresses; they either hunt with horses or with their souls.'[10]

The affair between Gabrielle and Westminster was a major item for the gossip columnists on either side of the Atlantic. Doing their damnedest to follow every twist and turn of this dazzling relationship, they vied with one another in predicting the date of the engagement. Both Westminster and Gabrielle, however, would always remain coy about any plans they had to marry. Though many at the time believed Gabrielle's own lineage would have made this an impossibility, this may not have been correct. At forty-six, Bend'Or was in a position where he no longer felt the pressure to keep up that kind of public reputation. He had been divorced twice; he had done much in the way of fulfilling his public duty; he continued fulfilling his private duties regarding his estates and his employees; and his thoughts about marriage were now untrammelled by too much consideration for social nicety.

Above all, Bend'Or needed a woman who could 'manage' him, who could relieve his boredom with her vivacity, who was sophisticated enough to forgive his infidelities and, finally, who would provide him with more children than the two girls from his first marriage. He had only partially recovered from the death of his four-year-old son a few years earlier, and very much wanted a male heir. Gabrielle fulfilled all the above criteria: she was independent, strong, a self-made woman of great wealth who was also capable of compliance. Being Gabrielle, she was utterly clear in the maturity, and the Frenchness, of her comment here: 'A woman does not humiliate herself by making concessions.' She fascinated the Duke of Westminster and, for now, it seemed that the only stumbling block was whether she could present him with an heir.

For a time, she forgot her obsession with independence and remembered that, in her heart, she had always wanted the certainty of marriage and, now, children. Despite being wedded to her couture house, Gabrielle may have courted a proposal of marriage. She would quote an eighteenth-century Frenchman's remark: 'The English are the best people in the world at marrying their mistresses and asking them the least about their past.'[11] In 1927, Gabrielle was forty-four, and it appears that she did her best to become pregnant, including doing everything the doctors asked of her.

Meanwhile, Bend'Or was bored by Gabrielle's friends. She said, 'He couldn't understand Misia at all, and she couldn't understand the English at all. He was appalled by Sert, who sawed off swan's beaks so that they would die of hunger, and who pushed dogs into the Grand Canal in Venice.' Thus, when together, they socialized mostly with Bend'Or's set.

In an unconscious attempt to cement their relationship, Gabrielle and Bend'Or 'made' two houses together. The first was a simple seven-bay classical house in Scotland, never a well-known part of the Chanel–Westminster romance. This was Rosehall House, in Sutherland, bought by Bend'Or as a place in Britain where he and Gabrielle might be more intimately together. Gabrielle didn't like the decor and so had it redecorated in her now celebrated style. The house has been in a state of great disrepair for years, but its simplicity of decor, with trademark Chanel shades of beige, plus chimneypieces in painted timber, was significantly radical for the period. It is most unusual as the only house outside France, besides Switzerland, that Gabrielle would ever decorate.

Several of Bend'Or's friends had villas on the French Riviera, now a most fashionable place, in which not only the French but also wealthy British and Americans were beginning to take their holidays. Monte Carlo was also the site of one of Gabrielle's new salons. The second Westminster–Chanel house was to be La Pausa. At the top of a small village called Roquebrune, it was a site with magnificent views down over Menton and the Italian border on one side, and the bay and Monaco far on the other. Behind the site, the foothills of the Alps can be seen in the distance. Gabrielle bought the five-acre grove of ancient olive trees, in which there were already three buildings, to become a main house and two smaller villas for guests. Gabrielle's friend Comte Jean de Segonzac had had his own villa nearby restored by a young local architect, Robert Streitz.

Streitz was duly invited to meet Gabrielle and Bend'Or at a drinks party on board the *Flying Cloud*, moored off Cannes; they were there to attend the preview of an exhibition by Gabrielle's friend Picabia. Streitz swiftly drew up a magnificent plan, which Gabrielle immediately accepted. This involved demolishing the present house and starting over again. It also involved Gabrielle revealing to the architect a crucial aspect of her past. She wanted a great central stone staircase just like the one at the convent of Aubazine, worn in the middle from centuries of tramping feet, and Streitz was sent to look at it. There he met the mother superior, who said she remembered Gabrielle.

From the beginning, Gabrielle was thoroughly involved, coming down from Paris on the Blue Train at least once a month to scrutinize La Pausa's progress. She was a testing client, discussing every single detail, from the precise colour of the plaster, to insisting on the old handmade roof tiles, of which twenty thousand were required. The materials for the rest of the house were all new and costly, but Gabrielle was determined that La Pausa should give the impression of maturity, of having been there for a long time; this included the carpenter 'ageing' his carefully made shutters. Gabrielle signed Streitz's plans, 'the only signature between us. We never had a contract or any kind of correspondence. For me Mademoiselle's word was as good as gold. Nine months after the completion of La Pausa every bill had been paid on the nail.'[12]

When the house was finished, three wings each faced inwards on to a beautifully shaded courtyard, on to which opened graceful Roman-style vaulting. La Pausa was a classic Mediterranean villa, functioning as a modern house. Large fireplaces were built into the rooms – Gabrielle disliked central heating – eighteenth-century

English oak was used for floors and panelling and, under Bend'Or's influence, much of the furniture was from England. Before the costly interior fittings, decoration and exterior landscaping – highly original at the time, with lavender, masses of purple iris, and lawns starred with crocus and hyacinth – the building costs were six million francs, four times the initial purchase. Everything was done as the duke had instructed, 'with the best materials and under the best working conditions'. Which of the two bore the costs for it all is not clear, but the signature of ownership is in Gabrielle's hand, and dated 9 February 1929. La Pausa's beauty was to establish the architect's name, and he would always feel it had brought him luck.

Over the years, La Pausa was to gain a reputation with Gabrielle's friends as a remarkable place. The perceptive future American *Vogue* editor in Paris, Bettina Ballard, who came to know Gabrielle well in the thirties, would say that it was 'the most comfortable, relaxing place I have ever stayed in', and indeed the building's design, combined with Gabrielle's style of hospitality was then most unusual. In those days, when the Côte d'Azur was just coming into its own, Gabrielle led the way in creating a new style of living for the holidaying rich. Bettina Ballard continued:

> In her own home she wanted to be left alone unless she wanted to be seen, and her guests had the same privilege . . . the house was blissfully silent in the morning . . .
>
> If and when you came down, there were small unostentatious cars with drivers to run you down the mountain to swim or shop in Monte Carlo. No life was encouraged around the villa in the morning. Lunch was the moment of the day when guests met in a group and no one missed lunch – it was far too entertaining. The long dining room had a buffet at one end with hot Italian pasta, cold English roast beef, French dishes, a little of everything . . . Chanel hated having servants under foot, and Ugo somehow managed to run the house superbly and still keep everyone out of sight but himself.[13]

The first major-domo at La Pausa was a Russian refugee, Admiral Castelain, who gave the relaxed impression that there were no other servants, and whom Gabrielle treated as a friend.

During 1929, as La Pausa was being painstakingly erected for Gabrielle and Bend'Or, their affair, however, was to founder. Gabrielle's bid to become pregnant may well have been the trigger for Bend'Or's return to his old routine of dalliance with pretty women. Gabrielle was a most un-jealous woman, but Bend'Or's fling at this juncture provoked in her feelings of real insecurity. Failure to conceive was a grim reminder to this commanding woman of her ultimate inability to control life. We don't know the details, but it seems most likely that a botched abortion during her affair with Etienne Balsan had left her unable to conceive. (One wonders if Arthur Capel would have married Gabrielle if she had become pregnant.) Gabrielle was miserable and frustrated, and her feelings sometimes turned to anger, which she would vent upon Bend'Or. This was a very bad idea. Nevertheless, for some time to come, the man whom few dared to cross would recall why he wanted Gabrielle, and returned, bringing her gifts, and his old enthusiasm and affection.

Meanwhile, another problem had rumbled on beneath Gabrielle's determination to become pregnant: her devotion to her work. Inextricably interwoven with her life and who she had become, her need of work was ineluctable. She longed for a child but, every time she succumbed to a man, eventually Gabrielle began to hanker after work and its beloved companion, independence. In reality, she found equality with a man – perhaps with anyone – deeply challenging, which was why a man as powerful as Westminster had appeared such a good proposition.

While Gabrielle's predicament as a woman was a reflection of her times, she also found that inescapable element of any relationship, the weighing scales of power, impossible, really, to balance for more than a few years. The deeply feminine part of her would make the poignant comment, 'I never wanted to weigh more heavily on a man than a bird,' yet the other Gabrielle had an extraordinary drive to create, to organize and to lead. And she would voice her dilemma with tragic accuracy: 'It would be very difficult for a man, unless he were strong, to live with me. And it would be impossible for me, were he stronger than me, to live with him.'[14]

No matter what she did to avoid it, Gabrielle's work in the end was pre-eminent. The unresolved motives that drove her always proved stronger than the conflicting wish for emotional fulfilment and tranquillity. Yet, while Westminster tried to draw her back to him, at the same time, he himself had begun to drift away.

Gabrielle's pride was at stake here, and she was edging towards disillusionment. No longer young, she had lived too much of her life in the glare of publicity for her to support a public slighting. And, while her disappointment at failing to bear a child was secretly causing her such misery, as was her way, the woman perceived as so resilient, even heartless, hid her anguish from all but one or two.

One of those always there in times of need since Arthur's death was Misia Sert. Gabrielle would say dreadful things of Misia, most of which were true. Describing her as having no sense of moderation or rationality, she said she was like a nomad from the steppes:

> She has an acute thirst for success and a deep and sacrilegious passion for failure. For herself, whom she loathes, for the man she serves . . . She aspires to greatness, she loves to mingle with it, to sniff it, to control it and reduce it . . .
>
> She had absolutely no shame, no sense of honesty, but she had a grandeur and an innocence about her that surpassed everything one usually observes in women . . . it's because of this I adored her . . . In woman there is everything, and in Misia there was every sort of woman.[15]

Whatever Misia's faults, Gabrielle would, nonetheless, continue to love her. Indeed, she would claim that she was the *only* woman who remained her true friend.

For the moment, however, Misia suffered, too, and Gabrielle came to her rescue. At her insistence, Misia had joined the *Cutty Sark* with a party sailing along the Dalmatian coast. While there was intermittent tension between Gabrielle and Bend'Or, Misia's situation was more acute: her marriage was in ruins.

Sert had become besotted with a tall, narcissistic and self-destructive Russian princess, Roussadana Mdivani. Finding her beauty luminous, half of the Parisian *haut monde* appeared besotted, too. Roussadana's brothers' indigence led them to use their exotic charm and titles to make marriages with a series of American film stars and heiresses, acquiring for them the moniker, 'the marrying Mdivanis'.

Meanwhile, Misia had worked her way through the repertoire of attitudes for the long-suffering wife. But her accustomed open-mindedness, as she waited for another of her middle-aged husband's infatuations to subside, had, this time, been to no avail. And foolish Misia had herself also grown to love this self-absorbed and high-spirited young woman, who was destroying Misia's marriage.

When Misia had first met Gabrielle, Sert had been taken aback at her passion for another woman. Now his wife's ardour for yet another woman only heightened his own desire for Roussadana, who so intertwined herself with their lives that the three of them no longer understood their motivation or their emotions. Geared as Sert was to the world of 'fashion, the rich and the vaguely talented, he had moved from Misia's lightness, with its solid basis of art, to Roussy's frivolity, with its nihilistic base of chic'.[16] In time, Gabrielle became more than a little besotted herself with the captivating creature, but for now, in hour-long conversations on the phone, she admonished Misia for involving herself with the girl, telling her she was playing a dangerous game. Misia replied that the forces that drew people towards calamity had her in their clutches and that she was powerless to do anything but try and subdue disaster.

Gradually, her increasing doses of morphine failed to keep her far enough removed from her emotions, and she was faced with the despair she really felt. Paul Morand would recall his admiration for Misia's 'joie de vivre, always concealed beneath a mask of ill-humour; that perfect poise even in moments of despair'. It must have been hard work indeed for Misia and Gabrielle to retain their legendary poise while concealing their real feelings from everyone – except each other – on board Bend'Or's pleasure ship.

One day, Gabrielle and Misia received a telegram on board the *Cutty Sark* from Diaghilev's assistant, Boris Kochno, in Venice: Diaghilev was very ill; they must come at once. Gabrielle had Bend'Or sail the ship to Venice, and the two women went in search of their friend Diaghilev. There, in the Hôtel des Bains on the Lido, with sunlight shimmering off that endlessly lapping water, the beautiful young Boris Kochno and Serge Lifar, each at various times Diaghilev's lover, were beside him: he was dying. The diabetes that Diaghilev had refused to attend to with any discipline was in its final stage. As his temperature rose steadily, he passed in and out of consciousness. He was moved when he saw that Misia and Gabrielle had arrived. His temperature reduced, he grew more cheerful, talked of plans, of new trips. Two nights later, there was a call to the women's hotel and they rushed to his bedside. In the early dawn, just before the sun rose again on that watery paradise he had loved so much, the great Sergei Diaghilev quietly died.

As so often before, there apparently weren't enough funds in the Ballets Russes coffers, and it was Gabrielle who paid for her friend for the last time: she saw to all the details of his funeral. As the small procession left the hotel in the early hours of the following morning – so as not to upset the tourists – it is said that Kochno and Lifar fell to their knees, and began to walk like that. Gabrielle was heard to say curtly under her breath, 'Get up!', and they immediately obeyed. When the white gondola had 'ferried the magician's mortal remains' to San Michele, that lonely Venetian island of the dead, and the mourners watched as the coffin was lowered into its grave, they had to restrain Lifar, who tried to fling himself in after it.

Forty-two years later, Igor Stravinsky, arguably the twentieth century's greatest composer, died in New York. His request to be buried near Diaghilev was duly honoured.

Gabrielle's disillusion at Bend'Or's philandering had sent her back to spend more time with her own friends. Concerned for Misia, she also made a room permanently available for her at the Faubourg St-Honoré. Cocteau had already been there under Gabrielle's wing for some time, with his new lover, the writer Jean Desbordes.

Cocteau's mother had told the Abbé Mugnier that Jean was 'living at Mademoiselle Chanel's, in the gardens of the avenue Gabriele'. The Abbé Mugnier wrote:

> After having accompanied the Princess Bibesco here and there . . .
> went to Mlle Chanel who was expecting us. The Serts, Jean Cocteau,
> a young English woman [Vera Bate], who works with Coco Chanel,
> were there . . . In Mlle Chanel's garden . . . a vast fountain unfolds
> . . . back in the salon, heard Wagner on the gramophone, chatted
> with various people. I thought Mlle Chanel had a more charming
> face. Very kind by the way.[17]

Gabrielle's socializing was not only for friendship's sake. Maintaining her image in the face of society, often secretly awaiting her downfall, she gave particularly sumptuous entertainments and was much seen abroad. Not long before Diaghilev's death, she celebrated a Ballets Russes performance with Misia, Diaghilev and their entourage, the artists Picasso, Cocteau and Rouault, and the composers Stravinsky and Prokofiev. She gave another of her magnificent balls to celebrate the end of another Ballets Russes season. The Hôtel de Lauzan was awash with the best champagne, caviar spilled from soup tureens, the gardens were lit by lanterns, a black jazz band offered up the most fashionable contemporary music. Serge Lifar, now the Ballets Russes's principal dancer, and who would in time describe Gabrielle as his 'godmother', recalled the evening:

> We drank rivers of champagne and vodka . . . Coco drank as much
> as anyone else. As always she flirted with the men. She was very kit-
> tenish, even purring, pretending she was completely captivated,
> when suddenly pfft! Nobody there! She was like a little Cinderella.

She disappeared around two in the morning, so as not to miss her beauty sleep. She allowed men to think that everything was possible.[18]

In 1929, Henri Bernstein would record the sense of grandeur at her parties 'in the white violence of the multitude of peonies – subtle, gay, moving parties which made several people envious (all those who could not be invited in spite of the dimensions of the beautiful lounges of the Faubourg St-Honoré)'.[19]

By February of 1930, Bend'Or had found himself a new wife, Loelia Ponsonby, one of the 'Bright Young Things' and daughter of the first Lord Sysonby. Bend'Or had brought Loelia to Paris for an excruciating session, in which she met her future husband's ex-lover. Understandably, Loelia found Gabrielle unsympathetic, describing her as 'small, dark and simian . . . She was hung with every sort of necklace and bracelet, which rattled as she moved . . . I perched, rather at a disadvantage, at her feet, feeling that I was being looked over to see if I was a suitable bride . . . I very much doubted whether I or my tweed suit passed the test.'[20]

Meanwhile, Loelia's forthright cousin Lady Ponsonby was unimpressed by both Loelia and her new husband, and also by the growing idea of celebrity. Writing of the wedding party at St James's Palace, she said that although the Duke:

as a Rake may be, attractive & having style . . . his large flabby face mottled with dissipation . . . made me wonder . . . Apparently outside the registry office was the largest crowd ever seen at a wedding . . . To arouse real enthusiasm you must be either very rich or very immoral – & if you are very rich, very immoral and a Duke – most people now go off their heads.[21]

Sixteen years later, Gabrielle would say of her life with Bend'Or that she had grown tired of 'that squalid boredom that idleness and riches bring about'. Despite Gabrielle's wealth, idleness was never to be her problem; she never ceased working with great purpose, which was to secure herself, and others, in the modern world in which they found themselves. Thus she would say of Westminster's life, 'You have to wonder whether . . . this absurd fairyland . . . is not a bad dream.'[22]

> I had satisfied a great core of lethargy that hides beneath my anxiety, and the experiment was finished . . . Fishing for salmon is not life. Any kind of poverty, rather than that kind of wretchedness. The holidays were over. It had cost me a fortune; I had neglected my house, deserted my business, and showered gifts on hundreds of servants.

Yet Bend'Or told Gabrielle he wouldn't be able to accustom himself to living without her. Gabrielle knew that this was because her willingness to say 'no' to him impressed him. 'It was a shock for him; it threw him off balance.'[23]

As the duke's lover and his equal in many ways, for several years Gabrielle shared the life of a man a good many regarded as nothing more than a selfish playboy. Gabrielle did believe that, once she was gone, Westminster permitted some of the rich man's parasites to encircle him again. But a devoted employee and friend would write of him:

> He was in charge of the greatest landed fortune in the country for fifty-four years, from the reign of Queen Victoria to that of Elizabeth II, from an aristocratic to an egalitarian, if not socialist, society. Whatever his services to his country in war, his personal qualities and defects, he should be judged by his success or failure discharging the responsibilities brought by his wealth.[24]

And, after ceasing to be his lover, Gabrielle would say of him, 'We have remained friends. I loved him, or thought I loved him, which amounts to the same thing.'[25]

While Westminster was married to Loelia Ponsonby for

seventeen years, they had separated long before they were finally divorced. In Westminster's fourth wife, Anne Sullivan, he would at last find a woman who was willing to appreciate his qualities and negotiate his foibles, and with whom he would spend six good years before his death, in 1953.

The Crash

'The upheaval of values characterizes our era, some say. A somewhat naive statement, since only one value dominates our times: money – first through the plethora, then through its lack.' So wrote the diarist Elisabeth de Gramont, in her measured and sardonic tone, when the fevered pitch of the twenties finally reached its climax in November 1929 after the Wall Street Crash. De Gramont told how the preceding decade had seen 'all values, the only ones left in this world . . . going up like a column of mercury', and described the luxury cars – the Rolls-Royces, the Hispano-Suizas, the Mercedes, and the spendthrift lifestyle of the speculators and the war profiteers, and how artists called it a golden age, because 'from the masterpiece to the daubed, everything sold for exorbitant sums.' People previously of moderate means acquired new ambitions, buying châteaux, racing stables and yachts, and the price of property continued rising astronomically. When the banks failed, many people's assets were reduced by as much as 90 per cent.

A well-to-do Englishman, weathering the storm in a Paris hotel, described how a man shot himself in an adjacent room, an old American woman threw herself out of the window clutching her cat to her bosom, and another woman was only saved from an overdose of sleeping pills because her Pekinese barked and gave the alarm. The Englishman wrote, 'I lost lots of money, and Coco Chanel was in a panic, while Misia Sert . . . remained quiet in her flat on the top floor of the Meurice'[1] – the famous Parisian hotel.

Gabrielle was in certain panic in this period of great dearth, but she hid it well from her reduced number of clients, and still made money. This was helped by the fact that, in the few short years since its introduction, Chanel N°5 had become the world's highest-selling perfume.

Meanwhile, Adrienne Chanel's faithful lover, Baron Maurice de Nexon, had finally been released by his father's death to receive his inheritance and marry. And in April 1930, 'Mademoiselle Gabrielle Chanel, dress designer, residing at 29 rue Faubourg St-Honoré', was Adrienne's chief witness at the quiet Paris wedding. On that day, Gabrielle's thoughts must have dwelt on her initial fall from respectability, when she chose to live openly with her horse-mad Etienne Balsan. Did she regret? Probably not, but she must, nevertheless, have recognized the irony of having recently given up a man who had now married someone else, while her aunt was at last entering into her own marriage. Some of the old Royallieu friends, including Etienne, were present on that otherwise happy day.

That summer, Misia was Gabrielle's almost permanent guest at La Pausa. While she had not recovered from her desertion by Sert (she never would), Misia nonetheless enlivened the atmosphere for the villa's numerous guests. Dmitri Pavlovich was also in the south of France, and introduced Gabrielle to the present tsar of Hollywood, Samuel Goldwyn. As America's economic crisis worsened with each month, Goldwyn was doing his best to counter it by turning Hollywood into an even greater star attraction than it had so far been. He engaged Gabrielle in earnest discussions. She was reluctant, but Goldwyn persevered: he wanted her to come to Hollywood.

When millions of Americans were now jobless, Goldwyn understood that reducing his costs would be a mistake: he must make his films even greater extravaganzas of escape. Recognizing the need to encourage a more middle-class audience to his films, he believed that women would be more attracted if they knew they were to see the very latest fashions from the hand of the most famous Parisian couturier. He would pay Gabrielle the fabulous sum of $1 million a year if she would visit Hollywood twice a year to dress his female stars, both on and off the stage. The great salesman Goldwyn failed to comprehend Gabrielle's hesitation. She would be clothing the women who peopled the dreams of millions. They would not only advertise Chanel in every dream-palace in the world, but also every time they set foot in any public place. Gabrielle finally consented.

In the spring of 1931, she set sail for Hollywood with Misia as her companion. It was an extraordinary enterprise, and there was no question that, in these testing times, her enormous bursary would come in useful. Whatever came of Gabrielle's attempt at dressing Hollywood, she and Misia would distract themselves together. Gabrielle was not at all concerned at the thought of dressing some of the most famous women in the world. But could she convince them her style was what they wanted? On her arrival in New York, word had already gone out, and Gabrielle was besieged by journalists. She told *The New York Times*:

> It's just an invitation. I will see what the pictures have to offer me and what I have to offer the pictures. I will not make one dress. I have not brought my scissors with me. Later, perhaps, when I go back to Paris, I will create and design gowns six months ahead for the actresses in Mr Goldwyn's pictures. I will send the sketches from Paris and my fitters in Hollywood will make the gowns.[2]

The reporters found Gabrielle taken aback at the scores of interviewers and the reception committee crowding out her suite at the Hotel Pierre. She answered questions, declaring that longer hair would be back in style, that a chic woman should dress well but not eccentrically. She said that flower-based perfumes were not mysterious on a woman, that men who used scents were disgusting, and that where, previously, people of elegance had led fashion, it was now the young who set the tone.

In a second interview, Gabrielle spoke about giving the films fashion authority, although saying she wasn't quite sure how it was going to work out once she arrived in California. The *New York Times* reporter found Gabrielle 'a woman whose business is charm in dress. She does not make speeches, nor has she any theatrical affectation or exhibition – her answers are simple, direct.' Gabrielle said that she never saw her clients at her salon; that her work was 'impersonal'. A gown was designed on a model, and that ended it for her. She seldom had the opportunity to see a frock, and even more seldom the inclination. Typical Gabrielle! Once something was done, it was gone; she was bored and on to the next thing: 'I needed to cleanse my memory, to clear from my mind everything I remembered. I also needed to improve on what I had done. I have been Fate's tool in a necessary cleansing process.'[3]

Her brief was to clothe the greatest stars of the time: Norma Talmadge, Clara Bow, Gloria Swanson, Lillian Gish, Ina Claire and Greta Garbo. Interestingly, the records for rue Cambon show that the witty and intelligent Ina Claire had already become a private customer of Gabrielle's, in 1926. Indeed, it was Ina Claire's Chanel wardrobe that became one of the best advertisements for Gabrielle in the States. Meanwhile, the film and fashion worlds were laying bets on whether Gabrielle really could impose her fashion dictates on the notoriously petulant and self-willed actresses of the silver screen, a group neither known for their decorum nor for the elegance of their style.

When Gabrielle and Misia arrived in Hollywood, Gabrielle was once again mobbed by reporters. The French guests were entertained at a celebrity reception in Gabrielle's honour, and here she met several of those actresses she was due to design for, such as Greta Garbo, Marlene Dietrich and Claudette Colbert. The renowned directors George Cukor and Erich von Stroheim were also at the party, and von Stroheim charmed Gabrielle. She said of him, 'Such a ham, but what style.' Meanwhile, Goldwyn's chief publicist dubbed Gabrielle 'the biggest fashion brain ever known'.

At another party, George Cukor introduced Gabrielle to his new 'find' Katharine Hepburn.

Gabrielle was taken around the studios, saw how films were made, saw the clothes, met the costumiers, understood what the camera wanted, and that her role was to create clothes that accentuated the personality of the stars. She was supposed to design costumes that must still be in fashion two years after she had created them; that was how long it took to make a film. She wasn't impressed by Beverly Hills, and the ruthlessness of the studio system appalled the woman who had fought so hard for her own independence. She felt the stars were 'producers' servants', and didn't have much time for many of the actors either. She thought that 'once you've said the girls were beautiful and there were a lot of feathers around, you've said it all . . . You know perfectly well that everything "super" is the same. Super-sex, super productions . . .' Gabrielle would, however, enjoy quoting Garbo saying to her later, 'Without you I wouldn't have made it, with my little hat and my raincoat.'

The woman who put fashionable women into raincoats had met the stars, met the producers, wasn't that impressed and became impatient to get back to France. En route, she stopped again in New York, for what turned out to be a most useful set of encounters. She met Carmel Snow, now editor of *Harper's Bazaar*, Margaret Chase, editor of *Vogue*, and Condé Nast, the extraordinary magazine publisher, who had a gift for making money; he lived in a thirty-roomed penthouse on Park Avenue. Nast had amassed a fortune through his publishing company; this included *Vogue* and *Vanity Fair*. His manipulation and machinations were legendary, and Gabrielle would always have a difficult relationship with this gifted yet unscrupulous man.

Something that impressed Gabrielle perhaps the most about America, and was to have a lasting effect on her attitudes, was the way she saw clothes sold in the great metropolis of New York. Taking a trip around the most elegant department stores, including Bloomingdales, Macy's and Saks, she also visited the Seventh Avenue garment-making district, and was fascinated by Klein's, the huge discount store on Union Square.

Samuel Klein had begun, in 1912, with $600 and, by 1931, he owned the world's largest women's-wear store, selling as much as $25 million worth of clothes every year. This was then a vast sum. Klein made no attempt at aesthetics – the floors were bare, and there were no saleswomen. Riffling through crude iron racks, customers selected dresses (all copies of one kind or another) without assistance and tried them on in crowded public dressing rooms. Klein didn't advertise, relying on rapid turnover and a mark-up of around 10 per cent. If something on the $7.95 racks was there for more than two weeks, it was marked down a dollar. At the end of another two weeks, its price was cut again. Sometimes, dresses were sold for as little as $1. Large signs in Yiddish, Armenian, Polish and English read: 'Don't try to steal, our detectives are every-where.' Today, versions of this type of clothes shopping are common but, in 1933, Gabrielle was amazed.

S. Klein would become part of American mythology, and Gabrielle returned to France, confirmed in her prophesy to her fellow cou-turiers that copying was inevitable and Klein's selling policy was a sign of things to come. Refusing to believe this, the couturiers exerted themselves each season to prevent the pilfering of their ideas. And Gabrielle would say, 'Fashion does not exist unless it goes down into the streets. The fashion that remains in the salons has no more significance than a costume ball.'⁴ She said she wouldn't have been able to realize all her ideas, that she liked see-ing them used, and that copying was not the drama for her it was for other couturiers: 'What rigidity it shows, what laziness, what unimaginative taste, what lack of faith in creativity, to be fright-ened of imitations! The more transient fashion is the more perfect it is. You can't protect what is already dead.'⁵ (Gabrielle meant she had already moved on.)

By the twenties, Gabrielle had come to believe that haute cou-ture would inevitably be translated 'down into the streets'. And her increasingly unfitted and simple shapes could now be replicated relatively easily; they also required less yardage than previous dresses and could be copied in cheaper fabrics. New synthetics, such as rayon, were emulating much rarer textiles such as silk, and the haute couture copies were being made up at a fraction of the cost. The line of descent began with the unofficial drawings taken – secretly – from the shows. Specialist copying houses made a living out of less costly versions of designer clothes. This idea went down through women's personal dressmakers until it reached the cheaper, mass-market end of the garment trade and the 'woman in the street'.

Following through her thought that she was quite willing for her clothes to be copied, in 1932 Gabrielle presented a fashion exhibition at the Duke of Westminster's London house in aid of charity. (The two remained on close terms.) The idea was that dressmakers and manufacturers should come along with the express intention of copying Gabrielle's designs. Five hundred or so society and entertainment personalities attended, over the course of several days. The *Daily Mail* reported how 'many visitors bring their own seamstresses because this collection is not for sale . . . Mademoiselle Chanel has authorized it being copied.' The other designers in Paris went to great lengths to protect their designs and were absolutely opposed to Gabrielle's initiative.

Sam Goldwyn had been unconcerned about Gabrielle's return to France and agreed that she could design the costumes for Gloria Swanson's forthcoming film, *Tonight or Never*, when Swanson was in Europe. When she came over to Paris, Gabrielle's designs for her were deemed perfect. However, after two seasons of Gabrielle's fashion dictatorship, the stars rebelled, and refused to wear clothes designed by the same person in all their films. Confirmed in their belief that Hollywood was more significant than Paris, they didn't care if the designer they were rejecting was Coco Chanel. As a result, Gabrielle felt released from her contract with Goldwyn and didn't return to Hollywood. The *New Yorker* published a witty piece on the reasons for her retreat:

> The film gives Gloria a chance to dress up in a lot of expensive clothes . . . the gowns are credited to Chanel, the Paris dressmaker who recently made a much publicized trip to Hollywood, but I understand she left that center of light and learning in a huff. They told her her dresses weren't sensational enough. She made a lady look like a lady. Hollywood wants a lady to look like two ladies.

Gabrielle and Goldwyn remained, nonetheless, on the best of terms, for their relationship had been mutually beneficial. Gabrielle's success in Hollywood raised her status yet further in France; she had become grand on an international scale. It was also good for Goldwyn, who kept the prestigious association between the designer and his films.

While Poiret was going bankrupt – creditors seized all his assets – and many of Gabrielle's rivals cut their prices, her own two Hollywood stipends of $1 million were a considerable help in those tough years. She had lost a number of English and American clients, but while the Americans would eventually return in force, there were still many rich women in India and South America who could well afford her couture. *Vogue*, meanwhile, told the world that Coco Chanel had revolutionized Hollywood by putting the actress Ina Claire into white satin pyjamas.

Once again, as in the First World War, in difficult times Gabrielle's Hollywood endeavour had enhanced her reputation. Even so, the Depression of the thirties, following the Crash of 1929, had a devastating effect on virtually every country in the world. Despite Gabrielle's upbeat pronouncement – she said that, like Goldwyn, she believed the best way to survive lean times was to maintain the highest standards – this was a tense period. In 1930, while Gabrielle had a turnover of around 120 million francs and a workforce of around 2,400, in 26 workrooms, it has been said that in 1932 she was forced to cut her prices by half. And although managing to retain her huge workforce, she did temporarily reduce the luxury of some of her fabrics. Silk manufacturers, for example, were horrified when Gabrielle introduced the idea of evening dresses in cotton. She had been invited to do so by an English firm, Ferguson Brothers, to promote the use of their cotton fabrics. Thus, Gabrielle's spring 1931 collection included thirty-five cotton-pique, lawn, muslin and organdie evening dresses. It proved very popular.

In the end, however, not only did Gabrielle retain the custom of some of her richest society clients, such as Daisy Fellowes, Lady Pamela Smith, the South American Madame Martínez de Hoz and the Americans Laura Corrigan and Barbara Hutton, by 1935 business was very much improved for Gabrielle. Her clientele had grown sufficiently that her workforce had now reached four thousand. The Duke of Westminster had permitted her to adapt his nine-bedroomed Audley Street London house to her own requirements. From 1930 to 1934, this became the centre of Gabrielle's cosmetics venture; part of her drive to grow by diversifying, it included the expansion of her perfume range, with N°22, Glamour and Gardénia. Like other couturiers, in order to maintain a high profile, she also now endorsed products and designed for manufacturers.

During the Depression, a young New York heiress, Maybelle Iribarnegaray, discovered that her husband was having an affair with Gabrielle. It was 1933. Her husband, Iribe, as Paul Iribarnegaray styled himself, was a thick-set Basque with an impenetrable accent, who often utilized his incessant womanizing to further his extraordinary talent. Besides the great Sem, Iribe had been the most talented and successful French pre-war caricaturist, with a facile and sharp pen. He had then branched out and launched a successful design business, creating furniture, fabrics, wallpaper and jewellery. The success of his business had made him a significant arbiter of taste. Then, one year into the war, having dispensed with his first wife, the actress Jane Diris, who subsequently died of tuberculosis, Iribe left for America, scooped up Maybelle and spent the next ten years in America, most of them in Hollywood.

Iribe worked on some of the legendary Cecil B. de Mille's most important films, including *The Ten Commandments*, the largest-scale film yet made, and was promoted to Artistic Directorship of Paramount. By this point, he was also designing dresses and film sets, and was sometimes even directing. Iribe was witty and clever, with an unctuous charm, but he had also gained a reputation for being arrogant and argumentative. One day, when he reacted badly to de Mille's criticism of his sets for *King of Kings*, de Mille had had enough and fired him. Iribe had also had enough, and left Hollywood, returning to France with his wife and her two children. With Maybelle's money, Iribe now opened a shop on rue Faubourg St-Honoré – not far from Gabrielle's residence, Hôtel de Lauzan – and reapplied himself to designing furniture and jewellery. He had always been intent on riches, fame and acceptance by society, and was envious of Cocteau, an old acquaintance and colleague, who infiltrated the *haut monde* with such ease.

On his return to Paris, Iribe hailed luxury, artisanship and nationalism as the cornerstones of his beliefs. Enslaved to money, he appears to have made and lost it at a great rate. For the moment, however, Iribe made huge sums, acquiring a luxury car, a yacht and a house in St Tropez, the fishing village now transformed into one of the most select playgrounds of the rich. Colette hadn't visited for a while, and friends warned her that it was overrun by 'the sort of people photographed by *Vogue*'. Colette herself was in fact photographed by *Vogue*, but bemoaned the smothering of one of her favourite places with traffic and tourists. One morning, she found a horde of them awaiting her as she left the stationer's, and wrote to a friend, 'I didn't hide what I thought of them.'[6]

Then, Iribe did less well, and his long-suffering wife hustled, and found him a commission from Chanel. Maybelle's parents were meanwhile pressuring their daughter to curtail their son-in-law's excessive spending; they were concerned he would bring them to ruin. This, combined with Iribe's serial infidelity, finally brought the marriage to an end, and Maybelle left for America with her two children.

When Gabrielle and Iribe's affair was still a well-kept secret, Colette and her lover, Maurice Goudeket, were inadvertently to discover it. (Gabrielle had met Colette at some point in the early twenties. They never became close but, with a number of friends in common, they met on numerous occasions.) At the end of 1931, 'strangled by the Depression', as Colette put it, and in financial straits –'Great God above, things are difficult for Maurice and me' – they were forced to sell their retreat outside Paris.

La Gerbière was a pleasant house surrounded by trees and high up in the village of Montfort-L'Amaury, where the composer Maurice Ravel lived. Gabrielle came down alone from Paris, and made the deal with Maurice Goudeket to buy the house as they walked around the garden. Colette had had no idea her partner was confirming the purchase of their house until it was all over. She then realized that Gabrielle intended bringing Iribe here for their trysts: 'a place for billing and cooing', as Colette put it.

At the end of the transaction, she was left with a sense of Gabrielle's decisive toughness. These two remarkable women may not have felt great warmth for one another, but they did feel a strong mutual respect. Gabrielle described Colette, correctly, as 'this highly intelligent woman', saying, 'The only two female writers who appeal to me are Madame de Noailles and Colette.'

In 1933, by which time everyone who was anyone summered in the south of France, Misia met Colette one day and gossiped about Gabrielle and Iribe's engagement. Colette then wrote to a friend: 'I've just been told that Iribe is marrying Chanel. Aren't you horrified for her? That man is a most interesting demon.'[7] Iribe's first wife had been a good friend of Colette's. Colette didn't like Iribe. Finding him fawning, she was suspicious of his thrusting drive to succeed. She described him as wrinkled and pale and said that he 'coos like a pigeon'. His friend Paul Morand felt rather differently.

> Back in Paris, having foretold the transatlantic cataclysm . . . having sensed that the time for misery was to come; Iribe felt that one had to fight against these curses and die, as a French artisan, for the individual and for quality. In love with the homeland he was returning to and disappointed by it, he was publishing *Témoin*.'[8]

Iribe had founded the magazine *Le Témoin* before the First World War, and now persuaded Gabrielle to fund its relaunch. With forceful Iribe graphics, this time, *Le Témoin* served to support a growing French nationalism. In one illustration, Marianne, female symbol of France, was Gabrielle, under a bench of sneering judges: Roosevelt, Chamberlain, Mussolini and Hitler. Iribe was now an arch-patriot who despised his nation's present government. Fierce anti-republican sentiment – the same that had brought Hitler to power in Germany not so long before – spawned a number of right-wing leagues, the aim being to overthrow the French Third Republic in favour of a strong, uniting individual. One of the most powerful right-wing elements, the Action Française, under François Maurras, wanted a restoration of France's monarchy. Iribe wasn't a monarchist, but he believed that democratic government was ineffectual.

As one element of the drive to patriotism, *Le Témoin* was anti-German and anti-Jewish. Above all, it was anti-foreign, claiming France for the French alone. However, in 1934, Gabrielle was as shocked as the rest of Paris when a demonstration by 40,000 right-wing associations and war veterans ended by being one of the bloodiest since the Paris commune of 1871. Sixteen people were killed, over two thousand were injured, the right was narrowly defeated and the communists and socialists were roused to sink their differences in a new party, the Popular Front.

After over a decade of entertaining and 'show', Gabrielle now gave up the Hôtel de Lauzan on the Faubourg St-Honoré, and moved into a large suite as a *hôtel pension* in the Ritz; her rooms were situated on the rue Cambon side. The furniture and objects she wished to keep were moved into a third-floor apartment she had made for herself in her rue Cambon building, at number 31. Here, she would keep her clothes. For the rest, when Gabrielle felt the need of a home, she could travel south to La Pausa.

This move [into the hotel] had possibly come about after some prodding from the demanding Iribe. He had told her he thought her way of life was corrupting and didn't understand why she needed so much. If she lived more simply he might live with her. He said he hated complex people. Gabrielle apparently obliged, moving into two rooms in a family house nearby. After a short time, Iribe asked her, 'Do you think I'm accustomed to living in such hovels?', and went to stay in the Ritz. Not long afterwards, Gabrielle moved to the hotel too.

This transition from the Faubourg St-Honoré to somewhere with its own servants meant that Gabrielle brought to an end her long association with her devoted major-domo, Joseph. Joseph had arrived when 'given' to her by Misia on the eve of her wedding sixteen years before. Gabrielle and her manservant parted on bad terms: her ability to be unsentimental was at times quite ruthless. And yet, the loyal Joseph would never make any public criticism of his ex-employer.

Between Gabrielle's fashion house and her textile and jewellery workshops, her expenditure was large. The effects of the Depression and the need to cut costs may have been another contributing factor in her move from the Faubourg St-Honoré to the Ritz. She now permitted herself to lean on Iribe. After years of grumbling resentment against the distributors of her perfumes, the Wertheimers, Gabrielle had begun a legal tussle with them over her 'abused rights'. Iribe was sufficiently bullish that Gabrielle overestimated his abilities as a negotiator and asked for his assistance.

The serious lawsuits Gabrielle now brought against the Wertheimers drove them to attempt removal of her as president of the board. In September 1933, Gabrielle had given Iribe power of attorney, and he presided over a board meeting. But he was reckless enough to refuse signature of the minutes, giving the board just the ammunition it wanted; he was voted off by a majority. Continuing with the company's reorganization, the Wertheimers succeeded in removing Gabrielle as president in 1934. Outraged, for the moment there was little she could do.

In 1934, Gabrielle was again in Roquebrune for the summer, at La Pausa. Friends staying included the composer Poulenc, the dancer Serge Lifar, and Horst P. Horst, a young German photographer. Another friend who often stayed at La Pausa was the Italian Conte Luchino Visconti, the future film director. Gabrielle had known Visconti for several years. At this time, Visconti's self-consciousness about his position as a nobleman of leisure drove him to put much of his energies into his racehorse breeding. He met Gabrielle and her friends in Venice at the Lido, or at his sisters-in-law Madina and

Niki Arrivabene's Venetian palazzo, and in Paris. Serge Lifar recalled how it appeared as if all society was in Venice, and they all thought themselves:

> unique, exciting and beautiful . . . During those years . . . at Venice there were the great popes, like the Visconti, and the Volpi 'doges'. Between Paris and Rome, society communicated and intertwined continuously. In Paris, those who welcomed me were the same ones I met in London, Rome or Venice, all capitals on that axis of triumphant worldliness.[9]

Visconti's biographer wrote that 'Visconti loved Natalie Lelong [half-sister of Dmitri Pavlovich], who had an affair with Serge Lifar and several women as well; Chanel had an affair with Visconti, who also loved Niki Arrivabene – they all loved each other and were all beautiful, bisexual and attractive.'[10]

When Visconti had arrived in Paris, despite his painful shyness his background and his handsome looks gave him a natural entrée into the Parisian version of the sophisticated Venetian milieu. When he was there, he had an open invitation to Gabrielle's much coveted lunches and dinner parties, where he found 'the most glittering, famous and interesting wits at her table'. One or other of Visconti's sisters-in-law sometimes accompanied him, and one of them remembered these occasions as 'so chic, one could die'.

Although Visconti's understanding of Gabrielle wasn't comprehensive, he came to know her well. Describing her as *La Belle Dame Sans Merci*, he recalled 'her sufferings, her pleasure in hurting. Her need to punish, her pride, her rigour, her sarcasm, her destructive rage, the single-mindedness of the character who goes from hot to cold, her inventive genius'.[11] Visconti was a connoisseur of interiors, making a number of fine ones himself, and admired what Gabrielle had created at La Pausa. He added that the gardens were 'special again', saying that Gabrielle 'was the first to cultivate "poor" plants like lavender and olive trees, discard lilies . . . and flowers of that kind. The house was decorated in beige leather and chamois sofas, pieces of Provençal and Spanish furniture, then totally out of fashion, and everything was in soft colours like a painting by Zurburan.'[12]

After years of wrestling with his homosexuality, Luchino Visconti had finally reached an accommodation with himself. This in turn led on to some major decisions. Rejecting a conservative aristocratic existence, and the comforts of family – in which, nonetheless, he believed profoundly – Visconti had decided he would make his mark on the world through art. In company with a number of others, he had fallen passionately in love with the photographer Horst, who had recently cemented his reputation with a set of alluring photographs of Gabrielle. Horst remembered that she:

> had had a row with *Vogue* [in fact, Condé Nast] and no photograph of her was allowed to appear in the magazine. I was sent to her: I photographed her and she said that the photographs were good of the dresses but looked nothing like her. 'How can I take a good photograph of you if I don't know you,' I answered. So she asked me to dinner. At that time she had had a row with Iribe . . . and she was thinking of him when I took my photographs. She adored them. 'How much are they?' she asked. 'Nothing,' I said. 'To be able to take a photo like that of you was wonderful' – and we became friends.[13]

In the summer of 1935, Gabrielle was at La Pausa awaiting Iribe, who had spent the previous weeks in Paris. He called to say he would arrive on the sleeper down from Paris the following morning, and suggested they could begin their day with a game of tennis. According to some sources, Iribe was warming up when Gabrielle joined him. Halfway through the first set, she went over to the net to ask him not to hit the ball so hard. Looking at her over the rim of his sunglasses, he stumbled and then collapsed. He had suffered a massive heart attack. Two days later, Iribe died in a nearby clinic, never having regained consciousness. Years later, Gabrielle would confess to believing she had caused his death, because she'd persuaded him to resume the game when he'd complained of feeling faint.[14]

Gabrielle was in a terrible state; it felt as if her own life was finished. Her affair with Iribe may have been a tempestuous one, but she had felt both stimulated and supported by this dominating man. Unusually, she had allowed herself to lean a little.

At night, Gabrielle's anguish grew worse as she lay alone, rigid with wakefulness and grief. Misia rushed to La Pausa. The doctor was summoned and prescribed Gabrielle with a sedative, Sedol, to calm her and ensure some sleep. Gabrielle would later say that it wasn't so as to live she had taken it, but simply to 'hold on'.

Once again, a man had 'left' her and, once again, she was alone. Each time Gabrielle lost someone, she appears to have re-lived her desertion by her father, and been plunged into an emotional crisis. But this time the effect was bad indeed. Not only did she feel again that desertion, she also experienced the most terrifying reminder of her own mortality. The night was impossible without the sedative. For a few hours, it numbed her grief and protected her from the sense that, every time she closed her eyes, she was no longer alive. Gabrielle quickly became dependent on this blessed release from pain and, after this period of abject misery, continued injecting herself each night with Sedol to help her relax and find sleep.

Years later, in the sixties, Gabrielle's Swiss doctor would tell her assistant, Lilou Marquand, that, when on a skiing trip to Switzerland, Gabrielle had broken her ankle. This was most probably the year following Iribe's death, when Gabrielle was indeed on a skiing trip, with Etienne de Beaumont and other society friends. She was given morphine to combat the pain from her broken ankle, and Lilou Marquand went on to say, 'The pain disappeared, and habit did the rest.' Saying that 'this story was not well known' and that Gabrielle seemed to have forgotten it, Marquand, who knew Gabrielle well, speculated that, even if her doctor might not have told her everything, 'Did she really believe she was only injecting a little bit of morphine in a liquid with added vitamins?'[15] However, Gabrielle always had her own truths and, as time went on, one of these would be that what she injected herself with was a simple sedative.

When Gabrielle came to describe her relationship with Iribe, we understand something of what it had meant to her. She said he was:

> a very perverse creature, very affectionate, very intelligent, very self-seeking and exceptionally sophisticated . . . He was a Basque with astonishing mental and aesthetic versatility, but where jealousy was concerned, a real Spaniard. My past tortured him. Iribe wanted to relive with me the whole of that past lived without him and to go back through lost time, while asking me to account for myself.[16]

One suspects that, perhaps along with Reverdy, Iribe was the other man to whom Gabrielle confided the most about her past. She and Iribe had set out 'on the trail of my youth' and visited the convent at Aubazine, far away in Corrèze.

Yet, years later, Gabrielle also said that:

> he wore me out, he ruined my health. My emerging celebrity had eclipsed his declining glory. He loved me, subconsciously . . . so as to be free of this complex and in order to avenge himself on what had been denied him. For him I represented that Paris he had been unable to possess and control . . . I was his due.[17]

At the end of August 1935, following Iribe's death, Gabrielle was not yet in a fit state to return to Paris, and stayed on in the south until late autumn. For the first time, the enthusiasm that drove her to make each new collection failed to draw her back to Paris. She was the same age Iribe had been – fifty-two – and she felt worn out. Perhaps Gabrielle was having an intimation that her phenomenal energy was finite. She managed, by giving instructions for the following spring's collection in long conversations over the phone to Paris. Years later, one of her long-term artisan employees lost his father, and Gabrielle asked him to come and see her at the Ritz:

She sat me down beside her. She told me, and I'll always remember this discussion, which lasted for over an hour . . . 'I wish you a lot of passion, a lot of love, this happens in life! But against grief, there is only one true friend – when you knock on the door, he is behind it: work!'

And, as work had become her habit, it was the only antidote Gabrielle knew of that calmed her many woes. In work, she approached a state of something akin to peace. Thus, when she returned to Paris, that was what she did.

Cocteau now asked her to design the costumes for a new play he was about to write, *Oedipus Rex*, and Jean Renoir asked her to do the same for his forthcoming film, *The Rules of the Game*. It was Gabrielle who had recently introduced her sometime young lover Luchino Visconti to her friend Jean, the painter Renoir's son. She explained to Renoir that the young Italian count wanted to work in films. Despite Visconti's painful shyness, he and Renoir got on, and Visconti went to watch the great director at his work. A year later, Renoir was sufficiently impressed that he included him in his film crew. Some time later still, Visconti was generous enough to give Gabrielle the credit for being the instrument that helped him find his true path.

When Gabrielle returned to Paris that autumn, she had not only returned to work, she had returned to do battle. She was setting about overcoming a professional obstacle, growing steadily over the last couple of years, but which she had so far refused to countenance. For the first time in over fifteen years, she had a serious competitor: her name was Elsa Schiaparelli. There were other competitors – Mainbocher, Marcel Rochas – but it was 'that Italian woman', as Gabrielle called her, who was beginning to attract as much attention as Gabrielle had been accustomed to since the First World War.

Schiap had lots of it but it was bad

Schiaparelli was a talented, eccentric Italian aristocrat who had begun by making sweaters and skirts. These were a great success. While also making clothes lauded for their understated elegance, Schiaparelli was soon to become better known for her witty and outrageous designs. From the mid- to late thirties, these were often done in collaboration with Salvador Dalí. (In this period, Dalí was also to work with Gabrielle, Cocteau and Balanchine on various stage projects.) As a mark of Schiaparelli's success, her work graced the cover of British *Vogue* for Christmas 1935. The young British photographic star Cecil Beaton took pictures of the much admired Indian princess Karam of Kapurthala wearing Schiaparelli evening saris, and shot a series of her clothes with Surrealistic backdrops. Schiaparelli was flamboyant where Gabrielle was understated, and produced a series of pieces in a colour she called 'bright, impossible, impudent, becoming, life-giving, a shocking colour, pure and undiluted'. This 'shocking colour' was the famous pink.

Anita Loos, of *Gentlemen Prefer Blondes* fame, Mae West and Daisy Fellowes were some of Schiaparelli's best-known early clients. Having triumphed by establishing herself on the magnificent place Vendôme, just around the corner from Gabrielle at rue Cambon, Schiaparelli would say, 'Chanel launched sailor sweaters, the short skirt, I took her sweater, changed the lines, and there, Chanel is finished!' Gabrielle believed the idea implicit in Schiaparelli's most daring clothes – that the world is amusing, absurd and futile – would not last. But with Schiaparelli's 'fish-shaped buttons, monkey hats, fox-head gloves and skunk coats', her outrageous, surreal nonsense was a perfect reflection of the times. Bettina Ballard perceptively observed that:

> She branched out into the couture to glorify the hard elegance of the ugly woman ... Hard chic made her exactly right for those extravagant years before World War II. Shocking pink ... was a symbol of her thinking. To be shocking was the snobbism of the moment and she was a leader in this art ... Paris was in a mood for shocks, and Elsa Schiaparelli could present hers in well-cut forms and with an elegance no one could deny.[1]

Pre-First World War, shock tactics had already become part of the *raison d'être* of artistic modernism. For the post-war Dadaists and Surrealists, to shock was virtually orthodoxy.

Schiaparelli not only surrounded herself with artists, just as Gabrielle had, she also persuaded them to work with her on her creations. (Gabrielle believed that art came before artisanship and, when working with artists, put herself very much in second place.) Schiaparelli was forever pushing her artists to experiment, the more suggestively and outrageously the better. Bettina Ballard quoted the great couturier Cristóbal Balenciaga commenting wryly that Schiaparelli '"was the only real artist in the couture", which didn't mean that he thought that art and dressmaking were good companions'.[2] These, of course, were exactly Gabrielle's sentiments. Balenciaga was one of the only colleagues for whom she had real respect.

Gabrielle was on the defensive, but her understanding of fashion was profound. And she now declared that novelty was not necessarily modern. She went further, saying that superficial seasonal changes were not what she offered. What she offered was 'style', and that wasn't the same as fashion. When Gabrielle objected to Schiaparelli's work, she was accused of going against that very avant-garde couture she had led since before the First World War. She retorted that her own modernity derived from placing herself in the classic tradition and understanding something more fundamental about her times. At her best, Gabrielle had created a style that was almost 'beyond fashion'. In creating clothes for a century whose art had lost much of its elitist character, her underlying theme had been inspired by a powerful aesthetic: super-refinement without elitism. Angered at feeling misunderstood, she lashed out with the brilliant comment that Schiaparelli's 'futurism' was an optical illusion that had 'nothing to say of the future'. Looking carefully at what Gabrielle meant, it is correct that Surrealism is an 'optical illusion', and this was not what Gabrielle believed dressing, or style, was about.

During the thirties, women's bodies had gradually re-emerged, and the angular tyranny of *la garçonne* – the flat-chested, Eton-cropped figure of the twenties – was banished. Clothes remained slim-line, but had rediscovered the curves of women's bodies and now followed the line of the bust, the waist and the hips. Smooth, sultry fabrics such as satin were much in vogue, and cutting cloth on the bias, so as to accentuate the curves of the body, became popular. The bodice was often slightly bloused, waists were emphasized with tight belts, while, below the fitted hips, skirts were very feminine and billowed out and flowed. Bias-cut clothes were the invention of Madeleine Vionnet, a couturier admired by Gabrielle for her simplified 'architectural' styles. She disliked anything distorting the curves of a woman's body, and her clothes were sought after for accentuating the natural female form. Influenced by Greek sculpture, the apparent simplicity of Vionnet's styles belied their lengthy process of creation: cutting and draping fabric designs on to miniature dolls before re-creating them on life-size models.

Gabrielle began using big bows at the neck, and shoulder-pads (Schiaparelli is supposed to have introduced them), to exaggerate the smallness of the waist. The hemline had dropped significantly to approximately six inches above the ground, while full-length evening dresses were once again the mode. As an escape from the challenging financial climate of the period, evening wear became more luxurious and sometimes exaggeratedly feminine. Pale satins were the rage throughout the thirties, and Gabrielle succumbed too, making her own versions of the fashionable white, cream and peachy pinks.

At this time, her suits were made of gently fitting tweeds with contrasting open-necked white shirts, showing cuffs, or crisp frills around the neck. Gabrielle's signature look for the time became these same white collars and cuffs as the contrast on a black dress. Black and white had become the underlying theme to many of her day clothes, with hints of green, red, brown, purple and mustard. From the mid-thirties, she used the new patterned elasticized fabric Lastex, afterwards called latex, an up-to-date version of her favourite, jersey.

Schiaparelli was now making jackets with tightly pulled-in waists and stiffly jutting peplums, set over narrow skirts of pin-thin pleats. Gabrielle had come to be regarded by some as the designer for unassertive, self-conscious women whose elegant reserve made them fear, above all else, the epithet 'bad taste'. Schiaparelli's increasingly avant-garde designs were for the woman who saw herself as daring, and who was acquiring a new kind of notice with the designer's intentional 'bad taste'. This group of Schiaparelli devotees were self-assured exhibitionists who loved the attention caused by their red eyelashes, black gloves with red fingernails, pancake hats and blue satin leggings, revealed under the lifted hem of a black evening dress.

The magazines and newspapers luxuriated in the rivalry of these two very different designers, and *Vogue* reported that the new mode 'is neither streamlined nor sentimental, it is casual, bold and chunky'. In 1934, *Time* put Schiaparelli on its cover and made a definitive statement, saying that Chanel was no longer the leader in fashion. Instead, Schiaparelli was one of 'a handful of houses now at or near the peak of their power as arbiters of the ultra-modern haute couture . . . Madder and more original than most of her contemporaries, Mme Schiaparelli is the one to whom the word "genius" is applied most often.' Schiaparelli's Surrealist clothes were challenging the notion of good taste, giving exotic and outrageous flights of fancy an allure previously confined to fancy dress for a costume ball. There was no doubt: Schiaparelli had made Surrealism the utmost in chic.

Schiaparelli and young Dalí's evening dress had a skirt printed with a life-size lobster, complemented by a bodice bearing a scattering of 'parsley'. It was received with a fanfare of publicity, when Beaton photographed it being worn by the Prince of Wales's lover, Mrs Wallis Simpson. Dalí's one regret was that he was forbidden to splatter the dress with real mayonnaise. The young Balenciaga, whose austere clothes were yet feminine and ultra-modern, and are to some the ultimate in twentieth-century elegance, would make an astonishingly acute observation: 'You see, Coco had very little taste, but it was good. Schiap, on the other hand, had lots of it, but it was bad.'

In the spring of 1936, France went to the polls. To the dismay of the right, there was a huge turnout, and a left-wing coalition was now in charge of France. Many believed that the new Popular Front would be the party that would finally push through long overdue reforms. Those to the right with privilege were fearful that the country was teetering on the brink of communism, while the left luxuriated in the May Day celebrations. Léon Blum, the socialist leader of the coalition, was openly taunted in the Chamber for his Jewishness by the right-wing deputy, Xavier Vallat. He said, 'For the first time this old Gallo-Roman country will be governed by a Jew. I dare say out loud what the country is thinking, deep inside: it is preferable . . . to be led by a man whose origins belong to his soil . . . than by a cunning Talmudist.' This reflection of growing anti-Semitism was confirmed in one of the dailies' headlines: 'France under the Jew'.

Meanwhile, concerned at the possibility that the longed-for improvement in their rights – paid holiday, family support, unemployment insurance – might not happen, the workers came out on strike in the largest working-class demonstration France had ever seen, and before the new prime minister had even taken office. Aeroplane-factory workers came out, car-factory workers came out and, after a while, a virtually unheard of thing happened: the textile workers went on strike too. The country was in turmoil. To Gabrielle's amazement, this contagion even spread to her own workers. One morning, she found that her way was barred to the rue Cambon salon by a group of her saleswomen, who were smiling at the cameras. Gabrielle's fury made no difference. They refused to let her in, and she was forced to beat a retreat over the road to the Ritz.

Her lawyer, Réné de Chambrun, was called, and advised an irate Gabrielle to stay calm and be moderate. He persuaded her to meet her workers. But when Gabrielle again crossed rue Cambon over to Chanel from the back of the Ritz, she was once more turned back. Chambrun advised her to wait and see. Eventually, the new premier, Léon Blum, sat down with a workers' delegation, with whom he spent the night drafting an agreement. This was to gain for French workers a set of rights they had never known before.

The strike continued for several days longer but, by the end of it, Gabrielle's workers, too, had gained the right to wage increases, the right to belong to a union, a forty-hour week, and an annual two-week paid holiday. Germany and Britain had both already achieved the principle of collective bargaining, but it was only with this, the Matignon agreement, that France had done the same. Gabrielle was outraged and instantly sacked three hundred of her workers, but Réné de Chambrun and her financial directors advised her that if she didn't relent, and quickly, she would be unable to present her forthcoming autumn collection. Years later, Gabrielle still railed against what she saw as domination by a workforce who should have been grateful to her for employing them. To all intents and purposes, Gabrielle's stance was that of the classic conservative from a modest background. She had worked tremendously hard to achieve, so why shouldn't her workers?

As always, however, Gabrielle was contradictory and frequently paradoxical. And, while her politics were not particularly sophisticated, one should never forget her intelligence or that, at some residual level, she remained deeply anti-establishment. As a result, her politics were more ambivalent than straightforward provincial conservatism. Despite her apparent dislike of left-wing politics, in 1936, for example, Gabrielle designed the costumes for her friend Jean Renoir's film *La Marseillaise*, which hailed the rights of the French people united against exploitation. In that same year, she was the second financer of Pierre Lestringuez's powerfully left-wing magazine, *Futur*. She would also, as mentioned, make the costumes for Renoir's *The Rules of the Game*, his lacerating satire of the establishment.

In these years leading up to the Second World War, the rich in France had little confidence in the government. As a consequence, they exported their capital, the Banque de France lost billions and the political climate was increasingly unstable.

In December 1936, Winston Churchill had come to Paris with his son, Randolph, and dined with Gabrielle (and Cocteau) in her suite at the Ritz. Churchill was there to prevail upon his friend Edward VIII not to marry his lover, Wallis Simpson. During the course of the evening, Churchill was reduced to tears at the thought of the abdication of his king. However, a few days later, he was obliged to help the king with alterations to his speech in which he was doing just that. The following year, when Edward VIII's abdication had made him the Duke of Windsor, he married his divorcee, Wallis Simpson, and Gabrielle sent gifts. Shortly afterwards, Léon Blum's Popular Front government was out of power, replaced by Camille Chautemps. After several rapid changes of French government, in March 1938 Hitler sent troops into his native Austria and was cheered, as the country united with the Third Reich.

In the late thirties, Gabrielle had been drawn, uncharacteristically, into the flourishing theme of escape then popular amongst the couturiers and their clients. Ornate and extravagant romance, inspired by a revival of nineteenth-century style, nostalgically recalled apparently better times. Hand in hand with the political turmoil of the period, these years saw a crescendo of particularly extravagant themed balls, to many of which Gabrielle was invited as one of the star attractions. She attended the Comte de Beaumont's ball, the American ambassador's party, and the astonishing Lady Mendl's party for seven hundred at Versailles. In diamonds and white organdie, the hostess was ringmaster to ponies, clowns and acrobats in white satin. Gabrielle's escort that night was Arthur Capel's old friend the Duc de Gramont, and the guests danced on a floor built upon thousands of tiny springs that swayed to their movements.

While Gabrielle's day clothes retained their typical simplicity of line, one could argue that, with evening wear, her famed restraint sometimes deserted her. This may well have been because she was neither immune to the political turmoil around her, nor to the competition she was experiencing from a handful of talented newcomers such as Balenciaga. Unusually, one glimpses a hint of indecision in Gabrielle's work, giving an impression of less self-assurance in this period. And, while her attacks on Schiaparelli's inadequacy were essentially correct, at the costume ball of the season, Gabrielle let slip her position of haughty superiority, revealing her defensive feelings.

The painter André Durst's mansion, already more stage set than home, was conceived as the house from Alain Fournier's elegy for those times recently lost, *Le Grand Meaulnes*. Durst wanted his ball to be a re-enactment of the one in the novel. Bettina Ballard was there:

> His guests fell quickly into the mood of fantasy. They made their entrances by the pool; one group came as a flight of birds; another as three trees walking solemnly towards the guests . . . Maria de Gramont, as a leopard, glided across the fields with Bébé Bérard as a frolicking lion . . .
>
> [T]here was a near disaster when Chanel . . . dared Schiaparelli . . . to dance with her and, with purposeful innocence, steered her into the candles . . . The fire was put out and so was Schiaparelli – by delighted guests squirting her with soda-water. The incident added enormously to the anecdotes about the party that provided Paris with conversation for many days.[3]

Careful to remain in the public eye, Gabrielle continued socializing and was noticed at one great costume ball after another wearing dramatic revivalist outfits. Interestingly, to the modern eye, for the first time, she looks a little dated. Having contributed so much to the look of her century, somehow the clothes of the previous one just don't look right on her. It is ironic that the woman who had become successful through her radical simplification of women's dress in the years before and after the First World War, on the eve of the next cataclysm joined in this escapist attention to the past.

★ ★ ★

Hôtel Ritz letterhead, dated 1938
Dearest Coco

I arrived just when you had left rue Cambon after an afternoon of colossal 'gnawing pains'. Don't forget about me! I would like to see you tomorrow morning . . . I will telephone you . . .

Dear Beautiful little Coco

I will write to you . . . Earlier, when Hugo told me you were clinging on to the other end of the phone, it scared me to death . . . and my legs were shaking a little bit . . . a compulsive tenderness seized my throat . . . After this phone call I had a . . . representation of your little face, there was a kind of melancholy which I had never seen before . . . a kind of melancholy which is probably . . . absolutely exclusive to you . . .
I give you my love. No one of us must ever die.

La Pausa
1938
Dear beautiful Chanel

. . . It scares me more and more to telephone you, it gives me palpitations, anguish seizes me by the throat and I understand absolutely

nothing of what you're telling me . . . I have to tell you where I stand
. . . and it is better to write it to you than not to tell you.

I give you my love and I love you.
Your Salvador

La Pausa, Roquebrune
Late 1938
Dear beautiful little bird

. . . Gala [his wife] is gone . . . While you were here you have truly
enchanted La Pausa. One gets used to not seeing this little image . . . One
thing is certain is that our meeting is becoming very 'good' and very
important . . .

I give you all my love
Your Salvador[4]

Salvador is Salvador Dalí and, for several months, he and Gabrielle
had been having an affair. A few years later, she would brush the
romance aside and say she only indulged in it to annoy Gala. Reading the series of Dalí's letters to Gabrielle, one can see that he,
however, had clearly both fallen in love with Gabrielle and was
amazed by her. In spite of his (intentionally or not) surreal way of
communicating, one sees that Dalí was no fool, and he undoubtedly
appreciated something of the great breadth of Gabrielle's character. This included 'seeing' her melancholy. He would no doubt have
agreed with her comments when she said: 'I provide contrasts . . .
which I cannot get used to: I think I am the shyest and the boldest
person, the gayest and the saddest. It's not that I am violent; it's the
contrasts, the great opposites that clash within me.'[5]

Gabrielle's horror of loneliness left her still yearning for love and
companionship. But, after Iribe's death, disillusionment would
harden her. She seemed resigned to the thought that nothing lasts
and you take what you can while you can. And, for all her growing
self-presentation as invincible and hard, as much as anything, this
was because of those violent contrasts she had described. On the

one hand, she was very strong; on the other, her vulnerability never left her. Thus she could say, 'Anyway, that is the person I am. Have you understood? Very well, I am also the opposite of all that.'[6] Thus, one is not entirely convinced by Gabrielle's protestations that she was untouched by her affair with Dalí and that her only thought had been to spite his wife, Gala, extremely annoying though Gala Dalí was.

Gabrielle came and went from La Pausa, regularly allowing one or more of her friends to stay for lengthy periods in her absence. During the thirties, one of these guests had been Pierre Reverdy. While Reverdy had exiled himself to the monastery outside Paris in the twenties, periodically, he found the life of an ascetic insupportable and returned to the outside world. For some time, this had also involved an intermittent 'return' to Gabrielle.

In that summer of 1938, Dalí's letters to Gabrielle repeatedly stress how they are 'terribly anxious about this nightmare you are living with Roussi'. This was Roussadana, the Russian girl who had married José Maria Sert.

Some time before, Roussadana had become addicted to morphine and, in recent months, she had also been reduced to a painful thinness. When she and Sert arrived to stay at La Pausa, Roussadana looked terrible; she was permanently feverish and coughing. Gabrielle took over. Sert didn't 'believe' in illness and, anyway, he was far too selfish to take a proper interest in his wife's failing health. Gabrielle insisted they take Roussadana to a specialist for X-rays, and the verdict did not surprise her: Roussadana was in an advanced stage of tuberculosis. The doctors insisted she must enter a sanatorium, but the ravaged young woman absolutely refused to do so. Finally, Gabrielle used the ruse of paying a visit to her doctor in Switzerland. Would Roussadana come with her? When their train had set off, Roussadana showed Gabrielle the bruises given her by Sert in his fury at seeing her leave. She called them 'Sert's last gifts'.

Arriving in Switzerland, Gabrielle persuaded her to enter a clinic.

On receiving the news in Paris, Misia rushed to Switzerland to see her but, once there, was repeatedly refused entry. She was told that the smallest upset could be fatal for Roussadana. Distraught, Misia returned to Paris, convinced it was Gabrielle, not the doctors, who had prevented her from seeing the dying young woman. She may well have been correct. Misia suffered terribly at not being able to see the woman who had not only destroyed her marriage but whom she also adored.

As a final pathetic twist, tradition has it that Roussadana's morphine addiction was now so relentless that, although mortally ill from tuberculosis, she could survive only short periods without a new fix. Ever the resourceful one, Gabrielle procured a substantial quantity, then brought Roussadana a large basket of marzipan 'flowers', ordered from Fauchon in Paris, into each one of which she had inserted a 'dose' of morphine.[7]

Not long after Roussadana and Sert had married, the Abbé Mugnier dined at the Robert Rothschilds'. The Abbé talked with Misia about what he called her 'peculiar social situation'. Painting a touching portrait of her, he was amazed at her lack of vitriol, saying that she 'didn't speak ill of her husband either'.[8] And when, on 16 December 1938, Roussadana Mdivani Sert was released from her suffering, Misia had been prevented from bidding her farewell. Jean Hugo (great-grandson to Victor, and the writer and artist whose benign personality led Sachs to describe him as having no enemies) wrote that Roussadana lay smiling as the Reverend Conan Doyle administered the last rites. The insane Sert had arrived with a blue eiderdown in which he wanted to wrap Roussadana's body. The eiderdown was too big for the coffin, but he was determined. Gabrielle was also determined to have her lilies in the coffin, and they argued; a depressing image.[9]

A few weeks earlier, on 21 September, the western powers had abandoned Czechoslovakia to its fate, agreeing to appeasement rather than confrontation with Germany. The following day, Churchill had voiced the opinion of many when he wrote to *The Times*:

The division of Czechoslovakia, under pressure from England and France, is equivalent to the total surrender of western democracies to threats of Nazi force. Such a collapse will bring peace and security to neither England nor France.

His words would of course prove correct, and time was running out.

War

The Paris spring collections for 1939 continued, meanwhile, with their escapist historical theme. *Vogue* said that 'Paris, the worldly, the sophisticated – Paris, where a woman is hardly considered a passable beauty until she is thirty-five – this Paris has suddenly gone completely innocent, quaint, modest, girlish.' Describing the 'modest grace' of the evening clothes, the magazine said, 'You can choose between the provoking gypsy modesty of Chanel's bodice-and-skirt dresses, Mainbocher peasant types, or the eighteenth-century modesty that is in every collection.' Gabrielle's day clothes remained simple but, for evening, she 'did' charming peasants, too, and had full skirts in multicoloured taffetas, puff-sleeved and embroidered blouses, short bolero jackets and handkerchiefs tied at the neck. And, while her signature (fabric) camellia flowers were pinned to shoulders and necklines, she also had several pieces taking up a Tricolour theme, trimming them with red, white and blue. For the first time, Gabrielle was interviewed by the American National Broadcasting Corporation (NBC) in Paris. Schiaparelli was interviewed, too, but separately.

In January 1939, Franco's fascists' success had driven almost half a million Republican soldiers and civilians to flee across the border into France; in February, the Republican government had followed them into exile. With the army routed, Madrid was left to the fascists and starvation. In March, Hitler invaded Czechoslovakia; three weeks later, Mussolini invaded Albania, opening up a route into Greece. France's coalition leader, Edouard Daladier, declared the introduction of emergency powers, and began talks with Britain and the Soviet Union on an alliance to prevent Hitler from invading Poland. To the consternation of London and Paris, Stalin now chose to sign a non-aggression treaty with Germany. This gave him the possibility of regaining territories in the Baltic, Romania and Poland, taken from Soviet Russia at the end of the First World War, and also meant that the balance of power had swung in Germany's favour.

No sooner had Gabrielle returned to Paris from La Pausa than Daladier called for general mobilization. Shortly afterwards, the brilliantly authoritative *New Yorker* correspondent in Paris for fifty years, Janet Flanner, wrote of a transformed capital:

> The greatest emotion was centred around the Gare de l'Est, where thousands of soldiers have entrained for the northern frontier . . . Mostly they have been in uniform and steel helmets . . . Also, mostly their mothers, wives, fathers, and sisters have shed no tears, till the troop trains have pulled out . . . There are no flags, flowers or shrill shouts of vive la patrie! as there were in 1914. Among the men departing . . . the morale is excellent but curiously mental. What the men say is intelligent not emotional. '. . . Let's stop living in this grotesque suspense and get it over once and for all' . . . Few Frenchmen are thrilled to go forth to die . . . Yet all . . . seem united in understanding that this war, if it comes, is about the theory of living and its eventual practice.[1]

Amongst the millions called up was Gabrielle's nephew, André Palasse, whom she asked to visit her en route for induction into the army. André's health had never been robust, and Gabrielle was concerned. As predicted by those in France and Great Britain, who believed that appeasement was a waste of time, Hitler now invaded Poland. On 3 September, Britain and France together declared war upon Germany.

Three weeks later, Gabrielle put into effect a most dramatic response to the announcement of war: she closed down her couture house and laid off most of the workforce. Only the boutique at 31 rue Cambon would remain open, selling the perfumes and jewellery. Gabrielle was now almost unanimously reviled. Many of her workers believed her decision was in retaliation for their strike action in 1936; others felt that she was deserting her 'responsibilities'. Some in Paris whispered that she had felt eclipsed by Schiaparelli. Speaking of the plight of her workforce, the trade union tried to dissuade her. When this failed, they appealed to her sense of responsibility to her customers. Gabrielle remained adamant. After a few weeks, the government stepped in and begged her: would she not work 'for the prestige of Paris'? She said that no one could make her work against her will. She would not re-open the House of Chanel.

It has been said that, having profited from the last war, Gabrielle had decided against it in this one to atone for her guilt. More convincing is her occasional comment that, while making her name in the last war, she didn't feel there would be a place for fashion in this one. She intended tidying up the loose ends of her business and, whenever the hostilities ended, would move on to something else: 'I had the feeling that we had reached the end of an era. And that no one would ever make dresses again. [She was referring to haute couture.]'[2]

Gabrielle was no longer young, but her intuitions were still remarkably accurate. With hindsight, one can see that the war was indeed to strike the death knell for the great tradition of haute couture. From the monastery at Solesmes, meanwhile, her friend Pierre Reverdy wrote approving of her actions, saying, 'The point in life . . . is to find equilibrium in what is inherently unstable.'[3]

While soldiers from opposing armies faced each other across the Rhine, Gabrielle heard from her nephew that he was in the first line of defence. Gabrielle now set about severing all but two or three links with her past: she wrote to her brothers, Lucien and Alphonse, saying that she could no longer support them as she had done. She said, 'You cannot count on me for anything as long as circumstances stay the way they are.' Lucien was touched by her plight and wrote offering her some of his savings. Gabrielle was, of course, still very rich and had no need of them.

She replaced her chauffeur, who had been called up, kept a car ready just in case and consolidated her rooms at the Ritz. She paid for a staircase to be built from her two-roomed suite up to a small bedroom in the attic, which was very simple, even austere, and contained little more than her bed. For decoration, there was nothing except the beautiful Russian icon given her by Stravinsky, two statues on the mantel and Arthur's watch, given to her by his sister, Bertha. It still kept perfect time. On the white walls there were no pictures. She said, 'Ah no, none of that here. This is a bedroom, not a drawing room.'⁴ However, even in her drawing room, Gabrielle had only one picture, a painting of wheat by Dalí. It is often said that Dalí gave it to her. He didn't; Gala Dalí had connived to make Gabrielle buy it. Gabrielle didn't *need* painting the way she needed sculpture. Sculpture was, like her couture, a three-dimensional thing, unlike painting, which only *plays* with three-dimensional space. Indeed, Gabrielle surrounded herself with sculpture of all kinds, from her small herd of large animals, particularly deer and lions, to the classical busts, the large Buddha, and the bust of Arthur's disgraced priest uncle, Thomas Capel. We don't know whether Gabrielle kept this link with Arthur in the mistaken belief that Thomas was distinguished, or whether in fact she was amused by his dubious reputation.

With the advent of hostilities, many male servants had been called up, so a good number of the better off closed up their establishments, sent their children to the country and, with their jewels and artworks hidden, moved into hotels. Amongst those living at the Ritz alongside Gabrielle were Schiaparelli and her beloved daughter, Gogo; the fabulously wealthy society figures Lady Mendl and Reginald and Daisy Fellowes; various aristocrats and women whom nothing would budge from Paris; a number of significant politicians; and the actor Sacha Guitry. In the weeks after war was declared, when there was no fighting and the soldiers were all idle, the hostilities seemed unreal. Gas masks remained unused, and people began to relax; there appeared little need for sacrifice, benefit galas proliferated and most theatres and cinemas re-opened. That winter of 1939, when social life almost returned to normal, became known as the 'Phoney War'.

By February 1940, Daladier was out, and a new French premier, Paul Reynaud, had been voted in. Suddenly, the Phoney War was over: Hitler attacked and occupied Denmark and Norway, and the Luftwaffe bombed the airfields of northern France. Jean Renoir's *La Règle du Jeu*, with the actors dressed by Gabrielle, had had its premiere just prior to the war and had been booed off the screen. The film, with its satirization of the upper classes as capricious and self-indulgent, was banned a few weeks into the war as 'unpatriotic'.

German tanks crossed into Holland and Belgium, and armoured divisions moved on the Ardennes. Neville Chamberlain resigned on 10 May, and Winston Churchill, who promised naught but 'blood, toil, tears and sweat', became Britain's new prime minister. By the end of May, the Allies had suffered a disaster, causing panic in London and Paris as General Rommel swept across northern France towards the Channel, driving the Allies ahead of him. Whenever a break in the weather allowed it, the Luftwaffe fired on the hundreds of thousands of Allies hoping for rescue on the beaches of Dunkirk. Between the end of May and the first days of June, in the most famous rescue operation of the war, instead of the thirty thousand or so Churchill had believed were all that could be rescued, well over three hundred thousand were ferried to safety in England by the Royal Navy, plus a huge flotilla of volunteer boats of all shapes and sizes.

By 4 June, the Germans were bombing the outskirts of Paris. The government instructed everyone who was able to leave the city to do so. Ahead of an advancing German army, millions of men, women and children, in any vehicle to be found, or otherwise on foot, were now fleeing Paris. Along the big west and south highroads, motor and horse-drawn vehicles were 'piled high with babies' cribs, luggage, pets, bedding, and food, all under a hot summer sun'.[5] 'The exodus', as it came to be known, was followed ten days later by the government, itself fleeing south to Tours in a convoy of limousines.

After war had been declared, Dalí wrote to Gabrielle from a villa at Arcachon, not far from the Spanish border, to which he and Gala had withdrawn. He was concerned about Gabrielle, saying he had

> sent you two telegrams and we are constantly waiting for a sign from you to know that you are running your little face somewhere. I imagine that you are snowed under with worries, for you cultivate such a 'fanaticism of responsibilities' in everything! . . . Only enormous and very 'important' things will be 'visible' in the times that will follow . . . When will we meet, where?

Then, in another letter, he tells her about the night bombings at Arcachon and regrets not being able to look at her: 'How sweet it is to grab you on the corner of a tablecloth . . . Whatever you do, be careful, I know that you have a crazy and useless carelessness, that you run like a cockerel without being scared of anything.'[6]

In the first week of June, along with most of Paris, Dalí's 'crazy' Gabrielle escaped, just ahead of the advancing German army. On closing her couture house and laying off all her workers except those in the boutique, Gabrielle had instructed her director, Georges Madoux, to remove all the accounts and archives and take them to a makeshift office he was to set up in the Midi. Madoux, however, had been called up and decided his first priority was to save his family and his own possessions before the administrative hub of the House of Chanel.

Stories differ as to Gabrielle's precise movements in those hazardous days, but we know she left Paris with a hastily recruited driver in his own car. Petrol had been rationed, and fear walked abroad. Gabrielle decided against her own house, La Pausa, as a refuge. In response to a Royal Air Force attack on Turin, the Italians had declared war on the Allies and begun bombing the Riviera. Cocteau had fled to Aix-en-Provence with the Aurics, but Gabrielle decided not to go there.

Having managed the long journey down through France, she reached Pau, in the Pyrenees, before turning off further into the mountains and the small village of Corbères-Abères. Here, André Palasse had his château, and Gabrielle came to a halt there for a few weeks. She had bought the château for André in 1926 – the sale was negotiated by Gabrielle's old lover Etienne Balsan, living nearby – and, most summers, Gabrielle had spent time there with André and his family.

Other refugees soon began to arrive. Gabrielle Labrunie, André's daughter, tells how these were her great-aunt's employees, who had nowhere else to go. In all, there were about fifteen. Madame Labrunie remembers that some of them 'were rather lost, confused . . . they were quite old . . . and no longer able to work . . . We'd heard that Paris was going to be very dangerous, so they all came to Corbères.'[7] One of the refugees was a pregnant girl, called Annick. She was the daughter of Madame Aubert, the redhead who had been Gabrielle's right-hand woman for so long. Another of those who ended up at Corbères-Abères was Gabrielle's friend the socialite Marie-Louise Bousquet.

On 14 June, the Germans occupied Paris; Reynaud's coalition government then collapsed, and Marshal Pétain was chosen as France's new premier. On 16 June, he requested an armistice. At dawn, a week later, Hitler arrived in Paris accompanied by his entourage, including his architect, Albert Speer, and the neo-classicist sculptor Arno Breker. With them he made his notorious lightning tour of the defeated city. Stopping at the Opéra, the party continued down the Champs-Elysées and on to the Trocadéro. Hitler posed for the infamous photograph in front of the balustrade overlooking the Seine and the Eiffel Tower. At Les Invalides, he stood musing over Napoléon's tomb. He was impressed by the proportions of the Panthéon but was uninterested in other monuments signalling the illustriousness of Paris. The rue de Rivoli, however, delighted him, and the military governor of Paris requisitioned the Hôtel Meurice there for himself and his associates.

By 9 a.m., Hitler had finished his tour. He told Speer, 'It was the dream of my life to see Paris. I cannot say how happy I am to have that dream fulfilled.' He later told Speer that he had often considered having to destroy the city, but it was clear that instead they must continue with the new buildings of Berlin, so that 'when we are finished Paris will only be a shadow.'

France had agreed to accept its military defeat. On 21 June – in a clearing in that same forest of Compiègne that Gabrielle had ridden through many times with Etienne Balsan and their friends – and in the same carriage in which the Allies had watched the Germans sign their defeat in the First World War, the Germans now dictated their terms to the French delegation. On hearing the news in the far-away Pyrenees, Gabrielle Labrunie tells how her great-aunt shut herself up in her room for several hours and wept, scandalized at Pétain's surrender without a fight.

After a few weeks of hiding in the hills, Gabrielle decided it wasn't for her. Dalí was right: she wasn't really 'scared of anything' – with one exception: being abandoned. On 14 July, she sent a telegram to a Spanish sculptor friend of Picasso's, Apel les Fenosa, who had fled Paris for Toulouse, and told him that she would be 'reaching Toulouse Monday afternoon. Please find me somewhere to stay ... Greetings. Gabrielle Chanel.'

Apel les Fenosa was an exiled Spanish Republican sculptor who had arrived in Paris in 1938 with nothing. Picasso had helped him escape from Spain, and Cocteau had introduced him to Gabrielle in early 1939. By this time, Fenosa's work was selling well, and Gabrielle commissioned him to sculpt her. (For some time, Picasso had failed to persuade his friend to sculpt him, but Gabrielle finally encouraged Fenosa to do so.)

Fenosa was a dynamic, attractive character and, not long after their meeting, he and Gabrielle were launched into an affair. She offered to move Fenosa into the Ritz, where she was already living, but the communist sculptor found himself uncomfortable in the bourgeois confines of the hotel, so Cocteau made a deal with him. He would swap his apartment in the place de la Madeleine with Fenosa, and Cocteau would take the room offered by Gabrielle at the Ritz. In the late autumn, Fenosa was diagnosed with double mastoiditis, and Cocteau told his boyfriend, the matinee idol Jean Marais, away in the army, that Gabrielle's doctors were looking after Fenosa, who was very ill. Away from Paris, Gabrielle had telegrammed asking for news of his health.

The affair between the couturier and the sculptor continued for a year or more, and they were said to be very close. Dalí had intuited correctly that he had 'been left a widow'. Fenosa felt great admiration for Gabrielle and would later say that 'she was highly intelligent, she was good for me. She never left anything to chance.' But, in the end, it was he who felt driven to break off their affair, saying there were two reasons for their separation. Apparently, 'there were two or three stories about men around her, as was often the case with her . . . but mostly it was drugs!' Fenosa was vehemently against drug use. Adamant that he didn't want to become habituated to them himself, he said, 'It was drugs that pulled us apart. If you love someone who takes drugs, either you take them yourself or the other person quits.' Fenosa had told Gabrielle, 'Either you quit drugs, or I leave!' He left.[8]

After the war, Gabrielle railed against some of those she knew, such as the writer and future statesman André Malraux, who were 'destroying' themselves with drugs. But, while Gabrielle denied those things she didn't wish others, or herself, to believe about her, as her future assistant would say, 'This didn't stop her from lying a lot.'[9] While Fenosa objected to Gabrielle using drugs at all, Gabrielle was able to convince herself that she didn't, because she was always able to keep it under control.

Gabrielle stayed at André Palasse's château for a few weeks and then made her way to Toulouse. Fenosa contacted several of their mutual friends, such as Cocteau, who were not far away, and ordered them to come to Vernet-les-Bains, where they spent time at the house of friends. Cocteau was relieved at the arrival of Jean Marais, demobilized after the collapse of France, and Pétain's armistice. Marais had starred in Cocteau's *Oedipus Rex* in 1937, for which Gabrielle had designed the costumes.

Once she knew that the Germans wouldn't bomb Paris, she wanted to return, and soon set off with Marie-Louise Bousquet and a female doctor on a journey busy with event. Bousquet knew someone who had forty-five or so litres of petrol, which they had to carry with them in the sweltering summer heat. Reaching Vichy, the women were down to their last litre of fuel. Now that Vichy was the capital of the southern half of France, which Hitler had chosen not to occupy, the travellers were obliged to stop here for papers, in order to be allowed to cross into the occupied northern sector of the country, and Paris. Pétain and Pierre Laval's government was ruling 'Vichy' France from a series of the spa town's hotels. (Laval had two terms as head of the Vichy government, signing the deportation papers of many Jews to the death camps, for which he would be executed after the war.) The US ambassador, William Bullitt, talked with the new government officials, then sent to President Roosevelt, saying:

> The French leaders desire to cut loose from all that France has represented during the past two generations. Their physical and moral defeat has been so absolute that they have accepted completely for France the fate of becoming a province of Nazi Germany ... the simple people of the country are as fine as they have ever been. The upper classes have completely failed.[10]

This failure, of course, had been the implication in Renoir's satire, hence its banishment from the screen. As someone who remained ambivalent towards this class, it seems appropriate that Gabrielle had designed the film's wardrobe.

In Vichy, Marie-Louise and Gabrielle ate at the Hôtel du Parc, where they were taken aback by the general air of celebration. Gabrielle said, 'Everyone was laughing and drinking champagne.'[11] Her ironic comment on this festive atmosphere provoked a man to confront her, and his wife had to calm him down.

Where were the travellers to spend the night? 'A gentleman offered me his bed on condition that I share it with him. I managed to persuade the owner of the hotel and they put me up in the garret where the heat was killing. I got up every hour and went into the bathroom just to breathe.' Marie-Louise had a chaise-longue placed in a linen room for her.[12]

Assisted by the prefect of police, they managed to obtain more petrol, and Gabrielle, Marie-Louise and the doctor set off once more for Paris. Reaching a roadblock, no one was allowed through, except Belgians returning home. The women attempted side roads, but these were jammed with cars trying to do the same thing. Moving forward slowly, wherever they stopped, they could find nothing to eat. Finally, reaching another spa town, where everyone was very jittery, because the hotels were all booked but no one had turned up, the travellers were offered three large rooms, each with its own bath.

Gabrielle went out for a walk and was duped by a child into giving him some money. This he immediately gave to his mother and told Gabrielle, 'Now we'll be able to eat tonight.' The woman had another child with her and was pregnant. When she revealed her almost empty purse, Gabrielle was struck by her destitution.

When the travellers finally reached Paris, on the rue de Rivoli and place de la Concorde they could only see German soldiers. A swastika was flying above the Ritz, as it was from all the major hotels. The MBF, the Wehrmacht military command in France, had its seat in the Hôtel Majestic on avenue Kléber. Here was centred the administration, the management of the economy and the maintenance of order. Here, too, Joseph Goebbels had his Propaganda-Abteilung (Propaganda Division) immediately begin its work. Posters were up everywhere announcing that 'the English and the Jews have brought you to this sorry pass.' Food and cigarettes were distributed, as was a poster of a Nazi soldier caring for some little children which bore the slogan: 'Abandoned peoples, put your trust in the German soldier.' German street signs, instructions and banners were everywhere.

A large number of overlapping organizations now ruled the French. Many Nazi officers worked in France under direct orders from Berlin while, in Paris itself, the MBF was always skirmishing with Ribbentrop's Ministry of Foreign Affairs – in this case, the German embassy. Eventually, Ribbentrop's protégé, Otto Abetz, became arguably more important than the MBF, and was dubbed King Otto I.

All requisitioned hotels had armed soldiers posted at their doors. Gabrielle was barred entry to the Ritz without an *Ausweis* (permit), and told she must seek permission from the commandant. There are several versions of what happened next but, eventually, Gabrielle was given leave to remain at the Ritz. However, her grand suite of rooms was now inhabited by German officers. She was offered one small room on the rue Cambon side of the hotel. She agreed.

26

Survival

Misia was appalled at Gabrielle's acceptance of a shabby room, and at her choice to remain in a hotel requisitioned by the enemy. However, to Gabrielle, these considerations simply weren't relevant. For all her beautiful houses and elegant possessions, her attachment to these only went so far. She was always able to withdraw from attachment to things. Her strongest sense now was survival. And her means of survival – her shop – was just over the road on rue Cambon. Gabrielle didn't care what people thought, and she asked Misia what was the point of going somewhere else. Sooner or later, all the hotels would be 'occupied' anyway. At 31 rue Cambon, meanwhile, the Chanel boutique was busy: German soldiers were buying Chanel N°5 for their womenfolk back home. Albeit limited in its production, the perfume would continue being sold throughout the four years of France's occupation.

Despite the occupation, ten or so of Gabrielle's fellow couturiers had remained open to carry on their work. Shortages of all materials, which would continue throughout the war, meant they were struggling to bring out their new collections. Schiaparelli and Mainbocher would go to America; Edward Molyneux fled to London. For those who stayed, the shows were attended by some French women, German embassy staff and some of the German command. They escorted their wives, including Emma Goering and Suzanne Abetz, wife to the man the Reich called the German ambassador. Following lengthy and delicate negotiations, Lucien Lelong, president of the Chambre Syndicale de la Couture Parisienne, dissuaded the German command from moving the entire Parisian couture business to Vienna and Berlin. He argued that Parisian fashion could *only* be made in

Paris. He also succeeded in keeping 80 per cent of couture's work-force, against constant demands for extra labour from German war industries intent on rapid expansion. Lelong even obtained special dispensations for the couturiers to buy costly fabrics without using their ration tickets. But a change in their clients was quickly noticed by all the fashion houses. Lelong would say:

> A new class of rich person, black marketeers and collaborators, thanks to their wives, provoked a sudden change in the dress world. The old wealthy and aristocratic clientele was ... replaced by the butter, egg and cheese people [the BOEF], the spoiled darlings of the war. These nouveaux riches caused a deluxe ready-to-wear, unknown to the public before 1939 ... and the new clientele brought an enormous success to this fashion, which was not high fashion but imitated it very well and was cheaper into the bargain.[1]

Gabrielle would describe this period as 'singularly lacking in dig-nity'; it was 'a filthy mess'.[2]

The races at Longchamp opened again, and German officers, who had free entry to the enclosure, mixed with Parisian society. A good section of this society chose to 'believe' in the propaganda regard-ing Franco-German cultural exchange. Much was made by those Germans and the Germanophile French of the fellowship of all art-ists and the meaninglessness of national boundaries. And the 'gentlemanly' German officers began to be welcomed into the re-emerging salons. The socialite Marie-Louise Bousquet, for example, maintained her renowned Wednesday lunches, keeping her trad-itionally good table well furnished with black-market provisions. To her Wednesdays, she invited a variety of the German command, including the propaganda director, Gerhard Heller, and the equally cultivated novelist officer Ernst Jünger. (After the war, Nancy Mit-ford and Evelyn Waugh were happy to be found at Marie-Louise Bousquet's lunches.)

Ernst Jünger found Hitler and the Jews equally distasteful, and socialized with Vichy-sympathizing Parisians, including the writer Paul Morand, who had wasted no time in offering his services to the Vichy government. He was for a time the film censor and, later, Vichy's ambassador to Romania. Misia Sert's ex-husband, José Maria, had returned to her after his young wife's death but, on his visits to Madrid, was conducting an affair with the wife of the German ambassador. Throughout the war, Sert's connections were unclear, but he always managed to have good food, entertained well and was untroubled by the inclusion of Germans at his gatherings. Another salon where conquerors and Parisians mixed freely was that of the American heiress Florence Gould.

While several writers, such as André Gide, André Malraux and Colette, chose to remain in the south, beyond the occupied zone, Cocteau had hurried back to Paris, saying that 'Miracles are happening everywhere, and I am intensely curious.' He wrote to his fellow opium-addict artist friend Christian Bérard, 'I find these days exciting, too bad Martel was so lacking in curiosity.'[3] Thierry de Martel was one of France's finest brain surgeons, and had lost his son, and himself been severely wounded, in the First World War. At the recent armistice, Martel had felt so disillusioned in his country's values and the international catastrophe that he had taken his own life. France was deeply shocked. Cocteau was fully aware of these circumstances, and the callousness of his remarks was thus appalling. But, by now, he had become incapable of appreciating the physical and moral enormity of the occupation, or of sensing the depth to which his conquerors might be capable of sinking. Cocteau's orgy of opium and cocaine consumption over the last few years had stupefied and desensitized him to a considerable degree.

There were many Frenchmen who, as Ambassador William Bullitt had put it, would remain 'as fine as they have ever been'. Yet, while it is difficult to write briefly about something as momentous as the occupation without gross simplification, Cocteau's repugnant detachment reflected one aspect of the tragedy of France in 1940. Intellectual and artistic life had taken on a darker intensity since the debilitating horrors of the First World War. The French experience had convinced many that violence and irrationality ruled, and that European society was in crisis. The poet Paul Valéry had written, 'We realized that a civilization was just as fragile as a life.' Since the First World War, the country had been at political loggerheads with itself – between left and right, between Catholic conservatism, fascism and communism – and many went into this new war already in a worn-out state of pessimism. 'Frenchmen had exhausted, in the charnel house of the First World War, their reserves of national pride, of confidence in those who led them, even of horror and indignation over their own fate.'[4] Afterwards, many would simply want to forget those 'Dark Years', as those between 1940 and 1944 became known.

The battle for France had lasted no more than six weeks, concluding in a total military defeat. Pétain had signed an armistice with Germany, and half of the country, including Paris, was occupied by thousands of German troops. Unprompted by Germany, Pétain's Vichy government now threw out democratic institutions and set about persecuting what it saw as the three most unwanted social elements: Freemasons, Jews and communists. From the outset, Vichy also had a policy of collaboration with Germany. By the end of the war, 650,000 civilian French workers would have been put to work in German factories; another 60,000 had been deported to German concentration camps; 30,000 French civilians were shot as hostages or members of the Resistance and, aside from about 4,000 Jews who died in French camps, almost 80,000 others would be sent from there to die in Auschwitz.[5]

The late Charles Péguy, taken up as a hero by both the Resisters opposed to Vichy's anti-Semitic laws and also by Vichy itself, had written: 'In wartime he who does not surrender is my man, whoever he is, wherever he comes from, and whatever his party . . . And he who surrenders is my enemy.'[6] That opposing sides were able to take this same man as one of their heroes is representative of the complexity of French reactions to the occupation. It reveals the extent to which 'antagonists might share as many assumptions with their enemies as with those on their own side.' Since the sixties, it has been shown that de Gaulle's 'heroic re-interpretation of the Dark Years . . . in which most of the horrors inflicted on France had been the work of the Germans alone . . . and in which de Gaulle and the Resistance had incarnated the real France' was a gross exaggeration. De Gaulle's propaganda, that the mass of French people, apart from a handful of traitors, was solidly behind him and the Resistance, was constructed in the belief that this was the way to get his countrymen back on their feet.

However, in the sixties, when the French came to challenge de Gaulle's heroic version of their past, and when they were increasingly reminded that millions had revered Pétain, they also saw that the laws of Vichy France were representative of much of France. And the country largely faced the fact that it was Vichy that had discriminated against Jews and Freemasons, that it was French policemen, not Germans, who arrested the Jews and communists and sent them to concentration camps. The Resistance was a very small minority, and most people had been *attentistes* – those who would wait and see. A gradual redressing of the balance in France has meant that this attitude is no longer hidden. It is overwhelmingly recognized that the history of the occupation should not be written in black and white, but in many shades of grey. This has much bearing on our understanding of how Gabrielle was to spend a good part of the war.

The prestige of intellectuals in France meant that the war invested their actions with particular significance. Although a good number fled to the unoccupied south, for many, the surest – almost the only – means to avoid compromising oneself was to go abroad into exile. A large number of artists and intellectuals were helped to do this early on, by the French, and by a number of foreigners. One of the most significant groups was the hastily organized American Emergency Rescue Committee. Most of the escapees – many of them known to Gabrielle, and a good number of them her friends – went to America. The artists included Salvador Dalí, Max Ernst, André

41. (*top*) Skiing with society; Gabrielle (*centre*). Behind are Etienne and Edith de Beaumont.

42. (*left*) Gabrielle in jersey suit, *c.* 1931; note the return of the waist.

43. (*right*) In New York, 1931, on Gabrielle's triumphant first trip to the US.

44. (*top*) Gabrielle with English society models, 1932; Lady Pamela Smith stands.

45. (*middle*) With and photographed by Cecil Beaton, *c.* 1937.

46. (*bottom*) Gabrielle, her jewellery designer Fulco di Verdura and his work, 1937.

47. With Salvador Dalí, *c.* 1938.

48. Apel-les Fenosa sculpts Gabrielle, *c.* 1939.

49. (*below left*) Gabrielle's close friend Maggie van Zuylen and the dancer Serge Lifar.

50. (*below right*) Baron von Dincklage at fifty-four, Gabrielle's lover during and after the war.

51. Gabrielle's 1954 suit, in the US *Vogue* photo shoot instrumental in resuscitating her name.

52. Suzy Parker, in one of the three outfits shot for US *Vogue* in 1954.

53. On the famed staircase at 31 rue Cambon, before Gabrielle's 1954 comeback show.

54. Some of the models who added lustre to Maison Chanel: Marie-Hélène Arnaud, Gisèle Francome, Paule Rizzo and Mimi d'Arcangues in 1958.

55. Gabrielle, once again famous, in characteristic pose, 1959.

56. Gabrielle's sculptures seen in the salon at rue Cambon: in the fireplace a Jacques Lipchitz; on the mantle, classical torso and masks.

57. At rue Cambon, the bust of Thomas Capel on mantle, Gabrielle's astrological lions on the table and a Coromandel screen behind.

58. An elderly Gabrielle in her salon with her chandelier of personal symbols, *c.* 1965.

59. Gabrielle's funeral mass in the Madeleine church, 13 January 1971, her coffin draped in flowers. Her models, in Chanel, stand at the front.

Breton and Jacques Lipchitz, Man Ray and Fernand Léger. Amongst the film directors were René Clair and Jean Renoir. The many writers who left included André Masson, the Catholic philosopher Jacques Maritain, and Antoine de Saint-Exupéry.

After legal or forged visas had been found for them, some sailed from Marseille; others were smuggled over the Spanish border. A few, such as the Russian émigré painter Marc Chagall, were slow to realize that they, too, must escape. The benign-tempered Chagall had gullibly believed his French citizenship would protect him from anti-Semitism, and only left France having been reassured that there *were* cows in America. Marcel Duchamp sailed for New York in 1942. Those who left France behind were often vilified for deserting their country 'in her greatest hour of need'. The artists were, of course, a minute fraction of the population and, for a time, many of those who remained saw Marshal Pétain as their best hope. Wanting a return to some kind of stability, they could convince themselves that returning to work was not only necessary so as not to starve, it was also their duty. This fitted perfectly with German strategy for a compliant France.

Otto Abetz, the German ambassador, was a protégé of the German foreign minister, Joachim von Ribbentrop. Although both were great Francophiles, their underlying motivation was sinister. Abetz admired French culture and its food and wine. He had a French wife, too. He also believed that the French should know their place.

The plan he had presented to Hitler entailed France becoming a 'satellite state', obliged to accept its 'permanent weakness'. To bring this about involved playing on the country's internal rivalries and hopes of an entente with Germany. Knowing that an attitude of confrontation would unite the French against Germany, Abetz was in concordance with his instructions from Hitler: 'Everything must be done to encourage internal divisions and thus the weakness of France.' Nonetheless, Abetz's was always a careful approach, with a good deal of effort placed on propaganda, while the Propaganda-Abteilung and the embassy permanently vied for control. The

Propaganda-Abteilung had a staff of 1,200 and controlled the press, radio, literature, propaganda, cinema and culture, including theatre, art and music. The objective was to promote German influence, to undermine and erase the dominance of French culture in Europe, and to promote collaboration. Abetz believed his seductive approach was superior to the Propaganda-Abteilung's more heavy-handed one, which involved assassination and reprisal. In 1942, Abetz won this battle, and his German Institute became a centre of cultural collaboration, with exhibitions, lectures, popular German-language classes, and concerts promoting the most distinguished German musicians.[7]

From the outset, Abetz was courteous, encouraging a return to 'normality' as quickly as was possible following the occupation. The remarkable Jacques Copeau, whose career had been devoted to challenging the stuffiness of bourgeois boulevard theatre, became the director of the Comédie Française, the national theatre, while Gabrielle's friend the Ballets Russes dancer Serge Lifar became the Vichy-appointed director of the Paris Opéra Ballet. Ever-sinuous and insinuating, Lifar wasn't too concerned by having to ingratiate himself with his Nazi masters. He toured in Germany, and notoriously paraded the claim that Hitler had 'handled' him on his visit to the Opéra. Hitler admired the place so much he apparently knew its floor plan by heart.

The Free French in London got wind of Lifar's bragging and, broadcasting via the BBC, had soon condemned him to death. Gabrielle's sometime friend Comte Etienne de Beaumont, as unperturbed by the Nazi presence as Lifar, had desperately wanted his post, but his attempts at ingratiation had been to no avail. Maurice Sachs, who had swindled Gabrielle over her library, was one of those who turned the war into an escapade in the transgression of every moral code. He also managed successfully to hide his Jewishness. After the occupation, he lived for a while with a German officer, began playing the black market, and also spent a period in a homosexual brothel. In early 1942, he went to Germany, where he became a crane operator, and was delighted when the Gestapo discovered how skilful he was at informing. His death by lynching, when the Allies occupied Germany, is supposed to have taken place at the hands of his fellow prisoners.

Under the watchful eye of Abetz's propaganda staff, cinemas and theatres in the occupied zone were re-opened. The making of new films was encouraged, and newspapers and publishers were permitted to recommence printing. The attitude of their masters was, at the same time, repressive regarding anything 'decadent', anti-German or pro-Jewish. Not long after the armistice, when the Pétain government in the south began to put anti-Semitic prohibitions into practice, most of the intellectual right across the country, and some of the left, had already joined in spirit this aspect of repression.

France was by no means unique in its anti-Semitism. Many Europeans, including Great Britain, were mildly anti-Semitic; some less mildly than others. The more extreme in France wanted a fascist France allied with Germany, to build a cleansed Europe. Otto Abetz was assigned the project of 'safeguarding' all objects of art: public, private and, especially, Jewish-owned. Abetz embarked on the job with enthusiasm. Many works of art were taken from their owners and stored in the Parisian Jeu de Paume Museum, while much else was hauled off to Germany. The worst perpetrator of this theft was Goering, who 'pillaged on a heroic scale'. If there hadn't been so much internecine warfare between the different German departments, a great deal more art would undoubtedly have left the country. Despite the plundering, some works were regarded as just too decadent and, in 1943, a pyre was secretly lit at the Jeu de Paume on which were burnt works by artists such as Picasso, Jean Miró and Max Ernst. Picasso, meanwhile, was selling work to those German officers who, secretly, recognized his gifts.

With occupation, there was an understandable wish for escapism and, although France was really a huge prison, with a captive audience like never before, for those in the arts prepared to 'collaborate' enough to have their work put on, this period proved to be strangely fertile. While the occupation has often defied description by those who experienced it, it has also caused utter bafflement in those who did not. One thing, though, is clear: it was virtually impossible not to collaborate with the conquerors if one was to work at one's profession. Almost all activity required a licence, and none were issued without strict German approval. If licences were not sought, this meant refusal for the publication of books, the production of plays, the showing of films and exhibitions and the performing of any concerts. The extremely courageous artists who gave up working under these conditions were very few in number. Any signs of anti-German sentiment were forbidden, and any artistic Jewish presence whatsoever was eliminated.[8]

The apparently relaxed cultural policy of the conquerors emerged from the principle that cultural distractions would keep the population unaware and contented. Meanwhile, the real attitude of the Germans towards French culture was a divided one, involving jealousy and contempt. There was jealousy at the pre-eminence of French culture in Europe, combined with contempt at its perceived artistic decadence. German Francophilia was, then, double sided; admiration co-existing with an attitude of superiority. And those very French attributes that made the country so attractive – the refinement and *douceur de vivre*, the pleasure of civilized living – were also what condemned her to the second rank in the eyes of her invaders. However, a good number of intellectuals and artists were so relieved at the urbanity and admiration shown by some of their masters they failed to observe what actually lay beneath. Serge Lifar and Jean Cocteau, who continued working, like many artists before and after them, were staggeringly politically naive. What we are to make of the record of Gabrielle's war years, however, remains to be seen.

Late in that summer of 1940, when Gabrielle had been reinstated at the Ritz, having accepted the one small room offered her, she sent all her best furniture back to her apartment above the salon on rue Cambon. And, whatever her private thoughts about the occupation, there were two immediate tasks Gabrielle was now obliged to fulfil. One was a task she wished to perform; the other was an onerous one she was forced into.

When she had closed her couture house, her workers had been left without work or compensation. After the armistice, when the German propaganda campaign was intent on letting it appear that France was getting back on its feet, educational establishments, businesses, the law courts, etc., were re-opened. And, at this point, Gabrielle's rejected workforce succeeded in taking her to an industrial tribunal. Under the excuse of 'act of war' or 'emergency action', Gabrielle had dismissed them without any notice or compensation. The court rejected this plea, and she was obliged to pay her employees the redundancy they were due.

Gabrielle's second duty was this. That September of 1940, when the Germans began releasing most of the 300,000 pre-armistice prisoners, her imprisoned nephew, André, was not among them. Preoccupied about his delicate health, his aunt was determined to bring about his release. A young aristocrat of her acquaintance, Louis de Vaufreland, told her he knew a German who might be able to help her. This gentleman was named Hans Günther, Baron von Dincklage. He spoke fluent French and English (his mother was English) and was the archetypal Aryan. Tall, blond, blue-eyed, von Dincklage was the embodiment of entertaining charm. He suggested that the person Gabrielle needed was an old friend of his, a cavalry captain, Theodor Momm.[9]

Momm's family was in textiles, and he had been deputed to mobilize the French textile industries, with a view to siphoning off the profits for the German war effort. Gabrielle's persuasion was effective, and Momm re-opened a small textile mill in the north of France. He then convinced his superiors that the owner was the famous Chanel, and that her nephew was the person needed to run the reinstated mill. Gabrielle was hugely relieved when André was at last released.

By this time, Gabrielle and von Dincklage had had cause to meet on a number of occasions. Gabrielle found the German's charm and well-bred attentiveness throughout these proceedings most seductive. If she may have experienced any initial doubts about associating herself with the enemy, they were put aside, and she and von Dincklage became lovers. This affair was to endure for several years.

Gabrielle was careful to appear discreet, confining herself a good deal to her apartment on rue Cambon, her room at the Ritz and visits to an inner circle of friends, including the Serts, Serge Lifar, Jean Cocteau, Antoinette d'Harcourt and Marie-Louise Bousquet. Aside from that, there was her handsome lover. In an occupied city, where it was soon impossible not to take sides, Gabrielle appears to have convinced herself that she could have an affair with a German and live immured. For someone of her intelligence, she cannot possibly have believed that such catastrophic events in her own country and beyond didn't concern her.

But Gabrielle's attitude didn't have much to do with intelligence; it was something more elemental than that. She had learnt young to put self-preservation before most other things, and one of her clearest intentions throughout the war was just that: survival. As someone recently observed who was acquainted with her then, when a boy: 'I don't think it was a question of politics. [She] wanted to serve her own interests and maintain her lifestyle.'[10] While this may have been ignoble, there were many who felt the same. Gabrielle and most of her friends were reluctant to ask too many questions about the oppression by their conquerors.

It has often been said that, while Gabrielle was very wealthy, if ever the health of her business was in doubt, like many another who had started out poor, she reacted with an irrational fear of returning to that state. And, perhaps to salve the guilt she must have had for pleading poverty and cutting off her brothers, she took up various public charitable activities, such as the patronage of Jean Marais's regiment in the first months of war. Gabrielle had time on her hands and threw herself into the project, looking after every last detail. Other examples of Gabrielle's charity were kept strictly private. For example, large sums were donated to a mental home in which the ex-courtesan Liane de Pougy was involved.[11] In her later years, she contacted the solicitor at Aubazine and made a secret donation to the convent. (It is also said that, over the years, she made occasional very discreet trips to the convent to visit the nuns.)[12]

Returning to Gabrielle's liaison with her German, one explanation for her actions was that her repeated losses in love had hardened her. Indeed, Cocteau would say that Gabrielle was 'a pederast'; that her sexual appetites were virile and that she set out to conquer like a man. This attitude, while serving Gabrielle's sexual needs, did little to ground her emotions. But, while she was not without blame in failed loves, Gabrielle had lost love so many times already that she had little faith in the possibility of it enduring.

There was no question that, had Arthur Capel asked her, all those years ago, Gabrielle would have married him. Quite possibly, in the end, this marriage would have foundered. While always believing in preserving the differences between men and women, Gabrielle also wanted desperately to be taken as an equal. However, her times, her upbringing and her social position, in combination with her powerful personality, had seen to it that this rarely happened. In her youth, women were seldom allowed that kind of scope. And, for all Capel's forward thinking, in marriage he had chosen the more traditional woman. Ironically, Diana Wyndham's own position regarding scope was that she hadn't easily accepted her husband keeping a mistress.

Gabrielle was more than equal to most men but, without the example of an even half-decent parental relationship, where the balance of power – despite its ups and downs – ultimately swings back and forth so that each partner believes themselves loved, needed and found worthy, she had no positive example. Despite her belief that a long-term, stable relationship was what she wanted, in many ways, Gabrielle had not developed the emotional maturity to make it happen. When young, she had luxuriated in being feminine and seduced, but this way of being wasn't sufficient, hadn't given enough scope for her intelligence and abilities.

Sadly, she appears to have found it impossible, really, to conduct a relationship without either dominating or being dominated and, each time, this led, eventually, to her frustration. She was remarkably able at managing the practicalities of her own and others' lives; friends were many, many times deeply grateful for her vital support. But, like her great contemporary and semi-friend Colette, who so publicly wrestled with squaring the problem of love and independence, Gabrielle found real mutual love near impossible. They were two highly intelligent women, whose lives and loves epitomized versions of the same problem: 'Is there love without complete submission and loss of identity? Is freedom worth the loneliness that pays for it?'[13]

In her own way, Colette had arrived at a better accommodation than Gabrielle ever would. Gabrielle remained vulnerable to emotional insecurity and loneliness. With time, suffering and disillusionment, she had become as much the seducer as the seduced. And she had long since learnt to enjoy a sexual relationship that didn't necessarily involve love. But, while harbouring few illusions, at the same time, she was also vulnerable in that she was alone and wanted to feel loved.

While Gabrielle was a sophisticated and worldly woman, von Dincklage was a suave and practised lothario, and a great many women had already fallen victim to his charms. In addition, Gabrielle was no longer young – she was fifty-eight to von Dincklage's forty-five – and this man left her feeling she was still attractive. Meanwhile, what von Dincklage's position was, in regard to the occupying forces, and what Gabrielle believed it was, obviously has considerable bearing upon the way we judge her collaboration.

If, during the occupation, Gabrielle was seen in public less than before the war, and was careful not to show herself in public places with her German lover, she did not, however, spend the occupation holed up in her room at the Ritz. Yet her powers of denial were as tremendous as Colette's, who wrote of this period, 'A credulity, a forgetful exhaustion endowed me with delusion.'[14]

Colette needed money to help support herself and her Jewish husband, Goudeket, and was neither amongst those who refused to write, nor did she work for the Resistance. Indeed, she wrote for 'some of the most repellent of the pro-Vichy and pro-German publications and maintained cordial relations with their editors'.[15] And when Colette was asked to sign a petition against the arrest of the Jewish director of the Bibliothèque Nationale, she refused on the grounds that it might call attention to her husband. At the same time, the couple socialized at the collaborationist salons of José Maria Sert and Florence Gould.

In August 1941, a mutual friend of Gabrielle and Colette's, the celebrity singer and actress Arletty, had a small party to celebrate her new apartment. Here she was to live with her lover, a German officer. Amongst Arletty's guests were her friends Lili de Rothschild (to die in the Ravensbrück concentration camp), Colette, Maurice Goudeket, Marie Laurencin, Misia and Gabrielle. When Arletty was later challenged, she dismissed the idea that her sexual choices made her unpatriotic, with the famous comment: 'My heart it is French but my ass is international.' At the liberation, Arletty would be tried and imprisoned as a collaborator.

Antoinette's d'Harcourt's son recently offered the opinion in an interview that Gabrielle's relationship was 'mostly in order to get material advantages. It was different from Arletty's behaviour during the war. Arletty, it was a coup de coeur [literally, "a blow of the heart"], whereas Chanel, they were coups de portefeuille ["blows of the wallet"].' While describing Gabrielle's attitude to von Dincklage as 'all about money' is too simple, Jean d'Harcourt's last comment is, nonetheless, interesting. 'You know, she kept a car, and a driver, and petrol throughout the war: that was most unusual, unless you were a Minister from the Vichy government but, otherwise, no one had that!'[16]

Gabrielle fairly regularly attended events in support of friends working under, if not directly for, the enemy, such as Serge Lifar, who ran the Opéra, and also socialized with others who were in the habit of consorting with the Germans. André de Segonzac made a tour of Germany and Austria in the company of a party of French artists. Sacha Guitry entertained for the Germans on the stage, at their receptions and their dinners. On other occasions, Gabrielle dined with the Morands, where guests might include Cocteau, the right-wing poet Jouhandeau and his wife, Caryathis, the writer

Louise de Vilmorin, Misia and José Maria Sert, and a smattering of the German command. One of the favourites at French gatherings was Gerhard Heller, important in the literature section of the Propaganda-Abteilung. Almost ubiquitous at Parisian salons, Heller cast his spell of utter charm. Seducing many French writers into believing he wasn't intent on destroying French cultural hegemony, Heller would again hoodwink large sections of the French public with his memoirs, in 1981.

In 1941, Misia was almost seventy and began dictating her memoirs to Boulos Ristelhueber, Sert's young secretary. In addition to Boulos's extreme thinness, his pallor was deathly and, to conceal it, he wore dense make-up. Sadly, this only added to the bizarreness of his appearance. He and Misia had a number of friends in common, shared an equal passion for music, and Misia found this painfully delicate creature a gentle and sympathetic companion. Their friendship was an unexpected boon for the ageing muse, whose loss of sight was rapidly narrowing her world. Boulos Ristelhueber greatly admired Misia and, during the war, saw her almost daily.

While Misia had never stopped loving Sert, after the young Roussadana's death, he had been desolate. Misia once again took on the role of hostess at her ex-husband's table and, while he supported her financially, they did not return to living in the same apartment. Sert, meanwhile, violently anti-German and hating the occupation, found little difficulty in accommodating himself, becoming Franco's ambassador to the Vatican, no less. Misia hated the occupation too. Yet, though fiercely pro-Jewish, she also closed her eyes to some of Sert and her friends' questionable activities.

Boulos Ristelhueber's diary gives us a glimpse of Gabrielle and her friends' occupied Paris:

Dec 17. Paris sadder than ever. An atmosphere of catastrophe. False rumours running wild. One knows nothing, nothing!

Dec 19. . . . Serge Lifar speaks about the concert tonight . . . [The great conductor Herbert von Karajan, penalized at the end of the war for his notorious membership of the Nazi party, was conducting.]

Dec 20. Dined with Misia on her bed. Picasso sinks onto it and speaks of his unhappy divorce from Olga . . .

Dec 21. Rather sad lunch with Jean Cocteau . . . I deposited him at Colette's . . . and went to see Jean Marais. At four o'clock called on Coco Chanel, so nice to me that she did me good . . .

Dec 27. . . . the anti-Jewish laws . . . turn Paris into a prison . . .

Dec 28. . . . At last night's dinner at the Barnes's, Misia . . . confronted an important German official . . .

Dec 29. Spent the evening at Misia's with Coco Chanel and François d'Harcourt. Coco goes into a tirade against the Jews. The conversation is dangerous, given Antoinette's origins [Antoinette d'Harcourt was a Rothschild] and the presence of the Duke. [Duc François d'Harcourt was Antoinette's husband] . . . Sert's chauffeur drove me home in such blackness that half the time we were on the pavement.

New Year's Day 1942. Thick snow. Paris covered in white: grey-green uniforms everywhere. With its deserted streets – just a few horses and men pushing hand carts – Paris looks like a city in East Prussia.

Jan 22. Jean Cocteau . . . shows me some great photographs from the old days . . . Gide at fifteen . . . Georges Auric and Raymond Radiguet, stark naked in a small clump of reeds . . . Misia and Coco in ju-jitsu outfits.[17]

On 11 January, Boulos commented on Misia's distress at Sert's departure for Spain and a sojourn with his mistress, and then described going with Cocteau and Marais to an all-night pharmacy 'to fill in a prescription'. Marais had almost succeeded in weaning Cocteau off his opium, so this must have been a prescription 'for the morphine to which Misia and Boulos were both hopelessly addicted'.

Over the years, Misia and Gabrielle had made numerous trips to Switzerland together, apparently to visit this or that clinic. Almost certainly, one of the major reasons for these trips was in fact to collect not only Misia's new supply of morphine, but also Gabrielle's.

In the post-war period, Gabrielle had someone else pick up her 'prescription'. Her assistant Lilou Marquand said she knew that 'someone would go to Switzerland to get her morphine with the protection of Chanel Inc.'[18]

Parisians were now pretty desperate for distraction from their privations, and entertainment of all kinds – theatres, cinemas, the opera and ballet, as well as music halls, cabarets and brothels – were doing a roaring trade. Cafés and restaurants were filled with celebrities, the old rich, the black-market new rich, as well as many Germans, keen to sample the famed pleasures of 'Gay Paree'. Those revellers unwilling to call a halt to their evening and brave the rigours of the metro at the 11 o'clock curfew hour – virtually everyone had to use it; private cars were almost unknown – stayed on at the clubs and cafés, frequently open all night. Colette wrote to a friend that the composer Georges Auric, out with Marie-Laure de Noailles and a German officer, had his leg badly injured: 'Nightclub, two in the morning, champagne, accident'.[19]

Intelligent and sensitive though Boulos Ristelhueber was, he could only partly comprehend the history and complexity of the friendships recorded in his diary. Perhaps most complex of all was that between Misia and Gabrielle. Since their meeting in 1917, they had fought, hurt, envied, loved and sometimes hated one another. Gabrielle was drawn to the mad Slav in Misia, who was, like her, as Morand said, extraordinarily rich in 'that singular commodity called taste'. And, while they each had a gargantuan appetite for gossip and intrigue, these were just as readily used against one another. Each of them was also probably the only woman the other knew to whom she could unfailingly turn. From its initiation, their friendship had been an intensely close one, often provoking gossip. Their many mutual friends were completely divided as to whether Gabrielle and Misia were lovers. At various times, it is almost certain that they were.

Gabrielle and Misia were connoisseurs of women's beauty, and bedding each other – or another woman, for that matter – was not something that would have concerned them in the least. They were libertarians who had lived through an era that was increasingly open to sexual experiment. Gabrielle also spent her working days moulding her artistry on women's bodies. As she would say, it was a woman's body itself that was one of the things that inspired her designs. She was also enough of an artist that Coleridge's assertion in many ways applied to her: 'A great mind must be androgynous.' In like manner, Virginia Woolf's conviction was pertinent: 'It is fatal for anyone who writes [or makes any art] . . . to be a man or a woman pure and simple; one must be woman-manly or man-womanly.'[20] With time, despite loving and wanting to be loved by men, it seems that Gabrielle turned more often to her own sex for both exhilaration and consolation.

In the period immediately before and during the early part of the war, one of her lovers was the woman mentioned above, the Duchesse Antoinette d'Harcourt. This beautiful and rather tormented woman apparently needed her beloved opium in order to better express her passion and intelligence. Her son, Jean, remembers Gabrielle visiting them often before the war, at the d'Harcourt château in Normandy.[21] Gabrielle was apparently having an affair with Antoinette. The younger woman appears to have enjoyed the extra frisson of running another female love affair at the same time. Her second lover was Arletty. One day, it seems that Antoinette misjudged her timing, or perhaps her 'mistake' was intentional. As Gabrielle was leaving her tryst with the young beauty, she met Arletty arriving.[22]

In 1943, Salvador Dalí wrote a roman-à-clef, *Hidden Faces*, cataloguing the viciousness and vacuity of much of *le tout* Paris. Cécile Goudreau, the sharp-tongued, knowing and witty sophisticate, is, apparently, Gabrielle,[23] and Dalí depicts her as both a devotee of opium and an enticingly predatory lesbian: 'As she spoke Cécile Goudreau stretched herself out and drew up the lacquered table with the smoking accessories set out on a level with her chest. Betka came and lay down beside her, pressing her own body lightly against hers. Then Cécile, with a quick casual movement, passed her arm around her neck.'[24] But, before Betka's seduction, Cécile, 'with the consummate skill of an old mandarin', introduces her young companion to the rituals of smoking opium.

With time, Gabrielle would become more circumspect about displaying any of these attitudes for public consumption. Indeed, as her legend would become transformed into a myth, she would staunchly deny any sexual or narcotic transgressions. During the war, meanwhile, she continued her affair with her German. Afterwards, she would defiantly proclaim, 'People believe that I exude rancour and malice. They believe ... well, they believe anything, apart from the fact that one works, one thinks of oneself and one takes no notice of them.'[25]

Gabrielle and Arletty were, of course, only two of the most high-profile of many French women who had affairs with German men. These liaisons with the enemy were to become the aspect of collaboration that most exercised the popular imagination and, in the purges that followed the liberation, thousands of women would be accused of 'horizontal collaboration'. Notoriously, many would have their heads shaved and swastikas daubed upon their skulls. Some were paraded naked through the streets; others were murdered before they reached any formal kind of trial. Prostitutes were treated with particular harshness.

In this period, any woman even found in the company of a German risked being accused of horizontal collaboration. To a large extent, while they were sometimes 'turned in' by other women, the feeling against them derived as much from the sense of personal and national emasculation felt by French men, living under an occupying army. While post-war prosecution of these women was seen as a kind of cleansing process, they were also used as scapegoats for the sense of impotence their menfolk had experienced during the war.

Whatever the resulting censure, these liaisons nonetheless took place. Frequently, these women were vulnerable in one way or

another: they might be young, single or divorced, and their first
contact with a German was often in the workplace. By the middle
of 1943, approximately eighty thousand women from the occupied
zone were claiming support from the Germans for the children
resulting from these liaisons. In Gabrielle's case, with a ruthlessness
attendant upon her fear of growing old, combined with her underlying loneliness, she, too, had her own particular vulnerability.

Who then, was Gabrielle's German lover, the man, like her, who
professed to hate war?

Von Dincklage

Amongst certain upper sections of Parisian society, Hans Günther von Dincklage had been known for a number of years before the war, as a handsome and engaging German diplomat of eminently respectable pedigree. An acquaintance remembered that 'he possessed the kind of beauty that both men and women like . . . His open face indicated an innocent sinner. He was very tall, very slender, had very light hair . . . He danced very well and was a dazzling entertainer.'[1]

Von Dincklage was born in 1896. His mother, Marie-Valery Kutter-Micklefield, was English and his father, Baron Georg-Jito von Dincklage, came from an impoverished but distinguished line. The boy grew up at the family castle in Schleswig-Holstein and, at seventeen, joined his father's cavalry regiment, the King's 13th Uhlans. Hans Günther proved himself a gifted horseman – 'his body possessed the suppleness of a rider's' – and he excelled at the game of polo.[2] After fighting on the Russian front during the First World War, at its conclusion, he was a senior lieutenant. Lacking any 'civilian' education and without a profession to look forward to, he drifted into a series of occupations. It appears he had few qualms about how principled these were. 'At first he was a member of one of those volunteer corps which organized civil war in the Republic and for years threatened it with uprisings . . . then, during the inflation he turned his hand to profiteering.'[3]

By 1924, he had joined a textile manufacturer, with whom his family had important interests, and he represented the firm in various European countries, including Switzerland. In that same year, von Dincklage had seduced a well-born young woman, Maximiliana von

Schoenebeck, into running away with him. Catsy, as Maximiliana was often known, was the daughter of Baron von Schoenebeck, an art-collecting aristocrat whose *Schloss* was at Baden. Catsy's mother was Jewish. Her half-sister, the writer Sybille Bedford, described her as 'an attractive, happy-natured, life-enhancing, vital young woman', whose family would come to believe that von Dincklage was 'a disaster of lifelong consequences'.[4] In 1928, the young couple moved to Sanary, in the south of France. Until a few years before a modest fishing village, Sanary had transformed itself into a select seaside resort. Discovered by a few French artists, including Cocteau, the little town had become particularly popular with von Dincklage's compatriots.

The stock market crash of 1929 saw him lose his partnership in the textile firm and, in 1930, he was describing himself as 'an independent merchant', who had acquired a post in Sanary overseeing transport.[5] In early 1933, von Dincklage became the national representative for a French cash register firm, and travelled regularly to Germany, ostensibly to study the cash register's manufacture. These trips were in fact a cover for what had become the other source of his employment: the new German government.[6]

Having helped Catsy go through her considerable inheritance, after Hitler's rise to absolute power, at the beginning of 1933, von Dincklage had 'placed his hopes in National Socialism'. As a result, in May of that year, he was resident in Paris with his wife, for 'the purpose of making contacts'.[7] One is drawn to contrast this particular polo player with that other polo-playing lover of Gabrielle's during the previous war. Arthur Capel had suffered from the *ennui* of his times and had been capable of emotional carelessness. Yet, drawn into the war, and finding himself torn between Gabrielle Chanel and Diana Wyndham, despite his ultimate failure, he was a man who appeared to have grown in emotional and moral stature. Capel and von Dincklage could not have been more different.

With Hitler's increased hold over Germany, a number of distinguished German Jews made their escape from the Gestapo to Sanary, where they took up exile. Soon, the resort became something of an artistic German colony, acquiring the sobriquet, 'capital of German literature'. Amongst its illustrious refugees were Mahler's widow, Alma, Bertholt Brecht, Arnold Zweig, Ludwig Marcuse and the magisterial Thomas Mann and his extended family. A small contingent of English émigrés included Aldous and Maria Huxley, Julian Huxley and his wife, and D. H. Lawrence and his German wife, Frieda.

Catsy's mother (a hopeless morphine addict) had taken up residence in Sanary with her new Italian husband some time before, and they had befriended a number of important local German figures, including Ute von Stöhrer, whose husband was then German ambassador in Cairo. Unbeknown to anyone in Sanary, including Thomas Mann and his family, who were staying in the von Stöhrers' villa, von Stöhrer was also in the employ of the German intelligence service.[8]

In the summer of 1933, von Dincklage was appointed to the post of cultural attaché at the German embassy in Paris. A notoriously vague position, this frequently involved undercover activities. Indeed, by this time, the French Deuxième Bureau, the country's external military intelligence agency, was constructing a file on von Dincklage. By August 1933, he in turn had sent a propaganda report back to his Nazi superiors in Germany.[9]

At around this time, Catsy's younger sister, Sybille, was made party to a conversation that left her deeply shocked. Sitting with her friend Aldous Huxley in Barcelona, awaiting take-off in a plane bound for Sanary, they were directly behind a well-groomed German couple. After a few moments, Sybille realized they were talking about her sister and von Dincklage. The woman said:

> 'Maybe they owe him now . . . there always was that rumour of his having been mixed up with some extreme right-wing students' gang during our Revolution, so called . . . Gave a hand when they put down the Communist putsch, some say he was in at the Rosa Luxemburg murder [in 1919].'
>
> 'Too young,' he said. 'He may have been there – standing guard by the wall . . .?'

'When the woman tried to get away through the window,' she said. 'You make me shiver . . . He's *very* decorative . . . international polish . . . adds up to a reassuring presence for the French. But aren't we forgetting that his wife's Jewish?' . . .

'You know, I think I hear that the von Dincklages are divorcing. No one outside Germany is supposed to know.'

'Ah . . . that would square it. Racial purity at home, liberal attitudes abroad. A quick, quiet divorce arranged by our authorities . . .'

[Young Sybille looked at Huxley.] I knew he had understood . . . He put his hand inside his coat and pulled out . . . the leather-bound travelling flask . . . he unscrewed the cap and held it over to me.[10]

Meanwhile, when von Dincklage officially left his post at the embassy in June 1934[11] he told friends that he had been ejected from his position as cultural attaché because he was married to a Jew. Assuring Catsy that there was nothing personal in his departure, von Dincklage now left her. Catsy loved her husband and was forgiving. She believed von Dincklage's stories and hoped he would return to her. Meanwhile, she moved back to Sanary, where her mother and stepfather still lived.

Von Dincklage now travelled widely, performing various missions for Hitler's government, in Athens and various Balkan states. He happened to be in Marseille just one day before the assassination of King Alexander of Yugoslavia and Foreign Minister Barthou of France. He happened to be in Tunis at a time when systematic and violent anti-French agitation was in progress.[12] He also went to stay periodically at Sanary with Catsy. He liked her well enough; he also needed her to keep their separation secret, not wanting her distinguished, and useful, Parisian friends to think ill of him.[13] Von Dincklage had been suspected of being an agent in diplomat's disguise by some at Sanary for a while.[14] Suspicions eventually to be confirmed. While von Dincklage kept an eye on the activities and whereabouts of the important Jewish émigré community, he was simultaneously collecting information on the nearby port of Toulon, the most important naval base in France.

But von Dincklage had to be seen to have a job. A Russian émigré friend, Alex Liberman – a future friend of Gabrielle's and eventually editorial director of Condé Nast Publications in New York – found von Dincklage employment as a journalist.[15] Then, in 1935, von Dincklage suffered a serious setback in his propaganda work for Hitler's government. In January of that year, a book entitled *Das Braune Netz* (*The Brown Network*) was published in Paris.[16] Its subtitle was *How Hitler's Agents Abroad are Working to Prepare the War*, and its aim was to alert the West to the potential 'Nazi espionage and fifth column activities outside Germany'. The book contained a list of all known Nazi agents, country by country, and the French list was headed by Otto Abetz (future ambassador). But one of the most prominent on the list of agents for France was von Dincklage.

A series of reports for his superiors had been stolen from von Dincklage and used as one of the central pieces of evidence for the book's claims. Printing a selection of von Dincklage's weekly reports back to Berlin, the book exposed his activities and showed 'the many channels used by Goebbels and the Gestapo in common for the execution of their work abroad'. A letter from von Dincklage to the Paris correspondent of a major German newspaper alerts one to his nickname: 'Kofink visited me today, I will probably be able to use him. He will phone you soon and have news for Mr Spatz. I am Mr Spatz. When this is the case, would you please inform me immediately by telephone.'[17]

(Spatz, meaning a sparrow, garrulously hopping from one place to another, was the name von Dincklage jokingly gave himself with French friends.)

The Brown Network goes on to say that 'every legation has its Dincklage. Gangster, profiteer, Gestapo agent – this admixture characterizes Hitler's diplomats . . . His reports show the many lines along which foreign propagandist activity is conducted, and how these lines converge at one common point: espionage.'[18] In page after page, von Dincklage details observations, connections and suggestions for his Nazi masters. He talks of his 'large French circle' and says that 'day by day this circle grows' and, through it, he hopes to be able to carry out his 'social mission most satisfactorily'.[19]

Although this extraordinary book was first published in German, French- and English-language editions were published in 1936 and gradually those in Paris got word of it. This exposé of von Dincklage's activities must have unsettled him a great deal. While he was a master at deception and duplicity, and would have been most convincing in his persuasion that *The Brown Network* was a scurrilous fabrication, the episode cannot but have been a serious bar to his promotion to the highest ranks of Nazi espionage.

Understandably, after the book's publication, von Dincklage absented himself from Paris for some months. During this period, he persuaded Catsy that he must divorce her. Their divorce papers don't give the real reason – in other words, Maximiliana von Schoenebeck's Jewishness – instead, the cause is stated as their failure to have children.[20] When von Dincklage returned to France, although Catsy felt bitter, she still cared for him, and agreed to keep their divorce a secret.[21] In Paris, while her ex-husband had continued at the fine addresses where he always managed to live, he also maintained his extensive reputation as a Don Juan. Marriage had in no way held up the progress of von Dincklage's conquests; it had simply given them an extra frisson. And he now asked Alex Liberman if he would introduce him to the Comtesse Hélène Dessoffy.

Hélène Dessoffy and her husband, Jacques, 'had enough money never to need to work, and channelled most of their energies into buying and redecorating their houses. Hélène was the daughter of a high-ranking naval officer, a horsy, long-legged, chain-smoking woman with . . . a wry, swift wit.'[22] Wasting no time, von Dincklage was soon launched into 'a torrid affair' with her. Unknown to Hélène Dessoffy, when her lover travelled south to spend time with her at Sanary (she and her husband lived 'rather separate lives and usually inhabited separate villas'),[23] he would also visit his ex-wife nearby. At the same time, von Dincklage continued his long-term surveillance of the Jews of Sanary and the French naval port of

Toulon across the hill. Now that he was divorced, his affair with Hélène Dessoffy gave him another alibi for being in the south.[24]

While the above gives some insight into von Dincklage's character and his multifarious activities, he continued to charm and amuse his way into the lives of an expanding Parisian circle, and we find the odd tantalizing glimpses of him in the late thirties. Here, also, we discover some of the conflicting information that would later circulate about both von Dincklage and Gabrielle. Remembering that von Dincklage wanted his divorce kept secret, the following is at first puzzling: 'Baron Hans Günther von Dincklage was celebrating his recent divorce by practically living in the bar at the Ritz, where he clearly demonstrated his expertise with women, wine, food and cigars . . . He flitted about, making friends, telling the latest jokes.'[25]

On one occasion, the manager of the hotel was outraged and told von Dincklage to leave his office, when he attempted to organize a black-market deal with the hotel to buy German wines. He had said it was 'at the request of our mutual friend Joachim von Ribbentrop. You know of course, how important he now is in my government, the Third Reich.' The manager was furious, and expelled him from his office. He told his wife that von Dincklage was 'free to move around the hotel where I cannot stop him. But I can stop him from access to the offices and the cellars!' He then said to her: 'Don't think I'm suffering from paranoia when I tell you the invasion of France has already begun. That man is a spy!'[26] As Germany's power had grown, von Dincklage presumably felt less concerned about his divorce becoming public, which explains his celebration of it at the Ritz.

After the 1938 signing of the Munich Pact, when Italy, France and Britain permitted Germany's annexation of the Sudetenland – effectively allowing her to take over Czechoslovakia – those Jews with enough foresight acted promptly. This included Alex Liberman, who advised all his friends in Paris to cut off relations with von Dincklage and any German nationals whom they knew in France. Liberman had alerted Hélène Dessoffy to the fact that von Dincklage might well be a German spy. On Liberman's advice, with great reluctance, she ended her affair with von Dincklage. Liberman's suspicion was now acknowledged by Hélène Dessoffy's friends, and she was both furious at von Dincklage's duplicity and depressed at losing her lover.[27]

According to a Swiss report quoting French intelligence,[28] in 1938, von Dincklage was ordered to leave France because he had been 'burned' by the Deuxième Bureau. (Although *The Brown Network* had appeared almost three years earlier, at the time, many of the implicated agents must have persuaded the French that it was simply anti-German propaganda.) Von Dincklage, however, soon slipped back into France. At the outbreak of war, he was once again banished, and again went to Switzerland. Until France was occupied, he shuttled back and forth between France and Switzerland, regularly thrown out under suspicion. Continuing surveillance, the Swiss next discovered von Dincklage at a clinic 'to cure his nerves', but noted, 'This fact is symptomatic because it is now well-known that German spies have recently adopted this system to escape police control more easily.'[29]

Shortly after the German occupation of Paris, in 1940, we find von Dincklage again ensconced in his favourite city, this time having acquired the house of one of his most recent lovers, a wealthy Jewish woman, who had fled with her husband to the unoccupied south. Police reports confirm that, some time between April and November 1940, von Dincklage had become a 'civil servant' in charge of pricing for the textile department of the German military administration in Paris, the MBF. No doubt this cover came about through the auspices of Theodor Momm.[30]

Shortly after the armistice, in June 1940, when half of Paris, and Gabrielle, took flight in 'the exodus', Alex Liberman's Russian lover and future wife, Tatiana du Plessix, also fled to the occupied zone with her small daughter. They eventually met up with Liberman and waited nervously for visas for America. In the meantime, the intrepid Tatiana decided she must make the hazardous trip back to Paris to gather crucial papers and possessions. Lying to Liberman, who would have forbidden her from making the trip had he known, Tatiana said she was going to Vichy to settle the papers of her recently deceased husband, a Resistance hero. She then made the journey into Paris in the back of a truck, hidden under some mattresses. Travel in and out of the capital was strictly controlled, however, charging large sums, underground groups transported people back and forth.

Halfway through Tatiana's assignment, walking down the avenue Kléber, she was startled to hear a man calling out her name. Turning, she saw von Dincklage, dressed as an officer, and climbing out of a Mercedes. As we saw, almost no one but German officers drove cars. When Tatiana asked von Dincklage:

> 'What are you doing here?' he replied:
>   'I'm doing my work.'
>   'And what is the nature of your work *now*?' Tatiana demanded.
>   'Same as it's been for decades,' von Dincklage cheerfully responded, 'I'm in army intelligence.'
>   Tatiana told him he was 'a real bastard! . . . You posed as a down and out journalist, you won all our sympathy, you seduced my best friend [Hélène Dessoffy], and now you tell me you were spying on us all the time!'[31]

It transpired that von Dincklage knew everything about Tatiana's recent movements and warned her not to stay long in Paris. He asked her to deliver a message to Comte Dessoffy, his lover Hélène's husband. Hélène's letters to von Dincklage had been intercepted by French intelligence, and she was now in prison. If her husband could get word to her, telling her to say that she knowingly collaborated with von Dincklage, he could get her out of prison. Tatiana did get the message to her friend, but Hélène Dessoffy refused to perjure herself. After the war, she was acquitted of the charge of collaboration.[32] During this period, Gabrielle herself was to have her own (modest) experience of a collaboration charge.

★ ★ ★

One day, in the summer of 1942, the Ritz was suddenly 'alive with German soldiers', deployed outside the entrance, while, inside, they had been ordered to search every room . . . Early that morning, two Resistance fighters had appeared and kidnapped Gabrielle from her suite. According to the management, their entry was a mystery (in fact, the manager's wife was a Resistance sympathizer), and Gabrielle, who had been blindfolded, had no idea where she was taken. Three hours later, having been questioned about her relationship with Lifar and von Dincklage, she had been brought back to her room. The Resistants had told her that collaborators could face disfigurement or death, and instructed her to change her ways: 'You are a French woman, and an important one. You are good for France, and France has been good to you.'[33]

Von Dincklage was furious at Gabrielle's treatment and, with General von Stülpnagel, demanded an explanation from the Ritz director. He said he could give none.

Meanwhile, a woman who worked in the Chanel boutique, and who met von Dincklage on a number of occasions, recalled that she had *never* seen him in a uniform. Perhaps in Tatiana du Plessix's anger she misremembered von Dincklage's outfit. If, however, he did wear uniform, he took care never to do so when he visited Gabrielle at her apartment on rue Cambon. The couple also spent time together outside Paris. Holidaying in Switzerland more than once, they travelled through the occupied zone to stay at La Pausa. In the autumn of 1942, the architect Robert Streitz, a member of an important Resistance network, asked von Dincklage to intercede on behalf of a Jewish physicist, arrested by the Gestapo. Apparently, von Dincklage tried to help, but someone else would be more successful in bringing about the physicist's release.[34]

Contrary to the impression that Gabrielle had nothing to do with any Germans except von Dincklage, the son of her previous lover Antoinette d'Harcourt remembers going several times to rue Cambon with his mother for entertainments given by Gabrielle. At these gatherings, there were a number of German officers present: 'I don't know exactly what their ranks were but they were very senior officers. Most people spoke in French, not German, but they had a German accent.'[35] It appears that, on these occasions, Antoinette d'Harcourt was intent on gathering information for a nationalist organization, the Synarchist Empire Movement (Mouvement synarchique d'empire), a secret right-wing anti-communist movement, launched in 1922.

In the following spring, 1943, we find that von Dincklage made the extraordinary offer – as a secret police document put it – of the 'services of Coco Chanel (lesbian), from the famous perfume house' in order to exploit her Anglo-Saxon relations in aid of German intelligence services'.[36]

We will almost certainly never know to what extent Gabrielle was aware of von Dincklage's activities. In having an affair with a German, she had made all sorts of accommodations. And if, like her friends, she turned a blind eye to much that went on, it is most likely that Gabrielle conducted her liaison with her German in much the same way Arletty conducted hers. Hers was a collaboration of chosen 'ignorance'.

Most importantly, one should bear in mind Gabrielle's primary motivation during the war: like Colette – and millions of others in France – she was determined to survive. Whatever our thoughts about this, it does not follow that Gabrielle was prepared to spy for the Germans. Did von Dincklage ask her outright? One suspects that he knew she would have refused and, with his accustomed deviousness, was offering her services to his superior without her knowledge. (While in no way proof of her innocence, Gabrielle was always strongly pro-British and had wept when Germany occupied France.)

When she and von Dincklage returned from La Pausa at the end of that summer, 1943, the Maquis (the rural French Resistance) sent word that von Dincklage was now on their death list. Busily consorting with the enemy, the dancer Serge Lifar was also back on the Resistance list. At this point he and von Dincklage secretly moved into the Ritz, where they now lived intermittently with Gabrielle. Although, in the liberal view of Ritz personnel, it was hardly worth more than passing notice that Coco Chanel was living with two men, what gave added spice was that both her men were known to be actively pro-German. The wife of the manager said that Gabrielle:

> ... never appeared anywhere in the hotel with either of them. Nobody gave a damn, but she really worked hard to keep them secret. I knew about them because I had a direct pipeline through the floor maid. She kept me up to the minute. She was envious, not because the Madame was a great couturier – that didn't mean a thing to her – but living with two impressive guys was her idea of paradise. What luxury![37]

In early 1944, Antoinette d'Harcourt was arrested by the Gestapo. She had begun the war as an ambulance driver on the battlefields, but then used the ambulance to ferry people to the border between France and Switzerland, for example. Her son, Jean, says: 'After a year she was "burned", so she had to stop – those activities are probably the reason why she was arrested.'[38] The young duchess was treated harshly and placed in solitary confinement for six months in the notorious Fresnes prison, then moved to another one, Romainville, also outside Paris. From there, she narrowly avoided deportation to Buchenwald concentration camp.

Arletty's biographer describes Synarchy's work as 'fairly pro-Mussolini ... [it] had as members some of the most powerful figures in the French establishment intent on maintaining national French unity.'[39] Preferring, as Jean d'Harcourt says, the idea of 'revolution by the elite rather than revolution from the street ... Synarchy's aim was to serve as a link between Pétain and Laval on the one side, and on the other, de Gaulle and Massigly [one of de Gaulle's senior diplomats] and therefore avoid a bloodbath' when France was liberated.[40]

When Antoinette's son, Jean, then only a boy, was permitted to visit his mother, they were both so overcome that, for the permitted fifteen minutes' visit, they could do no more than remain clasped in one another's arms. Jean d'Harcourt recalled how 'after the war, my mother refused to speak with Chanel and never set foot in her shop again.'[41] Before the war, the duchess had been dressed by Gabrielle. Jean also said:

> My mother greatly admired Arletty. She considered that her affair with the German was just a sentimental matter . . . There was never a betrayal on her part . . . My mother was faithful in her friendships. The only person with whom she broke up because of the war was Chanel, who played a double or triple game.[42]

While one appreciates Antoinette d'Harcourt's suspicions about Gabrielle, unfortunately proof will almost certainly never be possible – especially as Antoinette d'Harcourt's papers were all burnt in a fire.

In 1943, Gabrielle was to take part in a bizarre episode. Possibly at von Dincklage's suggestion, she apparently decided she should help negotiate a peace settlement. Gabrielle was by no means alone in believing that this would be the speediest end to the war. (Her friendship with men of standing such as Westminster and Churchill may have encouraged her.) Her first step was to summon Captain Momm to the rue Cambon to lay out her plan. Momm, we remember, was von Dincklage's friend and the person who had interceded on André Palasse's behalf to get him out of prison.

Gabrielle's plan had her act as messenger to initiate peace talks between Churchill and the German High Command. Churchill was due to visit Madrid after the Tehran Conference, and Gabrielle said that he had agreed to see her on his way back. At first stupefied, Theodor Momm was eventually won round, and took her 'peace proposal' to Berlin. With Momm as her emissary, Gabrielle's scheme was at first brushed aside. But then the new director of German Foreign Intelligence, the ambitious young Colonel Walter Schellenberg, became interested. Risking execution if discovered, he was himself looking for a way to negotiate with the Allies, and agreed, naming Gabrielle's mission 'Operation Modelhut' (model hat). Even more extraordinary than that, in early 1944, Gabrielle apparently visited Berlin to meet Walter Schellenberg, with von Dincklage as her escort. (Our one piece of evidence for this is Schellenberg's testimony in his subsequent trial.)[43]

Schellenberg decided Gabrielle should travel to Madrid to set up her meeting with Churchill via Sir Samuel Hoare, the British ambassador. As her safety net with the British, however, Gabrielle wanted the Germans to bring along Vera Bate-Lombardi – from internment in Italy – an acquaintance of Winston Churchill's. At this point, the two women's stories diverge. Vera afterwards claimed that Gabrielle sent a German officer to Italy with a letter asking her to return to Paris and help Gabrielle re-open Chanel.[44] Having refused, Vera was subsequently arrested as a British spy. (Vera believed Gabrielle had caused this.) According to Gabrielle, she waded in on Vera's behalf and got her out of a Roman prison.

Vera next came to Paris, and later said that, instead of re-opening her salon there, Gabrielle told her that it was in Madrid she wanted help with a salon. Vera went along with this, although, as it turned out, neither she nor Gabrielle trusted each other. When they arrived in Spain, Gabrielle apparently went to see the British ambassador to present him with her plan. He informed her that Churchill was not now visiting Spain; he was unwell and returning to England via Cairo and Tunisia. (It is highly unlikely that Churchill had ever agreed to meet Gabrielle in these times.) Meanwhile, in Gabrielle's discussion with the ambassador, she omitted to tell him that Vera was also in Madrid. This was a mistake because Vera herself, meanwhile, had arrived at the embassy and was in another room denouncing Gabrielle as a German agent.[45]

Vera's request to be returned to Italy was refused her, and she duly wrote to Churchill. Telling him she wasn't a spy but a loyal British subject, she begged for his assistance. Gabrielle also wrote to Churchill, explaining that she was 'obliged to address someone rather important to get her [Vera] freed and be allowed to bring her down here [Madrid] with me'. She went on to tell Churchill that she realized that this had put Vera in a compromising position; her Italian passport had a German visa on it and Gabrielle understood 'quite well that it looks a bit suspect'. She suggested that a nod from Churchill would facilitate Vera's return to Italy, where she wanted to find her husband. Gabrielle signed herself affectionately, and asked after his health and that of his son, Randolph.[46]

Information on Gabrielle's bungled mission is somewhat muddled. She appears now to have returned to Paris. But Vera was kept in Madrid, from where she sent various missives to Churchill begging him to help her. The British had, however, already been suspicious of Vera Bate-Lombardi. She had remarried in the twenties an Italian, Colonel Lombardi, and for some time before the war the couple had been suspected of spying by the French Interior Ministry. As one of their associates, from 1929 Gabrielle had also come under investigation. While much of the information in the final dossier on Gabrielle was ludicrously inaccurate,[47] the French suspected the Lombardis of being double agents.[48] While another investigation was ordered in 1931, in the end, the French didn't have enough concrete evidence against the Lombardis, and nothing against Gabrielle.[49]

The British Foreign Office, Allied Force Headquarters and the prime minister's office conducted an investigation. After several months, in December 1944, they concluded that, while there was no indication that Vera was 'sent to Madrid by the German Intelligence Service, it is equally clear that Mme Chanel . . . exaggerated Mme Lombardi's . . . position in order to give the Germans the impression that if she were allowed to go to Madrid she might be useful to them. Mme Lombardi seems to have had some curious notion of trying to arrange peace terms.' While the prime minister's office concluded that Vera should be allowed to return to Italy, she was, nonetheless, 'by no means anti-Fascist', had not been 'completely cleared of all suspicion', and was 'still under a cloud'.[50] Whatever the lost details of this murky episode actually were, and whether the megalomaniac scheme to be involved in ending the war was really Vera's or Gabrielle's, it had come to naught.

★ ★ ★

While fashionable Paris persevered in its refusal to face the tide of events, there was no longer any pretence by the authorities of Franco-German cultural exchange. Meanwhile, the theatres were full, and Cocteau and Gabrielle set to work on the restaging of his *Antigone*. Gabrielle also moved herself back to her apartment in the rue Cambon. Was she taking care to separate herself from any connection to the German command?

On the morning of 6 June 1944, D Day, the Americans, Canadians, British and the Free French began the phenomenal Normandy landings. Over a stretch of fifty miles of beaches, this was the launch of the Allied invasion of France. More than 150,000 men were landed in what was to be the most complex and largest amphibious invasion ever undertaken. Simon, Lord Lovat DSO, MC, the son of Arthur Capel's sister-in-law, Laura – in other words, Arthur's nephew – was amongst those on the Normandy beaches. In defiance of recent orders not to permit such foolhardy action in battle, Lord Lovat famously ordered his personal piper, young Bill Millin – wearing the kilt his father had donned in the First World War – to pipe the men ashore. Lovat then led his commando brigade in what became one of the most iconic images of these famed landings. The Germans later said the only reason they hadn't shot Billy was because they thought he was mad. This piece of bravado would have appealed to Arthur Capel.

With Parisians anticipating the arrival of their liberators, a fierce battle was taking place in Normandy. But, in Vichy, as Pétain proclaimed that 'the battle which is taking place on our soil does not concern us,' the Allies moved slowly towards Paris, fighting all the way. By 26 June, de Gaulle had landed and proclaimed a new government and, by early July, the Americans were on the outskirts of Chartres, fifty-six miles south-west of Paris. With de Gaulle's master plan, the notoriously divided Resistance agreed that there was no question: Paris must be seen to liberate itself.

Yet, while German troops had begun a sporadic retreat, they also continued arresting and deporting people to the camps, and the swastika still flew over the senate in the Luxembourg

Gardens. Within a day or so, the major institutions were in the hands of the liberators yet, a week later there were still some Germans in Paris.

As Von Dincklage left with his compatriots in retreat, apparently he asked Gabrielle to come with him. He told her they could quietly slip away to neutral Switzerland, but Gabrielle refused. She was defiant, and would face whatever happened. By 17 August, the most senior collaborators were being evacuated by the German army: over twenty thousand French militia and fascists fought their way on to the retreating trains and lorries. At intervals, these were bombed by the Allies and sabotaged by the Free French, who were staging an uprising against the Germans in Paris. The Resistance and de Gaulle were determined that it would be the French who liberated their own capital, and not the advancing Allies. Serge Lifar heard that he was to be evacuated with the Germans, and sought refuge with Gabrielle in the rue Cambon. With the remnants of the Vichy government, Pétain, who claimed he was a prisoner, was taken by the Germans to the Hohenzollern castle of Sigmaringen, near Stuttgart. Paul Morand was already there.

Gabrielle and Lifar saw the last German tank roll away down the rue de Rivoli, heard the last street fighting between the Germans and the Free French, and saw fire-fighters hoist the first French flags up over the Théâtre de l'Opéra. The Supreme Allied Commander in Europe, General Eisenhower, hadn't regarded Paris as a primary objective. The German forces were retreating towards the Rhine: the aim was to reach Berlin before the Red Army, and there put an end to the conflict. And, while Eisenhower had thought it was premature for any battle for Paris, de Gaulle would now force his hand. In de Gaulle's determination to be seen to 'free' Paris, he threatened the Allies that he would order the French 2nd Armoured Division into the capital.

As the seat of government, Paris was the prize sought by the numerous Resistance factions and, despite a large anti-Gaullist Resistance wing, expelling the Germans united them. To this day, opinion is divided over the military governor General Dietrich von Choltitz's claim that he was 'the saviour of Paris'. Despite repeated orders from Hitler that the city 'must not fall into the enemy's hand except lying in complete ruins', von Choltitz disobeyed and, on 25 August, he surrendered at the Meurice hotel, the newly established headquarters of the Free French.[51]

On the following day, when de Gaulle marched his troops through the place de la Concorde to the Arc de Triomphe, and half of Paris turned out to welcome them, José Maria Sert gave a party for fifty to watch the triumphant parade from his balcony. Gabrielle, Lifar and Etienne de Beaumont were there, alongside many of their fellow 'collaborator' friends. As de Gaulle was getting into his car, a shower of sniper's bullets shattered Sert's windows, and his guests leapt for cover under tables and behind doors. When they finally dared to emerge, as a typical mark of Sert's bravura, he had remained on the balcony, and apologized for the 'inconvenience'.

On 29 August, with the arrival of the US Army's 28th Infantry Division, diverted en route to Berlin, a combined Franco-American military parade took place, again past the Arc de Triomphe. As the vehicles drove down the city streets, more joyous crowds greeted the Armée de la Libération and the Americans as their liberators.

With the liberation, the purging of the collaborators began. Before any organized legal trials could get under way, the *épuration sauvage*, the summary courts, were hastily set up by the Free French, or sometimes by vindictive crowds, initiated, as often as not, by a personal vendetta. In several thousand cases, these episodes resulted in execution. At the same time, in towns and rural areas across the country, women accused of 'horizontal collaboration' were dragged out of their houses and publicly humiliated. Although shaving women's heads for sexual infidelity wasn't new, it isn't clear why between ten and thirty thousand of them were treated to this, plus the added indignity of being paraded naked through jeering crowds. What people expected from these public acts and their construction of what was collaboration is still being debated. While appalled by the ferocity of this popular retribution, de Gaulle's fragile government had little effective power and let the vengeance run its ghastly course. These are some of the most terrifying images of the liberation.[52]

Gabrielle was a high-profile figure and was to experience an attempt to 'cleanse' her when she was arrested by two representatives of the Free French. With an icy dignity, she made her way as quickly as possible out of her room at the Ritz; she didn't want them to find Serge Lifar, hiding in her bathroom. There has been much speculation over the years as to why, following a few hours' questioning, Gabrielle was released. What did she say in her defence, when her friend, Arletty, who had also lived with a German, was imprisoned for four months then put under house arrest for a further eighteen? We have one small piece of information. A 'top secret' letter, from the chief of staff of Allied Force Headquarters, was written in December 1944 referring to Vera Bate-Lombardi's imprisonment in Spain. Following Gabrielle's Modelhut debacle, she and Vera Bate-Lombardi gave different versions of what had come to pass. They both wrote letters to Winston Churchill; letters which contradicted one another.

Amongst several reports and letters from Allied Force Headquarters, there is one recording that 'Mme Chanel has been undergoing interrogation by the French authorities since that time'; in other words, throughout December 1944. While Vera was stuck in Spain begging Churchill to help her get back to her husband in Italy, the British were also concerned to clear up what had been the purpose of the women's visit and whether either she or Gabrielle were German agents.[53]

Did the Allied forces ever know, however, that Gabrielle had apparently returned to Berlin to inform Schellenberg of the failure of her mission? We don't know what possessed her to do such a thing. Aside from believing that she was a German agent – for which we have no proof – perhaps there is only one conclusion to be drawn from her visit. While her mission to Spain sprang from a grandiose egotism, her slightly cracked belief that she could take a hand in ending the war may have emerged from a desire to be

known for something besides haute couture. Years later, her assistant would say:

> Every morning she read the papers in great detail, from the short
> news items to the results of the races. To . . . the head of *France Soir*'s
> surprise, she knew everything about international news. She couldn't
> help it: Chanel put herself in the place of heads of State. She thought
> about the decisions to make . . . She felt concerned, both as a national
> symbol and as a company director. Listening to her, one could even
> have thought that she was responsible for the situation. Mademoiselle
> found it regrettable that great men didn't consult her. Already, during
> the war, she had taken it into her head to make Churchill sign peace.
> She had projects for Europe, which Mendès France judged discerning,
> and she wondered why *L'Express* didn't repeat them.[54]

Like a handful of thoughtful, rather than merely clever, fashion
designers, Gabrielle came to believe that fashion was essentially
worthless. Yet she had pinpointed more accurately than almost anyone before her what it was really about.

And her claim to be a maker of 'style', rather than mere fashion, was of particular significance to her, because it signified
something less ephemeral. She had staked her life on work, and
this work had been the creation of a couture house. Without it,
Gabrielle would have lost her *raison d'être*. She was quite right
when she said, 'I have a boss's soul,' and she needed to feel significant. The success of her political mission would have put her into
the history books in a way she felt was commensurate with her
intelligence. Her return visit to a man as powerful as Schellenberg
must have been a kind of proof to herself that she had been taken
seriously on a far grander scale than merely for the creation of
dresses. In company with many exceptional artists, Gabrielle
understood her own worth, because she lived so wholeheartedly
in the present, but she also underestimated the value of what it
was she had done for her century. Through dress and her lifestyle,
she had made a genuine contribution towards the first century of

modernity; facing up to what it was, something more than many of those in the political sphere ever managed.

With almost nothing to go on, we are left to speculate on the reasons for Gabrielle's prompt release by the Resistance. Remembering Arletty, whose popularity with her compatriots had not been enough to set *her* free, Gabrielle's fame alone can't have been sufficient to procure her release. The routine speculation is probably the closest to the truth: an influential figure let it be known that no proceedings were to be taken out against Gabrielle. It is said that, when the British forces reached Paris, some officers had been deputed to make sure of her safety. They couldn't find her. She was no longer at the Ritz or the rue Cambon, and none of the staff was forthcoming. Gabrielle was eventually found, keeping a low profile at a modest hotel on the outskirts of the city. It was said that the orders to discover her whereabouts had come from Churchill himself.[55]

Churchill liked Gabrielle, and one of his closest friends, the Duke of Westminster, was her ex-lover, with whom she had remained on close terms. Westminster may have stepped in and asked the prime minister to help her. Churchill's possible intervention may have been encouraged by the knowledge that Gabrielle might have had things to say about the rumoured pro-Nazi sympathies of the Duke and Duchess of Windsor, with whom she was acquainted. This would not have gone down well.

While many of Gabrielle's compatriots were amazed at how she 'got away with it', a young English journalist, Malcolm Muggeridge, marvelled. He wrote:

> By one of those majestically simple strokes which made Napoleon so successful a general, she put an announcement in the window of her emporium that scent was free for the GIs, who thereupon queued up to get the bottles of *Chanel No.5*, and would have been outraged if the French police had touched a hair of her head. Having thus gained a breathing space, she proceeded to look for help to right and to left . . .

thereby managing to avoid making even a token appearance amongst the gilded company – Maurice Chevalier, Jean Cocteau, Sacha Guitry and other worthies – on a collaborationist charge.[56]

Gabrielle's lawyer, Réné de Chambrun, as the son-in-law of the Vichy prime minister Pierre Laval, was himself living very discreetly. He advised Gabrielle that she ought to do the same thing, and outside France. Gabrielle knew and liked neutral Switzerland, and that was where she chose to go into voluntary exile.

Before she left, however, she received a postcard from a young GI, who had called on her at the Ritz early in 1945.[57] Hans Schillinger told her he had been sent by her friend, the now-celebrated photographer Horst, who had fled France for the United States early in the war. Horst had managed to get his compatriot Hans Schillinger to the States, where the young man then joined the US army. Horst had told his friend that, if he was in Paris, he must 'give my love to Coco', and this Schillinger had done. The story is usually told that Gabrielle, in turn, asked Schillinger, if ever he came across someone called Hans Günther von Dincklage, would he please write to the Ritz and let her know.

Schillinger had indeed come across von Dincklage, and is supposed to have written Gabrielle a postcard telling her that he had secured his release from a POW camp in Hamburg. In reality, the sequence of events was appreciably different. Gabrielle had given Hans Schillinger the considerable sum of $10,000 and asked him to 'go to Austria, find von Dincklage, give him the money and if possible conduct him to his home in Schleswig-Holstein'. This we know because Schillinger and von Dincklage were arrested by the British Military Authorities in the spring of 1945. The military recorded that Schillinger 'was apparently accompanying Baron von Dincklage with a view to taking him to the latter's family estate at Gettorf. Von Dincklage was in possession of US dollars 8,948 which were impounded on his arrest.'[58] There was no possibility of getting von Dincklage back into France and, with the burden of Gabrielle's own blackened reputation acting as a spur, by the winter of 1945 she had made her judicious move to Lausanne.

Exile

While Gabrielle's life had been one of almost perpetual motion for decades, her Swiss exile launched her on an empty nomadic period. For several years before the war, she had spent her days in the rue Cambon and her nights across the road in the Ritz. Forever on the move, she also regularly left Paris for a few days; staying in the house of a friend, at resort hotels, or La Pausa in the south of France. However, in leaving Paris for Switzerland, Gabrielle had lost something more important to her than any dwelling place – she had lost her business, her all-important *work*. At the rue Cambon it had always been possible to distract oneself from too much thought. Either a collection was in progress or it was the aftermath of the one just gone. There were the new season's accessories to be discussed with the appropriate craftsmen and women; the hours with the models on which all ideas must be tried out; the friends, sycophants and employees proffering queries and comments.

Gabrielle's lack of occupation during the war had been frustrating enough but, in Switzerland, she didn't even have the consolation of rue Cambon nearby. Aside from a handful of friendships, for over twenty-five years, her work had represented the one permanent fixture in her life. Her lovers, her friends, her family, where she lived – these were forever changing. Gabrielle was almost a caricature of the Heraclitean notion that the essence of life is flux, and to resist this change is to resist the heart of our existence.

Whatever she might have sometimes said to the contrary, she had chosen change as her life, and would say, 'I am scared only of becoming bored.' Constant movement was the one thing that would keep this fear at bay. She also knew that moving on, carrying no baggage from the past, was the climate out of which she was best able to create. Gabrielle came closest to being a revolutionary when understanding that, within her there was a 'deep taste for destruction and evolution'. This was what she meant when she said, 'Fashion should express the place, the moment . . . fashion has a meaning in time but none in space.'[1]

Without her business – both the building and the exercise of designing – as the fixed point in her life, Gabrielle's incessant movement had lost its meaning and acquired an aimlessness that did not suit her. Leaving Lausanne, she wandered from one grand Swiss hotel to another and back again. With her energies previously harnessed creatively, she now had no outlet for her restlessness and 'revealed a certain weariness', a disenchantment with life, as her old friend Paul Morand put it.

Morand, who had worked for the Vichy government, had recently taken refuge in Switzerland with a number of other political exiles like himself, so as to avoid any legal judgements being meted out by his homeland. He had lost almost everything. As an impoverished and vilified ex-member of the French literary establishment, in the winter of 1946, he took up Gabrielle's invitation to visit her in St Moritz. There, at the Badrutt Palace Hotel, they sat together over the course of several evenings, and Gabrielle told Morand her story. With nothing to do, with her youth now behind her, inevitably, she looked back. (These were the evenings referred to at the beginning of this book, and the record of which, years later, Morand would publish as Gabrielle's 'memoir', *The Allure of Chanel*. In his introduction, Morand would recall that 'with nothing to do for the first time in her life', Gabrielle was 'champing at the bit'.)

Reflecting on her heart, which 'unburdened the secret of a taciturn disposition', Morand remembered Gabrielle's voice 'that gushed forth from her mouth like lava, those words that crackled like dried vines, her rejoinders, simultaneously crisp and snappy . . . a tone that was increasingly dismissive, increasingly contradictory, laying irrevocable blame, I heard them all'.[2] He heard her doubts about when to return to the rue Cambon, and how she felt both 'trapped by the past and gripped by time regained'. She was part of an age which was suddenly 'foreign to her . . . black bile flowed from eyes that still sparkled, beneath arched eyebrows increasingly accentuated by eyeliner.'³ And although Morand's Gabrielle was formidably alert and well informed, her star was no longer in the ascendant.

Sitting in the palatial opulence of the Swiss hotel, she talked. Far too intelligent not to be self-aware, she said of herself, 'I lack balance . . . I talk too much,' but she added, 'I forget quickly, and furthermore . . . I like to forget. [Emptying her mind enabled her to create.] I throw myself at people in order to force them to think like me.'⁴ The contradictions came thick and fast and, while she did always forget, this woman of paradox also declared, 'I have never forgotten anything.' Saying that 'ageing is Adam's charm and Eve's tragedy', Gabrielle now had more time than she wished to contemplate the possibility of her own decline. On the one hand, she despised women who faced ageing without dignity and, on the other, she was unable to comprehend the thought of her own non-existence. She would say that the idea 'of youth is something very new, who talked about it twenty years ago?'; she also said that 1939 was the first time it had occurred to her that she was no longer young: 'It hadn't occurred to me that I could grow old. I'd always been among bright, pleasant people; friends. And all at once I found myself alone, separated from everyone I liked. Everyone I liked was on the other side of the ocean [she means those who had fled to the States].'⁵ But there were distractions. A few old friends, such as Visconti, visited her, there was a handful of new Swiss friends, and a new female companion, Maggie van Zuylen.

Marguerite Nametalla was an Egyptian (it was said she had been a violet seller), married to the diplomat Baron Egmont van Zuylen, whose home was the immense medieval-style castle Haar, in Holland. Maggie was elegantly beautiful, with pale skin and green eyes, and enjoyed dramatizing her 'un-wealthy origins'. Her son-in-law, Guy de Rothschild, described her as 'witty and gay, lively and provocative, she combined audacity and fantasy. Completely natural and devoid of timidity, her sense of humour . . . her repartee, her gift for imitation, made her seem like a character in a play.'[6] André Malraux would proclaim that 'Chanel, General de Gaulle and Picasso are the three most important figures of our time,' and, of Maggie van Zuylen, he said, 'Hers is intelligence in its purest state, since it is unencumbered by any intellectual baggage.'

'Maggie could participate in any conversation for, while conscious of her lack of culture, she never gave it a second thought.'[7] Her vivacity was seductive, and Gabrielle felt renewed in the company of this worldly and vital younger woman. She also became her lover. In the winter of 1945–6, they entertained one another uproariously with their sparkling and acid wit. Writing many years later in his journal, Paul Morand would say that, before Gabrielle 'became exclusively lesbian, I lived with her and Mme. de Zuylen at the *Beau Rivage*, shared their private life . . . in Lausanne. They didn't hide when I found them in bed together.'[8]

Gabrielle had so far outwitted her demons, by 'never resting'. Still on the move from everything she found too painful, she was obliged to use her hotel-hopping as a new method of forgetting.

Did she make herself forget, too, the mounting deaths of her friends, lovers, family, that reminded her of time passing? Her two brothers, whom she had cut off so peremptorily at the beginning of the war, were both dead, Lucien felled by a heart attack early in the war, and without seeing their sister again. Gabrielle rarely referred to her family. She was one of those who had so outgrown their roots that in doing so she had rejected them, left them far behind. They pulled her back, did nothing but remind her of a childhood that she said she remembered every day and which she spent her whole life trying to avoid. Either through a sense of social inadequacy, or a genuine impatience with the roots that were of no use to her emotionally, psychically or financially, Gabrielle had made the decision, and ruthlessly thrust them aside.

Excising almost all her family from her life, Gabrielle appears to have retained only her aunt Adrienne and her nephew, André Palasse, and his family. She brought André and his family to Switzerland, in an attempt to improve his health, but André would eventually die of tuberculosis.

In 1942, Gabrielle's friend Max Jacob had died in the appalling Drancy internment camp, in Paris's outer suburbs; his sister and brother already sent to be gassed in Auschwitz. That same year, Duke Dmitri Pavlovich had died in another kind of prison, a sanatorium in Switzerland, where, for over a year, he had struggled with tuberculosis. In 1948, Vera Bate-Lombardi died in Rome. But, before Vera, Gabrielle's old friend, José Maria Sert's death was announced. Theirs had been what Gabrielle called a relationship 'with all the ripples that the clash of characters as entrenched as ours can stir up'. Sert, 'as munificent and as immoral as a Renaissance man', had done nothing to curb the pace of work, food, drink and the drugs that his doctors had said would kill him. One day, in November 1945, while labouring on his huge mural in the cathedral of Vichy, he dropped dead.

Misia had been quite unaware that Sert was close to death, and was bereft, afterwards writing, 'With him, disappeared all my reasons to exist.'[9] Her beloved brother had already died; and her divorced niece, now living with her, would be killed in a car crash, leaving Misia more alone than ever. The dosage and frequency of her morphine increased. It was her only way of keeping at bay the inevitability of loss and its sibling, pain, made worse by the sequence of her own ageing. She survived by spending increasingly long periods shielded from reality under her cloak of narcotics: 'Chatting at dinner parties, or wandering through the flea market, she would pause to jab a needle right through her skirt.'[10] And here was one of the great differences between Misia and her friend and sometime lover Gabrielle. Both of them had long ago reached a state where they could not live without their drugs. But, where Misia's addiction meant that she became utterly controlled by it and used her narcotics in increasing quantity, Gabrielle was never in that position. She was dependent, but her great force of character never allowed the morphine to control her; *Gabrielle* controlled the morphine.

Procuring Misia's drugs had become dangerous, yet she bothered less and less about concealing her habit. 'Once, in Monte Carlo, she walked into a pharmacy and asked outright for morphine, while a terrified Gabrielle pleaded with her to be more careful.'[11] In those post-war years, Misia travelled to Switzerland to spend time with Gabrielle, and also to collect her supplies, as she and Gabrielle had done together so many times before. But Misia's name was now found on a drug-dealer's list in Paris; she was arrested and thrown into a cell with fellow addicts, prostitutes and down and outs. Friends got her out after twenty-four hours but, at seventy-six, she was greatly shaken by the experience.

Now frightened to answer the door, Misia turned ever more to her chemical oblivion. In September 1950, when there was little of herself left to destroy, Misia made her last trip to Switzerland to visit Gabrielle and collect her latest consignment of drugs. Not long after returning to Paris, she withdrew to her bed. A month later, her maid called friends to her bedside; she was dying. Gabrielle came, and stayed until Misia retreated into that silent space before death. Late that night, her breathing quietly stopped. Early the following morning, Gabrielle took charge, as only she knew how. She had Misia's body removed to Sert's great canopied bed, then set to work to 'perform her last rites for her friend'.

She arranged Misia's hair, made up her face and decorated her with her jewels. In white, on a bank of white flowers, a pink ribbon across her breast, at its centre one pale rose. Thus, Misia was presented by Gabrielle to her mourning friends. Misia's biographers would say that Gabrielle had made the years fall away and that Misia looked 'more beautiful than ever'. With more realism, in a typically arch aside, the novelist Nancy Mitford wrote, 'Dolly . . . had just come from the deathbed of Misia Sert. Mlle Chanel was there doing up the corpse. "Well, Coco was doing her nails – I thought it was kind of her – but I must say, she had overdone the make-up."'[12] The funeral was held in the Polish church, in rue Cambon, close by the Chanel boutique.

First Sert and now Misia were gone. Whatever dreadful things Gabrielle might have said of Misia, these two had been a source of strength and comfort to one another in an enduringly passionate friendship, lasting for over thirty years. Gabrielle said, 'Whoever mentions Sert mentions Misia,' and so it must have been in her own heart. With the death of the prodigiously unreconstructed Sert and his woman, a crucial aspect of Gabrielle's life's entertainment, exasperation and support was gone, leaving her world a diminished one. While declaring that 'I am much more frightened of women than I am of men,' she added, 'Women never amuse me. I feel no friendship for them ... They don't play the game, but expect it to be played for them.'[13] Meanwhile, Misia, who, like Gabrielle, was 'neither good nor bad', was also the one about whom Gabrielle would say with stark simplicity, 'She has been my only woman friend.'[14]

As she sat in that Swiss hotel with Paul Morand, Gabrielle's now unsparing tongue demonstrated the formidably tough exterior few were brave or imaginative enough to challenge. Yet, hidden in her armoury of words, every now and then, alongside the unrelenting worldliness, Gabrielle revealed her other self, a diffident, fragile and lonely creature. This vulnerable woman, who admitted, 'I have only ever found loneliness ... at the age of six I am already alone,' went on to say defiantly, 'It is loneliness which has forged my character, which is bad-tempered, and bronzed my soul, which is proud, and my body which is sturdy.' At the same time, she said, 'I have a horror of loneliness and I live in total solitude. I would pay so as not to be alone.' (In fact, she often did. On her annual trips to Italy, for example, she took lovers, saying later, 'One doesn't go to Italy for gentlemen. But I always paid.'[15]) And, reading her comment, 'I would have the duty police constable sent up so as not to dine alone,' the thought of von Dincklage, there in the background, springs to mind.

Since his arrest by the British in 1945, von Dincklage had been living in Schleswig-Holstein (British zone) with his aunt, Baroness Weber-Rosenkranz.[16] But, in September 1949, we find him once again in Switzerland, staying at the Hôtel Beau-Rivage in Lausanne. Between December 1949 and January 1950, Gabrielle was also at the hotel.[17] Von Dincklage and she had somehow arranged to meet.

With Gabrielle, von Dincklage was able to enjoy a well-appointed lifestyle, while Gabrielle didn't have to send for the 'duty policeman' so as not to dine alone, or fend off the idea that 'if I let myself slip, I know that melancholy awaits me, open-mouthed.'[18] Von Dincklage was still an attractive man, who retained that unctuous charm. Even if there was a modicum of sincerity in his feelings for Gabrielle, it is difficult to believe it was much more than convenience that put him at her side.

Meanwhile, Gabrielle, who was as powerful and forthright as she was vulnerable and alone, would recall Arthur Capel's comment to remember she was a woman and say that, to remind herself, she would stand in front of the mirror where she saw her:

> two menacing arched eyebrows, my nostrils that are as wide as those of a mare, my hair that is blacker than the devil, my mouth that is like a crevice out of which pours a heart that is irritable but not selfish . . . My dark gypsy-like skin that makes my teeth and my pearls look twice as white; my body, as dry as a vine-stock without grapes; my worker's hands . . .
>
> The hardness of the mirror reflects my own hardness back to me . . . it expresses what is peculiar to myself, a person who is efficient, optimistic, passionate, realistic, combative, mocking and incredulous, and who feels her Frenchness. Finally, there are my gold-brown eyes which guard the entrance to my heart: there one can see that I am a woman. A poor woman.[19]

This same 'poor woman' believed she had been put here for a purpose and said, 'That is why I endured, that is why the outfit I wore to the races in 1913 can still be worn in 1946, because the new social conditions are still the same as those that led me to clothe them.' Remembering the revolution she had initiated, she described how 'I was working towards a new society.' She described clothes until then as being for women who were 'useless', who did nothing for themselves or with their lives. Saying she designed for busy working women, she added that 'a busy woman needs to feel comfortable in her clothes. You need to be able to roll up your sleeves.'[20] And in the drive to fulfil her destiny, and her deep urge for independence, Gabrielle also understood, and regretted that 'I belong to that breed of foolish women, women who think only of their work.'[21]

While saying that she had never really known happiness, she also said, 'I have never had the time to be unhappy, of existing for another human being, or having children. It is probably not by chance that I have lived alone.'[22]

Asking herself where she would go now, Gabrielle continued looking forward: 'I don't know, but I'm going somewhere and it's not over.' Saying that her reaction to being told that Europe was in ruins made her think that, while she felt that Europe was her mother, if it was lagging behind in the world, she would readily leave it behind, as she had done her family, and begin her new life: 'I want to be part of what happens. I will go wherever is necessary for that . . . It will be necessary to do something else. I am ready to start all over again.'[23]

This refusal to be bowed by circumstance, plus the willingness to 'start all over again', was most impressive in a woman of sixty-three. For all her tenacity and verve, however, Gabrielle didn't have quite the same energy she had possessed thirty years earlier. And yet, the icon Coco Chanel had become so intertwined with whoever Gabrielle was, she was unable to relinquish it. As it turned out, what she would take up wasn't as novel as she might have envisaged when she spoke these words in 1946.

When Gabrielle had agreed with her lawyer, René de Chambrun, that she should leave France and live in Switzerland for a while, she also asked him if he would help her in taking on her partners, the Wertheimers. Gabrielle believed that, during the course of the war, they had once again defrauded her, and told Chambrun, 'I want revenge.'[24]

For several years before the war, convinced that their initial agreement had been a bad one, Gabrielle had intermittently skirmished with the Wertheimers. In the early thirties, for example, they had begun making Chanel perfumes with their own company, Bourjois. They gave sales rights to foreign subsidiaries they had created; from these they also gave Gabrielle her 10 per cent profit. This infuriated her. As the business had grown, Gabrielle was increasingly frustrated by what she saw as a reduction of quality in her creation, and had insisted on being released from the original agreement. While the war had interrupted Gabrielle's initiation of a lawsuit, the conflict between her and her partners only intensified.

At the onset of the war, before leaving France for America, the Wertheimers had cleverly entrusted their business to a cousin, who in turn cleverly appointed a non-Jewish industrialist, Félix Amiot, to be the 'front' for the family. He had continued marketing the Chanel perfumes during the occupation. At the same time, the Wertheimers had set up production of Chanel N°5 in America, where they made yet more perfumes, using natural essences from the south of France, which didn't follow the original formulas.

These activities, for which Gabrielle was given ridiculously small royalties, continued after the war. Chambrun and the president of the French Bar Association, called in to assist him, advised Gabrielle that 'an amicable settlement will bring you much more than litigation.' But relishing the thought of a fight, Gabrielle would not agree. The Wertheimers argued that they had made a major financial contribution to Parfums Chanel, had built it into a worldwide business, and that Gabrielle's contribution was no longer relevant. She was no longer a public figure, and was too old to offer the talent, youth and celebrity she had possessed when she had launched N°5. Gabrielle was incensed: 'So I'm too old! They think I'm too old, those — bastards!'

In the two months before the case came to trial, Gabrielle was very busy. Eventually, she handed Chambrun several tiny phials and asked him to give these to his wife. Could she make up phials like this from her own home? Chambrun said she could, with the proviso that they must be presents. Josée de Chambrun declared the perfume exquisite, as did a Russian 'nose' called in to confirm her opinion. Gabrielle then instructed the perfumer in Switzerland to make up a hundred bottles of her various perfumes. The bottles were not the same design as the originals and were prefixed with the word 'Mademoiselle', making them 'different' perfumes, too. Gabrielle then sent them as 'gifts' to all the smartest department stores in New York. The Wertheimers asked her lawyer, 'But what does she *really* want?' Not long afterwards, they made a settlement out of court.

While the Wertheimer brothers had played rough with Gabrielle during the war, they were also distinguished losers, and the terms of the new agreement were most favourable to Gabrielle. She had the right to make Mademoiselle Chanel perfumes anywhere in the world: a good threat to her partners she never acted upon; she was to be paid substantial damages, with interest, for the sales of Parfums Chanel in the US, Britain and France; she was to have a kind of monopoly conceded to her in Switzerland – 'her fief, her kingdom' – and she would be paid a royalty of 2 per cent on all gross sales of Chanel perfumes throughout the whole world.

At the conclusion of this intense legal battle, in which Gabrielle had joined with righteous indignation, tremendous enjoyment, and considerable low cunning, she was left a multi-millionaire. After the agreement had been signed, she took the Chambruns back to rue Cambon for a celebration. 'My dear Bunny,' she said to Chambrun, 'I have already made a great deal of money in my life, but, as you know, I've also spent a lot. Now, thanks to you, I shall never have to work again . . . I'm not going to do anything anymore.' That was in 1947.

After the Nuremberg war trials for the twenty-four major criminals, in the Ministries trials Walter Schellenberg was given the lightest penalty. In 1951, he telephoned Gabrielle. He had not long since been released from prison, and he and his wife would live in Switzerland under assumed names. Schellenberg had no money and was going to publish his memoirs. As the former head of Hitler's secret police, he was approached by a number of literary agents, and indicated that he would provide a full record of his experiences during the war. Whether Schellenberg told his agent, or the man discovered for himself the connection between Gabrielle and Schellenberg, is not known, but the agent blackmailed Gabrielle into paying him a 'large sum of money' to keep her secret.

The Swiss now told Schellenberg he wasn't welcome there. The Schellenbergs then moved to Italy and a house on Lake Maggiore, where, apparently, all their expenses were paid by Gabrielle. Schellenberg had developed cancer and, by early 1952, he had died. His wife would write to von Dincklage's friend Captain Momm that 'Madame Chanel offered us financial assistance in our difficult situation and it was thanks to her that we were able to spend a few more months together.'[25] When Schellenberg's memoir, *The Labyrinth*, was published, there was no mention of Gabrielle, or any reference to the mission to Spain with Vera Bate-Lombardi christened Operation Modelhut by Schellenberg. At the end of 1952, von Dincklage went to visit Mrs Schellenberg in Düsseldorf in order to collect two 'objects' she wanted to give Gabrielle. We have no evidence, but these 'objects' may well have been documents.

With time on her hands in Switzerland, Gabrielle had turned to thoughts of safeguarding the myth of Coco Chanel. As she was no longer perpetuating it in her couture, she wanted someone to take down a more formal record of her life than her earlier conversations with Morand. Her choice of 'ghost-writer' was the poet and novelist Louise de Vilmorin, a formidable character with a distinguished literary reputation. Amongst her numerous affairs, after the war, de Vilmorin became the lover of both the British ambassador Duff Cooper and his wife, Diana. In her last years, she was the companion of the writer André Malraux, by then the French Minister of Culture. Gabrielle admired de Vilmorin's cleverness, her urbanity and her irony and, in 1947, they sat down together in Venice to work through Gabrielle's life.

Notwithstanding de Vilmorin's lack of moralizing, she was unable to subsume her own personality sufficiently to permit her subject to settle into the foreground. De Vilmorin was also driven mad by Gabrielle's inability to be straight about her early years. Gabrielle wasn't pleased with de Vilmorin's account, especially when it failed to find sympathy with any of the American publishers. Their friendship did, though, weather this episode. Next, Gabrielle tried out one of the extraordinary Kessel brothers, Georges, the suicidally depressed ex-lover of Colette, whose opium-cocaine-morphine habit left him wasted before his time. This too was a failure. Undaunted, for the rest of her life Gabrielle tried to coax a succession of writers into helping her construct and reconstruct her legend.

Soon after Kessel, there was the journalist and novelist Gaston Bonheur, then came the young novelist Michel Déon, who had recently helped Salvador Dalí with his memoirs and brought out his own successful first novel. Michel Déon, who spent a good part of 1951 to 1953 in her company, recently described Gabrielle as an 'exceptional, and at the same time exasperating and brilliant woman'. Travelling with her from Paris to Lausanne, from Roquebrune to Rome to New York, he faithfully noted down her stories. Déon's mode was not to query what she said. She talked; he listened, and then wrote.

Déon is now a youthful nonagenarian and one of the grand old men of French literature. His irony and sly wit are countered by a prevailing warmth, and one can imagine Gabrielle being charmed by the young writer. In conversation, he alludes to a novelist's material-gathering. Describing himself as 'a robber', Déon was fascinated by her 'complexity and seductiveness'.

Telling how he listened happily to this woman forty years his senior, 'who had seen and experienced everything', he was moved by her admission that 'timid people talk a great deal because they can't bear silence in company. I'm always ready to bring out any idiocy at all just to fill up a silence. I go on, I go from one thing to another, so that there'll be no chances for silence. When people don't enjoy my company . . . I feel it right away. I have a kind of nervous flow. I talk vehemently. I know I'm unbearable.'[26]

Gabrielle made a remarkable admission to a young Jean Cau, then Jean-Paul Sartre's secretary, that in fact everyone intimidated her, from her mannequins to minor employees, to the delivery boy. And she added, 'Fortunately no one or almost no one knows this.'

Déon was both sufficiently observant and imaginative enough that, in spite of the flaws, he found Gabrielle sympathetic and tantalizing. She asked him to come with her to Switzerland in her Cadillac, but he preferred to remain independent, making the journey in his own car, a black MG. Gabrielle travelled 'with two black Cadillacs, one for her, driven by her chauffeur in livery, and another carrying her two personal maids, one of them clutching the famous jewellery box in detergent-worn hands. Travelling in convoy like this, halfway she stopped her car and got into my convertible, her head veiled in pink gauze like a motorist from the early 1900s.'[27] The young novelist was paid a monthly salary by Gabrielle and occasionally returned to Paris to write an article or pay his rent. In the end, Déon spent so much time away from Paris, listening to her, that his girlfriend got tired of waiting and dumped him.

On several occasions, Déon met von Dincklage in Switzerland and describes how Gabrielle 'continued with the pretence that he hadn't had anything to do with the war on France'. (In 1950, a Swiss police report had stated that 'Today, VD still comes across as a very cold man and tries to impose his will on every occasion.') Meanwhile, Déon wryly tells a story demonstrating how much the older man, by then aged fifty-seven, still retained his looks and his ability to ensnare. One night, Gabrielle had retired early to bed, and Déon and von Dincklage set off for a nightclub. There they met Déon's new German girlfriend, a club dancer. Von Dincklage worked his charm so effectively that Déon was amazed at the speed with which his girl dropped him for the older man.[28]

(Some time around 1953–4, von Dincklage disappeared from Gabrielle's life. All we know is Gabrielle continued giving him an allowance; he eventually settled on a Spanish island, and there he devoted his time to painting erotica.)

After considerable perseverance, by the end of 1953, Michel Déon had produced a manuscript of three hundred pages, recounting Gabrielle's life story. He waited for her judgement, but none came. Then, Gabrielle sent word through her friend Hervé Mille, editor of *Paris Match* and one of the arbiters of post-war Parisian taste: 'In these three hundred pages there is not a single sentence that is not hers, but now she sees the book, she thinks that it is not what America is expecting.'

Michel Déon understood Gabrielle's message. He had written down her words just as she had spoken them, without interpretation and with all the fantasies intact. He understood that, in her heart, she knew the truth perfectly well: that the fantasies that helped her survive were fine to expand on in conversation but, as he says, 'not to read black on white'. As a writer, Déon was sensitive to the very powerful hold her imagination had upon her, and says, 'What I found truly moving about her was her constant call to this strange, imaginary, quality of existence. [And] her charming impulses, a very delicate generosity – when one did not ask for anything – a remarkable intuition in music, poetry, drama.'[29]

Rather than criticizing Gabrielle's fantasy life, 'this strange, imaginary, quality of existence', Déon is subtle enough to see that she could not have survived without it. He also appreciated her respect for truth and the integrity of writing. Thus, when she said to him, 'Michel, it is my voice, but I don't want to hear it,' he told her he understood, and they remained friends. He then destroyed his manuscript. Asked why, Déon says, 'I knew that one day I would be approached to use it and, if I didn't have that unique copy, then I couldn't.'[30] In Michel Déon, Gabrielle had found a true ally: someone who appreciated her blend of understanding exactly what truth is, and her emotional need to fantasize. In this, Déon did not judge her. Rather, he felt great sympathy for Gabrielle's childlike fears; her 'inability to abandon her dreams in order to face reality'.

Return: 1954

In the spring of 1953, Gabrielle travelled to the United States. For three months, she was the guest of Maggie and Egmont van Zuylen in New York. On weekends, they mostly socialized with people Gabrielle already knew. Out on Long Island, for example, she spent time with the photographer Horst. Then there was Mona Williams, later von Bismarck.

Mona had been named by several designers, including Gabrielle, the best-dressed woman in the world; her fame had triggered Cole Porter's lines 'What do I care if Mrs Harrison Williams is the best-dressed woman in town?' Her husband (who would die that year) was reputedly the wealthiest man in America. Gabrielle had often been a visitor at the Harrisons' villa on Capri, originally belonging to the emperor Tiberius. Before the war, she and Harrison had a brief liaison. He had told Gabrielle that his beautiful socialite wife – most famously photographed by Cecil Beaton in Chanel – 'is a fashion model, just a model', and had attempted to capture Gabrielle for himself. She said if he'd asked her a year earlier she would have gone. As it was, 'It felt too late.'

Gabrielle's visit to the States was in part motivated by the prospect of work. Chanel Parfums New York had asked for her assistance in redesigning their new offices. Gabrielle relished the challenge and created a luxurious yet restrained interior. To accompany the group of signature Coromandel screens she had brought with her from France, Gabrielle included another signature: her beige carpets. These worked as soothing background to the honey-coloured straw-cloth walls, and the warm wood of the antique pink-beige leather-covered French chairs. Around the rooms was a mixture of African bronzes and paintings by Renoir and Henri Rousseau.

In Gabrielle's years without designing, she almost never spoke of it. Events, however, were leading her towards it once again. While she was in New York, she made a point of being introduced to Alex and Tatiana Liberman, who had escaped France to safety in America in 1940. Liberman was both talented and tremendously ambitious, and had risen to become the art director of *Vogue*. He recalled how Gabrielle's business manager, Count Koutouzof, introduced to her by Dmitri Pavlovich, 'brought Chanel to our house, and we became great friends'. This was that same Alex Liberman who had charged his Parisian friends to break off their friendship with von Dincklage, shortly before the war.

Liberman enjoyed Gabrielle's company: 'I loved the Proustian aspect . . . the stories, the legends, and her involvement with Diaghilev and Picasso and Cocteau and Reverdy. She was a constant lesson in refinement . . . Tatiana and Chanel got along well on the surface, although I don't think there was ever much warmth between them.'[1] Quite possibly this was because of Gabrielle's liaison with von Dincklage, who had deceived Tatiana's close friend Hélène Dessoffy so badly.

In 1950, Schiaparelli's sensational style had run its course, and she was obliged to close down her house. Between the First and Second World Wars, some of the most distinguished and influential Parisian couture houses had been directed by women, but several were now gone. Jeanne Lanvin died in 1946; the great Madeleine Vionnet had closed her house in 1939. Admired by Gabrielle, Marlene Dietrich, Katharine Hepburn and Greta Garbo, Vionnet had described herself as 'an enemy of fashion', stating that her interest was in expressing a timeless vision of woman.

The post-war designer Christian Dior, who had shot to overnight fame in 1947, would write that the earliest twentieth-century designers gained variety largely by 'trimmings of exquisite craftsmanship'. After the creation and decoration of Poiret:

It was Madeleine Vionnet and Jeanne Lanvin who finally transformed the profession of couturier, by executing the dresses in their collections with their own hands and scissors. The model became a whole and at last skirt and bodice were cut according to the same principle. Madeleine Vionnet achieved wonders in this direction: she was a genius at employing her material, and invented the famous cut on the cross which gave the dresses of the women between the two wars their softly moulded look. Freed from the trimmings of 1900 and decorative motives of Poiret, dresses now depended entirely on their cut.[2]

Another woman, Nina Ricci, was one of the best designers for elegant older women, and Germaine Krebs, known as Madame Grès, was a sculptress whose house had opened in 1942. The last of the couturiers to develop a ready-to-wear collection, Grès called it 'prostitution'. Christian Dior knew his subject well, describing the inter-war period as 'the age of the great couturiers. Outstanding among them was Mlle Chanel, who dominated all the rest . . . In her personality as well as in her taste, she had style, elegance, and authority. From quite different points of view, she and Madeleine Vionnet can claim to be the great creators of modern fashion.'[3]

Meanwhile, Marcel Rochas, Lucien Lelong, Jean Patou, Edward Molyneux, Cristóbal Balenciaga, Mainbocher and a handful of other young male designers were now the dominant figures in the couture. At the same time, many commentators agreed with Dior that post-war fashion lacked purpose and was often rather ugly: 'Hats were far too large, skirts far too short, jackets far too long, shoes far too heavy . . . and worst of all there was that dreadful mop of hair raised high above the forehead in front and rippling down the backs of French women on their bicycles.' Appreciating that this *zazou* style had originated in the desire to 'defy the forces of occupation and the austerity of Vichy', nonetheless, as fashion, Dior found it repellent.[4]

Paris had become cut off and impoverished during the war, while American ready-to-wear designers and manufacturers had forged a place amongst the leaders of female taste, and were absolutely set on making New York the world's new fashion capital. At the same time, with backing from the textile magnate Marcel Boussac, a young Dior set out to reinstate France's premier role. In February 1947, it was freezing cold and the French press was on strike, yet word had got round that something unusual was about to happen. Dior's first show, at his elegant avenue Montaigne premises, was oversubscribed. On the day, the crowded salon was tense with anticipation. Society, fashion's attendants and its commentators were there, including Carmel Snow, the omnipotent American editor of *Harper's Bazaar*. Close by was the *Vogue* team, led by Michel de Brunhoff, his famous joie de vivre never to return after the Nazis had shot his son.

Suddenly, stepping out fast, the first girl made her entrance; others followed in quick succession. The audience was stunned. The pace of fashion shows was traditionally extremely sedate, as the models gave journalists and buyers time to take in the new collection. Instead, Dior had instructed his girls to walk fast and seductively, heightening the sense of drama. Each girl moved 'with a provocative swinging movement, whirling in the close-packed room, knocking over ash trays with the strong flare of her pleated skirt, and bringing everyone to the edge of their seats in a desire not to miss a thread of this momentous occasion'.[5]

The response was unanimous: the show was a triumph. Madeleine Vionnet, now in her seventies, told Dior, 'It has been a long time since I have seen anything as beautiful.' But it was Carmel Snow's comment that travelled like lightning around the world: 'It's . . . a revolution. Your dresses are wonderful: they have such a *new look*!' she told Dior. She had named it. The clothes trade was in an uproar. Millions of dollars were invested in new stock which, if outmoded by this New Look, would be made obsolete overnight. Buyers cabled the States from Paris predicting 'catastrophe. Women will go for this look like bees for honey.' Carmel Snow was interviewed on NBC: 'God help those who bought before seeing Dior's collection. He is a genius. He has changed everything.'[6] And he did.

After years of austerity, with strictly regulated yardage for clothes, Dior's New Look (actually entitled 'Coralle', after the petals of a flower), did away with the hard, squared-off padded shoulders and short lengths of the ubiquitous military influence almost overnight. He presented instead softer, feminine, waisted jackets, and dresses and skirts using yards and yards of fabric. Moulded shoulders, flattering flared skirts, tightly corseted bodices and provocatively defined breasts helped signal the impression of bodies that were archetypes of the female form.

Describing his couture as 'ephemeral architecture, dedicated to the beauty of the female body', for his first collection, Dior was violently criticized by the establishment for not working in the spirit of austerity. Britain's President of the Board of Trade objected, there were accusations of decadence and 'lowering the standards of public morality'. Some women complained about covering up their legs and, during a photo shoot in a Paris market, the models were attacked by women stall holders over the profligacy of their dresses. But all that really mattered was that both women and men fell in love with Dior's glorification of all that was delicate and feminine.

With great speed, the New Look re-established Paris as the epicentre of the world's fashion. Recalling the response to these luxurious and exaggeratedly feminine clothes, one socialite said, 'Women had been deprived of everything for years and they threw themselves on fashion like hungry wolves.' Indeed, the New Look was so successful that, by the beginning of 1950, approximately 75 per cent of French couture exports came from the House of Dior. Within a year, he had become the most famous designer in the world.

Gabrielle was curious; angry at what she saw as unwarranted attention, and came back to France to see this New Look for herself. Meeting her friend Christian Bérard, who had illustrated Dior's collection, she berated him for working for someone participating in 'the ruin of French couture'. Now hopelessly addicted to his opium, Bérard was also a classic Parisian celebrity, noted for his theatrical decors, his fashion sketches, his gossip and his wit. Annoyed by

Gabrielle's arrogance, he retorted, 'Oh stop taking yourself for France and crowing "cock a doodle doo!"'

Much more, however, than Gabrielle's pique at the brilliance of Dior's success, she was appalled at the reintroduction of so many aspects of women's dress from which she had worked so hard to free them. It was ironic that Dior, a gifted, gentle and retiring homosexual, had returned women to an updated version of the Belle Epoque. Woman was once again to be worshipped as an image. She was an immensely elegant, padded, corseted and constrained symbol. With her tiny waist, voluptuous breasts and elegantly female hips, she was costumed as a beautiful ideal. For all its undoubted beauty, this image presented woman as an adored object, who moved with less freedom than she had done for many years. Some of these lovely and graceful costumes were so structured that they could almost stand up on their own. Whatever else it did, Dior's couture symbolized the more reticent role women were expected to revert to in the years following the war.

When Gabrielle was met by reporters on her 1953 visit to the States and asked what she thought of the New Look, wearing one of her own suits from a pre-war collection, she answered, 'Just take a look at me.' The exquisite couture Dior and his fellow designers created throughout the late forties was the antithesis of everything in Gabrielle's sartorial philosophy.

For many years, the upper floors of Gabrielle's rue Cambon boutique had been deserted. After the war, she sometimes returned to Paris and 'walked through the silent workrooms where pieces of fabric, dress dummies fallen over on to tables, and rusting sewing machines, were left miserably about. Life had stopped there.'[7] Without the work that had filled Gabrielle's days, all her houses, her money and jewels rewarded her only with boredom.

In 1954, while American *Vogue* would say that Gabrielle probably meant nothing more than the name on a perfume bottle to those born after 1939, for those born before it, the rumour of her return had sent a frisson round a series of inner circles. Gabrielle denied it and played coy. Then, finally, after considerable planning and guile, involving recalling some of her best *premières*, and the employment of some of the most well-born girls in Paris as models, Gabrielle re-opened her couture house in early 1954. If she was yielding to the need to throw off the boredom of these last years, perhaps she also hoped her return might be recompense for what she had sacrificed and lost in the name of the House of Chanel. Speculation was rife. What had made her, at *seventy-one*, decide to reopen? What on earth would her first collection be like?

If boredom was one of the drivers for Gabrielle's return, so was her dislike of present fashions. But a visit to Switzerland by Pierre Wertheimer was probably the final trigger that spurred her on to act. In the summer of 1953, Wertheimer came in person to give her some worrying news. Despite the magazines all quoting Marilyn Monroe's claim – a famed Chanel N°5 promotion – that she wore nothing else in bed, for the first time in thirty years, N°5's sales were down. Wertheimer was soothing: Gabrielle should not concern herself, profits were still substantial. She did not react with the anticipated indignation, instead quietly suggesting they launch another perfume. Wertheimer told her that this wouldn't be good business. On the one hand, Paris no longer had automatic precedence in the world of fashion, perfume and cosmetics; on the other, the life of these things was becoming shorter each year. Gabrielle didn't persist, and Pierre Wertheimer was relieved to see that, at last, she was mellowing. He was wrong.

Very shortly after this meeting, Gabrielle returned to Paris, reinstated herself at the Ritz and set about getting rid of her buildings on rue Cambon, with the exception of number 31. Here, she refurbished the boutique on the ground floor, the grand salon, where she had always shown her collections, plus her third-floor apartment and workrooms above. Once again, Gabrielle spent her days working and entertaining at rue Cambon, and her nights over the road at the Ritz. She also sold her beautiful house in the south of France. La Pausa was bought by Emery Reves, literary agent and friend to Winston Churchill. It seems fitting that not only was Churchill to spend much time in his last years at this, one of Gabrielle's most perfect creations, he would also write a good part of his war memoirs there. Gabrielle would later buy a house in Switzerland for retirement, but no longer kept a home in France outside Paris.

She sold La Pausa knowing she would need every centime she could lay her hands on. As much as anything, however, letting it go was a return to her real life: her work. La Pausa had represented the discreet yet luxurious leisure Gabrielle had been one of the first to develop. There she had shared some of the best aspects of the life she had created. Gabrielle was controlling, but she was also its contrary, non-judgemental, and life at La Pausa had been very non-judgemental of its guests. Gabrielle had said, 'It pleases me infinitely more to give than to receive, whether it is at work, in love or in friendship.'[8] In relinquishing La Pausa, she was taking stock before re-launching herself upon the world. Paramount was her belief in the future. In the end, houses and many objects were consigned to the past. Her rebirth was to be about work, not holiday. Connected with this thinking was a more profound move.

Returning to a hotel, to her work and the re-creation of her couture, Gabrielle was, once and for all, giving up on a life that was private. Given her times, her upbringing and her own character, she had failed in her search for long-term emotional contentment. Indeed, she no longer believed it was possible. Work and her public face were the only places where fulfilment had always followed her, so she would devote the remainder of her life to living in the public gaze. From now on, she would cultivate her legend.

Gabrielle's faith – perhaps 'credo' is a better word – that only she knew how to dress women, nowadays sounds like bombastic exaggeration. But, while the couture of the contemporary stars – Dior, Givenchy, Fath – had made women look and feel beautiful in clothes that were sensational, opulent and romantic, it was also primarily about escape: escape from the realities of modern life. For some time after the war, that was exactly what the world had wanted.

Male designers now dressed women either as exquisite archetypes or as experiments in geometry and colour, sometimes with little thought for the body underneath. The sheath, the tent, the trumpet, the A line and the H line were executed in lemon yellows, pumpkin oranges and bright sky blue. Buyers began to complain that there was no decisive lead.

However radical and modern these styles appeared, essentially, they alluded to a past where woman was simply decorative. Subtly disempowering her, they implied that the realities of modern life she actually had to manoeuvre just didn't exist. Skirts were sometimes so tight one could hardly walk, and corsets, jackets and dresses had returned to the underlying whale-bone structure of women's grandmothers, squeezing them into the desirable hourglass shape. These clothes were not about comfort. They transformed woman into a beautiful kind of make-believe. Good dressing was dressing up; it was once again about theatre. Against this, Gabrielle's lament 'Dressing women is not a man's job. They dress them badly because they scorn them' at first sounded a dull, disgruntled note.

Meanwhile, hearing of her projected return, one of these, Balenciaga, a gentle and gifted man, who was also a great admirer of Gabrielle's work, declared, 'Chanel is an eternal bomb. None of us can diffuse her,' and sent her a heart-shaped bouquet. She was unable to let down her defensive shield; sadly, she diminished herself by scoffing at this distinguished admirer.

Gabrielle had spent her early professional life trying to dispel the notion that dress should be a disguise. Her success had enabled her to supplant the great creator of what she called 'costume', of make-believe, Poiret, as the Parisian couturier *par excellence*. But this great coup had come about for far more interesting reasons than simply because Gabrielle was a practical realist who didn't like 'costume'. In her own life and designs she was constantly telling her contemporaries that they lived in a 'practical' era. This meant fewer servants, more machines, a more urban life for the majority, and all at a faster pace.

Out of this, Gabrielle's great feat had been to encourage her contemporaries to accept the times in which they lived. Helping to dispel nostalgia and escapist fantasy about the past, she wanted them to accept, embrace and embellish this machine age, which, for all its faults and problems, was the only one they'd got. At their best, Gabrielle's clothes made women feel enabled and exhilarated about taking part in this new world, while at the same time looking sleek, seductive and elegant in an entirely new way. Many of the elements she introduced and made fashionable have become indispensable to a modern female wardrobe: women with short hair; in raincoats; in trousers both day and night; in swimsuits, with costume jewellery and sunglasses; handbags with shoulder straps; and the rightly ubiquitous 'little black dress'.

Gabrielle had promulgated the idea that, if a fashion wasn't taken up and worn by everybody, it wasn't a fashion but an eccentricity. This had helped bring about her greatest offering to the world: fashion that was democratic. This was also, however, her greatest dilemma. What she propounded was a democratic belief in a world (haute couture) at whose heart is the idea of exclusion of the majority (the exclusive). Unlike her fellow designers, who *only* understood the notion of exclusiveness, Gabrielle Chanel knew that any fashion not adopted by the majority was a failure. This, ironically, had also been the source of her waning influence before the war, when Schiaparelli and the Surrealists had led the dance in outrage, anti-taste and eccentricity.

The period before the war was groping its way towards two related thoughts: an increasing disenchantment with authority and the dystopias created, ultimately, as a result of the machine. Fritz Lang's film *Metropolis* had depicted this disenchantment as long ago as 1927. Emerging out of this disillusionment with the modern world, it had been feeling, emotion and the unconscious, as opposed to the rational and the non-feeling machine, which were explored as never before.

Before the First World War, Gabrielle had intuited that this would be the dilemma at the heart of her era. And, rather than shying away from it via nostalgia, she faced it, 'saw' it for what it was, and designed clothes accordingly. On into the period of tumult between the two world wars, her devastatingly simple clothes had sometimes seemed a little too grown up. And, though she would *never* have admitted it, it was very difficult not to be seduced by the powerfully escapist climate of thought in the later thirties and, for a while, she lost her way. Her chief *première* would later say, 'When she re-started, it's really then that she invented, re-invented her style. From my point of view, in 1935 she didn't have a precise style. It's when she came back she invented *le petit Chanel.'*[9]

Gabrielle had had fifteen years to think things over. Times had changed, but she affirmed what she called 'the integrity' of her clothes. Living most of her life at the heart of the narcissistic world of fashion, her puritanical streak led her to say, 'I am against fashion that doesn't last.' While understanding its ephemeral nature better than almost anyone, she had come to the radical belief that fashion's real purpose was not to redefine the way we look, but to tell us who we *are*. This was how she believed that it was a lasting, recognizable style that made women look beautiful and was the bedrock of the best fashion.

Meanwhile, Gabrielle had no intention of being left behind in her elegance, and was fascinated by much of what was new. An underlying shift taking place in her trade was reflected in one of the remarkable new synthetic fabrics, easy-care nylon. Gabrielle had foreseen that the days of haute couture were numbered, that the effects were related to the cost of labour and an age that had little interest in the artisan. An instant effect now mattered more to women than how something was made.

Since the war, every couture house had been preoccupied with how to balance its costs. The collections – meaning the sales of models to a wealthy private clientele of a few thousand women – no longer covered anything like the huge costs of running the couture house. (All labour costs had gone up, in particular the traditionally appalling wages of those at the artisanal level of couture, those who actually *made* the clothes.) Using the cachet of their labels, selling prêt-à-porter was the only path down which the cou-turiers believed they could go. Both a dilemma and contradiction for Gabrielle, like the rest, she saw that prêt-à-porter was an inevit-able part of the future.

Accordingly, through Marie-Louise Bousquet in Paris and Car-mel Snow in the States, she cunningly set up a most innovative deal that would fund her new collection. To coincide with its launch, she negotiated 'Coco Chanel' ready-to-wear originals in New York's fashion district, Seventh Avenue. Gabrielle calculated – correctly – that this would stimulate considerable interest around the world. Not only that, when Pierre Wertheimer got wind of her crafty plan, to his credit, he made an immediate and generous offer. He would like to underwrite half of Gabrielle's new collection's expenses. If it went well, they all knew that the sales of N°5 could only benefit. At seventy, Gabrielle had lost neither her market trader's shrewdness, nor her feminine touch. Once more, her old adversary and friend Wertheimer had been won over.

This coup was part of Gabrielle's carefully considered campaign, in which she refused all interviews. The resulting sense of anticipa-tion meant that, several months before her collection, journalists began dredging up and expounding on old articles and photographs: Gabrielle's thoughts on fashion, her look, her extraordinary friends, and all those famous affairs. The young were amazed by this woman, in whom the press were so interested.

With her retrieved ex-*premières*, to whom she said, 'Come quickly, we only have ten green years,' she had set to work. The *premières* were in only two of the old workrooms high up in 31 rue Cambon, while Gabrielle herself worked from one small room on the third floor, close by her private apartment. With one mannequin alone to work on, and one fitter, an elderly, white-haired woman, this was nothing like the past. But Gabrielle's scissors were, nonetheless, once again hanging authoritatively from around her neck. The task before her was almost insurmountable, and with all in Paris with the vaguest interest in couture waiting on this collection, Gabrielle permitted herself no indulgence, such as speaking of her fears.

Instead, she spelt out her criticism of other – male – 'pederast' designers, whom she decried for designing on paper, rather than on the model's own body as she did:

> To one of the few journalists who were lucky enough to talk to her in the winter of 1953, and who asked her what she was planning to present in her collection, Coco, superb as ever, answered, 'How can you expect me to know? Until the last day I alter, transform. I create my dresses on the mannequins themselves.'[10]

Meanwhile, for 20 December 1953, Jean Cocteau wrote in his diary: 'Sunday with Coco Chanel, Marie-Louise [Bousquet] and [Michel] Déon. Chattered from one till ten at night without saying one nasty thing about anyone. Coco amazingly revivified by re-opening her house.'[11]

The invitation everyone in Paris wanted for 5 February (always 5 to bring luck) 1954, was the one to Gabrielle's show. Select members of Paris society were invited, plus every journalist, photographer, magazine editor and buyer deemed worthy. The night before, as had been Gabrielle's custom, she lay flat on the floor in the grand salon as her models walked past; she was checking the length of their hems.

I prefer disaster to nothingness

Latecomers were locked out, and that even included the editor of the Parisian fashion bible, *L'Officiel de la couture*. Every newly painted gilt seat was filled; towards the back, the staff members of French, British and American *Vogue* stood on their chairs to see. The crush, the suspense were incredible. The first girl appeared carrying her number and walked slowly past the audience. The next girl walked just as sedately. Already, it was abundantly clear that Dior's triumph of a few years earlier was not about to be repeated. One commentator noted acidly:

> A black coat-suit, the skirt of which was neither tight nor loose, with a little white blouse . . . was followed by other suits in rather dull wools, in a wan black, matched joylessly with melancholy prints. The models had the figure of 1930 – no breasts, waists, no hips . . . offering nothing but a fugitive reminder of a time it was difficult to specify . . . What everyone had come for was the atmosphere of the old collections that used to set Paris agog. But none of that was left.[1]

The atmosphere was icy. Glances were exchanged. And when, at last, the show finished, there was a moment's dreadful silence. A pensive and tentative-looking Gabrielle stood in her old position at the top of those mirrored stairs. Traditionally, she had permitted twenty or so of her most privileged friends and admirers to sit on this, the 'spine of her house', to watch the show unfold. This time, unaware of the old protocol, many who hardly knew Gabrielle had crammed themselves on to those notoriously uncomfortable yet much sought 'seats'. *Vogue* would write:

> A spare, taut, compressed figure hung with jewels, Chanel looks as
> she did before the War, except that her widely spaced, lively eyes . . .
> deny the lines around them. That she is a monument to common
> sense, to logical stubbornness, can be seen in her broad, shrewd face
> with the wide mouth pulled straight across, the eyebrows deter-
> minedly pencilled. Her hands are powerful, broad-knuckled; her
> sculptor's strong fingers have unpolished nails.

Then, with the last dress, there was a sudden hubbub and the audience was in a rush to get away. Only a handful of friends remained,
including Hervé Mille, Maggie van Zuylen and Gabrielle's faithful
première, Madame Lucie. They strained to congratulate Gabrielle, but
she was devastated, silent. While her lawyer would say later, 'She
accepted defeat with a great deal of dignity, a dignity based on self-
confidence,' she also implored Madame Lucie to tell her, had she lost
her touch? Unquestionably, memories of Gabrielle's war record were
in the air. Nonetheless, while a good number in the fashion firmament had – to a greater or lesser degree – themselves been
collaborators, they would have ingratiated themselves quickly
enough if they'd thought Gabrielle's new collection passed muster.

Meanwhile, one of those whose judgement may in part have been
based on criticism of her war record was Lucien François. François, a
journalist from *Combat*, whose power enabled him to make or break
reputations, and who was secretly and passionately loathed, insinu-
ated that Gabrielle had had a facelift, and dismissed her: 'With the
first dress we realized that the Chanel style belongs to other days.
Fashion has evolved in fifteen years . . . Chanel has become a legend
idealized in retrospect.' He ended with the acid comment: 'Paris society turned out yesterday to devour the lion tamer . . . we saw not the
future but a disappointing reflection of the past, into which a pretentious little black figure was disappearing with giant steps.'[2]

While the French press described the beauty of the mannequins,
and declared that Gabrielle was still a 'personality', it also weighed

in with the opinion that, as a designer, she was finished. The response by the British press was just as negative. The headlines announced: 'Chanel Dress Show a Fiasco – audience gasped!' One article said, 'Once you're faded it takes more than a name and memories of past triumphs to put you in the spotlight.' In a daze, Gabrielle said quietly, 'The French are too intelligent, they will return to me.'[3] Afterwards, she blamed no one for the show's failure except the press – particularly the French press. There was, however, to be one major exception: the United States.

The outgoing Parisian editor of American *Vogue*, Bettina Ballard, was being assisted by Susan Train, a young American, who had come from New York three years earlier, in a 'cold and not that glamorous post-war Paris'. Sitting in the *Vogue* offices, in the magnificent place du Palais-Bourbon, with the experience of hundreds of collections now behind her, she recalls that day in 1954:

> All of Paris knew about it. And American *Vogue* had decided they were going to do a story on Chanel for the February 15 issue [in those days, *Vogue* came out bi-monthly], and the main collections issue would be in the first week of March . . . Although they cut it in the end, the article started like this, 'Trying to direct the flow of Mademoiselle Chanel's conversation is like trying to deflect Niagara with a twig,' which is absolutely brilliant, because so true!

With the photographer Henry Clarke, Susan was amazed 'to discover the mythical Chanel was still alive', and remembers that:

> People at French *Vogue* had a totally different take. Naturally, because they'd been here during the war and she was 'mal vue', viewed with disapproval . . . After all, staying on at the Ritz and having a German lover and so forth, that was not very acceptable. Particularly poor Michel de Brunhoff [editor of French *Vogue*] . . . He never got over his son, it broke his heart. What he thought and said about Chanel . . . he was outraged.[4]

Susan recalls how 'all Paris was in a buzz, and that practically every designer had paid tribute to Gabrielle's comeback by trying to anticipate what she would do with a little Chanely look some-where.' But when the day of Gabrielle's show arrived, 'it was a nightmare. It was like going back in a time capsule . . . Dior had changed everything.' Indeed, quite apart from the collection itself, Dior had transformed the idea of a couture collection from a sed-ate and rather stately masque, to a fast-moving, stylish and seductive show. In addition, he had decorated his svelte models with a brilliant display of accessories; something that Gabrielle had never done. And now here she was, stubbornly ignoring Dior's effect on the tenor and tempo of fashion. Susan Train remembers how:

At Chanel nothing had changed. The show took forever. There were no accessories . . . Just dresses, shoes. There were no hats, gloves, no jewellery . . . and clothes that had absolutely nothing to do with what was going on: 'It was famously a disaster' . . . We came out, we got into the car . . . there was this deathly silence, and Jessica Daves said, with her Southern drawl, 'Well, Bettina, do you really think that the collection we have just seen is worthy of the opening pages of *Vogue*'s Collection Report?'

Bettina Ballard told her young colleagues that, actually, it was no worse than some of Gabrielle's collections in the late thirties, and suggested a photo shoot to see what they thought. Accordingly, that evening, Susan went with Bettina Ballard and Henry Clarke to Cha-nel, where they selected pieces from the collection. Bettina chose three or four of these and sent Susan down to the boutique with instructions to gather up whatever jewellery she could lay her hands on. (There was apparently very little to choose from.) She recalls Bettina Ballard's familiarity with Gabrielle, saying, 'She had an intimate knowledge of how she dressed, and had lent Bettina clothes.' Bettina encouraged her young colleagues with the com-ment, 'There was always something in a Chanel collection that was worth it,' and Susan describes her 'picking out that suit. She just knew it was going to start a whole new thing.'⁵

Susan says that there was an American manufacturer, Davidol, who had continued making Chanel suits throughout the war, and on into the fifties: 'how much American women loved them . . . And the new one was easy, because it was so comfortable and yet elegant.' She continues:

> And Bettina Ballard bought that suit herself. She not only bought it but she wore it for the Fashion Group Import Show meeting in New York, where all the retailers were shown the clothes that had been bought and brought over from Paris. Bettina stood up in her Chanel suit and said, 'Mark my words; this is the beginning of a new thing.' And of course it was!⁶

This was the navy suit Bettina Ballard had Henry Clarke photograph, and worn by Marie-Hélène Arnaud. It was mid-calf (Dior's highly fashionable couture was only just below the knee), and made of jersey, with an easy skirt with pockets, a semi-fitted open jacket and a white lawn blouse topped off by a pert straw boater. This was Gabrielle's version of the Chanel suit she had initiated before the war. In 1954, to those who could see it, the suit gave an overwhelming impression of insouciant, youthful elegance, and Gabrielle was to continue perfecting it for the rest of her life.

The other two costumes Ballard selected for the *Vogue* photo shoot were worn by Suzy Parker, the magnificent, red-headed American, then perhaps the highest-paid model in the world. One dress was in a draped and clinging rose wool-jersey, while the other was a mad, strapless evening dress. *Vogue* described this as 'tiers of the most modern of fabrics, bubbly nylon seersucker in bright navy-blue, with huge full-blown roses attached'. Gabrielle explained to the magazine how she was now looking beyond the couture: 'I will dress thousands of women. I will start with a collection . . . because I must start this way. It won't be a revolution. It won't be shocking. Changes must not be brutal, must not be made all of a sudden. The eye must be given time to adapt itself to a new thought.'

Maggie van Zuylen's daughter, Marie-Hélène, who had married Baron Guy de Rothschild, had helped Gabrielle find her new models. They were, like Marie-Hélène Rothschild, well-bred society girls, who knew how to 'carry' clothes. Young women such as the Comtesse Mimi D'Arcangues, Princesse Odile de Croÿ, Jacqueline de Merindol, Claude de Leusse, Vera Valdez. They were all subjected both to the hours of 'posing' for Gabrielle, and the accompanying advice on life and love: 'There is a time for work and a time for love. That leaves no other time' was a much repeated adage. Gabrielle was ambivalent about these girls. While she liked to know about their private lives – who they were seeing, the details of their affairs – she also criticized them for going out with men who weren't particularly rich. They defended themselves by saying that their boyfriends were handsome and fun. Gabrielle was not convinced.

The girls later described how Gabrielle's instinct for promotion led her to give them Chanel couture for most of their wardrobe. Their connections meant that they 'went everywhere, and she knew it. People called us "les blousons Chanel".'

With Gabrielle's lacerating tongue, she would say, 'Yes, my girls are pretty, and that's why they do this job. If they had any brains, they'd stop.' She also claimed that, rather than needing beauty, her models must possess poise and style in the way they carried themselves: 'Only the figure, the carriage, the ability to walk exquisitely.' Several of them happened to be some of the most beautiful girls in Paris. Gabrielle believed her models were mistaken, in not using their looks more ambitiously, and in their goals, which were love and happiness. Their lack of ambition irritated her, and she charged them to 'take rich lovers'. Her own failure to remain with any man meant that Gabrielle was obliged to believe the independence she had worked so hard for was more important than enslavement to a vain search for happiness.

While Gabrielle would, on occasion, say that she didn't really like her models, she also became much attached to a handful of them, most famously, Marie-Hélène Arnaud. Indeed, for some time after Gabrielle's return to couture, this beautiful young woman was, apparently, almost 'like her shadow'. Some thought their relationship was too intense. When Marie-Hélène arrived at Chanel, she was seventeen, and according to Lilou Marquand loved Gabrielle:

> as one loves one's creator. She was incapable of contradicting her, or even of replying to her. She followed her everywhere as if she were her shadow, and never balked at criticism. Everyone was pushing her to express herself more, but she could barely finish a sentence. What use was it anyway? Mademoiselle loved her as much as she would her own daughter and that was enough for her. She had many suitors but none of them ever managed to take her away from the rue Cambon for more than a weekend.

Gabrielle encouraged Marie-Hélène to have steady relationships – but was also very possessive. Marie-Hélène said to Lilou Marquand, 'You understand, I have problems.'[7] The young woman was herself quite possessive of Gabrielle and, for a time, almost acted as an intermediary between the little court, soon dancing attendance upon her mistress and the outside world.

The gossips, meanwhile, assumed that Gabrielle's feelings for Marie-Hélène went beyond simple affection. The other models believed, too, that they were lovers. One of them says, 'At any rate that's what was being said in the *cabine* [the models' dressing room]. It didn't shock me at all, I thought it was very natural.'[8] Gabrielle stoutly denied the rumours, saying, 'You must be crazy – an old garlic like me. Where do people get those ideas from?' This was not the first time such rumours had been abroad about Gabrielle and, over the years, they would persist. Neither does one believe that Gabrielle really cared that much. For over fifty years, she had been the subject of gossip, and she had never let it make any difference to the way she chose to lead her life. And while *Women's Wear Daily* journalist Thelma Sweetinburgh would say that Gabrielle's bisexuality 'was a sort of known thing', a young French woman on the staff of American *Vogue* at the time remembers, 'I had to go once to see her, and was told to be careful. I believed, and all others did, too, that Chanel was bi-sexual. One assumed it to be the case. British and French laws were different. It wasn't illegal in France and people were just less fussed about it really.'[9]

Assisted by her atelier and her mannequins, Gabrielle had returned from Switzerland with the intention of overcoming her opponents: those who reviled her war record and those who believed her work was now part of history. And, during the course of 1954, what had at first appeared a disaster was set to become Gabrielle's triumph. In November 1954, *Elle* put Suzy Parker on its cover in a seductive red Chanel suit and a pill-box hat, all trimmed around in fur.

As Gabrielle's success became undeniable, she was asked why she had returned. She replied, 'I was bored. It took me fifteen years to realize it. Today, I prefer disaster to nothingness.' Laying bare the drive that almost became her curse, in the years without work, Gabrielle had been lost, up against her demons and her loneliness. But, by 1957, she was sailing triumphantly for America.

This was supposedly to accept what was then America's greatest fashion accolade, the Neiman Marcus Fashion Oscar, in Dallas. However, while Dior had been awarded the Oscar before her, and Gabrielle had refused to follow in his footsteps, she allowed herself to be enticed to America because it was the fiftieth anniversary of the Neiman Marcus stores. As ever, alert to a publicity opportunity, she agreed to an interview with the *New Yorker.* Gabrielle informed the reporter that, in 1954, her reaction to her initially poor reception – everywhere except America – had been defiance: 'I thought, I will show them! In America, there was great enthusiasm. In France I had to fight. But I did not mind. I love very much to battle. Now, in France they are trying to adapt my ideas. So much the better!'

Succumbing to Gabrielle's wiles, the reporter wrote:

We've met some formidable charmers in our time, but none to surpass the great couturier and perfumer, Mlle Gabrielle Chanel, who came out of retirement . . . to present a collection of dresses and suit designs that have begun to affect women's styles every bit as power-fully as her designs of thirty years ago . . . She was fresh from three strenuous weeks here in Dallas . . . at seventy-four, Mlle Chanel is sensationally good-looking, with dark-brown eyes, a brilliant smile, and the unquenchable vitality of a twenty-year-old . . . 'I liked very much Texas. The people of Dallas, Ah, je les aime beaucoup. Très gentils, très charmants, très simples.'

Not long after this, Bettina Ballard wrote of her disappointment that many women no longer appeared to think for themselves; that 'their very conformity in wearing what the stores or magazines tell them to, proves their lack of personal interest. They don't mind spending money; it is the time and the boredom of shopping they resent. If anyone will take the burden off their shoulders they are happy.' Ballard cites the then-new notion of personal dressers, describing it as like 'eating pre-digested breakfast food. Imagine a Daisy Fellowes or any of the pre-war ladies of fashion allowing any-one to choose a handkerchief for them! Fortunately for those who work in fashion, women now ask for nothing better than to be led, bullied, dictated to, and given as little freedom of choice as possi-ble.'[10] Ballard appealed to them, saying that they were the ultimate critics, they shouldn't always listen to the 'experts' and should think for themselves. She went on to say:

Another proof of this hidden power is the way women took the Chanel look to their hearts and bodies. It is true that the press, par-ticularly *Vogue*, spread the word . . . that Chanel was back designing after fifteen years, but left to the press, the rebirth of the Chanel look would have lasted at the very most two seasons. By the very laws of change, the press, the manufacturers, and the stores, would not have dared to go on promoting this look season after season, if women hadn't found Chanel completely to their taste and stubbornly demanded more of her type of clothes.[11]

Meanwhile, Gabrielle continued beguiling the *New Yorker* reporter with her undimmed allure. Flicking the ash off the last drags of her cigarette, she said:

As for myself, I am not interested any more in 1957. It is gone for me. I am more interested in 1958, 1959, 1960. Women have always been the strong ones in the world. Men are always seeking from women a little pillow to put their heads down on. They are always longing for the mother who held them in her arms as an infant. Women must tell them always *they* are the ones. *They* are the big, the strong, and the wonderful. In truth, women are the strong ones . . . It is the truth for me.[12]

Having first said she was 'too tired, too bored', Gabrielle agreed to attend a dinner given for her by the famously suave and yet eccentric *Vogue* editor Diana Vreeland, whom she had known since the thirties. Gabrielle would only attend on condition that the evening would be intimate and she wouldn't feel obliged to speak. Accompanied by someone Vreeland described as a 'very charming Frenchman', once there, Gabrielle spoke without ceasing. Halfway through the evening, she asked if 'Helena' could join them. When Helena Rubinstein arrived, she and Chanel withdrew to Vreeland's husband's study. After some time, their hostess went in to see if they were all right:

They hadn't moved . . . and stayed in there the rest of the evening talking about God knows what . . . They never sat down. They stood – like men – and talked for hours. I'd never been in the presence of such strength of personality . . . Neither of them was a real beauty. They both came from nothing. They both were much richer than most of the men we talk about today being rich.[13]

While saying that Gabrielle had 'an utterly malicious tongue', Vreeland also had great admiration for her, and added, 'But that was Coco – she said a lot of things. So many things are said . . . and in the end it makes no difference. Coco was never a kind woman . . . but she was the most interesting person *I've* ever met.'[14] Vreeland mixed with some of the most interesting people of her day.

Gabrielle had told the *New Yorker* reporter, 'I am not young, but I feel young. The day I feel old, I will go to bed and stay there. *J'aime la vie!* I feel that to live is a wonderful thing.' And, over the coming seasons, this youthful septuagenarian made strapless evening dresses of embroidered organdie, and quantities of others in satins, chiffons, plain and printed, brocades, velvets, lamés and some of the most avant-garde, manmade fabrics. Then there was the lace Gabrielle used to such effect for effortlessly chic and alluring below-the-knee cocktail dresses, or a longer, black-lace, boned, strapless sheath, with a trumpet-shaped skirt over stiffened, black net-petticoats.

As the fifties wore on, and her success continued, in each collection, there were always the variations on the suit: these were soon selling over seven thousand a year. More than twenty years later, Diana Vreeland would say, 'These post-war suits of Chanel were designed God knows *when*, but the tailoring, the line, the shoulders, the underarms, the *jupe* – never too short . . . is even today the right thing to wear.'[15]

And a new generation of the best-dressed women in the world was wearing Chanel Nº5, once more the most popular perfume in the world. Not only Gabrielle's old friend Marlene Dietrich, and other luminaries, such as Diana Vreeland, but also younger celebrities wanted to become her clients. These included the actresses Grace Kelly, Elizabeth Taylor, Lauren Bacall and Ingrid Bergman. In the sixties, Gabrielle would attract to 31 rue Cambon yet more young women from the stage and screen: Anouk Aimée, Gina Lollobrigida, Delphine Seyrig, Romy Schneider, Jeanne Moreau and Catherine Deneuve. And, while Gabrielle was particularly attached to Schneider and Moreau, she saw Elizabeth Taylor and her then husband Richard Burton on their visits to France. When Gabrielle was asked whether she didn't think Elizabeth Taylor wore her Chanel suits rather too tightly buttoned – over that famously ample bosom – she replied, 'There is one . . . who can do anything, that is Elizabeth Taylor . . . She is a real star.'

Bettina Ballard wrote:

> There was an unorganized revolt building up in women against the whimsy changes of fashion, many of which ridiculed the wearers, and Chanel came along . . . to be the leader of this revolt. The young joined as her followers . . . and now there is a whole new generation aware of the good-taste connotations of the 'Chanel Look'. She will certainly go down in history as the only couturier who spanned the taste space of almost half a century without ever changing her basic conception of clothes.[16]

In 1959, *Vogue* wrote:

> If fashion has taken a turn to the woman, no one can deny that much of the impetus for that turn stems from Coco Chanel – the fierce, wise, wonderful, and completely self-believing Chanel . . . it is not that other Paris collections are like Chanel's . . . But the heady idea that a woman should be more important than her clothes, and that it takes superb design to keep her looking that way – this idea, which has been for almost forty years the fuel for the Chanel engine, has now permeated the fashion world.[17]

This acclaim, from one of the most influential fashion magazines in the world, was also a precise rendering of Gabrielle's mantra: that clothes, rather than dominating a woman, should be the background to her personality. Gabrielle's comment that 'the eccentricity should be in the woman not the dress,' had been central to the most austere version of this philosophy, the now-legendary 'little black dress'. And, while Gabrielle herself was sufficiently characterful that she had always outshone her clothes, they also acted as her 'shield'. Her assistant, Lilou Marquand, would say, 'Maybe that was Mademoiselle's genius: her clothes were a protection. In my suit, I was certain to look my best. No more worrying about one's appearance, image, and line: I could think of something else. Living in Chanel gave a safety which, for Mademoiselle, was worth all the holidays in the world.'[18]

Although Gabrielle vehemently denied the criticism sometimes now levelled, that her collections didn't change, her suit, in particular, was endlessly refined and had become unfailingly recognizable as a 'Chanel'. While this description irritated Gabrielle, she did indeed repeat a formula with different materials, and rang the changes with the details – the buttons, the braids, the linings. But this was the point: wearing a Chanel suit, one had no need to worry about one's appearance. It has been said many times before, that these suits were a kind of uniform. But, as with a uniform, where everyone apparently looks the same, as Gabrielle said of her black 'Ford' dresses, in such clothing, the individuality of the wearer is brought out rather than submerged.

By the late fifties, Gabrielle had created all her signature elements: the 'little black dresses', the smart trousers, the costume jewellery, sling-back shoes with contrasting toe-caps, pert hats, the delicate lace evening dresses, the comfortable yet elegant jersey dresses, the suits of bouclé, or Prince of Wales check, with their distinctive Chanel buttons, all with chains to ensure the jackets sat well, and linings often matching the accompanying blouse, the 1955 quilted leather or jersey bags with those gilt chain shoulder straps, and now the big bows gathering up Gabrielle's models' short bouffant hair. And, no matter what may have been said about how often these elements appeared, they were also thought worth emulating by other designers, and by women across the world.

After Gabrielle's long hiatus, despite her seventy-one years, in 1954, her thirst for work seemed as unquenchable as ever. And, as had been her custom, she drove her models and her staff as much as she drove herself, almost to distraction. If those who worked for her were not strong enough, or didn't have enough respect for her, they left. It would be said that Gabrielle ruled by intimidation: 'As to really contradicting her . . . only her friend Maggie [van Zuylen] . . . dared to throw a glass of beer in her face; for the rest, her employees were too afraid of her.'[19] Gabrielle's small court – that kind that typically grows up around a couturier – of course had its sycophants, but all those who worked for her did not fear her. Like her friends, several had made the decision to accept her for what she was.

When the French philosopher and literary theorist Roland Barthes wrote his essays on the language of fashion,[20] he nailed Gabrielle as a classic rather than an innovator. While also declaring her a rebel, he described her recent declaration of war on the other designers: 'It is said Chanel keeps fashion from falling into barbarism and endows it with all the classical virtues: reason, naturalness, permanency, and a taste for pleasing rather than a taste for shocking.' Barthes described Gabrielle's unwillingness to take part in the annual fashion 'vendetta', where what has gone before is now dead. However, while his critique of Gabrielle is a good one, in the past she had been an innovator, and 'reason, permanency, [and] a taste for pleasing rather than shocking' are *not* the attributes of a rebel.

By 1964, Gabrielle did indeed feel that barbarism was walking the streets, with the advent of a new designer. André Courrèges was a former cutter at Balenciaga and had created a sensation with his 'modernist' clothes. Breaking with tradition, both in his styles and his use of fabric, such as plastic, he called his 1964 collection 'Space Age' and had his mannequins dancing 'the jerk' as they moved down the runway. In 1965, Courrèges, along with Mary Quant in Britain, would claim to be the inventor of the mini-skirt. Soon Gabrielle's favourite *bête noire*, Courrèges, refused to accept her criticisms and said, 'I am the Matra, the Ferrari, Chanel is the Rolls Royce: functional but static.' Courrèges's challenge to Gabrielle's notion of dress was genuinely original. And she sensed that his style was closer to the new spirit of the age than her own was.

Gabrielle felt further threatened when young Jeanne Moreau first 'defected' to Pierre Cardin, whose work Gabrielle loathed; she even went so far as to live with him. Gabrielle broke with her young friend.

In May 1968, when student protest swept the world, for a month

Paris was in chaos. And, just as de Gaulle had sounded out of touch to those political reformists, so Gabrielle now sounded out of date to many of her fellow couturiers, intent on their own rebellion. They were young and couldn't help but be affected by the anti-establishment youth culture of the late sixties. Raw, immature, naive, self-absorbed and idealistic as it was, their rebellion was also expressed in the new street-style of the young, deliberately breaking the old rules of elegance and luxuriating in a kind of theatrical 'anti-dressing'.

Gabrielle cried out in protest, 'They like the street. They want to shock. They try to be amusing. For me fashion is not amusing,' and she repeated her mantra: 'The eccentricity should be in the woman not the dress.' Gabrielle's own obsession with youth – she hated growing older – as a vital, creative thing was in opposition to what she saw as the destructive force abroad in the late sixties. But no matter how much the old lady thundered, the young were set against their elders and their elegance; it was anathema.

As Gabrielle grew more defensive about her competition from the young, she didn't confine herself to pouring scorn on Courrèges alone. In 1969, for example, she would use the announcement of the dreadful-sounding musical *Coco*, in New York, with Katharine Hepburn playing Gabrielle, to denounce her fellow designers, via journalists from press and radio invited to her apartment in the rue Cambon. Sitting in her salon on the famous sofa, Gabrielle spoke of the degradation of modern fashion. Its present meandering infuriated her. She hated the mini-skirt, said knees were horrible, and that 'fashion today is nothing but a question of skirt length. High fashion is doomed because it is in the hands of the kind of men who do not like women and wish to make fun of them. Men dress like women; women dress like men . . . No one is ever satisfied . . . Men used to woo and be tender . . . Boredom of every kind has become an institution.' These and more such remarks were calculated to stir up controversy.

Amongst fashion designers in France, there had long been a tradition of showing respect for Coco Chanel but, after Gabrielle's latest diatribe, several no longer bothered with such *politesse*. Paco Rabanne, Louis Féraud, Philippe Heim, Marc Bohan (Dior), Guy Laroche, Pierre Balmain – all retaliated with comments in their own way as withering as Gabrielle's. Pierre Balmain was more reserved and attempted to keep his comments impersonal. But he voiced the thoughts of all of them when he said:

> It is regrettable that Mademoiselle Chanel chooses to ignore the history of costume. But she knows that every period has been marked by a certain style of dress, imposing the tendencies and tastes of the times, which the designers can do no more than express, each according to his manner . . . Mademoiselle Chanel has every right to be against the short skirt. Nonetheless, this time, she is far from having the unanimous agreement of her colleagues.

What this young man, and most of his contemporaries, did not understand was that, rather than only having reflected her times – the accustomed description of fashion's role – Gabrielle had been amongst the few who had *led* hers.

Meanwhile, she still had a loyal following, plus the voyeurs who came to her shows, because she had become a kind of monument. However, there were also empty seats, and the audience wasn't jostling to congratulate her afterwards. And, while the fashion house remained a significant 'motivating force for the promotion and sales of the perfumes',[21] Gabrielle also admitted, 'The House of Chanel is doing well, but fewer orders are being turned down.'[22] In fact, she no longer 'made fashion news'. And, in those moments when she dropped her guard to reveal her vulnerability, Gabrielle was apprehensive and uncertain. At the same time, she was far too intelligent not to appreciate that society was going through radical changes, and observed that 'in the time we're living in now . . . Nothing any more fits in with the lives people lead.'[23] And her thoughts of more than half a century earlier spring to mind: 'One world was ending, another was about to be born . . . I was in the right place . . . I had grown up with this new century: I was therefore the one to be consulted about its sartorial style.'[24]

Gabrielle was, though, no longer the first to be consulted about style. Instead, she had become a public figure, whose time was bound up with serving her legendary name. How else was she to absorb that still remarkable physical and emotional energy? But while her frequently abrasive manner drove others to see less of her, there was a small group of young admirers who were more patient.

Gabrielle had always refused to be interviewed for television but, in 1969, her friend the Opéra Comique dancer Jacques Chazot, who had made himself into an indispensable young society figure, wanted to make Gabrielle the first subject of a television series on famous women. He was overjoyed when she agreed. Gabrielle saw much of Chazot and believed that she could trust him. Without any rehearsals or script, in that soft, low voice, belying the incisive authority of her manner, Gabrielle held forth on camera for twenty-five minutes. She concluded with the pronouncement 'Well, if they're not pleased with this, what do they want?'[25]

Editing the interview, Chazot was in a torment of indecision until, eventually, he decided he would cut nothing. Bringing along his friend, the rebellious and already iconic writer Françoise Sagan, they watched it with Gabrielle. Her trust in Chazot had been well placed; she pronounced it 'very good'. Having been rather slow off the mark, the French television service now realized the interview's potential and readjusted their programming schedule with it in a prime slot.

The response was tremendous. Chazot received all kinds of filming offers, and Gabrielle was gratified to receive a huge quantity of approving mail.

Meanwhile, the younger designers, irritated by Gabrielle's lack of indulgence over their work, were unable to see that much of their 'rebellious decade' was simply a mass-culture version of the cataclysmic changes Gabrielle had experienced with that small and extraordinarily creative group of people either side of the First World War. And, while her complaints were not all justified, essentially, they were more far sighted. And at the heart of her complaints was something more significant than an irritable old woman's aversion to change.

Gabrielle had not been uniquely responsible for changing women's appearance during the first decades of the century. While undoubtedly one of only a handful of initiators of a new, easy kind of female glamour, Gabrielle was different in that she herself *lived* the emancipated life her clothes were made for. Talking of having 'liberated the body', she had 'made fashion honest'. More than any other designer, Gabrielle had been responsible for the democratization of fashion; making it more accessible to the majority than ever before. Her own radical life and work had gone hand in hand with the rise of political *democracy*, yet as a fashion designer, she had overcome the dilemma this created for the couturier: how to be *exclusive*. An American's compliment, that she had 'spent so much money without it showing', delighted her.[26] Of all the couturiers, Gabrielle had walked the finest line in dressing the rich as the poor; in other words, with simplicity.

While often contradictory, the source of Gabrielle's reaction to the sixties was that she had never been interested in *attacking* culture. She had espoused a different – and in some ways more serious – kind of liberation for women. Gabrielle was now old, and critical, but she also understood that jeans (originally work wear) were subtly different from her appropriation of fishermen's tops or her lover's polo shirt for women. Their new glamour was based upon living more emancipated, modern lives. In Chazot's interview, for example, her point was serious when she said, 'I do not approve of the Mao style; I think it's disgraceful and idiotic . . . the idea of amusing oneself with such games, with such formidable countries, I think it's dreadful.'[27]

When it came to mini-skirts, while Gabrielle's objections revealed her age, she was also capable of saying, 'I have no right to criticize, because [the time] isn't mine. Mine is over . . . Frequently I feel so alien to everything around me. What do people live for now? I don't understand them.'[28] And then she made one of those typical comments, requiring a moment's trouble and reflection to understand,

and revealing her comprehension of those tumultuous times: 'I'm very well aware that everyone is out of date.'[29]

Age had some time ago crept up on the woman who had remained so perennially youthful, and her arthritis and rheumatism now grew more painful. To counteract the pain, and 'inconvenience', she swallowed quantities of vitamins, painkillers and sedatives. Then, despite her doubts and apprehension about the sixties, and while she had enough self-knowledge to be able to say, 'Sometimes I realize I'm ridiculous,' she continued, driven by work. Gabrielle had understood long ago that work is vital to who we are. However, setting aside the striving involved in creativity, work consumed her, was her *raison d'être*. In the process, it had become her demon master. But, as with the drugs – the only means by which poor Gabrielle could find any rest at night – she needed to dull her sense of isolation; in her waking hours, it was only through work that she found some sense of peace.

In a quieter moment, she would also confide to one of her last intimates her belief that 'a woman is a force not properly directed. A man is properly directed. He can find refuge in his work. But work just wipes a woman out. The function of a woman is to be loved.' And she confessed her feeling that 'my life is a failure. Don't you think it's a failure, to work as I work?'[30] This formidably powerful yet always feminine woman, who had found consolation in work, also believed that women 'ought to play their weakness never their strength. They ought to hide that . . . One ought to say "yes but" . . . in other words play the fish.'[31]

I only hear my heart on the stairs

Gabrielle's aversion to any kind of constraint had not diminished with the years; she was defiant: 'I never settle down anywhere, I've chosen freedom.' Stimulated by the unpredictable, she remained irritated by much organization, and 'loathed people putting order into my disorder or into my mind,'[1] declaring, 'Order bores me. Disorder has always seemed to me the very symbol of luxury.'[2] And, while the houses she had owned were beautiful and innovative in their design, she also said, 'It's not the houses I love, it's the life I live in them.'

In her Hôtel Ritz suite, and her apartment on the rue Cambon, meanwhile, Gabrielle had created sumptuous and atmospheric surroundings, luxurious interiors filled with private symbols. Yet the apartment at 31 rue Cambon was never at heart a domestic one. Gabrielle had entertained many friends there over the years, but she also conducted business there. Someone now very familiar with the apartment describes it as 'the place where she kept her memories, her links with her close friends, and her past. But if it had been a really intimate, personal apartment it would have had a bedroom. In some ways she lived her life like a man.'[3] Neither was there a kitchen at rue Cambon; Gabrielle had food brought in. And, while she could juxtapose grandeur with simplicity and the severity with comfort, in truth, Gabrielle had little interest in the hearth.

A hotel, where she slept and ate most of her meals, is essentially an un-domestic space, and its underlying atmosphere of transition precisely served Gabrielle's needs. Although she lived in the Ritz for more than seventeen years, in theory, at any moment she could be on her way: 'In a hotel I feel I am travelling.' An echo of her nomadic childhood – in whose recollection Gabrielle often spoke of trains – this existence also represented her undaunted and slightly cracked refusal to be tied down. Her openness to the possibility of change in turn represented the possibility of creativity, leading her to say, 'When I can no longer create, I'm done for.'[4]

By contrast, the symbols of others' rootedness affected Gabrielle more adversely as she grew older. For example, she hated Sundays. Traditionally the family day, it was also the one when her salon was closed, making it more difficult to divert herself – with work – from admitting her sense of isolation. She professed to dislike marriage, and children, and on occasion used her unerring capacity for fantasy to erase spouses and their progeny from the lives of those around her. In the same spirit, she was quite capable of trying to destabilize a relationship. Good ones unsettled her. Gabrielle could also quietly admit to the one member of her family with whom she remained close, her namesake, Gabrielle Labrunie, 'Actually, it's you who has been right in life. You are much happier than I am. You have a husband and children. I have nothing. I am alone with all my millions.'[5] Gabrielle told one of her favourite models, 'I envy you because I always wanted to have children, and I had an abortion and I could never have any. It's not true when I say that I find children disgusting.'[6]

In the late sixties, when Gabrielle was in her late eighties and had become more famous still, she was once again acceptable to most of France. Yet, while this enabled her to go anywhere and meet almost anyone, this usually left her unimpressed. There was, however, the odd exception. Claude Pompidou, elegant wife to de Gaulle's prime minister, had for some time been one of Gabrielle's clients, and she realized that Gabrielle would like an invitation to the Elysée Palace. De Gaulle's permission must be sought. Eventually, he agreed, and Gabrielle went – accompanied by her friend, ex-prefect of police and ambassador André-Louis Dubois – to dine alone with the Pompidous. Claude Pompidou found Gabrielle beautiful, wonderfully dressed; intelligently observed her complexity, her failings, her 'boldness', and yet still found her fascinating.

Gabrielle had many years ago nurtured her image, now she was tending her legend. And while saying, 'May my legend gain ground, I wish it a long and happy life!'[7] she had also become its victim. Unable sometimes to distinguish it from herself, she had said some years before, 'my legendary fame . . . each of us has his or her legend, foolish and wonderful. Mine, to which Paris and the provinces, idiots and artists, poets and society people have contributed, is so varied, so complex, so straightforward and so complicated at the same time, that I lose myself within it.'[8] Her friend, the novelist Michel Déon recently recalled to me how 'with time, she turned a cynical eye on her milieu . . . She didn't care, because being a celebrity no longer went to her head. I have rarely seen someone desire victory so much and then so disdain its rewards.'[9]

Gabrielle's friends were only temporarily able to hold back her solitude, in which she had become imprisoned and, one day, she posed a mournful question to one of them: 'What's going to happen to me? What can I do? . . . In bed at night I say to myself: "Why do you put up such a front? Why don't you dump all that?"'[10] But she couldn't. She talked on, through shyness and through fear. Indeed, years before, she had declared with that startling self-awareness, 'I prattled away out of shyness . . . How many windbags, mocked for their self-assurance, are simply quiet people who, deep down, are frightened of silence?'[11] Meanwhile, that 'prattling' public self made a habit of toughness and self-aggrandizement: 'So much insensitivity . . . the jewellery, the rings on her thin fingers . . . the monologues, the Chanel jargon, with the opinions, the judgements without appeal.'[12] It was as if poor Gabrielle had welded her armour of self-protection to her mind and frequently to her heart. Her inner plight, accurately described by a young friend as the 'truant furies', had overtaken her.

Her solitude had deepened even further with the deaths of her oldest friends and ex-lovers. Hardly had the war ended than José Maria Sert had gone. Then, in 1950, Misia, whom she had loved, and hated, for so many years, and who knew so many of Gabrielle's secrets they had both long since dispensed with any pretence. In 1953, the Duke of Westminster, with whom, as with Dmitri Pavlov-ich, Gabrielle had always remained on close terms, died of a heart attack, after only six years of his final and happiest marriage. The sympathetic, horse-mad Etienne Balsan, who had recognized that, in Sachs's words, 'Her spirit and her heart were unforgettable,' had rescued Gabrielle from her servitude: he died in South America. Following his daughter's marriage and removal to Rio de Janeiro, Etienne had gone there, too. His wish to die quickly had been answered, when he was run over by a bus, in 1954.

When Adrienne de Nexon (née Chanel) died, in 1955, she took to her grave the most intimate details and appreciation of Gabrielle's background. At Solesmes, in 1960, when Pierre Reverdy – the man for whom Coco 'would have gladly given up everything' – died, only his wife and the monks were present at his simple funeral. Like all the rest, Gabrielle only heard about it through the papers. In 1963, Jean Cocteau, whom she had supported and denigrated for more than half a century, died too. And, on Pierre Wertheimer's passing, in 1965, she lost the man who for so long had fulfilled for her the stimulating role of beloved adversary. In 1969, the ageing Paul Morand would write in his journal: 'We are the last ones, the survivors. We talk of people, of stories which only Cocteau, Poulenc, Radiguet, Etienne de Beaumont, Misia could understand. Only Chanel remains.'[13]

In 1960, when Gabrielle's favourite, Marie-Hélène Arnaud, had been employed by her for six years, she told Gabrielle that she didn't want to be a model for ever. Gabrielle tried to keep her by hiring her father, an academic, at a huge salary. Apparently, M. Arnaud had heard that Marie-Hélène was going to be made director of Chanel and would need help. In the hope of dissuading Marie-Hélène from leaving, Gabrielle had hinted at this herself. Marie-Hélène said she felt no animosity towards Gabrielle: 'I loved Coco ... it never crossed my mind that someday I would replace her.' But Gabrielle was unconvinced, felt threatened and, when the young woman did leave – her father followed soon after – Gabrielle spoke ill of them, hurt at what felt like rejection by the lovely Marie-Hélène. Gabrielle turned a good many friends away in these years in a similarly unjust fashion; a few, such as Serge Lifar, put up with her inconstancy, although even he tended to see her less.

As a solace, during these years, Gabrielle came to rely much on her small group of younger friends and assistants. This included her butler, Jean Mironnet – 'François', as she called him – and two or three young women. François, the son of Norman peasants from Cabourg, was a man who didn't speak too much and, unlike Gabrielle's more sophisticated and better informed friends, there was much she could teach him. Whatever his private thoughts, François looked up to her and, a few years before her death, Gabrielle promoted him as a kind of companion. He was often by her side, sat silently behind as she worked on her collections. He kept her pills, gave her the water to take them with, was ready to help if she needed an arm on the stairs, remembered anything she might have forgotten. He was invited to eat with her and accompanied her when she travelled, now only to Switzerland. 'Monsieur François' was Gabrielle's 'quiet gentleman-in-waiting', who did his best to make sure she was rarely alone.

Aside from her models, the significant young women in Gabrielle's life were her great-niece, Gabrielle (Labrunie); Claude Delay, daughter of the psychiatrist Jean Delay; and Lilou Grumbach (née Marquand), Gabrielle's assistant from the late fifties onwards. Lilou Marquand's actor brother was Christian Marquand, friend to Roger Vadim. He was also friend to the Mille brothers, *Paris Match* editor Hervé, and interior designer Gérard. (The Milles' rue de Varennes apartment was one of the most powerful post-liberation Parisian salons, and Gabrielle felt at home there. Hervé and Gérard were old friends, who had known her since 1935, and Hervé regularly did 'battle on her behalf'.) Lilou Marquand, meanwhile, had made a botched attempt at meeting Gabrielle, and asked the Mille brothers for their help. They told her they were going to dinner with

Gabrielle that very evening; why didn't she come along? Someone mentioned to Gabrielle that Lilou would like to work for her, but she made no comment. Then, as everyone was leaving, she said to Lilou, 'You're starting on Monday.'

After Marie-Hélène Arnaud's departure, Lilou found herself being taken more into Gabrielle's confidence. In theory, her job was handling press and public relations; in practice, her role was far more extensive than that. Among other duties, she acquired responsibility for photo shoots and was in charge of the dressing rooms, the *cabines*. Seeing Gabrielle almost every working day for the last fourteen or so years of her life, Lilou came to know her well. She was strong enough to withstand Gabrielle's rages and outspokenness and, while remaining an employee, she also became an intimate. In interview with the author recently, she laughed and said, 'We used to shout at one another. She would scream. You could hear everything we said downstairs, but she'd reply: "I don't give a damn!"' Lilou lost track of how many times over the years Gabrielle had sacked her.

As the sixties had worn on, by day, Gabrielle remained indomitable. As her friend Claude Delay says, she was 'very strong, very violent, not a sweet little character. She was a force. She was exigent. Demanding of herself and of others.'[14] However, in quieter moments, and by night, Gabrielle's vulnerability had grown more disabling. When the end of each working day forced her to halt for the rest she sorely needed, she was increasingly defenceless against the sense of abandonment that now overcame her each night on finding herself alone. The mark left by her mother's emotional and physical frailty had not equipped Gabrielle with that specific emotional strength required to have come to terms with her father's abandonment, and it had lain unresolved. In this way, throughout her life, Gabrielle had suffered inordinately when she felt herself 'left'; be it by man or woman, in life or through death. Her strength of character had enabled her to survive but, without the emotional tools to face her demons, with time, they had grown more frightening. Lilou Marquand would say:

Chanel was everything but serene. After the throes of work came what she called 'the evening's anguish'. Once the sun had set, and the rue Cambon had emptied, she felt powerless, almost without personality: in the now silent hive she remained alone with the guard. Her helplessness was so deep and so moving that I acquired the habit of staying there for dinner once or twice a week.[15]

Claude Delay tells how Gabrielle would say, '"I've wept so much, now I don't cry any more. When one doesn't cry any more it's because one no longer believes in happiness." But she said this because she loved romance. And secretly she always hoped that it might happen. She was always waiting for something to happen . . . But it never did.'[16]

Lilou Marquand, too, witnessed Gabrielle's fantasies, her dreams of an ideal man, and heard stories about Gabrielle's father as the personification of this ideal. On other occasions, he was a wastrel and drunkard. Lilou tells how 'in some ways Chanel had remained very romantic. She liked handsome, tall strong men. When she saw one in the street she always said, "You see, he's probably someone wonderful." She had spent some of her best moments in their company and she couldn't get used to their absence. "From time to time I need to rest my head on a shoulder. Too bad I don't have that, too bad. It doesn't matter."'[17] But of course it did. Gabrielle would say, 'When men were strong, they were chaste and gentle . . . Tenderness is strength watching over you.'[18] And Claude Delay recalled an episode that had touched Gabrielle deeply, when witnessing that tenderness she had lost and for which, above all, she longed. Returning to the Ritz one evening:

She saw a man who was drunk stumbling over his woman companion. He was paralysed. He must have wanted to have dinner at the Ritz. He was in a dinner jacket, very well turned out; she was in an evening dress. She stood in front of him and put both his arms around her neck, and they walked like that, she holding him up. She signed to the hotel people not to help her. I would have run to go with them at the least sign. But she didn't make it. And when the woman's hand went near the man's lips, he kissed it.[19]

And Gabrielle confessed to Claude: 'The only time I hear my heart now is on the stairs.'[20]

In company with the few who took the trouble to see through the carapace of Gabrielle's self-defence, Claude could not but be affected. As time passed, like Lilou Marquand, she was called upon more frequently to help relieve Gabrielle's isolation. She hated dining alone. Having alienated a good many, she had brought on her own head this reminder of her pressing solitude, but lamented, 'I cannot eat when I'm alone, when there's no one across from me to talk to.' Claude Delay recalls the poignancy of managing Gabrielle's suffering:

There was her primitive mistrust and her disconcerting feminine resistance . . . these were never to leave her. She knew very well what it was to be lost, to be miserable. But I had a husband; I had two little girls. I felt a criminal that I had to go back home. I had dinner with her at the Ritz, sometimes in her room. And at the end, at the door, you know, I felt a criminal. She hated to be alone. Because she hated to go back to her loneliness without love; to the terrors of the past, to the somnambulism of her childhood; to her dreams. Why? Because she lived again those things. Her father's abandonment, her mother's fragility, the deaths; and of Boy . . . The imagination, which is the opposite of the deadly ruthlessness of the world. It gives you peace . . .

She was a woman of life not death; that twin struggle between death and life, we carry on in every act of our life. But she felt life the right way. She had a healthy psychic attitude.[21]

Indeed, if Gabrielle had not in many ways had a 'healthy psychic attitude', she could not have withstood her past. Nevertheless, each time she was 'left', it was revived and she collapsed. Lilou Marquand remembered an event highlighting Gabrielle's disproportionate response. It took place on one of the regular visits to Switzerland with Lilou and François at the Grand Palace Hotel. (Gabrielle increasingly preferred the life of a hotel to the little house, Le Signal, she had bought beyond Lake Geneva and restored for her 'retirement'.) François was almost always by Gabrielle's side. She liked his sense of humour, appreciated his uncomplicated, unassuming presence. She gave him money, bought him an apartment, sent him to Switzerland for cures, took him ever more into her confidence. She would say of him, 'Ah, how restful they are these ordinary people who are what they are, natural. Not at all like the Parisians, all those liars.'[22]

As they sat in the hotel one day discussing the next collection, Gabrielle said to François, 'You don't understand a thing, my dear, I've asked you three times to abduct me to no avail. Are you pretending not to understand what I'm saying or are you deaf? I say it again in front of Lilou: will you marry me?' François got up immediately, left the table and checked out of the hotel. It took Lilou six days to find him, there in Lausanne, in another hotel, and she said:

> He was still in shock, furious that he might have passed for an old lady's gigolo. He couldn't believe that a character as extraordinary as Chanel could love him. I asked him to be generous, to understand that she still had the heart of a sentimental young girl and a romantic mind . . . He came back to the hotel and no one ever mentioned it again.[23]

In the absence of François, meanwhile, Gabrielle had been 'distraught. Distraught at the rejection. Then, instead of her single dose of Sedol each day to sleep, she took more. Three, four of them. For days she didn't go out. It was terrible, terrible. François was in her confidence, he was her support.'[24]

Back in Paris, François and Lilou had acquired the habit of playing cards outside Gabrielle's bedroom each evening, to be nearby as she went to sleep:

We had sworn to her that we'd never abandon her. But still Mademoiselle was frightened. My return was always a surprise. Simply to see me, to hear my 'Good morning' or my 'Goodnight' overwhelmed her. 'You see, when you're here the loneliness, the anguish, it all flies away!' Ah, if only night had not existed . . . If Mademoiselle had been able to go directly from the evening to the morning! She would have lived without the horrible suspicion that she was being abandoned.[25]

Gabrielle's unstill mind meant that the sleepwalking from which she had suffered intermittently since childhood had grown worse. In her sleep, she cut up curtains, bedspreads, towels; making them into new designs carefully laid out upon the floor or hanging up on hangers. She was found sleepwalking naked in her rooms; on other occasions, she wandered through the Ritz and was gently guided back to her suite. Once, she was discovered hurrying along a corridor in her nightgown in the small hours with a wild expression on her face. Her maid, Céline (Gabrielle insisted on calling each new personal maid Jeanne, no matter what her real name might be), once watched as Gabrielle walked into her bathroom, broke a comb then turned on the water in the basin. To a friend, she would make a most revealing comment: 'I've never known just what it was I wanted to forget. So, to forget, whatever it was – probably something that was haunting me – I threw myself into something else.'[26]

In order to make a life, when young, Gabrielle had re-created herself, and this had nourished and encouraged her for many years. In her heart, meanwhile, she knew the truth of what haunted her. But, lacking that emotional resilience, with time her frantic attempts to throw herself 'into something else' through work had grown ever less successful. Even in sleep, her need to forget no longer left Gabrielle, and she was obliged to fill that, too, with work. Finally, worried about embarrassing herself in sleep, Gabrielle told Céline and Lilou that she wanted to be tied down to her bed, leaving her unable to 'stray' through the corridors of the Ritz at night.

But the sadness of Gabrielle's trials was not to end there. One of her favourite models recently remembered that, after dinner with Lilou and Gabrielle one evening, she came with them to Gabrielle's rooms. The model was astonished at the ritual of Gabrielle's preparations for the night and, watching Lilou and Céline strap her to her bed, she objected, 'But are you mad, why are you tying her up, what's going on?' And Gabrielle told her that, the other day, she'd been found 'cornering the elevator man . . . and dragging myself through the hotel'. She continued:

> She'd been taking morphine for 25 years and morphine made her delirious. She told me,
>   'I want to make love.' She didn't say 'make love', she used the direct word.
>   'It's not because I don't want to fuck, it's because I'm ashamed of my body.'
>   So I think that at this moment (when she was injected with her morphine), she was delivered from her inhibitions, and then, she'd leave her room. Searching. So she explained to me that she started to have herself tied up to her bed. After that she was in her dream and said, 'We'll say goodbye now. Lilou, tie me up.'[27]

Gabrielle began falling over. She injured her leg, cut her nose, hurt her hand. But she was terribly wary of being treated by the doctors, fearful they would disclose her weakness to the press. (Rumours of Gabrielle's reduced health had indeed been going around the news offices for some time.) She had a minor stroke, was hospitalized, and felt humiliated at her infirmity. She was becoming very frail.

Her arthritis and rheumatism had made her less nimble; at work she would jab herself with pins. Sucking the injury, she would yell, 'Ouch, what was that?' and, while she was exhausted and would sometimes say, 'There are days I want to drop everything,' the underlying theme was always the same: 'I must think of my collection, because that's the future.' And, of course, as long as there was the possibility of another collection, of working, there was always the possibility of avoiding death.

By 1970, while knowing that it drew nearer, Gabrielle often found the thought of not existing an impossibility. Yet, in saying 'I don't believe much in death,' she was contemplating something further: 'The soul departs: the ordeal has lasted long enough. For the Hindus it's merely a transformation . . . "Give up one's soul to God" – I like that expression . . . what remains of us is what we've thought and loved in life.'[28]

On that Saturday in January 1971, Gabrielle had been particularly irritable with her assistants; she was even short with her devoted Claude Delay. Gabrielle's collection was almost upon her, and her nerves were raw:

> Coco had mood swings all the time. One day she was ruminating and I was there. And she was talking about women: 'Nowadays women don't need men! We're independent . . .' And she would hold forth like that for ten minutes all alone. And all my life, I see her, she walks two steps, she turns back and says, 'A woman without men, what's the point?' That was Chanel. An idea and its opposite.[29]

She changed her mind constantly, one minute telling Claude she was going to give it all up, that she wouldn't do it anymore; then, away from work, she was only waiting until it was time to go back to the rue Cambon. On her bedside table was Erlanger's *Richelieu*; she told Claude it was 'the best story there is in the history of France . . . it's better than Alexander Dumas, but it hasn't got so much passion.'

On that Sunday 10 January, Claude returned and lunched with Gabrielle, then accompanied her on her customary drive around the Longchamp racecourse. The sun shone pale through the wintry mist. Later, as they drove back through the place de la Concorde – the great square through which Gabrielle had fled, almost sixty years before, from Arthur Capel's truth about her business not making any profit – Gabrielle bowed, telling Claude she was saluting the moon. It was full. Bidding Claude farewell, Gabrielle told her, 'I'll be working tomorrow.'

In her suite, she told Céline that she was very tired and must lie down; Céline could only persuade her to remove her shoes. Gabrielle lay drowsing. Later, she told her maid she would eat in her rooms, read the restaurant menu, then cried out, 'I'm suffocating . . . Jeanne . . . the window.' Céline rushed to her side; Gabrielle's face was taut with pain and she held her hands over her chest. She was too weak to break the phial of morphine always by her bed and, taking the syringe, Céline injected her to relieve the pain. Gabrielle murmured, 'So that's the way one dies.' Céline immediately phoned the doctor but, when she returned, she saw that her mistress was quite still. She closed Gabrielle's eyes.

Next day, newspapers across the world announced the death of 'one of the greatest couturiers of the century', and tried to encapsulate her achievements as the woman who had become a legend in her own lifetime. Claude Delay returned to pay Gabrielle her own respects and found her 'very small under the white Ritz sheets drawn up to her heart'. On Gabrielle's bedside table was the beautiful icon Stravinsky had given her in 1921.

On 14 January, a funeral service was held for Gabrielle in the Madeleine, the great parish church of the Parisian elite, close by the rue Cambon. Gabrielle's small coffin was covered in a mass of white flowers, with the exception of two wreaths of red roses; one from the Syndicat de la Couture, the other from Luchino Visconti.

Whatever the personal feelings of her fellow couturiers, virtually all of them were there to render her homage, including Balmain, Balenciaga (whose graciousness and forgiving nature sent him there 'to pray for her' despite her having destroyed their close friendship with unkindness), Castillo, Marc Bohan and Yves St Laurent. Notwithstanding Gabrielle's criticism of most of them at one time or another, they cannot but have been conscious that her remarkable life's work had brought great credit to their profession. Gabrielle's friend Michel Déon made a plea for compassion in one's final judgement:

> One shouldn't turn one's back on Coco but, on the contrary, help
> her to erase everything that had embittered her so much it was making her suffocate. Between the imaginary world where she was
> taking refuge and the cruel world which had hurt her ... the gap
> remained impassable.[30]

Meanwhile, standing in the front row for the entire funeral ceremony were Gabrielle's models, all dressed in Chanel suits. Behind them were the forewomen, and men, the seamstresses and numerous assistants that made up the team at rue Cambon, without whom Gabrielle's ideas would have been impossible. A fascinated crowd joined Paris society, and Gabrielle's friends, who included Salvador Dalí, Lady Abdy, Antoinette Bernstein, Serge Lifar, André-Louis Dubois, Robert Bresson, the Mille brothers, Jacques Chazot and Jeanne Moreau, whose friendship Gabrielle's defensiveness had made her reject.

A much smaller group of mourners, including Gabrielle's great-niece, François Mironnet and Lilou Marquand, later followed Gabrielle's coffin to Switzerland, where she was laid to rest in the cemetery of Lausanne. Why Switzerland? While deeply French, Gabrielle was also ambivalent about her compatriots; just as some of them were about her. She had said, 'The French don't like me, it can't be helped.' She had also said, 'I have always needed security' and, in Switzerland, apparently, she felt secure. A marble headstone was raised to her, with the heads of five lions, her zodiac sign, carved in bas-relief. Below them is a cross, below that, simply:

GABRIELLE CHANEL

1883–1971

However many words were written on Gabrielle in the weeks after her death, typically, in death as in life, she would manage her legacy. In that remarkable memoir she had given to Paul Morand just after the war, she had 'written' her own epitaph:

My life is the story – and often the tragedy – of the solitary woman. Her woes, her importance, the unequal and fascinating battle she has waged with herself, with men, and with the attraction . . . and dangers that spring up everywhere.

Today, alone in the sunshine and snow . . . I shall continue, without husband, without children, without grandchildren, without those delightful illusions . . . My life has been merely a prolonged childhood. That is how one recognizes the destinies in which poetry plays a part . . . I am not a heroine. But I have chosen the person I wanted to be.[31]

Afterword: Those on whom legends are built are their legends

Gabrielle once said to Morand, 'Contrary to what Sert used to say, I would make a very bad dead person, because once I was put under, I would grow restless and . . . think only of returning to earth and starting all over again.'[1]

When one of her managers was asked had Gabrielle thought about the future of Chanel, he retorted, 'Certainly not. She was *much* too egocentric.' Yet while Gabrielle had told her Zurich lawyer that she 'longed for peace' and wanted no publicity after her death, she had also been thinking for some time about her successor, and her personal fortune. With regard to that fortune, she did her best to avoid giving any of it to the French state. Taking her lawyer's advice, that Lichtenstein was a superior tax haven to Switzerland, in 1965 she set up a foundation there – named Coga, after Coco-Gabrielle – and then made her will. This stated: 'I establish as my sole and universal heir the Coga Foundation.' Having thus bequeathed the majority of her personal estate, Gabrielle made certain bequests to a handful of people. Her added verbal instruction to help the needy, and gifted artists, was sufficiently vague that it is possible nothing has ever been put into effect.

Gabrielle's manservant, François Mironnet, was apparently at first informed he had 'inherited Mademoiselle', however, the document proving this was never found. The estate did, nonetheless, make an out-of-court settlement with Mironnet. Others who made claims on Gabrielle's estate were not so fortunate. Over the years, her bankers and lawyers have maintained a stony silence over the Coga Foundation, and its function remains a mystery. So does the extent of Gabrielle's personal fortune. In 1971, Mironnet claimed it was worth $1.5 billion. The Wertheimer family claimed it was $30 million. It has been estimated that, at the time of Gabrielle's death, the House of Chanel brought in approximately $160 million annually.

Gabrielle's manager was mistaken about her failure to contemplate a successor for, several years before her death, she had discussed it with more than one friend. Where her manager had been correct was in Gabrielle's inability to put anything into practice. The House of Chanel had become her final solace, her *raison d'être*. If she handed it over there would be nothing left for her but to die. In avoiding choosing a successor, Gabrielle implicitly staved off death.

When it finally came, there was much doubt as to whether Chanel could continue without her. While the owner, Jacques Wertheimer – son of Gabrielle's partner, Pierre, who had effectively bankrolled Chanel since 1954 – wished to continue, Chanel couture was to languish for some time. In 1974, Jacques's sons, Alain and Gérard Wertheimer, took over the running of the company. With the intention of maintaining Chanel as a family business, they refused to bring in shareholders; the number of outlets permitted to sell the perfumes was drastically reduced; Gabrielle's policy of employing Chanel's own perfumers, craftsmen and jewellers was continued, and large sums were spent on promotion.

For many years, the Wertheimers have been well served by a number of gifted employees, the most distinguished of whom have remained with the company for long periods, sometimes for most of their working lives. These include 'the eye behind the image', the late Jacques Helleu, Chanel's artistic director, who oversaw the changing image of Chanel. While the most famous advertisement for Chanel was Marilyn Monroe's quip 'What do I wear in bed? Why Chanel N°5 of course,' Helleu used some of the world's best photographers, such as Richard Avedon, Irving Penn, David Bailey, Luc Besson and Ridley Scott, to photograph and film some of the world's most glamorous women – these included Catherine Deneuve, Candice Bergen, Carole Bouquet, Nicole Kidman, Audrey Tatou and Keira Knightley – in expensive and influential advertising campaigns. With their underlying theme of luxury and mystique, these highly successful promotions fulfilled Alain Wertheimer's maxim: 'The secret of advertising is to make it real and a dream at the same time.'

By the end of the twenties, Gabrielle and Beaux's first perfume, N°5, had been so successful it became Gabrielle's chief source of revenue. In more recent times, Chanel's chief *parfumeur*, Jacques Polge, has ensured the continuing quality of this, the fragrance the company understandably refers to as its 'treasure'. In his long years at Chanel, Jacques Polges – a gracious and abstracted man, who speaks of the 'poetry of fragrance' – has admirably extended the company's repertoire, with several renowned perfumes of his own. Amongst them are: Coco Mademoiselle, Chanel N°19 and Beige.

When Gabrielle had told Beaux not to hold back on the costly ingredients for N°5, she had instructed him to make it the most exclusive in the world. Sixty years later, Alain Wertheimer was determined to follow the same principle, and set out to improve on what had become the perfume's slightly flagging image of exclusivity. In time, this goal was to prove successful for the perfumes, jewellery and accessories. But, for several years after Gabrielle's death, the dress designers employed to take up her baton made the mistake of trying to emulate her. Admittedly, their task was a daunting one; a friend of Gabrielle's had remarked on the fact that 'in the House of Chanel everything went through her, nothing could be conceived, let alone carried out, without her.'[2] As it was, Chanel couture appeared to have lost its way.

Since before the Second World War, prêt-à-porter had been a growing challenge to the far greater but more time-consuming skills of haute couture and, after the war, a growing number of couture houses would be forced to close their doors. Following Gabrielle's return in 1954, she herself had held out but, in 1977, Chanel took on a designer, Philippe Guyborget, to design prêt-à-porter. In 1983, the Parisian-trained couturier Karl Lagerfeld, then at the fashion house Chloé, was persuaded to take over this role. His rapid success led to an invitation from Chanel to design both their haute couture and prêt-à-porter. Speaking of the Wertheimers' brief, that he 'make something of Chanel', Lagerfeld recalls their telling him, if he couldn't, they would sell up.

Young Lagerfeld had arrived in Paris from Germany in 1953 or '54, intent on a career in fashion. He worked first as an illustrator for fashion houses, was taken on as an apprentice at Pierre Balmain, and then became a couturier at the house of Jean Patou. Lagerfeld's first collection, in 1958, was poorly received; the second was praised as having a 'kind of understated chic, elegance', while in the following year, 1960, the designer produced 'the shortest skirts in Paris'. This collection was criticized for being 'more like clever . . . and immensely saleable ready-to-wear, not couture'. Lagerfeld's work was seen as good but not ground-breaking. For the next couple of years, he effectively dropped out; he has said he spent 'a lot of time on beaches'.

By 1962, he was back in Paris, and for the next twenty years honed his skills as a freelance designer, collaborating simultaneously with numerous fashion houses, such as Chloé, Valentino and Fendi on prêt-à-porter and haute couture. In 1984, a year after he took over at Chanel, this phenomenally energetic designer also created his own label, Karl Lagerfeld, and continued forging his reputation, as one authority put it, 'through consistently strong work for the numerous lines he produces every year'. For the rest of that decade, while his designs were not the only reason for Chanel's growing profile, they were a major factor in its steady progress.

Lagerfeld says, 'When I took over Chanel, no one wanted to work for an old company. I accepted against everyone's advice, to breathe some life back into a house which was more than a Sleeping Beauty, it wasn't trendy at all.'³ From the outset, he knew that 'I must blow hot and cold. I must excite and enrage the high priestesses who'd say "Mademoiselle would turn in her grave."' He recalls his first few collections for Chanel with 'very short skirts, very wide shoulders, oversized jewellery, a bit "too much" of everything, but it was the right time to do it.' On another occasion, he describes having 'to push it, nearly, I wouldn't say into the vulgarity, but the

eighties were not really about distinction'. Creating endless variations on Gabrielle's signature themes, as the years passed, Lagerfeld
wittily combined elements of street-style with the simple elegance
of Chanel classics.

His ability to reflect his times, combined with skilled manipulation
of the grammar of Gabrielle's design, enabled Lagerfeld to reinvigor-
ate her design house with notable success. Throughout the nineties,
the House of Chanel grew still more successful and, by 2001, Lagerfeld was being dubbed one of 'the most high-profile designers of the
previous twenty years'. But this, he says, has been easy, because no
other fashion house has such immediately recognizable 'elements' as
Chanel. These are the markers, Gabrielle's signature pieces, long
ago core elements of twentieth-century women's dress. Indeed, a
woman's wardrobe today is virtually unthinkable without, at the very
least, one of Gabrielle's innovations: a 'little black dress', costume
jewellery, *any* bag with a shoulder strap, jumpers for women, trousers
for women, suits for women, sling-back shoes, a trench coat, a strapless dress and, finally, that perfume in its modernist bottle, so iconic it
has remained virtually unchanged for ninety years.

Lagerfeld says, 'All that together makes it that I can play with the
elements like a musician plays with notes. You don't have to make
the same music if you're a decent musician.'[4]

Using formidable designing skills, honed with rigorous couture
training, his enviable unself-consciousness has enabled Lagerfeld,
for a staggering fifty years and more, to design an immense body of
work with fluency and ease. (With Chanel Inc. as financer, he has
also helped preserve the highly skilled – largely Parisian – couture
artisans with the recent purchase of several distinguished companies, such as Lesage (embroidery), Goossens (jewellery), and Massaro
(footwear), whose time-consuming and, therefore, very costly work
would otherwise have led to their closure.) While Lagerfeld knows
his work 'has re-established Chanel's image', he is quite aware that:

> Not all this was very Chanel . . . but my job is to give the idea that
> this is what Chanel is. What it is in reality, what it once was or what

it might have been once doesn't matter. And it can have a certain magic which includes everything ... the name, the myth, the woman, myself ... but the whole thing must be something of today ... which is rooted in the past.'[5]

Enjoying his boast that 'I'm the first [fashion designer] who has made a name for himself with a name that wasn't his,' Lagerfeld made it seem smart to do this and highly profitable for Chanel. As a result, several long-established houses have been re-vamped by new designers. Meanwhile, Lagerfeld claims he is simply 'a visitor passing through', saying, 'I haven't made an empire with my name on it' but, like a mercenary, 'I go wherever they pay me. I don't have to think about marketing, or sales, that's none of my business.' (The pragmatist in him, nonetheless, adds, 'I like to be used by people who invest ... if you don't invest, if you don't spend – the box is closed.')

Gabrielle is mistakenly portrayed as a hard-headed businesswoman but, like Lagerfeld after her, she was pragmatic and business-like about her creativity, without it being *business* that motivated her. She would say, 'It was thought that I had a mind for business, I don't ... Business matters and balance sheets bore me to death. If I want to add up I count on my fingers.'[6] And, while her fights with the Wertheimers were about money, their primary source wasn't a financial one. Rather it was from Gabrielle's great pride, her insecurity and the fear of losing her independence. Her success arose from her recognition and anticipation of her times, combined with an intelligent employment of the right people to run the business for her. *Her* business, like her successor's, was, above all, designing.

Unlike Lagerfeld, Gabrielle never dreamt of working for anyone else. Neither did any relationship, or age, make her feel able to retire from the House of Chanel:

They didn't understand that, neither men nor the others, that still there was one thing I had done myself – the Maison Chanel is my only possession, the rest was thrown at me. It's the only thing I've made – all I've had, I didn't want anything . . . but everybody was giving me everything. I didn't want anything from anybody; I had made something on my own.[7]

As we have seen, Gabrielle's house became her *raison d'être*, and she identified with it more than anything: it *was* her. It also led her to great loneliness.

Lagerfeld, meanwhile, doesn't profess to having a vocation, or a message, and in interview with the formidable fashion journalist Suzy Menkes, he says, 'I have no direction, line, etc. I am not that serious. In fact, I'm not serious at all. That's why it works.' When asked what he believes his legacy will be, he replies, 'I never think what's going on after me. I don't care!'[8]

Multilingual, intelligent, ironic and pragmatic, Lagerfeld prides himself on his culture and appears driven to constant motion. In addition to his multifarious activities for several design houses, his designing portfolio includes costumes and stage sets for theatre and film, house interiors, and a steady stream of books, many of which are presentations of his own photographs.

While Lagerfeld's success at Chanel means he is almost synonymous with Gabrielle's house, the image he has cultivated has made him almost as iconic a figure as Gabrielle herself. Using her 'elements' with great ingenuity, Lagerfeld has gained for himself and Chanel even greater cachet with his interweaving of aspects of Gabrielle's personal story into his designs. He has created collections based on Russia (Dmitri, Stravinsky), or Britain (Arthur Capel), and made short films referring to episodes in Gabrielle's life, such as her love affair with Stravinsky. In combination with Lagerfeld's own image, his fashion has helped create a new version of Gabrielle. Albeit simplifying her, over the years, his endless re-creation of her designs has done much to perpetuate Gabrielle's personal legend for a modern audience. The atmosphere that now surrounds her reminds us that Gabrielle once referred to her life as 'the maze of my legendary fame'.

★ ★ ★

Evoking herself, Gabrielle said, 'Those on whom legends are built *are* their legends.'[9] In the latter part of her life, however, she need not have exaggerated her role as the person who had single-handedly revolutionized women's appearance, for she was, and remains, the most influential designer of her century.

The source of Gabrielle's phenomenal *success* lay in that instinctive understanding of the new epoch, and her anticipation, if not dictation, of what it needed. The source of Gabrielle's *greatness* lay beyond simple success. She believed she had been put on this earth for a purpose: 'I was working towards a new society.' And dress was only the most visible aspect of more profound changes she helped to bring about. During the course of her extraordinary and unconventional journey – from abject poverty to a new kind of glamour – Gabrielle Chanel had helped forge the very idea of modern woman, and would say: 'That is why I was born. That is why I have endured.'[10]

Notes

Epigraph

1 Paul Morand, *The Allure of Chanel*, p. 143

Prologue: *You're proud, you'll suffer*

1 Paul Morand, *The Allure of Chanel*, p. 40
2 Ibid., p. 34
3 Ibid., p. 41
4 Ibid.
5 Ibid., pp. 20 & 21
6 Ibid., p. 56
7 Ibid., p. 42

Chapter 1: Forebears

1 Jean Cocteau, *Past Tense*, vol. I, p. 50
2 Eugen Weber, *Peasants into Frenchmen*, p. 285
3 Ibid., p. 285
4 Ibid., p. 410

Chapter 2: The Bad One

1 Henry Gidel, *Coco Chanel*, pp. 21–5
2 Ibid., p. 30

Chapter 3: The Lost Years

1 Lilou Marquand, *Chanel m'a dit*, p. 45
2 Paul Morand, *The Allure of Chanel*, p. 22
3 Ibid., both references p. 22
4 Ibid., p. 23
5 Ibid.
6 Marquand, p. 61
7 Morand, *Allure*, p. 30
8 Ibid., p. 24
9 Eugen Weber, *Peasants into Frenchmen*, p. 325
10 Ibid., pp. 326 & 455
11 Ibid., p. 313
12 Ibid.
13 Morand, *Allure*, p. 19
14 Ibid., p. 20
15 Ibid., p. 19

Chapter 4: Things that I should be and which I am not

1 Paul Morand, *The Allure of Chanel*, p. 27
2 Ibid., p. 28
3 Charles Roux, *Chanel*, p. 79
4 Morand, *Allure*, p. 29
5 Charles Roux, p. 84
6 Morand, *Allure*, p. 31
7 Pierre Galante, *Mademoiselle Chanel*, p. 60
8 Judith Thurman, *Secrets of the Flesh: A Life of Colette*, p. 111. This superlative biography of Colette was a fascinating comparison in my gradual understanding of Gabrielle.
9 Hickman, p. 12
10 Liane de Pougy, *My Blue Notebooks*, p. 51
11 Galante, p. 54

Chapter 5: A Rich Man's Game

1 Paul Morand, *Venices*, p. 42

2 Judith Thurman, *Secrets of the Flesh: A Life of Colette*, p. 113

3 Paul Morand, *The Allure of Chanel*, p. 52

4 Ibid.

5 Ibid., p. 146

6 Ibid., p. 31

7 Shari Benstock, *Women of the Left Bank*, p. 46

8 Ibid., pp. 54 & 228

9 Thurman, p. 165

10 Valerie Steele, *Paris Fashion*, p. 164

11 Pierre Galante, *Mademoiselle Chanel*, p. 22

12 Morand, *Allure*, p. 56

13 Steele, p. 172

14 Ibid., p. 170

15 Ibid., p. 173 and Amy de la Haye, *Chanel: The Couturière at Work*, p. 9

16 Galante, p. 63

17 Ibid.

18 Morand, *Allure*, p. 39

Chapter 6: Captive Mistress

1 Paul Morand, *The Allure of Chanel*, p. 32

2 Ibid., p. 23 and Marcel Haedrich, *Coco Chanel*, p. 79

3 Katie Hickman, *Courtesans*, p. 6. Hickman was most instructive in my understanding of the courtesan's attitudes and milieu.

4 Morand, *Allure*, p. 33

5 Charles Roux, *Chanel*, p. 115 and Axel Madsen, *Chanel: A Woman of Her Own*, p. 55

6 Isabelle Fiemeyer, *Coco Chanel: Un Parfum de mystère*, pp. 37 & 53

7 Lilou Marquand, *Chanel m'a dit*, p. 65

8 Morand, *Allure*, p. 33

9 Marquand, p. 56

10 Morand, *Allure*, p. 33

11 Marquand interview with author, Jan. 2010

12 Fiemeyer, p. 50

13 Lourdes Font, *Fashion Theory*, p. 305

14 Morand, *Lewis et Irène*, p. 23

15 Ibid., p. 87

16 Ibid., p. 108

17 Morand, *Allure*, pp. 34 & 53

18 Morand, *Lewis et Irène*, p. 120

19 Morand, *Allure*, p. 34

20 Ibid., pp. 33 & 39

21 Ibid., p. 34

22 Morand, *Lewis et Irène*, p. 307

23 Morand, *Allure*, p. 34

24 Morand, *Lewis et Irène*, p. 306

25 Morand, *Allure*, p. 32

26 Henry Gidel, *Coco Chanel*, p. 53

27 Ronald Courtenay Bodley, *Indiscretions of a Young Man*, p. 122

28 Morand, *Lewis et Irène*, p. 307

29 Morand, *Allure*, p. 36

30 Ibid.

31 Ibid., p. 34

Chapter 7: Arthur Capel

1 Paul Morand, *The Allure of Chanel*, p. 20

2 Ibid., p. 34

3 Arthur and his father Arthur Joseph's birth certificates plus the Census records revealed Arthur's antecedents and their subsequent betterment.

4 Arthur Edward Capel was born at Bedford House, Marine Parade, Brighton.

5 Arthur Joseph Capel (From the London Post Office directory, between 1875 and 1884 one sees Arthur's father's rise to prominence as an

entrepreneur.) In 1874, he was a businessman, and agent for travellers to Paris, and by 1880 he had become a major agent for train and shipping companies in Ireland, England, France and Spain. In 1884, he was a founder of a Compressed Air Company, licensed to lay pipes through the streets (Bulletin of Warwickshire Industrial Archaeology Society, issue 5, summer 1995). This must have been a very lucrative venture.

6 Joseph's diverse business interests now required distant travel. In December 1884, he was at a coming-out ball for debutantes at Delmonico's, the most distinguished public dining rooms in New York (*The New York Times*). By 1885, it appears he no longer needed to work.

7 Philip Sydney, *Modern Rome in Modern England*, pp. 114–15

8 I am indebted to Father McCoog (Archivist at the British Province of the Society of Jesus, Mount Street, London), who pointed out the unlikelihood of Arthur's attendance at Downside, suggested Stonyhurst as his school, and passed me on to Bernardo Caparrini, who has worked on the history of Beaumont College. Bernardo recommended me to David Knight, Archivist at Stonyhurst College, who was assiduous on my behalf in discovering Stonyhurst's record of Arthur (including a photo of him with fellow Gentlemen Philosophers). In the Stonyhurst log, in Arthur's own hand, he details his place of birth and schooling. The information at Stonyhurst was invaluable in my search for this most elusive man.

9 From Bernardo Caparrini, I had these crucial references for Arthur's movements: 'The Beaumont Lists for Fifty Years, 1861–1911. Supplement to The Beaumont Review Old Windsor' (*The Beaumont Review* Office, 1911, p. 17) and 'The Beaumont Lists, 1861–1961' (*The Beaumont Review*, no. 207, Oct. 1963, p. 470). Bernardo also referred to 'a manuscript document at the Mount Street archives (box PE/2) entitled "Lists from 1887–1909 (with follow-up notes)" ... in which it says (folio 190) ... "Capel, Arthur Edward (entered Oct. 14, 1891; left Aug., 1897) b. Brighton 1881, was at a school in Paris. Went to San Sebastian in Spain. Was a Philosopher at Stonyhurst, where he carried off the Keating Prize ..." The "Keating Prize" was for the best essay on Christian Sociology.'

10 H. J. A. Sire, *Gentlemen Philosophers*, p. 5. Sire, suggested by Bernardo

Caparrini, details life at Stonyhurst College for the Gentlemen Philosophers.

11 *The New York Times*, 12 June 1902

12 Arthur Capel noted at a polo match at Deauville. *Le Gaulois,* 16 Aug., 1909

13 Paul Morand, *Lewis et Irène*, p. 61

14 Following polo at Deauville, Arthur is noted by *Le Gaulois* arriving at Dieppe on his yacht and then spotted the next day at the casino. Throughout the 1910s, he is regularly referred to in *Le Figaro*, *The New York Times*, etc.

15 Letter from Arthur Capel to Diana Wyndham: 'I hate the main road & the crowd. The world I know is of my own making, the other makes me sick. Their morals, their convictions, their ambitions mean nothing to me. Fancy, sympathy & illusion have ever been my bed mates & I would never change them for Consideration, Position or Power.' Capel correspondence, courtesy of Christopher Osborn. This letter is undated, as are all those from Arthur.

16 Valerie Steele, *Paris Fashion*, pp. 71–2. I based my argument here on Ms Steele's description of the *grisettes* in this thought-provoking book.

17 Ibid., p. 71

18 Ibid.

19 Charles Roux, *Chanel*, p. 113

20 Elisabeth de Clermont-Tonnerre née de Gramont , *Mémoires, vol. IV, La Treizième Heure*, p. 154

Chapter 8: Refashioning Paris

1 Vanessa Schwartz, *Spectacular Realities*, p. 229. Ms Schwartz informed my descriptions of the development of mass culture in Paris.

2 Colin Jones, *Paris: Biography of a City*, p. 410. I am indebted, for this section, to this excellent work on Paris.

3 Ibid., p. 365

4 Ibid., p. 386

5 Schwartz, p. 92

6 Paul Morand, *The Allure of Chanel*, p. 37
7 Ibid.
8 Ibid.
9 Arthur Capel, *What Will Tomorrow be Made Of?*, p. 77

Chapter 9: The Rite of Spring

1 *Revue de Paris*, t. 6, pp. 279 & 276. Blanche, regarded by some as ingratiating, was sharp tongued, a fine portraitist, and also made it his business to know everyone.
2 Modris Eksteins, *Rites of Spring*, p. 31
3 Ibid., p. 72
4 Ibid., p. 73
5 Sjeng Scheijen, *Diaghilev*, p. 454
6 'Diaghilev the Man', in Jane Pritchard, *Diaghilev and the Golden Age of the Ballets Russes*, p. 41
7 Eksteins, p. 39
8 Mary Davis, *Classic Chic*, p. 26. Mary Davis's seminal work was most helpful in the section on Poiret and the relationship between fashion and developing modernism.
9 Ibid.
10 Valerie Steele, *Paris Fashion*, p. 230
11 *Femina*, 1 Sept. 1913
12 Francis Steegmuller, *Cocteau*, p. 89
13 Paul Morand, *The Allure of Chanel*, p. 37

Chapter 10: The End of an Epoque

1 Paul Morand, *Lewis et Irène*, p. 124
2 Ibid.
3 Arthur Capel, *What Will Tomorrow be Made Of?*, p. 18
4 George de Symons Barrow, *The Fire of Life*, p. 149
5 Ibid., p. 151

6 Elisabeth de Gramont, *Mémoires, vol. III: Clair de lune et taxi-auto*, p. 36

7 Paul Morand, *The Allure of Chanel*, p. 43

8 Ibid.

9 Ibid., pp. 43 & 45

10 de Gramont, vol. III, p. 79

11 Ernest de la Grange, *Open House in Flanders*, 29 Dec. 1914, vol. III, p. 77

Chapter 11: Master of Her Art

1 Paul Morand, *The Allure of Chanel*, p. 46

2 All references in this section ibid., p. 52

3 Ibid., p. 45

4 Pierre Galante, *Mademoiselle Chanel*, p. 37

5 Amy de la Haye, *Chanel: The Couturière at Work*, p. 20

6 Baronne de la Grange, *Open House in Flanders*, 8 Aug. 1915, p. 143

7 Morand, *Allure*, p. 39

8 Galante, p. 38

9 Ibid., p. 37

10 Ibid.

11 Ibid., p. 39

12 Ibid.

13 Morand, *Allure*, p. 42

Chapter 12: The War Bans the Bizarre

1 Paul Morand, *The Allure of Chanel*, p. 38

2 Letter from 'the General Officer, Commander in Chief, the British Army in France' to 'the Secretary, War Office, London', 20 Mar. 1916, National Archives, Kew

3 C. E. Callwell, *Sir Henry Wilson: His Life and Diaries*, vol. I, p. 205

4 Morand, *Allure*, p. 42

5 Lord Egremont, *Under Two Flags: The Life of General Sir Edward Spears*, p. 27. This admirable biography was instructive in my understanding

of what Arthur Capel's work as a liaison officer would have been like. Spears's comments on Arthur (from Spears's diaries in Colonel Anthony Aylmer's collection) were another vital step in discovering Arthur's life.

6 *Cahiers André Gide*, vol. VIII, p. 214, J. E. Blanche to André Gide, 15 Feb. 1917

7 Charles Roux, *Chanel*, p. 162 and John Pomian, *J. Retinger: Memoirs of an Eminence Grise*, p. 35

8 Francis Steegmuller, *Cocteau*, p. 184

9 Sjeng Scheijen, *Diaghilev*, p. 323

10 Mary Davis, *Classic Chic*, p. 117

11 Scheijen, p. 331

12 Davis, p. 117

13 Ibid., pp. 128–9

Chapter 13: Remember that you're a woman

1 Charles Roux, *Chanel*, p. 164

2 Robert Fizdale and Arthur Gold, *The Life of Misia Sert*, p. 198

3 Ibid., p. 196

4 Ibid., p. 202

5 Ibid., p. 197

6 Paul Morand, *Lewis et Irène*, p. 144

7 Ibid., p. 135

8 Paul Morand, *The Allure of Chanel*, p. 143

9 Morand, *Lewis et Irène*, p. 142

10 Sir Jeremy Hutchinson in interview with author

11 Christopher Osborn in interview with author

12 Arthur Capel's correspondence, Christopher Osborn. These letters proved invaluable in 'reading' Arthur, and the relationships with Diana and Gabrielle.

13 Ibid.

14 Christopher Osborn, in interview with author

15 Arthur Capel correspondence, Christopher Osborn

16 Ibid.

17 Lord Egremont, *Under Two Flags: The Life of General Sir Edward Spears*, p. 66

18 Michelle Maurois, *Déchirez cette lettre*, p. 125

19 Edward Stanley, Earl of Derby, *Paris 1918: The War Diary of the British Ambassador*, 29 May 1918, p. 25

20 Georges Bernstein-Gruber, *Bernstein le magnifique*, p. 165

21 Arthur Capel, *What Will Tomorrow be Made Of?*, p. 79

22 Ibid., pp. 79–80

23 Ibid., p. 80

24 Maurois, p. 160

25 Morand, *Allure*, p. 43

Chapter 14: Alone

1 Paul Morand, *Lewis et Irène*, p. 140

2 Paul Morand, *The Allure of Chanel*, p. 37

3 Capel correspondence, Christopher Osborn

4 The Papers of Alfred Duff Cooper (1st Viscount Norwich), DUFC 12/8, 5 July 1918, Churchill Archives Centre, Cambridge

5 Ibid.

6 Scotland's People website, www.scotlandspeople.gov.uk

7 Edward Stanley, Earl of Derby, *Paris 1918: The War Diary of the British Ambassador*, 11 Aug. 1918, pp. 133–4

8 Georges Bernstein-Gruber, *Bernstein le magnifique*, p. 166

9 Benquet Agency letters

10 Earl of Derby, p. 161, 22 Aug. 1918

11 Michelle Maurois, *Déchirez cette lettre*, p. 15

12 Ibid., p. 160

13 Liane de Pougy, *My Blue Notebooks*, p. 54

14 Lady d'Abernon, *Red Cross and Berlin Embassy, 1915–1926: Extracts from the Diaries of Viscountess d'Abernon*, 28 Nov. 1918, p. 56. My thanks here to Lady Polly Feversham.

15 Christopher Osborn in interview with author

16 Ibid.

17 Viscount Norwich, *Duff Cooper Diaries*, 9 Apr. 1918, 29 Oct. 1918 and 5 Nov. 1918. The notion that Duff Cooper and Diana Capel had an affair (Justine Picardie, *Coco Chanel*, p. 88) is based on a misreading of these diaries.

18 Ibid., 11 Nov. 1919

19 Phillip Norcross Gross, Oscar Edward Fleming's nephew, has been helpful with new information on Antoinette Fleming née Chanel.

20 Norwich, 23 Dec. 1919. These diary entries proved crucial in the last piece of the Arthur Capel/ Diana Capel/ Chanel puzzle.

21 Axel Madsen, *Chanel: A Woman of Her Own*, p. 99

22 Norwich, 21 Jan. 1920

23 Charles Roux, *Chanel*, p. 178

24 Stonyhurst magazine and *Le Gaulois*, 2 Jan. 1920

25 Capel correspondence, Christopher Osborn

26 Ibid.

27 Ibid.

28 Morand, *Allure*, pp. 54–5

Chapter 15: Beginning Again

1 Colin Simpson, *Artful Partners*, pp. 168–78

2 Elisabeth de Gramont, *Mémoires, vol. IV, La Treizième Heure*, p. 154

3 Charles Roux, *Chanel*, p. 183 and Axel Madsen, *Chanel: A Woman of Her Own*, p. 106

4 Mairie de Garches

5 Churchill Archives Centre DUFC12/8, 17

6 Paul Morand, *Venices*, p. 121

7 Paul Morand, *The Allure of Chanel*, p. 59

8 Marcel Haedrich, *Coco Chanel*, p. 112

9 Ibid.

10 Charles Roux, p. 196

11 Morand, *Allure*, p. 62

12 Ibid., p. 60

13 Ibid.

14 Ibid., p. 63

15 Audio recording, Gabrielle Chanel, Bibliothèque Nationale de France (undated)

16 Richard Buckle, *Diaghilev*, p. 161

17 Morand, *Allure*, p. 84

18 John Richardson, *A Life of Picasso*, vol. III, p. 39

19 Buckle, p. 364

20 Mary Davis, *Classic Chic*, p. 226

21 Richardson, vol. III, p. 174

Chapter 16: The strangest and most brilliant years

1 Paul Morand, *The Allure of Chanel*, p. 107

2 Mary Davis, *Classic Chic*, p. 179

3 Morand, *Allure*, p. 127

4 Chanel interview BNF

5 Richard Buckle, *Diaghilev*, p. 412

6 Davis, pp. 183–5

7 Ibid., p. 179

8 Chanel interview BNF

9 John Richardson, *A Life of* Picasso, vol. III, p. 177

10 Gaia Servadio, *Luchino Visconti: A Biography*, p. 41

11 Morand, *Allure*, p. 128

12 Ibid., pp. 30–31

13 Ibid., p. 31

14 Morand, *Lettres du voyageur*, letter to Valentine Hugo, 2 Jan. 1921

15 Morand, *Allure*, p. 128

16 Ibid., p. 81

17 Chanel interview BNF

18 Arthur Rubinstein, *My Many Years*, p. 151

Chapter 17: Dmitri Pavlovich

1 Pavlovich diaries 9 Feb. 1921. For guiding my thoughts on Dmitri Pavlovich, and painstaking translations of all following diary entries, I am most grateful to William Lee. *homepage.ntlworld.com/ .../Will%20 Lee%20Sue%20Woolmans.html*

2 Marie Pavlovna, *A Princess in Exile*, p. 71

3 Ibid., p. 130

4 Ibid.

5 Amanda Mackenzie Stuart, *Consuelo and Alva Vanderbilt*, p. 158

6 Pavlovich., 9 Feb. 1921

7 Ibid., 10 Feb. 1921

8 Ibid.

9 Robert Fizdale and Arthur Gold, *The Life of Misia Sert*, p. 132

10 In conversation with William Lee

11 Pavlovich, 18 Mar. 1921

12 Ibid., 1 May 1921

13 Marcel Haedrich, *Coco Chanel*, p. 26

14 I am grateful to Philip Norcross Gross for this information.

15 Charles Roux, *Chanel*, p. 176

16 Haedrich, p. 26

17 Pavlovich, 4 May 1921

18 Ibid., 5 May 1921

Chapter 18: The Lucky N°5

1 *Vogue*, Oct. 1920

2 Robert Fizdale and Arthur Gold, *The Life of Misia Sert*, p. 201

3 Ibid.

4 Ibid.

5 Pierre Galante, *Mademoiselle Chanel*, p. 67

6 Ibid., p. 69

7 *Souvenir de Parfums*, Ernest Beaux, in *Industrie de la Parfumerie*, vol. I, no. 7, Oct. 1946

8 Galante, p. 74

9 Audio recording, Gabrielle Chanel, Bibliothèque Nationale de France (undated)

10 Patrick Doucet painstakingly described the development of Chanel perfumes and helped me towards a chronology of N°5.

11 Chanel catalogue, Chanel Conservatoire

12 Galante, p. 75

13 Ibid.

14 Audio recording, Gabrielle Chanel, Bibliothèque Nationale de France (undated)

Chapter 19: *Entirely in white and covered in pearls*

1 All references in this paragraph Paul Morand, *The Allure of Chanel*, p. 104

2 Francis Steegmuller, *Cocteau*, p. 268

3 Jean Cocteau, *Le Passé défini*, 6 Feb. 1956, p. 42

4 John Richardson, *A Life of Picasso*, vol. III, p. 87

5 Marcel Haedrich, *Coco Chanel*, p. 105

6 Marie Pavlovna, *A Princess in Exile*, p. 174

7 Axel Madsen, *Chanel: A Woman of Her Own*, p. 118

8 *Harper's Bazaar*, March 1937

9 Madsen, p. 118

10 All preceding quotes in this section: Marie Pavlovna

11 Gaia Servadio, *Luchino Visconti: A Biography*, p. 31

12 Steegmuller, p. 170

13 Ibid., pp. 241–2

14 Ibid., p. 301

15 Ibid., p. 308

16 Ibid., p. 276

17 Ibid., p. 297

18 Chanel to Etienne de Beaumont in the Institut Mémoire de l'Édition Contemporaine, fonds E. Beaumont

19 Chanel correspondence, Conservatoire

20 Chanel archive

Chapter 20: Reverdy

1 Paul Morand, *The Allure of Chanel*, p. 133
2 Charles Roux, *Chanel*, p. 370
3 Marcel Haedrich, *Coco Chanel*, p. 138
4 Jean Cocteau, *Le Passé défini*, vol. V, 3 April 1956, p. 91
5 Collection Chanel, by kind permission of the estate of Pierre Reverdy
6 Francis Steegmuller, *Cocteau*, p. 325
7 Roux, p. 230

Chapter 21: At the Centre

1 Paul Morand, *The Allure of Chanel*, p. 148
2 Ibid., p. 118
3 Ibid., p. 146
4 Ibid., p. 147
5 Ibid., pp. 145–8
6 Carmel Snow, *The World of Carmel Snow*, p. 31
7 Morand, *Allure*, pp. 122 & 151
8 Ibid., p. 123
9 Whitney Chadwick and Tirza Latimer, *The Modern Woman Revisited*, p. 89
10 Ibid., p. 89
11 Ibid.
12 Ibid., p. 82
13 Ibid., pp. 80–85
14 *Vogue*, 1 Mar. 1923
15 Morand, *Allure*, p. 47
16 Ibid., p. 155
17 Ibid., p. 131
18 Ibid., p. 133
19 Arthur Rubinstein, *My Many Years*, p. 125
20 Renée Mourgues, *La République*, 13 Oct. 1994
21 Pierre Galante, *Mademoiselle Chanel*, p. 155
22 Maurice Sachs, *La Décade de l'illusion*, p. 138

Chapter 22: Bend'Or

1 Jean Cocteau, *Lettres à sa mère*, vol. V, 24 May 1957
2 Marcel Haedrich, *Coco Chanel*, p. 125
3 George Ridley, *Bend'Or, Duke of Westminster*, p. 141
4 Ibid.
5 Ibid., p. 134
6 Winston and Clementine Churchill, *Speaking for Themselves*, p. 313
7 Ibid., p. 306
8 Paul Morand, *The Allure of Chanel*, pp. 158–9
9 Ibid., p. 160
10 Ibid., p. 165
11 Ibid.
12 *The Wendy and Emery Reves Collection* catalogue, Dallas Museum of Art
13 Bettina Ballard, *In My Fashion*, p. 49
14 Morand, *Allure*, p. 169
15 Ibid., p. 69
16 Robert Fizdale and Arthur Gold, *The Life of Misia Sert*, p. 271
17 Marcel Billot, *Journal de l'Abbé Mugnier*, 6 Aug. 1928
18 Axel Madsen, *Chanel: A Woman of Her Own*, p. 172
19 *Vogue*, Aug. 1930
20 Loelia, Duchess of Westminster, *Grace and Favour*, p. 159
21 Dorothy Ponsonby, *Diaries*, 20 Feb. 1930
22 Morand, *Allure*, p. 162
23 Ibid., pp. 165–7
24 Ridley, p. 167
25 Morand, *Allure*, p. 167

Chapter 23: The Crash

1 Francis C. Rose, *Saying Life: The Memoirs of Sir Francis Rose*, p. 154
2 Axel Madsen, *Chanel: A Woman of Her Own*, p. 186
3 Paul Morand, *The Allure of Chanel*, p. 151
4 Charles Roux, *Chanel*, p. 237

5 Morand, *Allure*, pp. 149–50

6 Judith Thurman, *Secrets of the Flesh: A Life of Colette*, p. 377

7 Charles Roux, p. 291

8 Morand, *Chroniques, 1931–54*, p. 314

9 Gaia Servadio, *Luchino Visconti: A Biography*, p. 40

10 Ibid., p. 42

11 Madsen, p. 210

12 Ibid.

13 Servadio, p. 52

14 Lilou Marquand, *Chanel m'a dit*, p. 108

15 Ibid., p. 137

16 Morand, *Allure*, p. 112

17 Ibid., p. 111

Chapter 24: Schiap had lots of it but it was bad

1 Bettina Ballard, *In My Fashion*, p. 61

2 Ibid., p. 62

3 Ibid., p. 140

4 Dalí letters to Gabrielle Chanel, Dalí correspondence, courtesy Fundació Gala-Salvador Dalí

5 Paul Morand, *The Allure of Chanel*, p. 170

6 Ibid., p. 172

7 I am most grateful to Jean-Noël Liaut for this and much other useful information.

8 Marcel Billot, *Journal de l'Abbé Mugnier*, 22 Feb. 1929

9 Jean Hugo, *Carnets*, 17 Feb. 1967

Chapter 25: War

1 Janet Flanner, *Paris was Yesterday*, p. 222

2 Pierre Galante, *Mademoiselle Chanel*, p. 170

3 Axel Madsen, *Chanel: A Woman of Her Own*, p. 226

4 Charles Roux, *Chanel*, p. 373

5 Flanner, p. 222

6 See previous Dalí reference

7 Madame Gabrielle Labrunie interview with the author

8 Nicole Fenosa and Bertrand Tillier, *Apel-les Fenosa: Catalogue raisonné de l'œuvre sculpté*

9 Lilou Marquand interview with the author

10 William Bullitt, pp. 481–6

11 Marcel Haedrich, *Coco Chanel*, p. 143

12 Ibid., pp. 143–4

Chapter 26: Survival

1 Marcel Haedrich, *Coco Chanel*, p. 178

2 Ibid.

3 Francis Steegmuller, *Cocteau*, p. 438

4 Ibid., p. 439

5 Julian Jackson, *France: The Dark Years*, pp. 360–63

6 Ibid., p. 4

7 Ibid., p. 199

8 Ibid., p. 308

9 Charles Roux, *Chanel*, pp. 324–5

10 Comte Jean d'Harcourt telephone interview, Adelia Sabatini

11 Archives of the Association Sainte Agnès, Saint-Martin-le-Vinoux, France

12 Chanel Conservatoire interview, Mme Tassin

13 Judith Thurman, *Secrets of the Flesh: A Life of Colette*, p. 197

14 Ibid., p. 437

15 Ibid., p. 436

16 Jean d'Harcourt interview

17 Robert Fizdale and Arthur Gold, *The Life of Misia Sert*, p. 290

18 Lilou Marquand, *Chanel m'a dit*, p. 136

19 Thurman, p. 445

20 Coleridge and Woolf quotes from John Kerrigan, *The Sonnets and a Lover's Complaint*, p. 51

21 Jean d'Harcourt interview

22 Jean-Noël Liaut interview

23 In Meredith Etherington-Smith's Dalí biography, *The Persistence of Memory*, 'the opium-smoking Cécile Goudreau is a thinly disguised portrait of Coco Chanel – Dalí gives the game away when he has her mention the Auvergne, Chanel's birthplace', p. 283

24 Ibid., p. 89

25 Paul Morand, *The Allure of Chanel*, p. 171

Chapter 27: Von Dincklage

1 M. Flügge, *Rettung ohne Retter*, p. 109

2 This information and much of what follows on von Dincklage is taken from M. Flügge, p. 109, and from two documents in the Swiss Federal Archives, which include letters from von Dincklage's lawyer. At the time, 1950, von Dincklage was trying to re-enter Switzerland.

3 *The Brown Network*, p. 98

4 Sybille Bedford, *Quicksands*, p. 90

5 Archives Fédérales Suisses (Bundesarchiv): Archiv des Schweizerischen Bundesstaates (1848–2009), File C.16-01373, 2 Feb. 1950. According to this report, he was '*directeur des transports*' in Sanary.

6 Ibid.

7 *The Brown Network*, p. 94

8 Flügge, p. 109

9 *The Brown Network*, p. 96

10 Bedford, p. 311

11 *The Brown Network*, p. 94

12 Ibid.

13 Bedford, p. 88

14 Charles Cotton interview, 10 Dec. 1982, in Jacques Grandjonc and Theresia Grundtner, *Zone d'ombres 1933–1944. Exil et internement d'Allemands et d'Autrichiens dans le Sud-Est de la France*, p. 51

15 Francine du Plessix Gray, *Them*, p. 170. The sections on von Dincklage

in this brilliant and absorbing memoir proved critical in my unravelling of that secretly repugnant man's chronology.

16 André Simone (pseudonym of Otto Katz), *Men of Europe*, pp. 16–17

17 *The Brown Network*, p. 95

18 Ibid.

19 Ibid., pp. 96–102

20 Von Dincklage's lawyer's statement and the Swiss Archive files cited above.

21 Bedford, p. 312. Here Bedford describes von Dincklage as 'made for the job [of spy], an effective charmer, a ruthless social butterfly with a heart of steel, ignorant of ideals, other human's pains'.

22 du Plessix Gray, p. 169

23 Ibid., p. 171

24 Ibid., p. 169

25 Samuel Marx, *Queen of the Ritz*, p. 106

26 Ibid.

27 du Plessix Gray, p. 170

28 Ibid.

29 Archiv des Schweizerischen Bundesstaates (E4320B#1990/266#1551*, file C.16-01373 P); 13 Nov. 1950 from the Chief of Police, Geneva, Switzerland to his counterpart in Berne, Switzerland. The French intelligence report adds that von Dincklage 'gave the impression he was trying to make deals with Germany and France ... [he] visits one Leonardo Dickens (suspected of being head of Gestapo in Lugano).'

30 The police reports confirm von Dincklage's position.

31 du Plessix Gray, p. 218

32 Dodie Kazanjian and Calvin Tomkins, *Alex: The Life of Alexander Liberman*, p. 98 (Charles Roux, *Chanel*, version of this episode on pp. 315–17).

33 Marx, p. 179

34 Axel Madsen, *Chanel: A Woman of Her Own*, p. 242

35 Jean d'Harcourt interview

36 Archiv des Schweizerischen Bundesstaates (E4320B#1990/266#1551*, file C.16-01373 P); 13 Nov. 1950 from the Chief of Police, Geneva, Switzerland, to his counterpart in Berne, Switzerland.

37 Marx, p. 174

38 Jean d'Harcourt interview

39 Denis Demonpion, *Arletty*, p. 225

40 Jean d'Harcourt interview

41 Ibid.

42 Ibid.

43 Charles Roux, p. 344

44 Ibid., p. 334

45 Letters between Churchill's office, the Foreign Office, Vera Bate and Chanel (CHAR 1/272/, CHAR20/198 A, etc.) in the Churchill Archives Centre, Cambridge

46 Ibid.

47 Courrier du Préfet de Police, Direction de la Sûreté Générale, Contrôle Générale des Services de Police Ad. No. 583. I am indebted to Marika Genty for this document.

48 Ibid.

49 Ibid.

50 Churchill Archives Centre documents referred to above

51 This section, see James McMillan, *Twentieth-Century France*, pp. 147–51 and Julian Jackson, *France: The Dark Years*, pp. 561–6

52 Jackson, pp. 577–92

53 Churchill Archives Centre documents referred to above

54 Lilou Marquand, *Chanel m'a dit*, pp. 113–15

55 Charles Roux, pp. 346, 349

56 Malcolm Muggeridge, *Chronicles of Wasted Time, vol. XI, The Infernal Grove*, p. 242

57 Churchill Archives Centre Documents referred to above

58 Documents and letters between the Foreign Office and the Zonal Executive Offices, Germany, between 1947 and 1948 http://www.nationalarchives.gov.uk/catalogue/displaycataloguedetails.asp?CATLN=6&CATID=1957690, and CATLN=6&CATID=3579445&j=1

Chapter 28: Exile

1 Paul Morand, *The Allure of Chanel*, pp. 146 & 147

2 Ibid., p. 12

3 Ibid.

4 Ibid., p. 170

5 Marcel Haedrich, *Coco Chanel*, p. 173

6 Guy de Rothschild, *The Whims of Fortune*, p. 216

7 Ibid.

8 Paul Morand, *Journal inutile*, 11 Jan. 1971

9 Robert Fizdale and Arthur Gold, *The Life of Misia Sert*, p. 292

10 Ibid.

11 Ibid., p. 300

12 Diana Mosley (ed.), *The Letters of Nancy Mitford*, p. 267

13 Morand, *Allure*, p. 140

14 Ibid., p. 65

15 Claude Delay, *Chanel Solitaire*, p. 52

16 Swiss Archive documents cited above

17 Morand, *Allure*, p. 171

18 Ibid., p. 143

19 Ibid., p. 73

20 Ibid., p. 120

21 Ibid., p. 169

22 Ibid., pp. 172–3

23 Axel Madsen, *Chanel: A Woman of Her Own*, p. 267

24 Charles Roux, *Chanel*, p. 380

25 Haedrich, p. 237

26 In interview and a number of telephone conversations, Michel Déon was most helpful in his non-judgemental attitude towards Gabrielle, including the fantasies crucial to her sanity.

27 Michel Déon interview with author

28 Ibid.

29 Ibid.

30 Ibid.

Chapter 29: Return: 1954

1 Dodie Kazanjian and Calvin Tomkins, *Alex: The Life of Alexander Liberman*, p. 205
2 Christian Dior, *Dior by Dior*, p. 16
3 Ibid.
4 Ibid., p. 4
5 Bettina Ballard, *In My Fashion*, p. 237
6 Pierre Galante, *Mademoiselle Chanel*, p. 197
7 Ibid., p. 200
8 Paul Morand, *The Allure of Chanel*, p. 120
9 Chanel Conservatoire interview, Jean Cazaubon
10 Galante, p. 207
11 Cocteau, *Le Passé défini: Journal*, vol. II

Chapter 30: I prefer disaster to nothingness

1 Marcel Haedrich, *Coco Chanel*, p. 169
2 Ibid., p. 171
3 Pierre Galante, *Mademoiselle Chanel*, p. 210
4 Susan Train interview with author. Ms Train's vivid recall of this dramatic episode was inspiring.
5 Ibid.
6 Ibid.
7 Lilou Marquand, *Chanel m'a dit*, p. 18
8 An ex-Chanel model in conversation
9 Lady Derwent interview with author
10 Bettina Ballard, *In My Fashion*, p. 311
11 Ibid.
12 Galante, p. 225
13 Diana Vreeland, *DV*, p. 132
14 Ibid., p. 131
15 Ibid., p. 130
16 Ballard, p. 60

17 *Vogue*, March 1959

18 Marquand, p. 87

19 Ibid., pp. 93 & 119

20 Roland Barthes, *The Language of Fashion*

21 Haedrich, p. 215

22 Ibid., p. 245

23 Ibid., p. 240

24 Paul Morand, *The Allure of Chanel*, p. 45

25 Galante, p. 268

26 Morand, *Allure*, p. 52

27 Galante, p. 269

28 Haedrich, p. 178

29 Ibid.

30 Claude Delay, *Chanel Solitaire*, p. 142

31 Ibid., p. 145

Chapter 31: I only hear my heart on the stairs

1 Paul Morand, *The Allure of Chanel*, p. 55

2 Claude Delay, *Chanel Solitaire*, p. 149

3 Marika Genty – whose knowledge and apprehension of Gabrielle is almost unrivalled – in interview with author

4 Marcel Haedrich, *Coco Chanel*, p. 222

5 Pierre Galante, *Mademoiselle Chanel*, p. 276

6 An ex-Chanel model in conversation

7 Morand, *Allure*, p. 21

8 Ibid.

9 Michel Déon in interview with author

10 Haedrich, p. 260

11 Morand, *Allure*, p. 38

12 Haedrich, p. 214

13 Paul Morand, *Journal inutile*, 3 June 1969

14 Claude Delay, in interview with author. Madame Delay's thoughts on her friend's inner life were instructive, and her comprehension of

Gabrielle as unable to survive without her fantasies are most perceptive.

15 Lilou Marquand, *Chanel m'a dit*, p. 43
16 Claude Delay in interview with author
17 Marquand
18 Delay, p. 147
19 Ibid., p. 161
20 Ibid.
21 Claude Delay in interview with author
22 Haedrich, p. 259
23 Marquand, p. 167
24 Claude Delay in interview with author
25 Marquand, pp. 150–51
26 Haedrich, p. 86
27 An ex-Chanel model in conversation
28 Delay, p. 164
29 Massaro interview, Chanel Conservatoire
30 Michel Déon, *Bagages pour Vancouver*, p. 276
31 Morand, *Allure*, p. 169

Afterword: Those on whom legends are built are their legends

1 Paul Morand, *The Allure of Chanel*, p. 175
2 Marcel Haedrich, *Coco Chanel*, p. 226
3 *Un Roi Seul*, Dir. T. Demaïzière and A. Teurlai, 2008
4 Suzy Menkes in interview with Karl Lagerfeld, *Herald Tribune*, Nov.
2010
5 *Un Roi Seul*
6 Morand, *Allure*, p. 21
7 Chanel interview BNF
8 Suzy Menkes interview as above
9 Haedrich, p. 17
10 Morand, *Allure*, p. 45

Select Bibliography

Works on Chanel

Baudot, François, *Chanel,* New York: Assouline, 2003

Bott, Daniele, *Chanel: Collections and Creations*, London: Thames and Hudson, 2007

Charles Roux, Edmonde, *The World of Coco Chanel*, London: Thames and Hudson, 2005

Charles Roux, Edmonde, *Chanel*, trans. Nancy Amphoux, London: HarperCollins, 1989

Delay, Claude (née Baillen), *Chanel Solitaire*, trans. Barbara Bray, London: Collins, 1973

Fiemeyer, Isabelle, *Coco Chanel: Un Parfum de mystère*, Paris: Petite Bibliothèque Payot, Editions Payot & Rivages, 2004

Galante, Pierre, *Mademoiselle Chanel*, trans. E. Geist and J. Wood, Chicago: H. Regnery, 1973

Gidel, Henry, *Coco Chanel*, Paris: Editions Flammarion, 2000

Haedrich, Marcel, *Coco Chanel*, trans. C. L. Markmann, London: Robert Hale, 1972

Haye, Amy de la, *Chanel: The Couturière at Work*, London: Victoria and Albert Museum, 1994

Leymarie, Jean, *Chanel*, Geneva: Editions d'Art Albert Skira, 1987

Madsen, Axel, *Chanel: A Woman of Her Own*, New York: Henry Holt and Co., 1990

Marquand, Lilou, *Chanel m'a dit*, Paris: Editions Jean-Claude Lattès, 1990

Other Works

Acton, Harold, *Memoirs of an Aesthete*, London: Hamish Hamilton (new edn), 1984

Acton, Harold, *More Memoirs of an Aesthete*, London: Methuen, 1970

Alexander, Grand Duke of Russia, *Always a Grand Duke*, New York: Farrar & Rinehart Inc., 1933

Association des Amis d'André Gide (ed.), *Cahiers André Gide*, vol. VIII, Paris: Gallimard, 1979

Ballard, Bettina, *In My Fashion*, New York: David McKay, 1960

Barthes, Roland, *The Language of Fashion*, Oxford: Berg, 2006

Baudelaire, Charles, 'The Painter of Modern Life', in *The Painter of Modern Life and Other Essays*, trans. and ed. Jonathan Mayne, London: Phaidon, 1964

Beaton, Cecil, *The Glass of Fashion*, London: Cassell, 1954

Beaton, Cecil, *Beaton in the Sixties, Unexpurgated Diaries*, ed. Hugo Vickers, London: Weidenfeld and Nicolson, 2003

Bedford, Sybille, *Quicksands*, London: Hamish Hamilton, 2005

Beevor, Antony and Cooper, Artemis, *Paris after the Liberation, 1944–1949*, London: Penguin, 2007

Benstock, Shari, *Women of the Left Bank*, London: Virago, 1994

Bernheimer, Charles, *Figures of Ill Repute*, London: Duke University Press, 1997

Bernstein-Gruber, Georges, *Bernstein le magnifique*, Paris: Editions J. C. Lattès, 1988

Billot, Marcel (ed.), *Journal de l'Abbé Mugnier (1877–1939)*, Paris: Mercure de France, 1985

Blanche, Emile, *Revue de Paris*, t.6 279: Au Bureau de Revue de Paris

Blanche, Emile, *More Portraits of a Lifetime*, trans. Walter Clement, London: Dent and Sons, 1939

Bodley, Ronald Victor Courtenay, *Indiscretions of a Young Man*, London: Harold Shaylor, 1931

Das Braune Netz – Wie Hitlers Agenten in Auslande arbeiten und den Krieg vorbereiten, Paris: Editions du Carrefour, 1935/ *The Brown Network: The Activities of the Nazis in Foreign Countries*, New York: Knight Publications, 1936

Buckle, Richard, *Diaghilev*, London: Weidenfeld and Nicolson, 1979

Callil, Carmen, *Bad Faith*, London: Jonathan Cape, 2006

Callwell, KCB, Sir C. E, *Sir Henry Wilson: His Life and Diaries*, London: Charles Scribners' Sons, 1927

Capel, Arthur, *Reflections on Victory and a Project for the Federation of Governments*, London: Verner Laurie, 1917

Capel, Arthur, *De quoi demain sera-t-il fait?*, Paris: Librairie de Médicis, 1939 / *What Will Tomorrow be Made of.* Published posthumously. Trans. Adelia Sabatini

Chadwick, Whitney, and Latimer, Tirza True (eds.), *The Modern Woman Revisited*, New Brunswick, New Jersey and London: Rutgers University Press, 2003

Chazot, Jacques, *'Chazot Jacques'*, Paris: Editions Stock, 1975

Churchill, Winston and Clementine, *Speaking for Themselves*, ed. Mary Soames, London: Black Swan, 1999

Clermont-Tonnerre, Elisabeth de, *Mémoires, vol. I: Au Temps des équipages*, Paris: Bernard Grasset, 1928

Clermont-Tonnerre, Elisabeth de, *Mémoires, vol. II: Les Marronniers en fleurs*, Paris: Bernard Grasset, 1929

Clermont-Tonnerre, Elisabeth de, *Mémoires, vol. III: Clair de lune et taxi-auto*, Paris: Bernard Grasset, 1932

Clermont-Tonnerre, Elisabeth de, *Mémoires, vol. IV: La Treizième Heure*, Paris: Bernard Grasset, 1935

Cocteau, Jean, *Past Tense: Diaries*, vol. I, London: Hamish Hamilton, 1987

Cocteau, Jean, *Past Tense: Diaries*, vol. II, London: Methuen, 1990

Cocteau, Jean, *Lettres à Jean Marais*, Paris: Albin Michel, 1987

Cocteau, Jean, *Lettres à sa mère*, Paris: Gallimard, 1989

Cocteau, Jean, *Journal 1942–1945*, Paris: Gallimard, 1989

Cocteau, Jean, *Le Passé défini: Journal*, vol. V (1956–7), Paris: Gallimard, 2006

Colette, *The Complete Claudine*, trans. Antonia White, New York: Farrar, Straus and Giroux, 2001

Colette, *My Apprenticeships Music Hall Sidelights*, London: Secker and Warburg, 1957

Colette, *Autobiographie*, Paris: Fayard, 1968

Corbett, Patricia, *Verdura*, London: Thames and Hudson, 2002

Craft, Robert, *Stravinsky: Chronicle of a Friendship*, New York: Alfred Knopf, 1972

D'Abernon, Helen Venetia Duncombe Vincent, *Red Cross and Berlin*

Embassy, 1915–1926: Extracts from the Diaries of Viscountess d'Abernon, London: John Murray, 1946

Dalí, Salvador, *Hidden Faces*, trans. Haakon Chevalier, London: Peter Owen, 1973

Davis, Mary E., *Classic Chic: Music Fashion and Modernism*, Berkeley, CA: University of California Press, 2006

Débordes, Jacqueline, *Coco Chanel*, Olliergues : Editions de la Montmarie, 2006

Demonpion, Denis, *Arletty*, Paris: Flammarion, 1996

Déon, Michel, *Bagages pour Vancouver – Mes arches de Noé*, Paris: La Table Ronde, 1985

Deslandres, Yvonne, and Muller, Florence, *Histoire de la mode*, Paris : Flammarion, 1978

Dior, Christian, *Dior by Dior*, trans. Antonia Fraser, London: V&A Publications, 2001

Duncan, Isadora, *My Life*, New York: Boni and Liveright, 1927

Egremont, Max, Lord, *Under Two Flags: The Life of General Sir Edward Spears*: Phoenix, 1998, first pub. London: Weidenfeld and Nicolson, 1997

Eksteins, Modris, *Rites of Spring*, London: Black Swan, 1990

Elgey, Georgette, *La République des illusions, 1945–1951*, Paris: Grasset, 1975

Etherington-Smith, Meredith, *The Persistence of Memory: A Biography of Dalí*, New York: Random House, 1992

Fenosa, Nicole, and Tillier, Bertrand, *Apel-les Fenosa: Catalogue raisonné de l'œuvre sculpté*, Barcelona: Ediciones Polígrafa, 2002

Field, Leslie, *Bendor: Golden Duke of Westminster*, London: Weidenfeld and Nicolson, 1983

Fizdale, Robert, and Gold, Arthur, *The Life of Misia Sert*, London: Macmillan, 1980

Flanner, Janet, *Paris was Yesterday*, New York: Popular Library, no date

Flügge, Manfred, *Rettung ohne Retter, oder, Ein Zug aus Theresienstadt*, Munich: Deutscher Taschenbuch, 2004

Flügge, Manfred, *Heinrich Mann: Eine Biographie*, Reinbek: Rowohlt, 2006

Font, Lourdes, *Fashion Theory*, vol. VIII, Sept. issue, pp. 301–14, Oxford: Berg, 2004

Franck, Dan, *Bohemian Paris*, trans. Cynthia Liebow, New York: Grove Press, 2001

Garafola, Lynn, *The Ballets Russes and Its World*, eds. Lynn Garafola and Nancy van Norman Baer, New Haven, CT: Yale University Press, 1999

Goncourt, Edmond and Jules, *Pages from the Journal*, ed. and trans. Robert Baldick, Oxford: OUP, 1978

Grana, César and Marigay, *On Bohemia: The Code of the Self-Exiled*, London and N. Brunswick: Transaction, 1990

Grandjonc, Jacques, and Grundtner, Theresia, *Zone d'ombres 1933–1944. Exil et internement d'Allemands et d'Autrichiens dans le Sud-Est de la France*, Aix-en-Provence: Alinéa, 1990

Grange, Baronne Ernest de la, *Open House in Flanders*, London: John Murray, 1929

Green, Julian, *Journal 1938–49*, Paris: Plon, 1969

Guitard-Auviste, Ginette, *Paul Morand, 1888–1976: Légende et vérités*, Paris: Editions Balland, 1994

Harrison, Michael, *Lord of London*, London: W. H. Allen, 1966

Heller, Gerhard, *Un Allemand à Paris, 1940–1944*, Paris: Editions du Seuil, 1981

Hickman, Katie, *Courtesans*, London: Harper Perennial, 2004

Home, Archibald, Sir, *The Diary of a World War I Cavalry Officer*, Tunbridge Wells: Costello, 1985

Hugo, Jean, *Le Regard de la mémoire (1914–1945)*, Paris: Actes Sud, 1983

Hugo, Jean, *Carnets (1946–1984)*, Paris: Actes Sud, 1994

Hussey, Andrew, *Paris: The Secret History*, London: Penguin Books, 2007

Israel, Lee, *Estée Lauder*, London: Arlington Books, 1986

Jackson, Julian, *France: The Dark Years*, Oxford: OUP, 2001

Jones, Colin, *Paris: Biography of a City*, London: Penguin, 2006

Kahn, Sylvia, *Music's Modern Muse: The Life of Winaretta Singer*, New York: University of Rochester Press, 2003

Kazanjian, Dodie, and Tomkins, Calvin, *Alex: The Life of Alexander Liberman*, New York: Knopf, 1993

Kerrigan, John, *The Sonnets and a Lover's Complaint*, London: Penguin, 1995

Kiste, van der, John, *The Romanovs*, Sutton: Stroud, 1998

Kochno, Boris, *Diaghilev et les Ballets Russes*, Paris: Fayard, 1973

Kochno, Boris, *Christian Bérard*, Paris: Editions Herscher, 1987

Laval, Michel, *Brasillach ou la trahison du clerc*, Paris: Hachette, 1992

Lifar, Serge, *Ma Vie*, trans. James Holman Mason, London: Hutchinson, 1976

Mackenzie Stuart, Amanda, *Consuelo and Alva Vanderbilt*, London: Harper-Collins, 2005

Malraux, André, *Antimémoires*, Paris: Gallimard, 1967

Marx, Samuel, *Queen of the Ritz*, London: W. H. Allen, 1979

Maurois, Michelle, *Déchirez cette lettre*, Paris: Flammarion, 1990

McMillan, James, *Twentieth-Century France, 1898–1991*, London: Arnold, 1992

McMillan, James (ed.), *Modern France*, Oxford: OUP, 2003

Morand, Paul, *Lewis et Irène*, Paris: Grasset, 1924

Morand, Paul, *L'Allure de Chanel*, Paris: Hermann, 1976

Morand, Paul, *Lettres du voyageur*, Paris: Editions du Rocher, 1988

Morand, Paul, *Chroniques, 1931–1954*, Paris: Grasset, 2001

Morand, Paul, *Journal inutile*, Paris: Gallimard, 2001

Morand, Paul, *Venices*, trans. Euan Cameron, London: Pushkin Press, 2002

Morand, Paul, *The Allure of Chanel*, trans. Euan Cameron, London: Pushkin Press, 2008

Muggeridge, Malcolm, *Chronicles of Wasted Time, vol. XI, The Infernal Grove*, London: Collins, 1973

Musée Cévenol, *Un secret Cévenol de Coco Chanel*, Le Vigan: Gard, no date

Norwich, John Julius (ed.), *The Duff Cooper Diaries*, London: Weidenfeld and Nicolson, 2005

Novick, Peter, *The Resistance versus Vichy*, London: Chatto and Windus, 1968

Pavlovna, Marie, Grand Duchess of Russia, *A Princess in Exile*, New York: Viking Press, 1932

Picardie, Justine, *Coco Chanel*, London: HarperCollins, 2010

Plessix Gray, Francine du, *Them*, London: Penguin, 2006

Poiret, Paul, *King of Fashion: The Autobiography of Paul Poiret*, trans. Stephen Haden Guest, Princeton, NJ: Princeton University Press, 1994

Pomian, John (ed.), *J. Retinger: Memoirs of an Eminence Grise*, Sussex: Sussex University Press, 1972

Pougy, Liane de, *My Blue Notebooks*, trans Diana Athill, London: André Deutsch, 1979

Pritchard, Jane (ed.), *Diaghilev and the Golden Age of the Ballets Russes* (exhibition catalogue), London: V&A Publishing, 2010

Ragache, Jean-Robert, *La Vie quotidienne des écrivains et des artistes sous l'Occupation, 1940–1944,* Paris: Hachette, 1988

Reverdy, Pierre, *Prose Poems,* trans. Ron Padgett, Brooklyn, NY: The Brooklyn Rail Black Square Editions, 2007

Reves, Wendy and Emery, *The Wendy and Emery Reves Collection,* Dallas: Dallas Museum of Art, 1985

Richardson, John, *A Life of Picasso,* vol. II, London: Pimlico, 1997

Richardson, John, *A Life of Picasso,* vol. III, London: Jonathan Cape, 2007

Ridley, George, *Bend'Or, Duke of Westminster,* London: Robin Clark, 1985

Rose, Francis C., Sir, *Saying Life: The Memoirs of Sir Francis Rose,* London: Cassell, 1961

Rothschild, Guy de, *The Whims of Fortune,* London: Granada, 1985

Rounding, Virginia, *Grandes Horizontales,* London: Bloomsbury, 2004

Rubinstein, Arthur, *My Many Years,* London: Cape, 1980

Sachs, Maurice, *La Décade de l'illusion,* Paris: Gallimard, 1950

Sachs, Maurice, *Au Temps du Boeuf sur le Toit,* 1939 reprint, Paris: Grasset, 2005

Scheijen, Sjeng, *Diaghilev,* trans. J. Headley Price and S. J. Leinbach, London: Profile Books, 2009

Schellenberg, Walter, *Schellenberg,* trans. and ed. Louis Hagen, London: Mayflower Books, 1965

Schiaparelli, Elsa, *Shocking Life,* London: J. M. Dent, 1954

Schwartz, Vanessa, *Spectacular Realities: Early Mass-culture in Fin-de-siècle Paris,* Berkeley, CA: University of California Press, 1999

Sert, Misia, *Two or Three Muses,* London: Museum Press, 1953

Servadio, Gaia, *Luchino Visconti: A Biography,* London: Weidenfeld and Nicolson, 1981

Simone, André, *Men of Europe,* New York: Modern Age, 1941

Simpson, Colin, *Artful Partners,* London: Unwin, 1988

Sire, H. J. A., *Gentlemen Philosophers: Catholic Higher Education at Liège and Stonyhurst 1774–1916,* Worthing: Churchman Publishing, 1988

Snow, Carmel, *The World of Carmel Snow*, New York: McGraw-Hill, 1962

Stanley, Edward, Earl of Derby, *Paris 1918: War Diary of the British Ambassador*, Liverpool: Liverpool University Press, 2001

Steegmuller, Francis, *Cocteau*, London: Constable, 1986

Steele, Valerie, *Paris Fashion: A Cultural History*, Oxford: OUP, 1988

Steele, Valerie, *Women of Fashion: Twentieth-century Designers*, New York: Rizzoli International Publications, 1991

Stendhal, *The Red and the Black*, trans. M. R. Shaw, London: Penguin, 1969

Stravinsky, Igor, *An Autobiography*, New York: W. W. Norton, 1962

Sydney, Philip, *Modern Rome in Modern England*, London: The Religious Tract Society, 1906

Symons Barrow, George de, Sir, *The Fire of Life*, London: Hutchinson, 1942

Thurman, Judith, *Secrets of the Flesh: A Life of Colette*, London: Bloomsbury, 2000

Train, Susan (ed.), *Le Théâtre de la Mode*, Paris: Le May, 1990

Vreeland, Diana, *DV*, New York: Da Capo Press, 1997

Walsh, Stephen, *Igor Stravinsky: A Creative Spring: Russia and France 1882–1934*, London: Pimlico, 2002

Weber, Eugen, *Peasants into Frenchmen*, Stanford: Stanford University Press, 2007

Westminster, Loelia, Duchess of, *Grace and Favour*, London: Weidenfeld and Nicolson, 1961

Wilcox, Claire (ed.), *Radical Fashion*, London: V&A Publications, 2001

Wilcox, Claire (ed.), *The Golden Age of Couture: 1947–57*, London: V&A Publications, 2007

Wilson, Edmund, *A Literary Chronicle of the Forties*, London: W. H. Allen, 1951

Wilson, Elizabeth, *Adorned in Dreams: Fashion and Modernity*, London: Virago Press, 1985

Archives of the Association Sainte Agnès, Saint-Martin-le-Vinoux, France

Archives Fédérales Suisses

Arthur Capel correspondence, courtesy of Christopher Osborn

Diana Capel correspondence to Duff Cooper, Churchill Archives Centre, Churchill College, Cambridge

Gabrielle Chanel correspondence, courtesy of the Chanel Conservatoire

Churchill Papers, Churchill Archives Centre, Churchill College, Cambridge

Dalí correspondence, courtesy Fundació Gala-Salvador Dalí, Figueres, Spain

Municipal Archives, Biarritz, France (Mairie de Biarritz, Service des Archives)

Municipal Archives, Garches, France (Mairie de Garches, Service Archives – Documentation)

National Archives, Paris (Fonds Chanoine Mugnier)

National Archives, Kew. Foreign Office records, FO 944/35 and FO 371/70892

National Archives, Kew. War Office Records, WO339/55790, Arthur Capel file

Pavlovich, Dmitri, *Diaries*, trans. by William Lee, courtesy of Prince Chavchavadze

Ponsonby, Dorothy, *Diaries*, courtesy the Hon. Laura Ponsonby

Acknowledgements

Of the many people who have helped me with this book, I owe the first debt of gratitude to my agent, Clare Alexander, whose idea it was. My initial doubts were soon transformed into an obsession. And, while Clare failed to curb this, she has my heartfelt thanks for her unfailing encouragement and professionalism. These were given with habitual good grace during the writing of this most difficult of lives.

Marie Louise de Clermont-Tonnerre, Director of External Relations at Chanel, kindly gave her support to the writing of the book, making my research at the Chanel Conservatoire possible.

The prime source for Gabrielle Chanel is Paul Morand's *L'Allure de Chanel* (copyright © Editions Hermann), and I am most grateful to Arthur Cohen, at Editions Hermann, who so readily gave me permission to quote freely from Gabrielle's extraordinary memoir. Edmonde Charles Roux was Gabrielle's first and supposedly exhaustive biographer, but no one can now think of writing anything on her without Morand's book, published two years after Charles Roux's.

An apparently endless stream of writing on Gabrielle has appeared since these publications. Pierre Galante's *Mademoiselle Chanel*, Marcel Haedrich's *Coco Chanel* and Claude Delay's *Chanel Solitaire* (particularly insightful with regard to Gabrielle's inner life) are all notable for their perception and sensitivity. These authors were all Gabrielle's friends, and I have drawn heavily on their work. Lilou Marquand's insightful *Chanel m'a dit* has been helpful.

Mary Davis's *Classic Chic: Music Fashion and Modernism*; Valerie Steele's *Paris Fashion: A Cultural History*; the contributors to *Modern Woman Revisited*; Judith Thurman's magnificent biography of Colette, *Secrets of the Flesh*; Francis Steegmuller's indispensable

Cocteau; and Eugen Weber's magisterial *Peasants into Frenchmen* were of great help in the development of my ideas.

I am much indebted to those below, who kindly gave me interviews and whose knowledge, memories and thoughts have informed this book.

Marika Genty, Director of the Chanel Conservatoire, courteously dispensed her encyclopaedic knowledge of Gabrielle the couturier and also contributed her thoughtful and perceptive observations on Gabrielle the person. Jacques Polge, Director of Parfums Chanel, was immensely gracious, and I thank him for a fascinating and thought-provoking conversation about perfume and the mysteries of Chanel N°5. This was aided by Christopher Sheldrake, Director of Research and Development. Patrick Doucet, at the Chanel and Bourjois Perfume Conservatoire, showed me the earliest Chanel cosmetics and N°5 bottles and ably described N°5's possible chronology. Julie Deydier, of the Chanel Conservatoire, helped me look through the remarkable collection of Gabrielle's designs, stored away on the outskirts of Paris; Odile Babin was always helpful; and Cecile Goddet-Dirles familiarized me with the large Chanel image database.

Claude Delay generously expanded on her memoir of Gabrielle, *Chanel Solitaire*, for me; Lady Sybille Derwent (previously of French *Vogue*), emphasized the unconcerned French attitude towards Gabrielle's sexual penchants. Lady Derwent also recommended me to Susan Train, of American *Vogue*, who described Gabrielle's 1954 comeback with great immediacy; in Ireland, Michel Déon collected me from Galway airport with his large hound and, while we ate shellfish by the sea, talked inspiringly about Gabrielle.

Madame Gabrielle Labrunie was most kind in sharing her memories of her great-aunt Gabrielle; Amanda Mackenzie Stuart's help was critical. Suggesting Francine du Plessix Gray's memoir, *Them*, Amanda also gave me much information on the Balsan family, and introduced me to William Lee. To William, my debt is considerable; for his painstaking translations of Dmitri Pavlovich's diaries, and for helping me to understand better this poignant man. Dmitri's grandson, Prince David Chavchavadze, has my warm thanks for allowing the first publication of Dmitri's diary excerpts regarding his relationship with Gabrielle.

Etienne Balsan's grandson and great-nephew, Antoine Balsan and Philippe Gontier respectively, told me about their delightful forebear, and have kindly permitted me to reproduce one of the few photographs of him still in their possession. Olivia de Havilland kindly wrote to me about what she knew; the Hon. Harry Fane's timely contribution is much appreciated; Philip Norcross Gross provided the most up-to-date information on Antoinette Chanel; and Lilou Marquand's astute observations to me were instructive.

I am very grateful to Comte Jean d'Harcourt for his memories, which were an informative and unsettling addition to the puzzle of Gabrielle's wartime activities, and to Hubert de Givenchy, who mourned Gabrielle's shabby treatment of their long-standing mutual friend Christobal Balenciaga, who yet brought himself to attend her funeral. On more than one occasion Danniel Rangel was the perfect ambassador on my behalf; Willy Rizzo's reminiscences of his friendship with Gabrielle are reflected in the quality of observation and sympathy evident in his photographs of her, some of the best that anyone made. Jean-Noël Liaut's recommendations, anecdotes and vignettes were valuable, and amusing.

My thanks to Father Tom McCoog, who directed me to Bernardo Caparrini's crucial scholarship, and to Bernardo in turn, who recommended me to the archivist at Stonyhurst, David Knight. David was most assiduous on my behalf, ferreting out school logs and photos of Arthur Capel, and thus I was set on Arthur's trail. This led to Arthur's son-in-law, Sir Jeremy Hutchinson, whom I warmly thank for his memories of Diana Capel née Lister, and his insistence on introducing me to his step-son and Arthur's grandson, Christopher Osborn. Christopher was extremely generous in lending me Arthur's letters; allowing me to publish them here for the first time; discussing Arthur, Gabrielle and Diana's dimly remembered story; and assisting me in sensitive negotiations.

The staff of the London Library were, as always, unfailingly helpful. I thank Lisa Dowdswell at the Society of Authors for her clear-headed advice; Lynsey Robertson at the Churchill Centre Archives; Kerry Bennet at the Scottish Civic Trust; the Association Sainte-Agnès, France; Mme Chantal Bittan, Directrice Générale, Polo de Paris; Christine Lauener, Collaboratrice Scientifique, Département Fédéral de l'Intérieur (DFI), Archives Fédérales Suisses (AFS); Christine de Metz, Municipal Archives, Mairie de Garches; Monique Beaufils, Municipal Archives, Mairie de Biarritz; Laura Potter at V&A Publications; and John Gray at *Dancing Times*.

I should like to thank the following for permission to quote excerpts from the cited works: Lady Polly Feversham, for *Extracts from the Diaries of Viscountess d'Abernon*; the Hon. Laura Ponsonby for Lady Dorothy Ponsonby's unpublished diary; the Chanel Conservatoire for the Pierre Reverdy dedication (in Rousselot and Manol) in their collection; and François Capon at the Maeght Foundation for the same; Fundació Gala-Salvador Dalí, Figueres, for the excerpts from Salvador Dalí's letters to Gabrielle; Christopher Osborn for Diana Capel's letters in the Churchill Archives Centre, and Arthur Capel's letters to Diana; Pan Macmillan and Alfred A. Knopf for *Misia*, copyright © Gold and Fizdale, 1980; Random House and M. Gabriel Jardin (English language copyright) for *Lewis et Irène*, originally Editions Grasset, 1924; for Marcel Haedrich's *Coco Chanel*, Editions Robert Lafont, copyright © 1971, English language translation copyright Little, Brown and Company, 1972; Editions Jean-Claude Lattès for Lilou Marquand's *Chanel m'a dit*, copyright © 1990; *Mercure de France*, for Pierre Galante's *Mademoiselle Chanel*, copyright © 1973. Every effort has been made to discover copyright holders. I will gladly make good in future editions any omissions brought to my attention.

In the early stages Clement Bosque was my able assistant. He was followed by Adelia Sabatini, whose ability to carry out research of all kinds, act as ambassador and fulfil numerous other tasks with intelligence, independence and good humour – including several discerning readings of the manuscript – have made working with her a great pleasure. I thank her for her tremendous contribution.

Acknowledgements

To my editor at Fig Tree, Juliet Annan, who commissioned the book, I am deeply grateful, both for her assured and reassuring editorial guidance and her great tact and forbearance. I also thank Jenny Lord for her helpful editorial contribution, and Sophie Missing for picture collecting. I thank my US editor, Alessandra Lussardi, who maintained her enthusiasm for the project.

My daughter Jessica brought her lucid and professional visual skills to bear as she expertly shepherded me through the difficult process of selecting pictures. She and her sister, Olivia, were also, as always, unfailingly wise and humorous advisers. My brother, Saul, was his characteristically hospitable self in France, as was Sira in London. While conversations with my father, Keith, were often critical, he also waded through a very long pre-edited manuscript. My other valiant readers were my sister Anna, Jessica, sister-in-law Vanessa, and friends Josephine Baker and Professor Jane Moody. Cheng Hao Zhou often kept me going. I owe them all a great deal for their thoughtful and astute observations, deletion of various howlers and sensitive recommendations. Jane's authoritative and judicious suggestions for trimming made the book more transparent. My exemplary copy-editor, Sarah Day, skilfully urged me on, spotted errors and suggested improvements, and I am very grateful. Meanwhile, any remaining flaws and errors are my responsibility.

This book took considerably longer than anticipated, and in the process I have neglected friends and family appallingly. Nevertheless, they continued to provide me with their support and good counsel, without which I could not have finished. They have my loving thanks. To Marcus I owe more than I can say.

Index